None Can Have Richer Memories

None Can Have Richer Memories

Polk County, Florida, 1940-2000

CANTER BROWN, JR.

POLK COUNTY HISTORICAL ASSOCIATION

UNIVERSITY OF TAMPA PRESS
TAMPA, FLORIDA

Manufactured in the United States of America
Printed on acid-free paper ∞
First Edition

The University of Tampa Press
401 West Kennedy Boulevard
Tampa, FL 33606

ISBN 1-879852-36-5 (cloth)

Browse & order online at
http://utpress.ut.edu

This book is distributed by the Center for Florida History
Florida Southern College, Lakeland, Florida
James M. Denham, Director

Library of Congress Cataloging-in-Publication Data

Brown, Canter.
    None can have richer memories : Polk County, Florida, 1940-2000 / by Canter Brown, Jr.-- 1st ed.
        p. cm.
    "Polk County Historical Association."
    Includes bibliographical references (p.   ) and index.
    ISBN 1-879852-36-5 (hardback : acid-free paper)
    1. Polk County (Fla.)--History--20th century. 2. Polk County (Fla.)--History--20th century--
Pictorial works. I. Title: Polk County, Florida, 1940-2000. II. Polk County Historical Association (Polk County, Fla.) III. Title.

    F317.P7B765 2005
    975.9'67063--dc22   2005002227

With respect and appreciation,

to Duane Peacock, Howard Beynon, Linda Cloud,

Carl Griffith, Esther Mayhall, Josephine Sthreshley,

Sally Hendry Waters, Lorraine Young, and

all of the other outstanding Polk County educators

who changed my life for the better

– C. B.

Contents

1. *Soon after its organization, the Polk County Historical Association began conducting video interviews of county "pioneers," eventually accumulating one of the largest collections of living local history available anywhere. During this 1985 interview, Carolynn Girtman (seated at right) helped to preserve the reminiscences of (from left) Lorry Mitchell, Mrs. E. F. Mitchell, and Leta Mitchell Wright.* FORT MEADE LEADER.

INTRODUCTION

Visitors and residents alike have known Florida's Polk County to be a very special place for thousands of years. Through the millennia they willingly and often have fought and, too frequently, died for the right to remain there in peace. The saga has reflected the experience of Native Americans, Spanish conquistadores and modern Hispanic settlers, free black warriors, independent pioneer women black and white, soldiers, sailors, Confederates and Unionists, cattlemen, citrus growers, farmers, miners, businessmen, movie stars, developers, saints, sinners, and more than a few scoundrels. That enumeration merely begins the list. In the circumstances it comes as no surprise to those who know the place that, by the twentieth century's second decade, its resources, diversity, and allure had prompted those who treasured it to begin calling the region Imperial Polk County.[1]

Through the years—and even though the passage of days witnessed tragedy, sacrifice, violence, injustice, and loss—Polk Countians often have proved more than willing to articulate their intense feelings about their home. The sentiments of two of them, expressed in 1977, typify those of numerous others. "I don't think the angels could make it no better," Lakeland's Gene Robson declared. "I don't have nothing but love for the county and the life it's given me and my family." LaCona Raines Padgett of Bartow concurred. "I love it," she proclaimed. "It's full of the old southern hospitality. The people are warm. We all stick together, especially in time of trouble." Padgett added: "This is about the only real Florida that people visiting the state are going to come in contact with. The glamor and glitter of the gold coast and the bigger cities, that's not Florida. Polk County and the style of life in Polk County, now that's the real Florida." Famed author Zora Neale Hurston preserved a remark made to her. "Course, Zora," a friend announced, "ain't you never hea'd dat in Polk County de water drink lak cherry wine?"[2]

So intensely have feelings run in this direction at times that local newspapers have urged their readers to share the depth of such sentiments with others. Lakeland's *Ledger,* for one, did so in 1965 in the form of a writing contest. Winner Linda M. Green's essay on Polk's place in the scheme of things asserted, "I am the heart of Florida, and steadily I

2. *On behalf of the Polk County Historical Association, President Edward Etheredge in 2002 presents Polk School Superintendent Jim Thornhill with copies of the association's* In the Midst of All That Makes Life Worth Living: Polk County, Florida, to 1940 *for each of the school system's libraries.* LAKELAND LEDGER.

beat my way forward," before concluding, "My lantern shines on strong, bright and steady, like a candle in the sun." Along the way Green found reason to mention a particular factor that played deeply in Polk's experience. "As I progress new ideas are formed," she insisted, "but I do not let them destroy my past."[3]

That linkage between the past and the present has resonated strongly in Polk's experience. Green, herself, noted, "The lantern of your ancestors burns on, never flickering." As she alluded—and unlike the circumstances in many Florida counties that have grown enormously in population during the past half century or so—Polk's claims on its residents have produced bonds of longevity over generations that, in turn, have kept alive a sense for and appreciation of history. Pioneer Lakeland resident Mrs. E. O. Flood illustrated the point during a 1952 interview. "Thinking back brings memories of ridiculous as well as serious things," she admitted. Still, the past and its lessons gripped her attention. "I don't know anything that I get more pleasure out of," Flood observed, "than just sitting down and thinking back to those [early] days."[4]

Polk Countians now have institutionalized their linkage with that past for nearly seven decades. This innovation arose after pioneer descendant Milton D. Wilson spurred action that prompted State Senator Spessard L. Holland in 1937 to secure for Polk the legislative creation of Florida's first county historical commission. Thereafter, Wilson, volunteer Lillian Rosa Carpenter, and scores of others labored to collect and preserve what ultimately amounted to a remarkable body of historical information. Eventually, and thanks in good part to the leadership of Polk County Clerk of Courts E. D. "Bud" Dixon, the collection grew and found a home in the highly regarded Polk County

Historical and Genealogical Library, housed in the restored 1908 Polk County courthouse at Bartow.[5]

The county also has benefitted greatly from the work of the Polk County Historical Association. A well-intentioned initiative spearheaded by individuals such as Dr. Charles Thrift, D. H. Sloan Jr., Wallace L. Storey, A. H. Blanding, W. H. Purcell, and others attempted to formalize an organization as early as 1958 but fell short of its goal. Then in 1974, as the nation neared its bicentennial, permanent success greeted renewed efforts. Glenn Hooker, the Polk County Historical Association's first president, thereafter offered guidance and stable leadership through 1991. Arthur Bissett, Lloyd Harris, Bob Bass, Freddie Wright, and Dr. Edward Etheredge have followed in the same tradition. The association presently claims a membership that ranks it among the premier local historical societies in the state.[6]

As the commission and the association pursued their missions, efforts moved ahead to build upon previous work in order to foster the preparation and publication of meaningful recorded history. Newspaperman M. F. Hetherington had penned his *History of Polk County Florida, Narrative and Biographical* in 1928. For the county's centennial in 1961 Ed McNeely and Al R. McFayden joined to produce *Century in the Sun, A History of Polk County*. Significantly, the Polk County Historical Association a decade later authorized publication of the *Polk County Historical Quarterly*. Launched by the capable hands of editor Louise K. Frisbie in June 1974, the *Quarterly* now has explored Polk's history and culture in depth for thirty years. Frisbie and her successors Dr. Charles Thrift, Freddie Wright, Hugh Wright, and Dr. James V. Holton deserve credit for offering the public a broad range of historical articles, many of which have pioneered studies of the lives and roles of women, African Americans, and other segments of the community. Frisbie additionally contributed an extended series of historical articles and photographs to the pages of the *Polk County Democrat* and authored two generously illustrated volumes of local history, *Peace River Pioneers* and *Yesterday's Polk County*.[7]

The efforts did not stop there. While officers and members of the Polk County Historical Association had taken great pride in that organization's accomplishments and the work of the *Polk County Historical Quarterly*, as the twentieth century neared its close they determined that time had arrived for the preparation and publication of a comprehensive county history. In 2000 the association under President Edward Etheredge assumed responsibility for bringing that goal to reality by contracting for a thoroughly researched and well-written two-volume series. Their charge to the author expressed a two-fold associational desire: that the work reflect the true diversity of Polk's experience; and that it be conceived and realized in a manner that would serve as a model for other localities in preserving their own heritage. The first volume, *In the Midst of All That Makes Life Worth Living: Polk County, Florida, to 1940* debuted in 2001. The present volume completes the series. The Polk County Historical Association offers both as a testament to Polk County's rich and diverse past and also as an aid to the present at a time when almost overwhelming change and challenge face not only the residents of Polk but those of the state of Florida as well.

ACKNOWLEDGMENTS

*T*he author's debt of gratitude extends to numerous individuals and institutions for kind assistance and encouragement. At the outset, this series and this volume would not have been written without the vision and commitment of the members of the Polk County Historical Association and, particularly, the association's officers and directors. When it commissioned this volume in 2000, they included Dr. Edward Etheredge, president; William Lloyd Harris, vice president; Sue Sellers, secretary; Paul Thornhill, treasurer; Freddie Wright and Hugh Wright, co-editors, *Polk County Historical Quarterly*; directors Ray Albritton, Hazel Bowman, Peggy Burr, Doy Copeland, James M. Denham, Betty McCall, Odell Robinson, Melvin Sellers, and Doc. S. Wesson, Jr; and honorary director Donald Wilson, Jr. As this volume reaches publication in 2005, Dr. Etheredge remains president and Paul Thornhill, treasurer. Other officers now include James M. Denham, vice president; K. C. Jarrett, secretary; and James V. Holton, editor, *Polk County Historical Quarterly*. The directors now also include Charlie Wilson.

Special thanks go, as well, to many others. Colleagues Dr. Larry Eugene Rivers, dean of the college of arts and sciences and distinguished professor of history, Florida A&M University; Dr. James M. Denham, director, Center for Florida History, and professor of history, Florida Southern College, Lakeland; Freddie Wright, Hugh Wright, and James V. Holton, editors, *Polk County Historical Quarterly*; and Joe Spann, director, Polk County Historical and Genealogical Library, assisted me greatly with encouragement and support. My talented wife and research partner Barbara Gray Brown uncovered much of the material and almost all of the best research findings included within this volume, and my brother John E. Brown of Fort Meade has never failed to offer generous assistance and his remarkable research skills. Florida Southern College student Shawn Nelson contributed, as well, with his growing research skills. Freddie Wright, Hugh Wright, Hazel Bowman, James M. Denham, and Barbara Gray Brown each read the manuscript and improved it with helpful corrections and suggestions. While asking pardon for names inadvertently omitted, thanks additionally are extended to (in alphabetical order): Susan McKay Bromwell, Auburndale; Wanda Moon Brown, Fort Meade; Richard Burnette, Florida Southern College; LaFrancine

K. Burton, Lakeland; Tenny R. Croley, Historic Bok Sanctuary; Mary Flekke, Florida Southern College; Gina Gary, *Lakeland Ledger*; Leland M. Hawes, *Tampa Tribune*; the late Robert Hawk, St. Petersburg; Clifton P. Lewis and Vendarae Lewis, Bartow; Donna Logan, Florida Southern College; Kevin J. Logan, Lakeland Public Library; Randall MacDonald, Florida Southern College; Dorothy Manley, Polk County Historical and Genealogical Library; Jody Norman, Florida State Archives; Mike O'Neill, Haines City; Tina Peak, Lake Wales Public Library; Andrew Pearson, Florida Southern College; Skip Perez, *Lakeland Ledger*; John R. Powell, Lake Wales; the late Robert W. Saunders, Sr., Tampa; Gail Seger, Polk County Historical and Genealogical Library; Geri Sparks, Florida Southern College; Spessard Stone, Wauchula; Robert P. Sullivan, Historic Bok Sanctuary; Nell Thrift, Lakeland; and the late Vernice Williams, Fort Meade. Many thanks to Peter A. Krafft, director of cartography at Florida State University, who produced the excellent maps used in these pages. Lastly, many thanks, as well, to Richard Mathews, Sean Donnelly, and the very talented graphic designer Ana Montalvo of the University of Tampa Press for producing such a beautiful book.

I alone am responsible for errors of fact and for the interpretation of events contained in this book. Note should be taken, as well, that incorrect spellings and usages within direct quotations appear as they do in the original. I additionally have avoided the use of "[sic]."

— *Canter Brown, Jr.*
Tallahassee, Florida

None Can Have Richer Memories

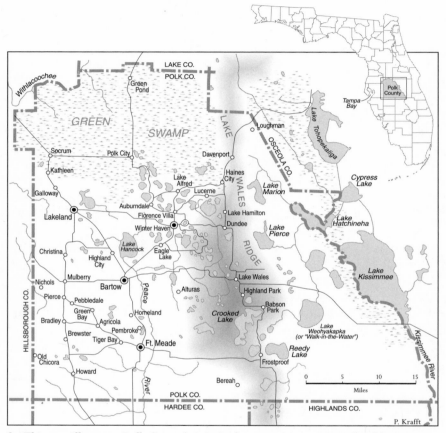

3. *This map illustrates Polk County's principal communities, topographical features, and transportation links as they appeared about 1940.* POLK COUNTY HISTORICAL ASSOCIATION COLLECTION.

"We were all in the same boat"

CHAPTER 1

〜

In Depression's Depths, 1940

*W*hen the decade of the 1940s commenced, Polk County's green vistas and glistening waters masked a harsher scene of residents struggling to cope with stresses that derived from a number of sources. The Great Depression of the 1930s had added to burdens that originated in the Florida "bust" of 1926 to cripple much of the county's economy, while the 1939 outbreak of World War Two in Europe had dealt a major blow to one of Polk's principal industries. As residents looked about them, state and county government rarely seemed able to address concerns meaningfully or successfully. Meanwhile, municipalities and schools faced bankruptcy; law enforcement reeled from the corrupting influences of illegal liquor and widespread gambling; and one quarter of the population found itself the victim of racial discrimination. Yet the county, despite its problems, stood on the verge of regaining lost stature and prosperity. In the short term specifically, it stood poised to produce a man to guide Florida through the trials and challenges of world conflict and to contribute meaningfully to the nation's victory in that war.

Challenges aside, Polk County in 1940 provided the Florida peninsula its heart and center. Created by the state's legislature in 1861, it covered a massive territory. County boundaries encompassed an impressive 1,310,720 acres, which is to say 1,875 square miles. This meant that Polk could claim precedence in size to the state of Rhode Island and equaled that of Delaware. In Florida, only the counties of Dade, Collier, and Palm Beach contained more land. To the north and northwest of Polk, above the Withlacoochee River, lay Pasco and Lake Counties, with Orange and its seat at Orlando situated to the northeast. Across the Kissimmee River to the east, sparsely populated Osceola County and the town of Kissimmee endeavored to expand economic horizons beyond the cattle business. To the southeast came Highlands County where the Depression had crippled Avon Park, Sebring, and Lake Placid. Due south, Hardee County fared worse than did Highlands. Hillsborough to the west presented a rosier picture, and its seat of Tampa furnished the region its only real city.[1]

Statements concerning the county's land area misled somewhat, since so much of its territory remained and remains under water. Almost 600 lakes, the majority of them in the county's eastern half, occupy from 7 percent to 9 percent of Polk's acreage depending upon weather conditions. They vary greatly in size. Fifty-eight lakes exceed 200 acres in area. Lake Wehyakapka, with its 7,532 acres, takes the prize for the largest.[2]

Numerous rivers and streams touch Polk, as well. As mentioned, the Withlacoochee and the Kissimmee help to form its bounds while the Hillsborough and Alafia Rivers connect the county with Tampa Bay and the Gulf of Mexico. Of central importance to Polk's and Florida's history, the Peace River supplies the county with a southerly connection to the Gulf at Punta Gorda and Charlotte Harbor. Originating in Lakes Hamilton and Hancock, the stream had offered its banks as sites for many of the county's earliest settlements.[3]

Water comprised a major element of another great feature of the county's topography, the Green Swamp. In northern Polk and adjacent areas of nearby counties, the swamp's 850 square miles dominate the scene. Its 220,000 acres in Polk consist of a series of wetlands, flat lands, and sand hills, rather than manifesting the appearance of a typical swamp. "It is actually a high, poorly-drained plateau that acts as a water retention area which feeds several major rivers in the state," declared one observer, "including the Peace, Withlacoochee, Oklawaha, and Hillsborough Rivers." Embracing an immensely fragile ecosystem, the swamp serves a key purpose in helping to maintain "the vast fresh water supply of the Floridan Aquifer."[4]

The Ridge stands out as another feature plainly evident to visitors and residents alike. Bisecting the county north to south roughly at its midpoint, these highlands parallel the Peace River to the west for much of their Polk County length. The Ridge in ancient times represented all of Florida's central and southern peninsula that remained above sea level. All told, one writer noted, "[it] stretches about 90 miles through portions of Highlands, Polk and Lake counties [and] is characterized by lakes and rolling hills." She continued, "Long and narrow (less than five miles wide at its narrowest), the Ridge appears from the air as a raised green spine." Made up mostly of "deep, well-drained sand," it offers a perfect home for citrus cultivation, especially since "warm trade winds blowing over the region help to protect the groves from severe frost."[5]

Otherwise, flatlands and gently defined rises and slopes dominate Polk's landscape. When the Ridge stood in its pristine majesty above primaeval waters, the rest of the county provided the Atlantic Ocean and the Gulf of Mexico with its adjacent bottom. Once water levels dropped with the decline of the last great Ice Age, the land emerged. Vast deposits of decayed and compressed marine life continued to underlay the surface, however. In time, these deposits transformed into phosphate ore, a substance of vital importance to manufacturing fertilizer and other commodities. The richness of the material produced grasslands that, in places, stretched beyond the horizon, beckoning eventually to cattlemen and their herds. By the late 1880s and 1890s, mining operations began to harvest the ore, altering the landscape while giving to the county an industrial base.[6]

Population and Diversity

In 1940, Polk County's population barely hinted at what it would become sixty years later. While the total had jumped nearly 10,000 during the 1930s, it had reached only 86,665 persons at decade's end. By comparison, Hillsborough contained over twice as many, and Orange

4. *As this 1930s photograph of Winter Haven's Fifth Street portrays, small town life marked the Polk landscape profoundly in 1940.* BURR, HISTORY OF WINTER HAVEN.

16,000 fewer. Osceola, Highlands, and Hardee meanwhile had crested at 10,000 or so. Florida as a whole then boasted substantially less than two million residents. Duval County placed second in importance statewide to Dade, the limits of which contained 267,000 individuals. As did the state, Polk split nearly evenly between men and women. Census takers divided them into only two categories, "white" and "negro." African Americans comprised 22 percent of the mix.[7]

Over the previous decades Polk's orientation increasingly had trended toward urban, rather than rural, life. The Great Depression, though, temporarily had reversed that trend. In 1930 a mere one-third of the county's residents had lived in rural areas. Five years later the figure had risen to 37 percent and, as late as 1945, would remain around the same level. Thanks to the careful drawing of corporate limits by legislators and local officials, African Americans tended more than whites to dwell in unincorporated territory.[8]

Its large number of municipalities, many of them incorporated, distinguished Polk from other urban and urbanizing counties in 1940 and has continued to do so since. The town of Fort Meade came first historically, but Lakeland with 21,650 residents in 1940 outranked all others. Bartow, where 6,158 persons lived, hosted the county seat. Winter Haven narrowly bested Bartow in number of inhabitants, with communities such as Lake Wales, Haines City, Auburndale, Mulberry, Frostproof, Lake Alfred, Eagle Lake, Davenport, Dundee, Lake Hamilton, and Polk City also registering their presence. Loughman, Waverly, Highland City, Kathleen, Socrum, Eloise, Babson Park, Homeland, Bradley Junction, and Brewster, among others, similarly claimed attention. Black neighborhoods and communities such as Villa Park at Fort Meade, Brittsville and East Bartow at Bartow, Moorehead and Teaspoon Hill at Lakeland, and Florence Villa at Winter Haven provided homes in incorporated areas, while Gordonville, Oakland, Jamestown, and Tripoli, to name a few, served the same purpose outside city limits.[9]

As the names of communities and neighborhoods separated by race suggest, Polk Countians in 1940 lived in segregated worlds that overlapped only occasionally. Given that fact, whites and blacks tended to look at the situation somewhat differently. "We always had interaction because even poor families, if they could afford it, would have a maid come in at times to clean up, wash, and what have you," William Ellsworth recalled from the white side of the divide. "If you were fortunate enough to have a yard man come occasionally, he brought maybe his children with him and you knew them, and things of that nature." Still, Ellsworth observed, "We were never conscious of segregation because it didn't enter our consciousness, because where you went there were your white kids." S. L. Frisbie, IV, shared his own thoughts on the topic. "For the most part, we didn't dislike each other, white people and black people," he wrote, "we didn't know each other well enough to like or dislike each other." Frank Byrd struck a similar theme. "Our family had many 'Black Friends,'" he recorded, "but there was no socializing much after dark." Byrd continued: "The Blacks stayed pretty much on their side of the tracks, and the whites stayed pretty much on their side." As Ellsworth recalled, most whites referred to black neighborhoods as "the Quarters."[10]

African Americans saw the situation, as a matter of practical necessity, in harsher terms. "We always had to be aware, even as children, of the status of blacks in society," explained future civil rights activist and Winter Haven mayor Lemuel Geathers. "It was something you questioned but had to accept," he added. Into the 1950s and early 1960s, as Florence Villa's James Henry Ammons, Jr., recollected, strict segregation remained a way of life for most. "The only time we saw or interacted with white people," he informed an interviewer, "was when we went to the shopping center or when we went to work for them."[11]

Racial segregation extended beyond residence to most public places and facilities. "Segregation was simply the way things were," a longtime resident insisted. Schools operated completely separately, while amenities such as theaters typically required black patrons to sit in the rear or else in a balcony reached by an outside entrance. The line of racial demarcation reached deep into the smallest manifestations of public life. "I tried to explain to my oldest boys why they couldn't drink water from certain fountains or use some restrooms," Geathers commented. "I would tell them: 'This is the law. It's not fair. You're just as good as anyone else. But you're not supposed to hate because of it.'"[12]

Attitudes that to modern readers may seem unjustifiable then appeared to be firm and enduring. "I have told my children, it may sound like the Dark Ages today," S. L. Frisbie related, "but in the 1940s and 1950s, that's just the way things were." There were reasons. In 1940, for instance, Civil War veterans and others with recollections of the era continued to reside in the county, a fact that kept memories of that conflict and supposed Reconstruction excesses alive. Lakeland's John B. Arnold, who well recalled meeting both President Abraham Lincoln and General Ulysses S. Grant, likely outshone many of the storytellers. One-time slaves such as Mulberry's Frank Lake added their tales. One of them, former Alabama bondsman Samuel Brunson of Lakeland, had helped to build the first railroad to that town in 1883. Charlie Smith—born in West Africa during 1842 and a resident of Texas before coming to Florida and Polk in the early twentieth century—would live another thirty-nine years in the county. Retired county sheriff James Dallas Tillis happily had spun yarns, many of them published, until his death in mid-1939. They had described an 1864 Union raid on the Tillis's Fort Meade farm but also reached back to an Indian attack eight years earlier.[13]

That proximity to the past—or, at least, what many believed the past to have been—touched lives, but so, too, did currents running deep in Florida, the South, and elsewhere in the nation. Racism existed as a fact of life virtually everywhere. All the while, white-on-black violence or the threat of such violence appeared pervasive to many in the African American community. The Ku Klux Klan had revived in 1915 and arrived in Florida and Polk County by the early 1920s. Lynchings fortunately had disappeared from the Polk landscape by the late 1930s, but Klansmen parading at Lakeland during 1938 had commanded national attention. Four years earlier county law enforcement officers had executed a former Marine, Frank Norman, who then was working to organize black grove workers for a national labor union. On the other hand, an all-white Polk County jury in 1936 courageously had convicted Klan-associated Tampa policemen of murder and other crimes in Judge Robert T. Dewell's Bartow courtroom. Despite such instances, though, African Americans necessarily walked a careful path. Thus, John D. Clark of Bartow's Crystal Ice Works could laud driver George Gammons for fidelity in not missing a day of work in almost twenty years. Gammons, on the other hand, knew well what price he might have paid had he, in fact, missed one of those days.[14]

An additional aspect of racial segregation deserves mention. The "Jim Crow" system, as it was called, indirectly encouraged the growth of a black business and professional class to address the needs of a community mostly forestalled from desirable access to white-owned businesses and professional services. Black physicians, such as

5. *The Ku Klux Klan maintained an intimidating presence in Polk County during 1940 and would do so for decades to come. Here African American residents of Lakeland refuse to back down during a 1938 confrontation.* LAKELAND PUBLIC LIBRARY.

6. *Dr. David J. Simpson's home, seen here, was situated in Lakeland's Moorehead neighborhood.* POLK COUNTY HISTORICAL QUARTERLY.

Bartow's Ledge Wynn Mc-Neill and Lakeland's David J. Simpson, earned reputations for excellent care. Dr. Alfonso William Blake practiced medicine in Bartow and Winter Haven before moving to Lakeland in 1941, while Dr. Thomas H. Adams had cared for dental needs at the same town since 1913. Numerous educators, too, evidenced professionalism of a high calibre. A few examples must suffice. At Lakeland, principals Q. J. Adderly and William A. Rochelle touched students' lives in enduring ways. James E. Stephens did so, as well, at Bartow's Union Academy.[15]

Black businesses thrived in each of the larger towns. Charlie Mc-Neill and Clifton P. Lewis have furnished looks at one community's experience by lovingly detailing several of the individuals who led Bartow in commercial and civic enterprise. They ranged from Fred Waldon, who ran "a creditable grocery store" to artisan, builder, and developer Lawrence Bernard Brown, whose home now graces the National Register of Historic Places. Thomas Franklin Burnett may have outdone all others, however, in variety of business interests. He partnered his grocery store with a funeral parlor. He then opened a multi-floor facility with a moving picture theater on the ground floor and a dance club, the Blue Room, on the second. In time Burnett launched a gas and service station and an ice cream and custard factory, as well. So profitable did his many ventures prove that, reportedly, he once loaned the City of Bartow $10,000 in a time of need.[16]

Black women also played roles of significance, as LaFrancine K. Burton has explored in Lakeland's case. Rosabelle Wilson Blake, to cite an example, would earn the honor of appointment as Polk's first "supervisor of Negro education." In that position she "coordinated pre-school conferences for black teachers" and "planned health-education programs for Polk County's schools, which included general physical examinations, health instructions and hygiene lectures." Rosabelle W. Blake Elementary School on Lakeland's Hartsell Avenue carries her name today.[17]

Women's contributions naturally made a difference in the white, as well as the black, community. The county's frontier heritage had wrought a tradition of fiercely self-reliant and capable women. Judith Breuggeman addressed that fact in discussing her grandmother Ollie Polk Futch, daughter of county pioneer J. C. A. Polk. "The most remarkable thing about my grandmother was that she and her sisters were all very independent women," Breuggeman explained. "Grandmother's sister Mary [Polk Willis] was infamous [to those who knew her] for leaving her husband a note on the kitchen table that she was driving to California," she continued. "She (Ollie) was the stability in her family," Breuggeman added. "My grandfather just seemed to drift from job to job and place to place."[18]

Polk's women desired a voice in political affairs, but the day remained distant when they would occupy official seats of power to any great degree. "[My grandmother] treasured the fact that women had gotten the vote during her lifetime," Judith Breuggeman recalled. Actually, Fort Meade and Auburndale female voters had cast some of Florida's first ballots following approval of the Nineteenth Amendment in 1920. Yet, twenty years later only a single woman served in elective public office within the county. Mada Burney Fraser (later Mada Burney Fraser Babcock McLendon) had achieved admission to the Florida Bar upon her 1932 graduation from Stetson Law School. Unable to practice her profession for four years due to Depression-era conditions, she nonetheless managed by 1938 to secure election as Lake Wales's municipal judge. She remained in the position for five consecutive terms, serving until 1948.[19]

Other women participated actively in politics and public affairs, even though they held no elective positions. Among them, Rebecca Caldwell acted in 1940 as vice chair of the Polk County Democratic Executive Committee and attended the Democratic National Convention that year as a pro-Roosevelt delegate. The previous year, a contingent of Winter Haven women, among them Josephine Burr and Dorothea Garber, helped to organize the League of Women Voters of Florida. The gathering elected Garber its first secretary. Beginning in 1941 and lasting until 1945, she presided over the organization. Deserving of additional mention, Mrs. Howard S. Warner had assumed responsibilities as Auburndale's postmistress in 1936. She would serve honorably in that office until the 1950s.[20]

Greater success or, at least, acclaim sometimes came for Polk women in venues outside the county. The celebrity of movie and radio star Frances Langford eclipsed that of all others. "When I'm rich and famous," she prided herself in telling audiences, "I'm going back to little old Lakeland down there in Florida, and settle down." Lakeland's Elizabeth Love gained renown, too. The late 1930s saw her featured in the popular network radio program "Big Sister," where she played Harriet Durant, "the scheming coquette-divorcee." As Harriet schemed, Laura M. Barrett delighted audiences with her singing. Following graduation from Florida A&M College, the Lakeland soprano played national venues, including the Chicago and New York World's Fairs.[21]

Religion, Education, Politics, and Government

Just as Polk's population diversity came down to a simple "white" and "black" in 1940, religious diversity consisted mostly of various Protestant Christian churches. The oldest continually operating congregations were Baptist. Socrum's Bethel Baptist Church traced its origins to 1851 (or, at least, not later than 1863), while First Providence Missionary Baptist Church members at Bartow believed that their congregation began when area slaves opted as early as 1856 to meet apart from white owners and their families. Methodism held sway in the county's southern reaches and among the families of many cattlemen. Homeland's Bethel Methodist Church operated by the late 1850s, with Fort Meade's First Methodist Church establishing itself in 1869. Other Protestant denominations followed. Notably, the Presbyterian Church coalesced at Bartow in 1882, while the Protestant Episcopal Church arrived in the county coincident with an influx of English visitors at mid-decade. The Church of God introduced itself into Florida near Fort Meade during 1898.[22]

The nature of religious worship varied according to the denomination, the locale, and the congregation's affluence. Numerous urban congregations had moved toward grander sanctuaries during the Florida "boom" of the early 1920s and the years thereafter. Bartow's First Baptist Church, for example, expended the considerable sum of $60,000 on a beautiful new building that would serve the congregation for the remainder of the century. Many sanctuaries and the worship they housed proved less grand, however. Harry Otis Prine has offered a helpful description regarding services at one rural church. "The Kathleen Baptist Church held one or two revival meetings during the year, which lasted for two weeks as opposed to the revivals today, which last only three to five days," he recorded. "At this period of time, preaching services were held twice a day, at eleven in the morning and at night," Prine continued. "The people were practically all farmers, so they could stop their farm work and attend the morning service easily." He concluded, "The other

7. *The imposing sanctuary of Bartow's First Baptist Church, erected during the 1920s, illustrated how far Polk County had come by 1940 from its humble pioneer roots of a century earlier.* FLORIDA STATE ARCHIVES.

denominations did not have morning and evening services, but some did run their revival for four weeks."[23]

Beyond Protestant Christianity, Polk Countians enjoyed the availability only of Roman Catholic and Jewish observances. While Catholic priests had worked in the county as early as the 1850s, Angola Catholic Church at Bartow organized only in the 1890s. A new mission church, St. Thomas, had risen there in 1913, ten years after St. Joseph Chapel began to welcome Lakelanders. St. Joseph Mission thereafter arrived at Winter Haven during 1914. Meanwhile, a small but growing number of Jewish families, including that of Cyrus "Cy" and Frances Wolfson, yearned for the comfort of a synagogue and regular opportunities for worship. They formed a Jewish Alliance at Lakeland in 1932. It soon established Temple Emanuel in an old church building.[24]

Even though most county residents professed adherence to one church or another, a note of caution or condition should be mentioned. Many area families, especially the men in those families, held themselves back from a close embrace of the specific tenets of any particular sect. A distrust of political involvements by preachers and churches went hand in hand with this tendency. Grace L. Snyder voiced the sentiments of many of these individuals. "My ideals are all tied up with a practical, functional approach to religion—not as a creed, but as a way of life," she explained. "Freedom to live and to grow, unshackled by any type of slavery (political or ecclesiastical)," Snyder continued, "is my dream for the coming generations."[25]

Even the most humble of Polk's churches prospered when compared with its school system. A low tax, low spend philosophy had kept schools lagging behind population growth through the 1920s boom and bust years; then, corporate arrogance had brought the county system to the verge of bankruptcy by the 1930s. Consolidated Naval Stores Company initiated the train of events by refusing to pay property taxes following the stock market crash of 1929 even though it possessed the resources to make the payments. Other corporations with large property holdings followed that lead. Chaos ensued to the point that, by summer 1931, the state's fourth largest school system stood last in teacher salaries. Scrip soon replaced cash as payment for educators. School closures and pay cuts followed. Assistance from President Franklin D. Roosevelt's New Deal beginning in 1933 allowed the system to continue operating, but economic downturn toward the decade's close resulted in the dismissal of every employee at the school board's Bartow headquarters. Then, on March 25, 1939, Superintendent C. I. Hollingsworth had announced that the board "may not be able to meet the future payrolls promptly for the remainder of the fiscal school year."[26]

Just when circumstances called most urgently for strong leadership, the school board itself had slipped into chaos. In March 1939 a grand jury had indicted three board officials on numerous counts of bribery and related crimes. Trials kept the story in the headlines for almost two years, embarrassing the county and further wounding the school system. Not guilty verdicts rendered in January 1941 failed to repair the damage.[27]

Polk did benefit through these difficult times from strong leadership from an outstanding educator, President Ludd Spivey of Florida Southern College. That Methodist-supported institution had moved to Lakeland in the early 1920s, with Spivey taking control in 1925. Despite the deteriorating economic conditions that followed the Florida bust the next year, Spivey refused to allow the college to close and, instead, undertook an expansion program that introduced remarkable growth to the Lake Hollingsworth campus. "A short, bald-headed man," respected journalist Leland M. Hawes observed, "Ludd M. Spivey exuded charm from every pore." Jean A. Battle, one of Spivey's deans, agreed. "He was the most popular man I've ever seen," he insisted. The dynamic educator reached out for financial benefactors by taking ocean liner trips to Europe during summer vacations, but his greatest catch proved to be Frank Lloyd Wright. The first of many buildings that the famed architect designed at

Spivey's request for the college began to rise in 1938. Built mostly with student labor and named for its donor, the Annie Pfeiffer Chapel opened for student use in 1941.[28]

Other institutions of higher learning also contributed to the Polk County educational climate. Webber College, for one, originated with the dream of Grace Knight Babson, who envisioned a school dedicated to teaching women from affluent families how to manage wealth. Her institution, named for granddaughter Camilla Grace Webber, opened April 6, 1927, on Crooked Lake at Babson Park. Initially, the students spent half the school year in Boston and half on the Polk campus, but in 1940 Babson abandoned the annual move and settled the college permanently in Polk. The next year, Webber would begin attracting national attention by commencing annual selection of the "Outstanding Young Women in the United States."[29]

While Grace Knight Babson delighted in the success of her college on Crooked Lake, black Baptists took pride in the Florida Seminary. Organized in 1901 at Bartow's First Providence Missionary Baptist Church as the Florida Baptist Seminary, the institution moved to Lakeland the next year. A two-building campus soon welcomed students and, by 1925, a state charter of incorporation had been obtained. Fire destroyed the academic building in the late 1920s, however, and not until 1932 could a new facility open under the guidance of Dr. J. P. McKinney, president, and the Reverend Willie Mack Davis, teacher. Following Dr. McKinney's death in 1933, Davis assumed the presidency and guided the institution through a decade of growth. White Hall on its campus honored Lucy White, an early promoter of mission and educational work at the seminary, and Davis Hall commemorated the service of President Davis.[30]

Educators of the calibre of Presidents Spivey, Babson, McKinney, and Davis unfortunately could do little to improve the tone and nature of Polk County politics. The problem stemmed partly from the Florida legislature's decision in 1889 to impose a poll tax for the privilege of voting. Aimed at African Americans, the measure threatened to wipe the rolls clean of poor people. It mostly achieved that goal, but, in the process, the law tended to corrupt the elections process by justifying the arbitrary exclusion of persons from exercise of their otherwise lawful rights. This fact emerged into public view in 1892 when Polk County's regular Democratic party officials, faced with a reformist challenge, arbitrarily closed polls, refused to allow residents standing in line to cast ballots, and took three days to announce results amid cries of "ballot-box stuffing."[31]

This situation produced a variety of results. For one thing, the Democratic party continued its uninterrupted rule in Polk County. A small electorate, representing the county's most-affluent and conservative voters, usually chose officials closely attuned to the interests of businessmen, citrus growers, phosphate companies, and the railroads. At the same time, individual politicians occasionally captured office by advocating rejection of the regular political establishment in the interest of reform. Several individuals stand out in this regard. Park Trammell, for instance, achieved election to the Florida house of representatives in 1902 and the state senate in 1904 before going on to serve as Florida attorney general, governor, and United States senator. The victory of Lakeland attorney J. Harden Peterson over Congressman Herbert J. Drane in 1932 symbolized the same dynamic, as did former county judge Spessard L. Holland's elevation to the state senate the same year.[32]

Democratic party dominance did not preclude individual Republicans from exercising substantial clout in local and state affairs, as well as in party councils. When Republicans controlled the White House, federal offices—including post offices—reflected the fact. Thus, one-time Civil War Unionist John L. Skipper reigned as Lakeland's postmaster and also unsuccessfully contested an election for the state comptroller's job in 1902. This partisan activity served as no bar to Skipper's later acceptance of a seat on the school board. Similarly, Lakeland's E. E. Callaway lent his name to the party's slate in the 1936 state elections. He did so as the Republican candidate for governor.[33]

Notwithstanding occasional reformist victories and a persistent—if ineffectual—Republican presence, Polk officials had resisted most efforts to prepare the county for future exigencies and, once the bust and the Depression had occurred, to provide for relief and recovery. Mostly, bickering between various elected officials characterized government in the 1930s. This fractiousness grew so intense

8. *J. Hardin Peterson of Lakeland emerged in the early 1930s as one of Florida's most influential political figures, serving as United States Congressman from 1933 to 1951. He is seen here prior to his election with law partner A. R. Carver and secretary Edna Wooten.* FLORIDA STATE ARCHIVES.

that it had reduced county government to stalemate by 1932. Frustrated by the situation, state senator Holland acted to take control in 1933 by securing enactment of a law creating a five-member budget commission appointed by the governor. With fiscal affairs now removed from day-to-day politics, county government began a slow process of maturing and learning how to reach out more effectively to the public.[34]

Meanwhile, corruption in government appeared rife as law enforcement seemed ready to break down. Prohibition had produced mountains of money for those involved in defying the law for profit, with plenty left over to bribe those charged with enforcement of the ban on alcohol sales and consumption. The problem persisted even after Congress during the Roosevelt administration repealed national Prohibition in December 1933. Controversial elections with questionable results maintained prohibition in Polk, other than for beer and wine, into the 1960s. Moreover, illegal gambling had spread to flood-tide proportions, especially the Cuban numbers game known as bolita. Police and sheriff's deputies usually looked the other way. "Lakeland and the entire county is a cesspool of dives, joints, bars, gambling dens etc. and any officer who does not know this is blind and dumb," E. E. Callaway informed Governor Fred P. Cone in 1937. He added, "They know." Bennett DeLoach amplified Callaway's remarks. "Politics were pretty rotten in Polk County," he remembered. "Especially the sheriffs: gambling, bootlegging," DeLoach continued. "Everybody talked about the sheriffs."[35]

Fortunately, a few leaders helped to guide Polk through this morass. As early as 1935 Ludd Spivey had grown so alarmed at the rise in crime and violence that he convened a county-wide conference on the subject. "[There have been] more murders in Polk county during the past 18 months," he declared, "than in all of Great Britain." As suggested earlier, Senator Holland also accepted responsibility and pushed for reforms. Among other initiatives, he joined with Dade County's state senator Ernest Graham in 1937 to convince the legislature to repeal the poll tax. Grateful for this and other accomplishments, Florida voters chose Holland as their governor in 1940. Thomas W. Bryant ranked high, as well, among those who contributed positively to county affairs. Although a state legislator in the 1920s, he declined electoral contests thereafter but did serve in various other capacities. As a Florida Board of Control member from 1936 to 1949, for instance, Bryant helped to guide Florida's system of higher education into the modern era and as a Lakeland Chamber of Commerce officer he fought for other needed improvements. "Tom Bryant is as blunt as he is honest," one journalist remarked of the man. "He was the wisest man I ever knew," son-in-law D. Burke Kibler added. "He loved education, and he was very instrumental in building the roads that let us grow." Bryant was, Kibler concluded, "A wonderfully progressive individual in wanting things to happen."[36]

Municipal governments required the leadership offered by men such as Spivey, Holland, and Bryant every bit as much as did the county. Complications of the bust and the Depression, coupled with property tax defaults by solvent corporations and an influx of jobless men from out of state, overwhelmed the ability of town and city officials to cope. They held out hope of recouping delinquent taxes on corporate-owned property until 1937. At that time the legislature approved the "Murphy Act," a controversial statute that permitted owners to redeem many delinquent properties simply by paying the state, as opposed to local, taxes due. By summer 1939 Auburndale had filed for bankruptcy protection. Other communities feared the need to take the same action in the not-too-distant future.[37]

Scenes of Depression

By 1940 the Depression's impact on Polk stood out starkly. Although pockets of affluence could be found in many areas of the county, the reality of the harsh times displayed itself all around. "Things went unkempt, things went unpainted, and the landscaping or anything like that was unattended because it was a matter of marshaling your funds and trying to get by," one resident recalled. "It was just a reversion back to nature somewhat until after the war," he added. Even at Mountain Lake, the county's millionaires' retreat near Lake Wales, directors grappled with budget shortfalls and personnel cutbacks. "It was a desperate time," local historian Freddie Wright has explained, "which only those who lived through it can understand."[38]

Hettie Lou Scanlin Whatley described conditions at Homeland in terms that applied in many county locales. "Everybody in Homeland was poor," she recorded. "We didn't know we were poor because everybody was in the same shape," Whatley continued. "We . . . could not afford shoes and when the soles of our shoes wore out we put cardboard in the bottom." She added: "If someone had a little mishap we passed an apron around. Each family would sew a coin into this apron and nobody knew who the coins came from, and then someone would deliver it to the person who needed it." Whatley concluded, "We were all in the same boat and there was no social stigma to it."[39]

Depression conditions actually had grown worse in Polk as the 1930s ended. Citrus industry overproduction during the 1938-1939 season resulted, as one historian explained, in "one of the most disastrous in the entire history of the Florida citrus industry." Drought deepened the crisis. Then, on September 1, 1939, World Two commenced with Germany's invasion of Poland. International trade constricted, but Polk's phosphate industry especially felt the blow. Germany had been Florida's number one foreign customer. "The companies have done everything they can during the depression to employ as many persons as possible," International Agricultural Corporation's general manager Barnwell Fuller proclaimed, "but the war puts a different complexion on the matter."[40]

At first, the new decade brought nothing better. "We all lived pretty hard for several years up to World War II," Frank Byrd well remembered. Conditions deteriorated particularly in late January 1940 when killer freezes, the worst in four decades, befell the citrus crop. "In January 1940, I saw a thermometer go down to eight degrees," Ben Hill Griffin informed one journalist. "Oh, 1940 was just terrible," he commented further. "Nearly all the oranges in the state froze. The fresh-fruit market was just about wiped out." William Ellsworth added, "A lot of your communities went bankrupt."[41]

Ironies abounded, with beautiful inspirations of the boom years and of times before offsetting current signs of desperation and defeat. As for inspirations, to cite an example, the magnificent Lake Mirror civic center at Lakeland set standards for urban design. "[It] without doubt is one of the most beautiful compositions of its kind in this country," a well-regarded magazine had declared. Just up the street the Lakeland Terrace Hotel welcomed guests with elegant hospitality and surroundings. To the east at Mountain Lake, golfers thrilled to play on the magnificent Seth J. Raynor course. They did so on the slopes of Iron Mountain, below Edward Bok's magnificent Singing Tower, itself set as a jewel within the grounds of the Mountain Lake Sanctuary. Upon dedicating Bok's gift to Polk's people in 1929, President Calvin Coolidge had declared its purpose as "preach[ing] the gospel of beauty."[42]

Lovely homes abounded, too. Perhaps the exotic and romantic Casa de Josefina, a Mediterranean-style mansion built by Josephine and Irwin Yarnell and located south of Lake Wales at Highland Park, resounded most deeply with echoes of past times. "Until the Florida real estate bust of 1926, life at the Casa was like an F. Scott Fitzgerald novel," one account detailed. "Hundreds of guests—millionaire friends, from New York and winter resorts around Florida, gathered for rounds of parties

9. *Although taken a few years later, this photograph preserves the image of Lakeland's skyline much as it appeared in 1940. Featured is landscape architect Charles Leavitt's beautiful 1928 Lake Mirror Promenade with the Lakeland Terrace Hotel appearing in the background.* LAKELAND PUBLIC LIBRARY.

where the champagne spilled from fountains and entertainment was often performances of Shakespeare's plays, contests or airplane rides around Polk County," the writer continued. "But with the loss of the value of much of his land in 1926, followed by further losses in the stock market crash of 1929 [and] the death of two of the couple's four children, the life at the Casa became more subdued," she added. "After Yarnell's death in 1935 Josephine desperately hung on to the Casa, selling off land, jewelry, antiques and eventually, the stories say, the Townsend diamond."[43]

The quiet that surrounded Casa de Josefina touched many of the man-made survivors of the boom years. Especially, partially completed structures, left unfinished when the economy collapsed in 1926 and 1927, punctuated the landscape as eerie reminders of past hopes. None commanded more notice than Fort Meade's "Skeleton Hotel." Its designers originally had intended that the Fort Meade Terrace Hotel dominate the juncture of the town's principal streets, described as "one of the busiest intersections in the Peace River Valley." Roofless when abandoned, it survived to 1940 only because seventeen local men paid to cover its top floor. Arguments flared as to its value or potential. Yet, the hotel's seven-story concrete frame glistened hauntingly in the moonlight, transformed in some eyes from an embarrassment to an object of abstract beauty. A suggestion that a "sort of multi-storied flower garden" fill the structure never came to fruition, although an open air market did, in time, occupy the ground floor.[44]

For many Polk Countians life by the early 1940s simply meant getting by day to day and week to week, and relatively inexpensive amenities available locally aided that pursuit immensely. "You just did your thing, grew up in a very isolated world, because of the radio and the news and movie shorts, you knew what was going on," a lad of the times recollected. "And its was a big world out there but nobody particularly cared." People did care, though, about politics. "Entertainment in Lakeland in the 1930s and 1940s consisted of radio, revivals, and political rallies," another observer commented. "Munn Park, in the center of downtown, was the scene of eight to 10 rallies a year." Lawton Chiles added: "Folks would sit on fruit boxes or on the front of their cars to listen. They would drive their cars downtown early in the day to listen to the speeches."[45]

In a land of lakes, rivers, streams, and springs, water sports drew thousands. Eagle Lake and Kissengen Springs offered two of the most popular such gathering spots. The Crystal Beach Pavilion, constructed at Eagle Lake during 1920, "boasted changing rooms, picnic supply canteen, shaded picnic areas, restrooms, a dance floor and a live band headed by Charles Proctor, the owner." Thursday night dances drew crowds. "There weren't many places around here to dance at the time so people would flock to the pavilion," J. D. Catrett explained.[46]

Kissengen Springs, situated between Bartow and Fort Meade, usually outdrew Eagle Lake. Owned by the family of one-time sheriff John Logan, it included a variety of accommodations, while encompassing an "underground stream [that] boiled out so fast that only the strongest swimmers could cope with it." The *Lakeland Ledger* attempted to explain its allure. "Kissengen was a grassroots place where people could put aside all pretense and be informal and have a general good time just relaxing and being sociable," it observed. "Much romance flourished at Kissengen," the journal added. "There is no estimating how many young couples first felt the idyllic young love fluttering in their inexperienced hearts at Kissengen." That did not exhaust the list of attributes. "It was a political spot, too," the report continued. "There at Kissengen candidates aspiring to serve the people have stood and said their pieces to large crowds. Gala occasions those were." It concluded: "There was lots of good eating. And there was lots of hand-shaking and visiting together by old-timers and young-timers assembled to consider the political destiny of the county, state, and nation."[47]

Water also offered a focus to one of Polk's newest popular gathering spots. Dick Pope's dreams of beautifying the swampland on Lake Eloise's north shore at Winter Haven had resulted by 1936, thanks to assistance from the New Deal's Work Projects Administration, in the opening of the mesmerizing Cypress Gardens. Inspired by "a wonderful grove of cypress trees extending far out into the lake," the gardens emerged within a short period as one of Florida's most frequented tourist attractions and a source of pride for county residents.[48]

Baseball offered leisure at low cost to many local fans. Amateur and school squads competed regularly, but professional teams generated excitement as well. The Detroit Tigers took spring training at Lakeland and had done so since 1934. As years passed, Winter Haven hosted the Philadelphia Nationals, Toronto opted for Haines City, and Milwaukee played at Lake Wales. Rochester meanwhile found a home at Bartow. Within the black community, the sport flourished with local teams and talents that participated in the Negro Baseball League. Benjamin Williams's Polk County All-Stars eventually took Florida state championships with squads that included Isaiah "Rabbit" Sabb, Ossie Green, Hardy Busbee, Reuben Williams, Hoagie Gordon, "Snooks" McDuffie, Sammie Williams, C. J. Gardner, "Pink" Dunlap, and Walter Perry. The Jimmy Hill Lakeland All-Stars likewise thrilled and entertained crowds that combined white and black patrons.[49]

No list of late 1930s, early 1940s, diversions would be complete without mention of the movies. From humble picture shows to motion picture palaces, the county offered moviegoers comfortable hours of enjoyment away from the cares of the day. Sometimes, a patron might receive even more since, once a week at many locales, lucky customers on "gift night" could gain a welcomed piece or selection of "Depression

10. *Top quality African American players regularly demonstrated their skills at baseball. Benjamin Williams (at left) owned the Polk County All-Stars, while Isaiah Sabb of Lake Wales stood out as one of the team's key players.* CLIFTON P. LEWIS.

glass" as a cheering prize. "My family would go once a week," Nancy Peterson commented. "We would dress up more than they do now," she added. "I would always wear a dress. We sat in the middle of the left-hand side, because that's where daddy liked to sit." Frostproof's Ramon Theatre, as could have been asserted of the comparable facility in any other town in the county, lived "as an immanent and active figure of Frostproof's cultural scene." The county's plushiest movie palace, Lakeland's "Venetian palazzo" Polk Theatre, featured a 100-ton air conditioner that, rumor had it, dimmed lights all over town when turned on by the manager. The theater came complete with a "twinkling night sky" and hand-carved columns. "At the Polk," an admirer related, "Lakeland saw the Depression's harsh reality and Hollywood's dream of prosperity."[50]

Betting on the Future

Times certainly appeared dismal to many Polk Countians in 1940. Despite President Roosevelt's campaign promises to keep the nation out of world war, that conflict, many believed, inevitably would draw the United States into the fighting. At home, an economy based upon agriculture, mining, and cattle grazing gasped for breath. A place that—during the twenty or so years preceding the early 1930s had been the wealthiest county in the nation on a per-capita basis—groaned now with the burden of state and national depression, not to mention especially cruel blows to the citrus and phosphate industries.[51]

Even in such difficult times, however, visionaries realized future potential and risked their all on its promise. At Lakeland, for instance, the William P. McDonald Construction Company stood out as one of the state's premier highway contracting firms, its backers understanding that population growth and the needs of military training necessarily would require road repair and construction. Likewise, from Mulberry the W. S. Badcock Corporation had endeavored to shake off the Depression's grip by innovative marketing, including pioneering dealer and consignment merchandising. In 1937 the company had expanded into quality bedding with the purchase of the Polk County Mattress Factory. The slogan "Badcock will treat you right" increasingly caught the attention of Floridians, and, as the years passed, would command the business of millions more.[52]

Certainly, Bertha Hinshaw also deserved to be described as a visionary. She and husband Carl had attempted in the 1920s to launch the Carlton Club, "a magnificent residential resort appealing to people

11. *When grocer George Jenkins opened the remodeled Publix Super Market No. 1 at Winter Haven in 1940, he helped to revolutionize an industry.* POLK COUNTY HISTORICAL QUARTERLY.

of culture and refinement" on Lake Suzanne near Lake Wales, but the bust took a heavy toll on their prospects. They dimmed further with Carl's death in 1931. Bertha, though, would not give up. Believing in the county and anxious to support her family, she took the resort's buildings and opened them for guests as the Chalet Inn. Meanwhile, she entertained up to 100 guests at a time with fine cuisine at the adjacent Chalet Suzanne restaurant. "I couldn't go into town for a job because I had two young children to look after," she explained. Hinshaw continued: "My hobby was gourmet cooking—it was the only thing I could do. So I decided to serve dinner in my home." She concluded, "Everybody said it wouldn't work." By 1940 the chalet's reputation for excellence had spread well beyond Florida, and Bertha stood poised to reap the harvest of better times to come.[53]

One individual may have epitomized more than anyone else those persons whose dreams of the future represented hope to a county mired in problems, and, as such, this chapter will conclude with his triumph as the 1940s opened on Polk County. George Jenkins, a Georgia native, had arrived in 1926 just as the boom turned to bust. He made do as a Piggly Wiggly grocery store manager until 1930 when he took a chance with borrowed money to open the first Publix grocery store, adapting the name from a failed theater chain. Dissatisfied with the quality of service generally available for grocery customers, Jenkins traveled the nation through the 1930s to view for himself innovations in store design, construction, and operation. Fortified with the results, he rejected the limitations of the past and seized upon the possibilities of the future. Specifically, the grocer commissioned the region's first modern supermarket. Complete with air conditioning and sliding glass doors, not to mention a bakery and other innovative services, his new Publix Super Market—opened at Winter Haven in November 1940—revolutionized the industry. "I've got an ambition," Jenkins quietly informed a friend soon thereafter of where his dreams had led him. "I want 50 stores," he declared, "just as nice as this one."[54]

12. *Many of Polk County's premier political leaders gathered at Kissengen Springs during the 1942 election season for an old-fashioned Democratic rally filled with stemwinding stump speeches and hours of good eating. Seen here, from the left, are county judge Chester M. Wiggins, state representative Perry Murray, criminal court clerk B. Lucian Durrance, tax collector Ray Clements, supervisor of registration Hugh Carlton, school board member Frank Myers, circuit court clerk D. H. Sloan, Jr., county solicitor H. Gunter Stephenson, Democratic executive committee chairman Dave Turner (at microphone), and Democratic party advocate A. D. Tomasello.* LOUISE FRISBIE COLLECTION.

CHAPTER 2

۔ە

All-Consuming War, 1940-1945

*W*hile World War Two fighting touched the United States directly only in December 1941, the conflict's shadow spread its looming presence over all of the decade's first half. At the beginning Polk Countians found themselves intent upon addressing challenges at home while praying for peace abroad, but increasingly they grew wary that something far more powerful than a national commitment to isolationism was about to engulf them. Once it did they vigorously supported their country at home and in the fighting overseas, often doing so with courage, distinction, and profound meaning for the future. As time would tell, seeds planted during those years would come to bear lush fruit in a dynamic era to come.

The period commenced in 1940 with county residents yet combatting the devastation of economic depression. The previous summer, war had flared in Europe, dealing the phosphate industry a heavy blow. In January, freezes crippled citrus production. Still, the year's toll had not been counted in its entirety as other events further dampened spirits and the economy. In the circumstances, school board finances dropped to such a low point by October that the Lake Wales city council approved a loan to pay teacher and bus driver salaries. Then, in mid-November temperatures dropped into the mid-20s, wreaking more havoc, especially to vegetable crops and other small plants. The month brought general misery, beyond freeze damage, with exceedingly cold weather. The *Lake Wales Highlander* labeled it, with only a little exaggeration, the "Coldest in History of Florida."[1]

President Franklin D. Roosevelt's administration and its New Deal thankfully persisted in combatting the economy's woes into the new decade. Numerous new public projects met with completion or else were announced by grateful local politicians and community leaders. The Work Projects Administration, for instance, moved ahead with plans to construct a commercial airport at Lake Wales, "complete with hangar, administrative building and lands costing $58,000." At Lakeland, civic leader Thomas W. Bryant managed to secure WPA funding for a new football stadium. Thankful for his efforts, local people insisted that the facility carry Bryant's name. That community's housing authority also signaled approval of the Lake Ridge project for black families. The grand scheme envisioned construction of twenty-one buildings encompassing 160 apartments on a tract that covered seven blocks. Plans called for tasteful landscaping, as well as modern conveniences including electric stoves and refrigerators. By July 1941 project files contained 150 applications for residences, and lucky tenants-to-be looked forward to an opening date in September.[2]

Almost all residents applauded the New Deal's helping hand, but by 1940 they had determined as well to compel state and local government to aid relief, recovery, and reform by cleaning up corruption and exerting more-positive leadership. The Democratic party ruled Polk and the state, so its May primaries decided contests for offices to be filled effective January 1941. Most significantly, state senator Spessard L. Holland of Bartow claimed the nomination for governor in a runoff with DeLand's Francis Whitehair, a one-time Winter Haven resident. Not too surprisingly, Governor Holland quickly reorganized the state citrus commission, designating Winter Haven's Thomas B. Swann as chairman. "The industry is looking to you with hope and anticipation," he informed his appointees. "The destiny of the industry is in your hands." Lakeland's Charles A. Stewart and Fred W. Davis of Lake Wales joined Swann on the panel. Other county residents also lent support to Holland's efforts to revitalize state government. Among them, Jack Futch Townsend of Lake Wales took a seat on the state road board; Jess J. Gilliam of Lakeland headed the state highway patrol; and Winter Haven's Henry Sinclair served the governor personally as his secretary.[3]

Regarding offices that lay closer to home, voters turned in good part to Winter Haven and a new generation of leadership in a time of trials and trouble. Youthful attorney Harry Eubank King captured Holland's state senate seat, serving thereafter for sixteen years and, in the process, becoming a force to be reckoned with in state politics. For the single most powerful county office, that of sheriff, the electors turned to Winter Haven police chief DeWitt Sinclair. Citrusman and Yale University graduate Francis Elbridge Brigham, a man willing to accept the formidable challenge of bringing order out of chaos for the county school system, emerged as school superintendent. Fellow townsman Don Register claimed the circuit judgeship. Meanwhile, Ray Clements took on the job of tax collector and Ben F. Conner of the Connersville citrus family achieved election as state representative. Unfortunately, Conner soon died in an automobile accident. Perry Earl Murray, a Frostproof attorney, succeeded Conner in the legislature and remained there, as will be seen, until 1955.[4]

It should be remembered that, notwithstanding all of the problems that faced Polk Countians before December 1941, the times remained relatively innocent compared to what was about to become the norm. Iris Sullivan Reese, then a student at Bartow's Summerlin Institute, recalled the era. "As the summer was coming to an end, we were enjoying picnics at Eagle Lake or refreshing dips in nice, cool Kissengen Springs," she recorded. "On the way back from the Springs, everybody gathered at John's Drive-in out on Highway 17 for hamburgers (smothered with John's special hot slaw) and Cokes," Reese continued. The girls, she remembered, typically wore "broomstick skirts with peasant blouses and penny loafers," the boys "khaki pants with shirts and loafers." For school children, the times seemed safe and mostly secure. "Most of us walked to school, rain or shine," Reese explained. "Life in Bartow was good, people were friendly, and we always had time to stop and visit with each other." She commented further: "Wilson and Bartow Drug were popular spots and they both featured curb service; we also had the Corner Drug and Soda Shoppe. Neither of the drug stores had doors or screens (except at night when folding doors closed the entry), and we parked our cars right in front for double-dipped ice cream cones and Cokes." Reese added, "Little did we realize that events were forthcoming that would change our lives forever."[5]

Romance could yet flourish and, when it did, have time to mature without a sense of urgency and fear that soon would be felt. During summer 1941, for instance, Texan Edward D. Wickersheim arrived late one afternoon at Winter Haven's Ridgeland Hotel, preparing to assume a job at the Lake Alfred Sun Dine Company plant. "Hungry and tired, he showered, dressed in a nice tan suit, Texas hat and boots, and headed downtown to the Home Kitchen Diner, the best cooking in town," an account of subsequent events related. "As he entered the diner and took a seat at a table, the most beautiful young lady he had ever seen was coming to wait on his table." At the time both Wickersheim and waitress

Oleda Darnell were engaged to others, but "love at first sight" prevailed. Despite warnings from her aunt that Wickersheim might be transferred out of the county, Leda welcomed the stranger and soon began to date him. On April 18, 1942, they married at Winter Haven's First Christian Church, thereafter maintaining their home and family in Polk into the twenty-first century.[6]

This sense of innocence persisted to some degree right up to the outbreak of war, as a Lakeland story published December 14, 1941, in a widely circulated newspaper suggested. "Members of the Junior Chamber of Commerce didn't classify themselves as home-wreckers until Secretary Glenn Higley got a frantic long-distance telephone call from an Atlanta husband who wanted the Jaycees to explain to his sobbing wife 'about the card I got in the mail from you,'" the item read. "This is the explanation of the phone call: Jaycees give away free orange juice here each Winter, later sending literature to tourists who register at the stands," it continued. "This Winter they took their lists of tourists and sent out picture postcards, signing names such as 'Bill,' 'John,' 'Mary,' and 'Sue' in order to personalize the publicity campaign while reminding visitors of the good time they had here last season." The article concluded, "The Atlanta husband happened to get his 'wish-you-were-here' card from someone who signed the name of 'Mary.'"[7]

War's Shadow

Distant fighting echoed in Polk after Germany launched World War Two by attacking Poland on September 1, 1939, but, at first, the reverberations seemed faint and not so threatening. For almost half a year a "phony war" quietly ensued until, in spring 1940, Nazi *blitzkrieg* or "lightning war" swept through western Europe leaving Great Britain as an "island fortress of democracy." As these events occurred, the people of the United States accepted President Franklin D. Roosevelt's assurance that "your boys are not going to be sent into any foreign wars." Roosevelt added, "Your President says this country is not going to war." What Roosevelt did do, however, was prepare for defense just in case. He endorsed a proposed Selective Service Act, and it passed the Congress in September. Beginning in mid-October men between the ages of twenty-one and thirty-five throughout the nation, including those in Polk County, signed up for the new military draft.[8]

Suddenly, the possibility of war and images of America's military capabilities seemed to present themselves more insistently. *Life* magazine on

October 28, for instance, presented a photo section on soldiers and sailors, featuring Lieutenant Commander W. R. Hollingsworth. The brother of Polk Superintendent of Public Instruction C. I. Hollingsworth, he served on the aircraft carrier *U.S.S. Enterprise*. By November military preparations had replaced mere images. Between the twenty-fifth of that month and January 6, 1941, Florida's national guard units mobilized. They included Polk's 116th Field Artillery Regiment located at Bartow, Lakeland, and Winter Haven. That unit later divided into two battalions, the 116th and 149th, with their members seeing combat in Europe and the South Pacific. William E. Backus, Robert L. Childress, Gillis R. Harris, Arthur F. Mathews, Harrell Lee Mullaney, Robert Sharpe, and Oscar M. Williams would give their lives.[9]

The pace of events quickened in 1941. Draft notices hit the mails beginning in February, with recipients receiving greetings from Uncle Sam as the months progressed. Meanwhile, the Florida Civilian Defense Council organized with a unit in each county. Winter Haven editor George L. Burr, Jr., at Governor Holland's request, served as executive director for the state effort. Women particularly contributed to the work. "Mrs. Elva Gibbs of Winter Haven, chairman of the division of Home and Community Services of the Polk County Defense Council," a notice published the next year declared, "reports 1083 women have completed the standard course in first aid, and 312 have taken advanced courses." The item added, "Qualified first aid teachers number 139, and 21 nutrition teachers are instructing the defense workers." In April a "Bundles for Britain" campaign opened at Lake Wales with Mrs. R. W. Bennett at its head, importing speakers from war-torn England and gathering needed supplies.[10]

War news and war preparations sparked genuine fears and, for a few, a sense almost of paranoia. "Polk County needs a little more activity in home defense work," one newspaperman proclaimed in May. "We are surrounded by traitors and fifth columnists, some of them not actively engaged in destructive work on material things, but there are a great many who are working on the line of injurious psychological sabotage, and they should be worked on," he continued. The editor went on to insist that "patriotic teaching should be stressed in the schools and churches, the lodge rooms and the public gatherings of all kinds." By August the school board had ordered all students fingerprinted "in the interest of national defense and to provide identification" and had urged the state board of education "to withdraw from the schools of Florida all text books termed 'un-American' by the American Legion's national Americanism committee."[11]

By that time the war truly had begun to come home to larger numbers of Polk residents. The reason lay in a United States Army decision, taken as early as September 1940, to train pilots at what would come to be known as the Lakeland School of Aeronautics, a facility associated with Albert I. Lodwick. Then, in spring 1941 a change in national policy permitted British Royal Air Force flight cadets and those of other British Commonwealth nations to train in the United States, and the Lakeland facility refocused its program under school director Harry Copeland to that purpose. The first contingent of ninety trainees arrived in June for the ten-week course. "The people of Lakeland warmly embraced the British cadets," historians Lynn M. Homan and Thomas Reilly have observed, "making the homesick young men feel as welcome as possible." Governor Holland on August 16 distributed diplomas at graduation ceremonies for the first class.[12]

Meanwhile a significant number of Polk County men prepared to fight. Lake Wales's John C. Linderman trained, for example, at the United States Military Academy at West Point, New York. Alexander Jenkins of Lakeland's Moorehead community served on the *U.S.S. Whitney*. Some others volunteered, including Fort Meade's Claude

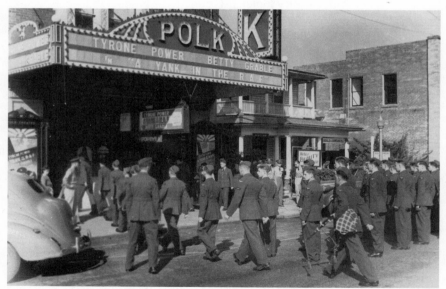

13. *The Lodwick School of Aeronautics at Lakeland drew British Royal Air Force flight cadets for training during World War Two's early years. Just as did Polk's young people at the time, the cadets often spent rare leisure hours enjoying the movies at the "fabulous" Polk Theatre.* LAKELAND PUBLIC LIBRARY.

Neil Wilcox who opted for service in the Canadian air corps and paid for the privilege with his life in 1943. Many received draft notices. Bartow's John Sanford Edwards, Jr., typically got his call from the army by mail. Edwards's only regret came from the fact that he just had purchased his first automobile. More men would follow the same path as draft registration recommenced in July.[13]

Still, the blow delivered by the Japanese Navy at Pearl Harbor, Hawaii, on December 7, 1941, caught the nation and Polk Countians by surprise. Alex Jenkins stood out as the first county resident to feel the surprise that Sunday since his ship then was moored at Pearl Harbor. All remembered the event as a defining moment of their lives. "I was with my sister and grandmother [at Lakeland's Polk Theatre]," Dyas Gregg recalled. "When we stepped outside, everyone was talking about war and the Japanese bombing us, and I couldn't figure out what was going on." Others echoed similar experiences. "I was at the Ernada Theater in Bartow," Meromay Boynton Davis explained. "They stopped the picture and announced that Pearl Harbor had been bombed." Davis added, "We all screamed and hollered and were scared to death."[14]

14. *Air bases and flight training facilities dotted Polk County during World War Two, contributing significantly to the war effort. This photograph offers a sense of the scale and intensity of those efforts at the Lodwick School of Aeronautics at Lakeland.* LAKELAND PUBLIC LIBRARY.

Iris Sullivan Reese recorded her memories as well, and they convey a telling sense of the time and place. "Most of us did what was usual for a Sunday morning," she commented. Reese then continued:

> We went to church and picnicked in the afternoon. Most of us did not have the radio on all day. The weather was sunny and pleasant, so we were outside enjoying it. When we heard the six o'clock news on the old Atwater Kent [radio], we were shocked. . . . When we got to school the next day, all was in turmoil. Many of the senior boys were talking about joining the Marines. At noon we filed into the auditorium to listen to the radio to hear President Roosevelt address the Congress ("a day that will live in infamy") and ask for a declaration of war. [15]

In a moment the world for Polk Countians had changed, far more decisively than at any other time in the past. Auburndale's Carl Allen articulated the point as he ruminated over 1941's end and the beginning of 1942. "New Year's came but it was different," he observed. "This year there were very few parties held to welcome the new year, and hardly anyone was feeling like celebrating or even thinking much about the new year," Allen continued. "There didn't seem to be anything to celebrate." He added: "People were afraid and now, for the first time, they began to realize that they hardly knew anything about the strength of our nation. We hardly ever saw a soldier or a sailor—although a few of the boys around Polk County had gone into the service—that was mostly for the sake of a job." Allen ended by stating, "It seemed like our generation was destined to have all the bad luck to come that there was, and now the new year was taking us into something that we knew nothing about." [16]

The Home Front

Authorities understandably lost little time in redirecting affairs to a war standing. Three days after Pearl Harbor Governor Holland, as expressed in an Associated Press report, "clamped on war-time economy" on state government. He restricted expenditures and "urged city, county and district governing authorities to do likewise." Rationing boards quickly organized, with first priority placed on automobile tires. Shortages of rubber to fabricate tires likewise introduced government price controls. *Lakeland Ledger* reporter L. F. Blankner reflected on what ensued thereafter. "Gasoline was rationed," he began. "Sugar was rationed; meat was rationed, including canned goods of various sorts; almost any meal included rationed articles." Blankner concluded, "The home front produced;

the home front conserved." Winter Haven's Josephine Burr added her recollections of blackouts, air raid warnings, and school superintendent F. E. Brigham's enhanced physical fitness program. "Practically everything that happened in the city," she insisted, "was for the war effort."[17]

A report from Homeland in late 1942 illustrated many of the home front efforts undertaken in support of the war effort. "The young men are gone to war and the older generation and the children have taken up their duties," the report observed. "When four youngsters will drag a big roll of four foot fence (did you ever try it?) two miles to their scrap pile, they know there is a war and that their country needs their contribution." The report added: "They've got a ground observatory post in Homeland, efficiently operated by a trained crew of airplane spotters. The grownups have taken first aid courses, incendiary and explosive bomb protection courses, nutrition and fire prevention training. They've contributed to USO [the United Service Organization], Red Cross, and they've bought war bonds and stamps."[18]

As the Homeland report mentioned, Polk linked itself with the Florida Defense Force through the Polk County Air Defense Unit. Watchers manned the tallest structures in each community nightly, charged with

15. *Young people, as well as adults, aided the war effort in Polk. The Bartow high school students portrayed here offer the popular "V for Victory" sign while sitting atop a pile of scrap they collected in November 1942. Those depicted include Dayle Taylor, Dot Butts, Andy Moore, Tommy Albinson, Thurman Whatley, Nellie Sutherland, Lonnie Knight, Murry Harris, Keil McCarly, Mrs. Mitchell, Mary Jean Crum, Bill Lawrence, Richard Peterson, Cleve Hamm, Bubba Boswell, Sonny Dieham Dieterman, Kenneth Paterson, and Mary Houghton.* POLK COUNTY HISTORICAL QUARTERLY.

reporting the passage of any kind of aircraft to a civil defense headquarters located in the county courthouse basement. Even the cupola atop the courthouse served as a watch station, a fact that gave rise to an interesting, although unsubstantiated, report. "One evening," according to the *Miami Herald*, "late workers nearby heard the [courthouse] clock begin to strike nine: bong, bong, bong, followed by a crash." The account added, "They thought the Nazis had bombed Bartow, but it turned out only to be the counterweight of the dome clock coming loose from its hook and smashing through the glass ceiling into the rotunda." Some evidence points to the truth of the tale. "Bartow's clock, which has told the hours from the dome of the courthouse for 34 years, finally became too rheumatic to carry on, and so it has been crated and shipped to Boston for rejuvenation," a local newspaper reported in early 1942. "The savants say that time heals all things, but time couldn't heal the clock," its article explained. "Indeed, it was time that dropped the 1,000-pound weight from the Polk clock a few weeks ago, and many a Polk countian who has viewed the gaping hole in the ceiling has felt extremely grateful that he wasn't standing underneath the weight that night it made its descent."[19]

The Civil Air Patrol, too, brought Polk's men and women into active support of the national struggle. It commenced operations on December 1, 1941, with Florida considered a location of immense importance to its work because of the damage that German submarines could inflict on merchant vessels in sea lanes off its coast. Florida's existing 1st Air Squadron merged into the CAP, with Haines City's Peter J. Sones acting in a key advisory capacity. In July 1942 Sones accepted command of Coastal Patrol Station No. 13, operating first from Tampa's Peter O. Knight Airport and then from Sarasota, with responsibility for patrolling sea lines and simulating bombing attacks. Not to be outdone, Sones's wife Eleanor Sones served back at home as a spotter from the roof of Haines City's Hotel Polk. Lakeland's Ruth Clifford, though, proved that women could participate directly as pilots in CAP work. "If, in my small way, I could contribute some little bit to the final success of the United Nations in this war," she recorded, "I would not have lived in vain." Clifford worked with Lakeland's Squadron 413-2 from November 1942 with the rank of second lieutenant.[20]

Besides spotters and CAP pilots, the regular military rapidly enhanced its presence in the county. In May 1942, to cite an example, officials ordered reactivation of Lakeland's Drane Field as the Lakeland Army Air Field. "Runways were laid, barracks were built and military men and planes began to swarm into the area," an onlooker reminisced.

"For several years," he continued, "Drane Field was used to polish off flyers before they were sent on overseas to join in combat." The next year Bartow Army Air Field opened on Highway 17 between Bartow and Winter Haven. The facility would become, according to its last commander, Lieutenant Colonel John A. Thompson, "one of the largest fighter pilot training programs in the Third Air Force." After May 18, 1943, it graduated over 1,500 combat fighter pilots.[21]

Lake Hancock, located in close proximity to the air fields at Lakeland and Bartow, particularly offered an inviting site for pilot training. For several years its waters often reflected the image of fighters and bombers, either practicing low-level flying or else engaging in bomber runs. "To this day," lake explorer Mike McDonald observed in 2003, "the lake bottom is still strewn with practice bombs and the pylons used to support the bombing target." McDonald should know because he and others from 1980 to 2003 recovered from its muddy bottom most of two Mustang P-51B fighter planes that crashed in late 1943, leaving their two pilots—best friends growing up in Decatur, Georgia—as casualties of Polk County training.[22]

Fatalities connected with Polk air fields, such as those involved with the Lake Hancock crash, enhanced residents' sense that they were a part of the war. Situations that called for as-yet-unskilled pilots to fly airplanes overtaxed by use scripted recipes for disaster. Time and again, planes crashed and pilots died. Days before Bartow Army Air Field opened for operations, for instance, a Drane Field bomber crashed killing thirteen. Six days later a similar tragedy occurred. Four days after the Bartow facility activated, two fighters crashed, leaving two dead. In September a Bartow trainee lost control near Drane Field. And, the pattern persisted until after Germany's surrender in 1945. On June 5 of that year, Flight Officer Robert B. Smith of Kansas City, Missouri, added his name to the list of servicemen killed in training. At Bartow Army Air Field alone, twenty-one pilots died by war's end.[23]

16. *Polk's communities, as this Auburndale billboard proclaimed, strove to honor local men and women who had answered the call to military service during World War Two.* POLK COUNTY HISTORICAL ASSOCIATION.

Sadly, as one report from Mulberry dated August 29, 1942, indicated, civilians might become fatalities as well as pilot trainees. "A medium army bomber flying low with six men aboard crashed late yesterday into a negro home about a mile from here and five of the crew and two women, sitting on the porch were killed," it declared. "Capt. J. C. Mayo, head of the Mulberry fire department, said the plane, flying low and west, bumped into a garage, then cut a Ford car in two before colliding with the negro house from the rear," it continued. "The small frame structure was knocked down and two negro women crushed to death instantly," the item concluded. "The plane, in flames, immediately ignited the house, as well as the one adjoining, both being burned to the ground."[24]

Everyone saw and heard fighter and bomber pilots training in the skies above, but some military activities remained known only to a few. Within the Green Swamp, for instance, the Army Corps of Engineers secretly tested chemical weapons. Specifically, according to a report issued a half-century after the fact, the army "evaluate[d] the action of mustard gas in semitropical environments" by "test bombing in 18,000 acres of the swamp." The initiative left more than 250 "undetonated, mustard-filled bombs." Experts quietly identified and removed that number of the devices in 1950.[25]

Polk also hosted two other war-related facilities that tied the county closer to world conflict. The first, a conscientious objector camp, opened at Prairie Pebble west of Mulberry on September 1, 1943, as a part of government efforts to require alternative service from men who refused the military draft for reasons of conscience. The Mennonite Church sponsored the camp, with all but two of the original twenty-four men assigned there being Mennonites. Harold S. Martin directed the program and supervised the men as they (among other things) built sanitary outhouses in connection with the state's anti-hookworm campaign. Each man labored at least fifty-one hours weekly, and each enjoyed a month's furlough annually. They lived in buildings leased from the International Minerals and Chemical Corporation's local phosphate subsidiary until the camp closed in 1947. "Our time in Mulberry was a tense period," recalled J. Virgil Miller. "We knew that there was a bloody war going on, and we endeavored to do alternate service of national importance," he continued. "Locally we tried to be good citizens as well. We visited local churches, and a number of us sang in choirs in Mulberry and Lakeland. We were able to take courses evenings and weekends at Florida Southern College." Miller added, "We had a good experience, first in seeing local needs and being able to make a contribution at the same time we were learning about the South."[26]

Meanwhile, German prisoners tended groves and maintained citrus packing plant operations a few dozen miles to the east of Mulberry. The war had brought labor shortages, partly because black workers demanded that they be paid a living wage. This prompted calls by businessmen for prisoner substitutions. "Putting German POWs to work in fields and groves, mine and forest, here and elsewhere, is only a logical development of the changed economy under which we live during war times," the *Winter Haven Daily Chief* insisted. The Winter Haven camp eventually opened April 15, 1944, with 250 prisoners. Initially, Orange Festival grounds and buildings housed the men, but by spring 1945 a "tent city" erected in a park "fifty meters from a beautiful lake" served the same purpose. "I remember walking down the railroad tracks toward Lake Silver just looking for a German," recalled Robert "Smitty" Smith, a future Winter Haven postmaster and mayor. "You thought they'd have spikes on their heads and all." Only one internee attempted escape, receiving aid at first from some members of the local black community. James Denmark, for one, noted that his family "fed [the man] milk and hunks of cornbread." After four days, though, Florence Villa grove caretaker Jesse Scott turned the prisoner in, and, by then, he was "exhausted from lack of food." Mostly, the men enjoyed their Polk sojourn. "Our 6th Company is hearty and dedicates much free time to gardening," Hans Bremer recorded. "Soccer, played with seven-man teams in limited space, is at a high level!"[27]

To say the very least, war's proximity stirred local emotions. "It was excitement, somewhat, because the entire area was covered up with service people because of our air bases and training camps and everything in Florida," William Ellsworth observed. "In some respects, you felt like you were part of the war with troops trains coming through, and Food Machinery [Corporation] out here on Lake Bonny manufacturing amphibian track assault vehicles, and they were training them at Lake Parker and Lake Bonny."[28]

For many the question became, in L. F. Blankner's words, "What to do with two or three thousand men out in the boondocks when they looked for recreation at the end of their workday?" Blankner then supplied the answer with respect to one community. "Well, the young women of the town organized the 'Victory Belles' and there were frequent dances and parties at the civic center," he began. "Bartow's lasses of the day had been faced with a terrific man shortage . . . and here were a fine, upstanding group of young men—the Army will tell you America's finest—shut up on the military reservation." Blanker continued: "But with overnight passes and a shuttle bus, they came to town.

The military, both student pilots and permanent base complement, got acquainted and became a part of the community."[29]

Polk Countians welcomed the military men in a variety of ways. As did others, Dewey and Vina Fields—cognizant of her four brothers then serving—opened their Bartow home and afforded personal hospitality. The Brewster community at the same time set up a recreation center hosted by Anna Mae Hooker in an empty home and welcomed soldiers stationed at Avon Park. More highly organized entertainment came with United Service Organization clubs. Bartow's "USO" operated at the town's civic center, a fact that prompted concerned parents of teen-aged girls to arrange a separate and supervised site for their recreation at the "Nut Hut," located upstairs over Hall's Grocery Store downtown. At Lakeland, a USO club for black servicemen opened August 15, 1943, at 1026 North Texas Avenue. Gatherings of up to 400 soldiers convened to enjoy dances and entertainment from groups such as Tampa's MacDill Field orchestra. The club provided welcomed hospitality for over two years, closing at last in November 1945.[30]

Many of Polk's attractions similarly strove to provide a warm welcome. Kissengen Springs, closed by the war, reopened in spring 1943. "Enlisted men have expressed much interest in having the swimming place made easily available," a notice advised. At Chalet Suzanne, Bertha Hinshaw—with son Carl Hinshaw away serving in the Army Air Corps—delighted officers and enlisted men with fine cuisine and accommodations. When fire destroyed the main house in 1943, as Carl's son Eric remembered, "the fact that many servicemen used the Chalet as a place for rest and relaxation was what got them the permission they needed [to rebuild]." Similarly, Cypress Gardens and its beautiful "southern belles" attracted servicemen's attention, with convoys ferrying men there from area bases. When a local newspaper ran a photograph of water skiers on the lake, in Dick Pope, Jr.'s, words, "some servicemen . . . showed up asking to see the ski show." With owner Dick Pope on active duty, wife Julie refused to disappoint them by admitting that there was no ski show. "She was a fast thinker," son Dick argued. So, Julie Pope "rounded up her children and some of their friends and goaded them into an impromptu performance." Thus commenced what become the internationally renowned Cypress Gardens ski show.[31]

Proximity of soldiers to Polk's female population naturally sparked more than a few romances. Van D. Howell, for instance, first saw Polk County in 1942, when he reported to Drane Field for B-24 bomber training. On a blind date later that year at Lakeland's Pipkins Ice Cream

17. *Servicemen who were stationed in Polk during World War Two utilized every opportunity to enjoy the county's many attractions.* LAKELAND PUBLIC LIBRARY.

Parlor, he met young Mary Smith and love blossomed. "After about a seven week courtship," Howell recollected, "we made promises that after the war we would see each other again." Such maturity failed to stem the tide of love. On January 2, 1943, the couple—in light of seventeen-year-old Mary's father's opposition—wed secretly at Bartow thanks to Judge Chester M. Wiggins's understanding. One night at Lakeland's New Florida Hotel sufficed as a honeymoon. Orders soon carried Van elsewhere, but his wife awaited him in Polk when he returned in late 1944. They remained together until Van D. Howell's death fifty-five years later.[32]

Romances bloomed for Polk women, as well, with civilians drawn to the county and also for Polk's men in uniform with women from distant lands. To cite an example, Shaw University graduate Altermese Smith was teaching high school science at Bartow's Union Academy when minister William Bentley captured her heart and subsequently moved her to Philadelphia in 1943. On the other hand, Winter Haven's Hamp Rogers, a paratrooper during bloody campaigns in Italy during 1944, saw love bloom after he received a well-deserved leave for rest and "rebuilding" in Northern Ireland. "[There,] he met an Irish lass who was later to become his wife," an account of Rogers's life explained. The couple married in September 1944, with Hamp and Gett Rogers greeting the arrival of their first daughter Marilyn in Northern Ireland in October 1945. Red tape delayed Gett's journey to a new Polk County home, but the family eventually settled at Winter Haven where Rogers, holder of the silver star and purple heart medals, entered upon a career in law enforcement.[33]

Conflicts and Transitions

Beyond war's direct impact on the home front, Polk witnessed changes that boded well and boded ill for the county's future. To the good, the nation's entry into World War Two and the bombing of Moroccan phosphate mines lifted local production of the ore from the doldrums, revitalizing the industry. "Seven phosphate mines produced a record of 16,526,647 long tons of the vital mineral during the war years," a Mulberry report issued just after the peace declared, "enough to fill a line of freight cars reaching from Tampa to Seattle, Wash." The report noted further: "Florida phosphate was not restricted to agricultural use during the war. About five percent of the 16 million ton production went into phosphorus bombs, explosives, hardening of metals, toughening lubricating oils, signal fires and smoke screens." It concluded, "This Polk county area . . . produces 90 percent of the pebble phosphate in the world." Enhanced production created jobs that caught attention well beyond the county's limits. Mabel and William Roberts, for instance, happily relocated from Leon County to Brewster. "My parents felt like it was home," daughter Carrie Roberts Oldham explained. "You had opportunity here."[34]

Citrus growers and processors enjoyed a boom very much like that experienced by the phosphate industry. War-related demands for Vitamin C and other citrus benefits resulted by February 1942 in shipment levels described as "high and steady." Later that year, the development of an early and barely palatable form of citrus concentrate had raised production goals to new levels. On its own, the Florida Citrus Canners Cooperative at Lake Wales in the five months beginning November 1942 dispatched one million gallons of concentrated juice to Great Britain under President Roosevelt's "lend-lease" program. A record crop followed during the 1943-1944 season only to be topped during 1945-1946. By 1945 Winter Haven claimed the title of "Citrus Capital of the World," as Polk County led the state by far in citrus output. Supporting this industry expansion, the Lakeland-based Florida Citrus Commission between 1942 and 1945 had supported researchers C. D. Atkins, Edwin Moore, and Louis Gardner MacDowell in perfecting the concentrate process. Their work by war's end had inaugurated a new era in citrus marketing and consumption.[35]

The cattle industry thrived, as well. Meat shortages prompted large-scale operators to boost beef production levels to previously unthought of heights. New Deal soil conservation activities had set the stage by improving grasslands, but the legislature's 1937 Murphy Act—so damaging to local governments by restricting their chances of recovering past-due taxes—had permitted cattlemen to purchase vast tracts of range for grazing on extremely favorable terms. So lucrative

18. *Polk County's output of phosphate ores and products contributed significantly to the war effort.* POLK COUNTY HISTORICAL QUARTERLY.

did the business become that some citrus growers, including Winter Haven's Lamar Beauchamp and Fort Meade's Minor Jones, abandoned their groves for the beef business.[36]

These industry gains produced a turnaround in Polk's economy of dramatic proportions. The example of two restaurants helps to make the point. During 1942, Clark's Restaurant on Bartow's Main Street closed "when business fell off during the slack period." By January 1943, however, conditions had changed to the extent that John and George Pittas felt confident enough to expand their John's Drive-In on the Fort Meade highway into a full-scale John's Restaurant, which they located in the old Clark building. "There is every reason to believe that the new restaurant will succeed," the *Polk County Record* commented. "The facilities that have existed have been strained to capacity for months," it continued. "None of the men and women who operate them will regret the opening of the new restaurant," the *Record* concluded. "They will welcome it."[37]

Statistics of various kinds underscored the economic revival. At Lakeland, for instance, construction expenditures jumped from less than $500,000 in 1942 to almost triple that amount three years later. Population in the county meanwhile had jumped 28 percent in five years, with most of the growth coming in Lakeland, Winter Haven, Bartow, Lake Wales, and Haines City. Lake Wales banker Hugh B. Alexander summed up the sentiments of many. "I can look back to 1933 and 1934 when good and progressive people were hard up," he recorded, "but we have had good times now for several years, and, by and large, any man in this community who has not gotten in good shape has only himself to blame."[38]

The good times extended unevenly through the county, however, and the gains had come at a cost, most particularly in race relations. Polk Countians black and white had departed to serve their country, leaving chronic labor shortages as the result. The unionized phosphate industry responded with the offer of good wages and other amenities, but citrus industry leaders preferred a different course. First, they pressured school board officials in fall 1942 to suspend black schools during December, January, and February to furnish a labor supply. This highly contro-versial step led in 1943 to release of a school calendar calling for Lake

Wales's Roosevelt School to close for one month during the Christmas break for the same purpose. As these events occurred, turmoil erupted in the citrus groves. The United Citrus and Allied Workers Union, an affiliate of the activist Congress of Industrial Organizations, attempted to organize workers in the interest of better wages and working conditions. Growers thereupon secured union official Otis G. Nation's arrest for "violating a state labor recruiting law." Lakeland attorney Bradford Williams rose to Nation's defense, but tensions boiled as the union man endured prosecution in Orange County.[39]

These circumstances led to what historian James V. Holton has characterized as "the first modern civil rights protest in Polk County." The action stemmed from the leadership of W. J. H. Black, a Baptist minister, and school teacher Jeresa Colvin Austin. They and their associates rejected the school board's decision to extend Christmas break at Roosevelt School. Their arguments convinced Citrus Exchange president Rollie Tillman to intervene in October 1943 with board members on behalf of black students. Acknowledging that industry labor needs crested in the spring, rather than at Christmastime, Tillman managed to convince the board to reverse its decision.[40]

That Black and Austin could achieve such success rested upon another 1943 development, the organization at Lake Wales of a branch of the National Association for the Advancement of Colored People. Its sixty-nine members held forty-two meetings during the year to further "investigation of [the] lawful authority to close negro schools in Polk County" and to "urge negroes to support and join the [United Citrus Workers], a CIO union, among fruit prickers here." Black served the branch as its president, with Gussie B. Griffin acting as secretary. Bernard Smith, D. J. Barfield, Joe Copeland, A. L. Brodie, J. C. Longworth, Mabel Carroll, and M. C. Brockington especially aided their efforts. Within two years the group claimed 308 members.[41]

Some steps were taken by white officials to recognize and begin to ameliorate concerns of African

19. *Polk's African American community supported the war effort in countless ways ranging from distinguished military service to conducting Red Cross and War Bond drives. Students at Lakeland's Washington Park High School illustrate that support for the camera by flashing the "V for Victory" sign.* POLK COUNTY HISTORICAL ASSOCIATION.

American residents. At Lakeland and with city support, for example, a "Negro Auxiliary Police Force" led by Paul A. Diggs organized as a division of the Civilian Defense Council. Restricted to patrolling black neighborhoods, according to community historian LaFrancine K. Burton, force members nonetheless received credentials and wore uniforms. The unit, it was believed, constituted "the only black auxiliary police force in the state of Florida with the authority to make arrests." Other leaders of the force included J. E. Sullivan, Bonnie West, and S. G. Baker. Similarly, Lakeland's Chamber of Commerce established an interracial council. Composed of ten whites and ten blacks, the panel met monthly "for the specific purpose of having white and negro leaders sit down together calmly at regular intervals to talk things over."[42]

One other development occurring during the war's last full year may help to explain the willingness to undertake such outreach. In April 1944 the United States Supreme Court in the case of *Smith* v. *Allwright* outlawed the practice of restricting Democratic party primaries to whites only. At Lake Wales in August, Harry T. Moore and Edward D. Davis created the Progressive Voter League as a political arm of the state NAACP. Many Polk residents supported the initiative and its future work in registering black Floridians as Democrats, among them Norris Woolfork, Paul Diggs, H. L. Stephens, Elsie L. Dunbar, O. L. Williams, Louise W. Diggs, R. H. Mobley, and J. W. Whipper.[43]

20. *Ceremonies honoring the service of Polk Countians in the military occurred repeatedly around the world. Here, Admiral Chester Nimitz congratulates Owen Hugh Wright for meritorious service as a Navy man in the Pacific.* POLK COUNTY HISTORICAL ASSOCIATION.

In the Military

Thousands of Polk Countians served their country in the military during World War Two, and hundreds sacrificed their lives in so doing. Despite growing racial tensions at home, however, no color line identified those whose valor carried them forward. Where Bartow's Edward Charles Flood, a white, could distinguish himself as a fighter pilot, Haines City's Canary Robinson, a black teacher, would earn accolades while soldiering in Europe. In the Navy, Yeoman George W. Trask could draw commendations from Admiral Chester A. Nimitz. Meanwhile, James E. Huger and Claude Woodruff were helping to integrate the United States Marine Corps.[44]

At first law and regulations prohibited women from enlisting, but that did not deter a number of Polk residents. "After Pearl Harbor, you couldn't keep me out of Washington," Brewster's Hazel Bowman recalled. She worked initially at code breaking for the Signal Corps before a desire for overseas duty led her to switch to Red Cross work. In China by 1944, Bowman faced threats the same as did those in uniform. "There was a time there for two or three weeks that we didn't know whether we would survive or not," she recorded. "We acquired a gun, and we were planning to take to the jungle rather than be taken prisoners by the Japanese."[45]

During 1942 the situation

21. *Eunice and Hazel Bowman of Mulberry stood out among the many Polk County women who served their country during the war years. Eunice joined the Navy's WAVES corps, while sister Hazel labored for the Signal Corps before extended overseas duty with the Red Cross. Brother Robert Bowman meanwhile opted as well for the Navy.* POLK COUNTY HISTORICAL ASSOCIATION.

changed, and the military opened its doors to allow women to serve in certain capacities. Hazel Bowman's sister Eunice Bowman Sloat, for example, quickly enlisted in the navy's Women Accepted for Voluntary Emergency Service or WAVES. CAP pilot Ruth Clifford of Lakeland opted for the army's Women's Auxiliary Service Pilots or WASPS, with Fort Meade's Caroline Varn Loadholtes entering the Women's Auxiliary Army Corps (later, the Women's Army Corps or WACS). One-time Polk deputy sheriff Edith Hughes Guthrie made history as the first woman provost marshal in the WAACS. Many followed in their wake, with a number contributing as nurses. Mulberry's Edythe Turner, who in time would rise to become the highest ranking woman in the nation's military services, volunteered for the army's Nurse Corps and contributed as chief nurse in military general hospitals located in England and France. Bartow's Ceila Zoe Pipkin also aided the war effort by nursing, as did Lakeland's Nell L. Fountain. Fountain received the bronze star medal for service as a hospital administrator in France. "I think the plain American has what it takes," she declared in words that applied to herself as well as to others.[46]

Polk Countians served in every theater and in virtually every major campaign and initiative of the war, from sailor Alex Jenkins's 1941 presence at the attack on Pearl Harbor to Dr. Marshall G. Holloway's contributions to perfecting the atomic bomb dropped at Nagasaki, Japan, four years later. General James A. Van Fleet, to name a very prominent example, led the 8th Infantry Division ashore at Normandy. Despite several wounds in the aftermath, his skills won him advancement from regimental commander to corps commander in seven months. "I am a soldier," he declared simply. Winter Haven's Colonel Charles Elder Frederick, killed in action in Italy during October 1943, had led the first U.S. troops into Palermo, Sicily. At the war's outbreak, retired navy captain Roy T. Gallemore returned to active duty as an administrator at the Norfolk, Virginia, Naval Training Center. Fort Meade's James Henry Mills received the Congressional Medal of Honor for heroism during the May 1944 landing at Anzio near Rome, while Dewey Norman fought at Iwo Jima the following February to count as one of only fifteen men in his company to walk off the island. Meanwhile, Brewster's John Vincent Atanasoff, working for the navy on aircraft research, had developed the basis for modern computer systems. These few examples obviously can only highlight the valor, sacrifice, and contributions of others.[47]

22. *At Fort Meade on November 23, 1944, a countywide celebration greeted the safe return of Medal of Honor winner James Henry Mills. Governor Spessard L. Holland of Bartow, standing here at the microphone, led the festivities. Behind the governor, from the left, stand Mills's mother Lessie Mills, the governor's wife Mary Holland, and Corporal Mills. This valiant soldier earned the Medal of Honor for valor during action connected with the invasion of Anzio Beach near Rome, Italy.*

County residents strove to keep in touch with their friends and loved ones in uniform, but all shared in the routine, the adventures, and the loss noted in letters and reports sent home and published in local newspapers. When it came to keeping in touch, Auburndale's "Mom Orchard"—postmistress Mrs. Howard S. Warner—probably came in first. She wrote weekly letters to the town's servicemen and women, keeping them informed about local news. A report regarding one airman's summer 1945 exploits in the Pacific, on the other hand, represented the communications link that civilian Polk maintained with the war's drama. Headlined "Bartow Pilot Makes Home Base With 'Half-an-Engine,'" the account pulsed with excitement. "With both engines riddled with Jap machine gun fire," it began, "a rescue Catalina plane piloted by Lt. Bryan W. Guess, 580 South Florida Ave., Bartow, was coaxed back to its home base on 'about one-half' a sputtering engine." After detailing the dangerous mission flown by Guess to the coast of Borneo, the item quoted the airman's words as he landed safely in the Philippine Islands. "I'm sure glad to see such a fine welcoming committee," Guess exclaimed, "but what's all the excitement." The report added, "Lt. Guess is a member of a rescue unit that has saved more than 570 allied airmen from capture or death on the open sea."[48]

As a letter from New Guinea pointed out to Lakelanders in summer 1944, ties with home for Polk men and women in uniform could extend around the world. "Upon my arrival in the South Pacific I found Lakeland negro boys performing outstanding jobs," Staff Sergeant Sidney E. Houston wrote to his father Z. E. Houston. "They had taken the best that Tojo and his gang could drop, yet they kept supplies moving. They kept supplies at the right place at the right time." Houston continued: "These boys have done everything from building docks, bridges and roads and performing a very excellent job of keeping roads open, which is a very difficult task. Some landed under bombardment, yet they kept their assigned jobs going." Among those whose presence Houston noted in

23. *Sergeant Sidney Eckhart Houston's letters home from the South Pacific noted his surprise encounters with other Polk Countians helping to wage the war effort.* LaFrancine K. Burton.

New Guinea were Sergeants Henry Rudolph, Marion Jackson, Pasco Dassie, Robert Brown, Timothy Lockliear, and Sanford Kelsey.[49]

The greater Polk County family abroad helped to sustain weary soldiers, sailors, marines, and others in uniform, but that did not take away from the fact that, at home, many families were called upon to contribute more than their fair share to the national defense. Numerous families claimed three children in service, such as those of G. A. Weeks at Lakeland and J. M. Bowman of Brewster. Others boasted more. The record for contribution, though, may have belonged to Bartow's Braxton B. McNabb clan. Five sons wore uniforms and, as if that were not enough, brother-in-law Alfred B. Manes earned the bronze star in the southwest Pacific.[50]

Whatever their family's size, Polk Countians joined the country in support of the men and women combating Axis military might and also in the pain that came with tragic sacrifice. To display the pride, residents proudly hung window flags with a blue star for each family member in service. Lamentably, many also displayed a gold starred flag for a loved one lost to the national cause. In words that applied well to Polk's people at large but that she directed to students at Bartow's Summerlin Institute, Iris Sullivan Reese recalled the impact at home when news of that ultimate sacrifice arrived. "One thing most of us will remember vividly," she recorded, "is the terrible sadness that clung like a heavy pall over the school when news came of schoolmates who had been reported killed in action." Understandably, then, after almost four years of war it was with a combined sense of pride, sadness, and relief that Polk residents awaited the end of four years of terrible conflict and that, at summer's end 1945, they finally could welcome victory and peace with joy.[51]

24. *Homecomings of World War Two veterans led to happy celebrations and more than a few photographs in commemoration. Such certainly proved the case with Lakeland's Wolfson family in 1945. Seen here are (top from left) Lieutenant Colonel Jack Wolfson, Major Wil Wolfson, and Second Lieutenant Herbert Wolfson, with parents Frances and Cy Wolfson and sister Irene Wolfson shown at bottom.* POLK COUNTY HISTORICAL QUARTERLY.

CHAPTER 3

౿ഌ

Peace and Prosperity, 1945-1950

*W*orld War Two's end ushered in a new and dynamic era in Polk County's experience. Trials of armed conflict and economic depression, coupled with ravages of nature, faded into the past. Now, golden sunshine streamed down to warm and to nurture. Longtime residents basked in opportunity, while newcomers in significant numbers exulted in semitropical breezes. Fortunes awaited the lucky and, for others, comfort could replace want. Adjustments came with the changes, but most welcomed the task for the progress that it promised. Only a few concerns appeared at first to call into question Polk's ability to find its way in this marvelous time. As the significance of these problems increasingly came to be understood, however, at least a few began to ask the price at which peace and prosperity could be realized.

The war and the environment created by it took a while to end. Victory in Europe or V-E Day came on May 7, 1945, with V-J Day following with Japan's surrender on August fifteenth. Still, men and women in uniform secured release from duty only slowly. Lakeland's Robert S. Herndon and Bartow's Harvey Dows likely savored the fact that they had arrived back in the states by November's end. Herndon's fellow townsman Harry M. Sweat awaited February 1946 before he could share that happiness. Frostproof's Glen Wise, Haines City's Charles Johnson, and Lakeland's Francis Howell came the next month, but they by no means were the last. A few who managed to return even found themselves soon headed back overseas. Lakeland police officer Walter Clark Stone, for one, departed for England in May to claim a bride. He and Doreen Tyrell had met in 1943, and she had waited for him as war ebbed and peace began to prevail.[1]

It took local people some time to realize fully that the war truly had ended. Into late summer casualty reports dampened spirits, such as when families and loved ones learned in August of the deaths of James Elliot Jones, a Marine from Mulberry, and Seaman James Gaston Paulk of Lakeland. The October crash of a National Airlines plane into Lake Parker dampened spirits further, with Lakeland state representative James L. Hardin called upon to identify the body of a friend, Sarasota County state senator Harrison E. Barringer. Community leaders at Lakeland, concerned about the lack of release from fear and loss, in November took extraordinary measures, calling for a "Cheer-Up Week" that resulted in the organization of a "Stretch Smirks Into Smiles Society." Society president Agnes Ashley claimed that she could "measure everything from a toothpaste-ad grimace down to the ghost of a grin by means of a special 'smile meter' designed by an ingenious Lakelander." She aimed her smile meter especially at "vinegar-faced store clerks," intending to "reconvert [them] to a peacetime basis." As she did, a "secret 'smiles' committee" endeavored to select a "Chief Sour-Puss," whom its members described as "the man who didn't crack a smile for seven long days."[2]

Despite difficulties in adjusting to peace, residents looked on as numerous events evidenced war's end. Bartow Army Air Field closed on October 26, for example, with officials deactivating Lakeland's Drane Field on November first. The Lakeland black community's USO club closed in November, as well, becoming a "Colored Youth Center" known as the Jolly Spot. Supporters believed it to be the first black youth center organized in Florida. Communities held dinners and other functions to welcome veterans home. Lakeland's American Legion Post. No. 4, under post commander Clinton Miller, did just that at the black community USO club only weeks before it closed. Veterans meanwhile flocked to join Legion posts and similar organizations. A new association designed for World War Two veterans only, the AMVETS, issued its third Florida charter to Lakeland Post No. 3 in September. J. T. Aiken had pushed the concept, with J. M. Blanton, B. F. Summerlin, D. L. Scott, B. B. Shaw, R. D. Fraser, J. R. Barnes, C. S. Spivey, J. D. Harrell, Jr., J. W. Hall, and C. W. Hodges aiding his efforts. A few days later Lakeland's Veterans of Foreign Wars post announced its expansion, with a new $40,000 meeting hall to be erected on Lakeland Hills Boulevard.[3]

The veterans looked forward to far more than a warm homecoming and socializing with their peers. Especially, the subject of service officer P. G. Mitchell's presentation at Lakeland's welcome home party for black veterans—the G. I. Bill of Rights—offered a topic of interest to all those yearning to restart civilian lives. Signed by President Franklin D. Roosevelt in June 1944, the measure addressed a variety of concerns. "[It] aimed to regulate the flow of returning veterans into the job market by offering them vocational training and higher education," one historian explained, "as well as housing and medical benefits while in school and low-interest loans thereafter for buying homes and starting businesses." For children of depression and survivors of war, it was a Godsend.[4]

For many, education came first. Back home from the Army Air Corps, Lake Wales's James Austin headed for Florida A&M College at Tallahassee. Similarly, Lakeland's D. Burke Kibler and Fort Meade's Richard Allen Fort joined others from Polk at the University of Florida in Gainesville. Additional institutions drew the county's veterans, as well, particularly Lakeland's Florida Southern College. "I . . . arrived on campus following a four year tour with the Navy in which I had been a part of a national effort to defeat the enemy and preserve our country," future county school superintendent Shelley S. Boone recalled. "The magic of Ludd Spivey and Florida Southern College was at work," he continued. "I had known hardships, experienced excitement and joy, seen the world and [now] needed only a college degree to complete my education!" Boone added, "I had chosen Florida Southern for that degree."[5]

The ups and downs of one such veteran's attempt to secure higher education even earned statewide publicity. "Bob Huffaker, of Bartow, was an ordnance captain in Europe," the *Florida Times-Union* of Jacksonville explained to its readers in October 1945. "He had five years of university training, then was out for five years," the article noted further. "He is now back to complete his law course, and he and his wife and child are living off the campus in an apartment for which they pay $55 per month. He said it was hard to get the hang of school again, but believes his five years of service not entirely wasted because it gave him time 'to grow up.'" The article went on to state: "He said he searched for five weeks for an apartment before he found a place to live off the campus, and rents in Gainesville are almost prohibitive for a student with a family. In the dormitory a man and wife pay $20.50 a month."[6]

The majority of veterans, though, simply desired to return to family, a steady job, and, perhaps, a new home. Dock Vaughn's example helps to illustrate the point. He and wife Ruby had married at Eagle Lake on August 12, 1933. Despite the responsibilities of a young family, Dock nonetheless accepted the call to wartime duties. A gunner's mate, he served mostly aboard the *U.S.S. Topeka*. Discharged in 1945, Vaughn returned to a home at Fort Meade and employment at the bustling Virginia-Carolina phosphate mine. Twenty-seven years later he would retire. By 2003 he and Ruby, still in Polk, enjoyed six surviving children, seventeen grandchildren, twenty-four great-grandchildren, and two great-great-grandchildren.[7]

Return of the Boom

Polk County exited World War Two with an economy as prosperous as any that had been seen since the 1920s, and better days yet were coming. True, an adjustment period brought a dip in employment in late 1945 and, for some, apprehension of an uncertain future. "Individual problems there will be, as there must be in every community," one journalist recorded. "The youngsters who went away to pilot a B-17 bomber will be home soon, and his old job is not going to look so good," the man added. "And some humble and deserving employees, others not quite so good, will be shoved out to make way for boys coming back." Mostly, he meant women. Florida Southern coeds had volunteered their labor during the war to help build the college's new library, and that effort echoed the actions of other women in most sectors of county

25. *Veterans hailing from Polk and elsewhere perceived the county's economic potential in the years immediately following World War Two. Signal Corpsmen Major Jack Brandstetter and Captain Lawrence A. Rollins, for example, joined with colleague Frederick L. Allman to establish a radio station at Winter Haven in late 1946. With assistance from program manager Richard P. Eyrich, WSIR broadcast its first programming on February 14, 1947. Show here, from left, are Eyrich, Mayor L. H. Recker, Chamber of Commerce official Ted Sanchez, Brandstetter, Allman, and Rollins.*
FROM BURR, *HISTORY OF WINTER HAVEN.*

economic life. Interestingly, one Florida Southern professor, Aldus M. Cody, discovered that newspapers had set limits on that female march into the marketplace. "Dailies are using more women on the editorial staffs," he had announced in 1943, "but [not, given] an adequate supply of help[, in] the business and mechanical departments." Constable Pat Gordon signaled, though, that enduring change had occurred respecting women in the public sphere. He designated Iris Caudill in 1945 as the first female deputy constable in state history.[8]

Optimism, in any event, far outweighed concerns as residents eagerly embraced future prospects. "Lake Wales Is Looking to Big Future," the *Tampa Tribune* proclaimed in August 1945, and so it was in Polk generally. "People have money, and now that the war is over they are itching to spend it," one banker observed. "Florida stands on the threshold of the biggest era of expansion it has ever seen," an industry publication added, "expansion caused by need, not by misguided speculation." By decade's end full-scale boom times prevailed. "A review of the past 12 months shows that Winter Haven enjoyed its year of greatest progress in its 65-year history," a report typically concluded in January 1949. Full of hope for the future, residents for the first time since before the Depression years embraced expensive civic improvements in recognition of their newfound prosperity. At Winter Haven, for instance, property holders by a lopsided margin opted to tax themselves the large sum of one-half million dollars for a single new elementary school that they intended to name in honor of county superintendent F. E. Brigham.[9]

Similarly and as early as January 1947, business representatives from across the county had decided to work in concert for needed civic improvements. Specifically, they created the Associated Chambers of Commerce of the Polk County Area to be led by chairman John R. Wright of Lakeland. Under its umbrella, Bartow, Winter Haven, Lake Wales, Auburndale, Lakeland, and other communities joined to push a variety of civic improvements, although none ranked higher than new and better schools. "One of the major problems of the county and state is our school system," Frank W. Myers expressed for the group, "and we must begin thinking about it." The organization proposed, as well, "area-wide advertising" of Polk's bounty.[10]

As white business leaders came together to further Polk's rising prosperity, so, too, did prominent members of the African American community. By October 1945, Lakeland's Negro Chamber of Commerce had reorganized under director E. T. Pickett. The same month, the Greater Bartow Negro Chamber of Commerce coalesced. This occurred thanks to the

leadership of con-
tractor-builder
Henry Silas and
businessman Lloyd
H. King who re-
cently had founded
the county's first
African American
newspaper, the *Polk
County Advertiser*.
The Bartow Negro
Chamber's organi-
zation was formal-
ized in January 1946
when its members
chose I. H. Green
as president. James
Waldon, Henry Si-
las, Mrs. L. C. B.

26. *Professor James E. Stephens (left), who headed Bartow's Union Academy from 1938 to 1968 and later would serve as chairman of the Polk Community College board of trustees, and respected businessman James H. Waldon (right) aided efforts in the immediate post-World War Two era to organize and encourage African American entrepreneurship. LOUISE FRISBIE COLLECTION AND CLIFTON P. LEWIS.*

Thomas, T. F. Burnett, Dr. L. W. McNeill, and Professor J. E. Stephens also served as officers. They opted, when the question of a first project arose, to honor veterans by "erecting a Negro Honor Roll board which is opposite the white service roll on Central Avenue."[11]

These initiatives, it should be mentioned, owed much to the continu-ing leadership in county affairs of Florida Southern College President Ludd Spivey. Already in 1943, Spivey had questioned Polk's future after the peace. He had warned members of the Committee of 100 for Post-War Planning, a group that he had convened on his Lakeland campus, about "industrial and commercial competition uncontrolled" and of the necessity for "men with brains to carry on our government." Spivey had added, "Men with brains should carry on without government help." But, he also had insisted: "Thousands of local communities will have new problems after the war. We must begin to plan now."[12]

Spivey's forecast proved reliable as every sector of Polk's economy steamed ahead in the immediate postwar years. The local citrus industry, to name the most prominent one first, already led Florida's counties during 1945 with 31 percent of total state production. That year frozen citrus concentrate first made inroads in the commercial market. Large crops brought some reductions in grower profits during 1946-1948, al-though the government's decision in late 1946 to purchase surplus juice for school lunch programs boosted prospects. Prices then began to advance in 1948 as consumers eagerly embraced concentrate and canned juice. Even better prices and higher incomes at decade's end resulted by 1950 in record profits. "Florida is in the midst of another land boom," one newspaper alerted readers that March, "and this time it is grove land or that suitable for citrus that shows amazing growth in value." Producing groves by then commanded up to $2,500 per acre, with experts speculating that a price of $4,000 per acre loomed in the near future.[13]

The phosphate industry faced an equally positive economic future. By war's end the county produced the overwhelming majority of the world's pebble ore. To handle expected enhancements in demand, the International Minerals and Chemical Corporation set a precedent by introducing a massive new "dragline" to its Peace Valley mine. It took 53 railroad cars to transport the various components of the "Bigger Digger" to the site in late 1945 and early 1946. When assembled, the massive machine's bucket, suspended from a 215-foot boom, could scoop almost 22 cubic yards of earth at a time. Industry innovations came in other areas, as well. IMC, for example, helped secretly to pioneer uranium production from phosphate ore. The industry expanded also into chemical fertilizer and sulfuric acid production. Then, when super processing systems aimed at increasing efficiency and capacity arrived in 1949, the limits of expectation rose even higher.[14]

27. *This historic "Polk O Dot" citrus packing label helps to illustrate the county's leading position in Florida's citrus industry during the late 1940s and the decades that followed.* POLK COUNTY HISTORICAL QUARTERLY.

Cattlemen, as well as citrus men and phosphate producers, saw gains. For one thing, they found that spraying cattle with the pesticide DDT, developed in Florida during the war, enabled beeves to put on weight much faster. As of then, DDT's harmful effects remained unknown. The discovery of fever

28. *Enthusiasts gather in Bartow during 1947 for the inaugural Polk County Youth Fair. Polk County Historical Association.*

ticks near Polk City in 1946 caused a scare, but the industry's prospects had helped by the next year to give birth, thanks to Grover Howell's imagination, to the Polk County Youth Fair at Bartow. In time the fair and its livestock competitions would become, as local historian Louise Frisbie has reminded, "the largest of its kind in the nation." Beef prices rose in these years, and cattle rustling, of all things, re-emerged as a serious problem. "The rustlers drive up to a herd on an isolated range, shoot as many animals as they can haul away and speed off in a fast truck," an expert advised. Still, in 1950 Polk contained more cattle than any other county in Florida, a state that yet claimed rank as one of the largest cattle-producing regions in the nation.[15]

The strength of the phosphate and cattle industries aside, their value for county residents paled by 1946 in comparison to the benefits of tourism. In Florida, the number of tourists nearly had doubled in the previous five years to an annual figure of 4.5 million. About 300,000 more came on the average in every year following for the next decade. As the visitors streamed in, Cypress Gardens emerged as a favorite destination with water ski shows building the attraction's popularity. Skiers such as Betty June Skelton awed and pleased crowds while honing skills to the point that she could claim the International Aerobatic Championship from 1948 through 1950. Chalet Suzanne, too, enjoyed the generous attention of Florida's visitors. "People who boast of turning a stable or barn into a country home can take a lesson from [Bertha Hinshaw]," one critic exclaimed. Meanwhile, headlines screamed "Polk County Jammed as Tourist Season Nears." By 1946 Lakeland was warning potential visitors about the lack of apartment and houses for rent. "Bartow," a report asserted, "frankly advises them to go somewhere else if they don't already have a reservation."[16]

When hordes of tourists needing reservations combined with returning veterans, a growing newcomer population, and a booming economy, the construction industry naturally benefitted enormously. At Lakeland, for instance, construction leapt from $1.4 million in 1945 to $4 million one year later. By 1950 the figure topped $6.5 million. Already by January 1947 local newspapers trumpeted "more housing activity than at any time since the fabulous boom days of the twenties." Other municipalities saw similar dynamics at play. The *Winter Haven News-Chief* in 1948 found that community's growth "astounding." Building permits for the previous year had climbed past the $1.4 million level. That year another $1 million in permits foretold construction of "scores of new and remodeled dwellings." Mayor L. H. Recker also proudly announced "approval by the State Improvement Commission of a citrus inspection and citrus exposition building to house offices and laboratories of the state and federal citrus inspection departments, a citrus museum, and an 1800-seat auditorium." A late 1949 item from Lakeland seemed to sum up sentiments in most of Polk's larger towns and cities. "Lakeland during the year saw civic improvements that have not been equaled in the municipality in the past several decades," it observed. "Few cities anywhere would seem to have a brighter outlook!"[17]

In these circumstances the construction industry claimed greater prominence than at any time since the early 1920s. For larger projects, especially road construction, firms such as Lakeland's John G. Dickson Construction Company competed statewide. Since much new construction involved use of concrete, allied businesses flourished by providing that material. Howard C. Stephens, to name one businessmen, arrived at Winter Haven in 1947 from Ohio to establish

29. *World War Two veteran Frank Byrd of Bartow launched civilian life by purchasing an automobile for $2,200 and building a house with $1,750 worth of materials.* POLK COUNTY HISTORICAL QUARTERLY.

the Stephens Concrete Co., the town's first quality concrete producer. E. R. Johns long had operated a similar business at Hesperides. Also in 1947 he established a new plant at Lake Wales to manufacture "concrete bricks, ready-mixed concrete and other concrete products." Reports insisted that "a demand for Johns products has been shown from a large area in Central & South Florida."[18] The residential housing industry, though, remained the domain of small entrepreneurs, many of them keying their offerings to those with entitlement to Veteran's Administration loans. Scott Kelly, a Madison native who relocated to Lakeland in 1949, discovered the easy opportunities available to an individual with initiative and the rather relaxed manner in which he could take advantage of them. "I picked up the building business," he explained to an interviewer. "I bought a house out here on Shore Acres on Holly Road that had two vacant lots, one on either side and one across the street ....," he continued, "and I started building." Kelly recalled that Lakeland then boasted no housing "developments" worthy of the name. "Lakeland was a laid back place," he stated, "nothing like it is now." In the circumstances, Kelly concentrated on "odd lots, mostly in south Lakeland." He concluded, "A lot of it was people coming to me to build on their lots."[19]

Naturally, the prosperous environment produced other businesses of significance that lent support to the county's growth. At Lodwick Field near Lakeland, Albert I. Lodwick launched Lodwick Aircraft Industries in late 1945, converting military DC-3 airplanes for use by civilian airliners. As Lodwick historian Waneta Sage-Gagne discovered, the plant also "exported converted planes internationally, sold aircraft parts and accessories, and operated a transport service." In another example, in 1946 Winfield Hugh Oglesby left his employment with Lakeland's leading manufacturing company Food Machinery Corporation and formed the Southern Machinery Corporation. It made innovative vegetable processing machinery. Meanwhile, brothers Austin Race, Jr., and Charles Race started the Race and Race, Inc., aluminum products plant at Winter Haven. Benefitting from the expertise of R. C. Wilson, they manufactured irrigation pipe, citrus picking ladders, and similar items useful to area industries.[20]

Population Growth and the Problems It Brings

Much of Polk County's 1940s population growth occurred during World War Two, but enough newcomers arrived in the subsequent five years to set trends in motion that would work significant differences as time passed. In 1940 less than 87,000 persons called Polk home. Five years later that figure stood at 112,000, and by 1950 it amounted to nearly 124,000. During the decade Lakeland had swelled by 50 percent, but little of that change resulted from postwar, as opposed to wartime, immigration. Winter Haven's 1945 total of 8,109 grew only to 8,605 five years afterward. Bartow's at 8,721 slipped to 8,694. The numbers at Lake Wales rose modestly, from 6,210 to 6,821. As these statistics suggest, much of the small increase came in unincorporated portions of the county since municipalities had not yet expanded their boundaries significantly to incorporate nearby growth areas.[21]

Many of the newcomers shared similar traits, although they represented a variety of backgrounds. They were relatively young, for one thing, and, of those arriving from 1945 to 1950, many were veterans. Minnesotan James Robert West, for instance, adopted Lakeland for his home in late 1945. A physician, West had attained the rank of captain as an army medical officer. William A. McRae, Jr., the son of a former Florida commissioner of agriculture, had studied law at England's Oxford University on a Rhodes scholarship. Ultimately an Army Air Force colonel, McRae opted upon discharge in 1946 to accept a law partnership with former Governor Spessard Holland at Bartow. However, such relative affluence and prestigious educations by no means served as a requirement for relocation to Polk. Micanopy native Samuel Berry took up his new home at Lakeland after a move from Winter Garden. In Polk, Berry accepted employment in the maintenance department of the Polk County school board. He maintained that job until retirement, while he and wife Willetta also contributed as members of Macedonia Primitive Baptist Church. Berry passed away, still at Lakeland, in 1996.[22]

Population growth that depended in good part upon the arrival of young families, a factor in county growth mentioned earlier, naturally prompted increased emphasis on schools. Here, school superintendent F. E. Brigham attempted to offer leadership. In 1945 he proposed a number of initiatives that would have improved educational opportunities significantly. For younger children, for instance, he urged kindergarten programs. "If citizens of Polk county decide, after careful consideration, that public school kindergartens offer advantages for a majority of the children in the county," Brigham declared, "then it becomes incumbent upon school officials to organize them where ever there is a sufficient number of children." Brigham also perceived the need for enhanced learning for older children and young adults. To address that problem he suggested creation of a junior college program by adding grades thirteen and fourteen at some high schools. As it turned out school board and county officials proved less than enthusiastic about increasing tax burdens, and Brigham's ideas gained no headway. Before his final term ended in 1949, the superintendent nonetheless pushed for school construction and more-efficient management of school funds. He worked, as well, with members of the Polk County Children's Committee—including Mrs. Tom Turnbull and T. D. Hayes—to authorize Polk's first school expressly for handicapped children. It opened at Winter Haven in September 1948. After leaving office the following January, the gifted educator dedicated much of his time to the American Legion. F. E. Brigham died August 4, 1952, shortly after his election as its state commander.[23]

Several other educational innovations fortunately made their debuts during this period. As to the first, in 1946 the South-Eastern Bible Institute relocated to Lakeland from Atlanta. The school operated on a temporary basis, school historian Rickey A. Cotton has explained, at buildings formerly occupied by the Lodwick School of Aeronautics. Permanent facilities as of 1952 permitted growth, and within four years the institution not only had begun to offer bachelor of arts degrees but had renamed itself as the South-Eastern Bible College. Further expansion would prompt another renaming in 1977. By the late 1990s and with the urging of President Mark Rutland, a fully accredited Southeastern College of the Assemblies of God eagerly would embrace the role and responsibilities of a liberal arts institution.[24]

Florida Southern College also pioneered new directions. In 1947, to cite an example, it established a school with immediate relevance to the local economy. The innovative program offered interested students "one, two, and four year courses in the production,

30. *Civic spirit and civic clubs typified community life in the late 1940s. Here, five Bartow Kiwanis Club members receive congratulations in 1948 for their community service. From the left and standing are N. E. Jordan, W. F. Bevis, Judge C. M. Wiggins, C. H. Barnett, and Bradley C. Wilson. At the table, seated, are, from the left, Lois Phillips, Mrs. Lennox Barnes, Mr. and Mrs. W. W. Weinkauf, Mrs. Richard Frisbie, and Richard Frisbie. Young attorney Chesterfield H. Smith, later president of the Florida and American Bar Associations, sits in the rear at the far right. LOUISE FRISBIE COLLECTION.*

packing, processing and marketing of citrus fruit." At the same time President Ludd Spivey announced a $500,000 science and research building that would complement the citrus school's work. Spivey's leadership also extended to outreach into the African American community with attempts to recognize creative talent. A 1947 art exhibit that featured work by several Florida A&M College teachers brought black students onto the Lakeland campus. The show additionally highlighted civic leader Paul A. Diggs's paintings, artwork that previously had drawn plaudits at the National Urban League's national exhibit at St. Louis, Missouri. The next year the school's art department invited Washington Park High School students to spend a day receiving instruction in art techniques and equipment, a visit that resulted in Florida Southern art professor Donna Stoddard demonstrating portrait painting at Washington High.[25]

Before passing on to other topics, it should be emphasized that— while Polk's public school system chronically suffered from weak governmental support and chronic funding shortfalls—individuals time and again brought credit to the county for their educational and professional attainments. The career of Elsie L. Dunbar provides an illustration. A longtime Lakeland teacher and librarian, she went on to become in 1947 the first person to earn a master's degree at Florida A&M College. Until 1954 Dunbar worked as librarian for the black branch of the Lakeland Public Library, after which she headed Rochelle Junior High School as its principal. Before her death in 1967, Dunbar also served, in addition to other roles, as president of the Women's Civic League, member of the Women's Division of the Chamber of Commerce, chairwoman of the Lakeland Canteen Corporation of the American Red Cross, member of the city-wide recreation committee, president of the Polk County Classroom Teacher Organization, and president of the State Library Committee of Congressional District Number One.[26]

The blossoming of young families in the immediate postwar era created pressing problems beyond placing heavy demands upon the school system. One such concern involved what people increasingly called juvenile delinquency. The first public hint that Polk faced trials in this regard came in fall 1945 when juvenile court judge William F. Bevis resigned, according to a report of the time, "because he felt the Juvenile Court work had reached the point at which the services of a full-time justice were needed." Governor Millard Caldwell quickly replaced Bevis with Bartow's G. Bowden Hunt, but, as an incident occurring at Lakeland in 1947 illustrated, a growing problem existed. "The relationship between

Lakeland and winter visitors who come here at Lakeland's invitation has reached a deplorable state because of disagreement over use of the civic center building tourists have used for years," the *Lakeland Ledger* reported. "This situation came about because tourists and Lakeland's teen-age young people were pitted against each other," the editorial continued. "It has become quite clear that tourists and teen-agers cannot get along harmoniously trying to use the same building," it added. "Such an arrangement is contrary to the laws of human nature[, and it] is especially important in this period of postwar transition that young people have a wholesome atmosphere in which to spend their recreational hours." The paper concluded, "There is only one practical solution—namely, a separate building for each group."[27]

The rising problem of juvenile delinquency in fact reflected larger trends in crime and violence generally. Most residents still slept behind unlocked doors in the late 1940s, but crime seemed to take on greater proportions as time passed. Some small incidents, as often happens, appeared to symbolize greater concerns. One occurred in December 1946 when thieves at Lakeland stole the public address system from St. Joseph's Catholic Church. "They also pried loose a poor box from a wall," a report of the incident declared, "lifted another collection box and broke into a case to get medals and two silver chains." The threat of violence posed by such crimes evidenced itself clearly in 1949 when a suspect shot Lakeland police officer Monroe Brannen in the face with a shotgun. Miraculously Brannen survived. The same luck attended Deputy Sheriff Carl Purvis the next year. As he questioned three burglary suspects near Drane Field, one raised a 32-calibre pistol and gunned down the deputy where he stood.[28]

The era's most publicized crime involved a schoolteacher victim and a judicial defendant. The crime, a murder, occurred at Lake Alfred in February 1948. Thelma Wilkinson Rollins, a Winter Haven teacher, suffered three gunshot wounds to the head and neck while sitting in her automobile. Husband Dewitt Rollins, a former Winter Haven city judge and supervising principal at Lakeland, at first reported an unidentified hitchhiking "stranger" as the culprit, but Deputy Sheriff Hagan Parrish soon focused on Rollins as the killer. Rollins subsequently confessed to quarreling with his wife, being slapped by her, and shooting her thereafter in a fit of rage. A jury in August found the defendant guilty of murder with a recommendation for mercy. Rollins served eleven years in the state penitentiary and later died at Chattahoochee's Florida State Hospital.[29]

Tensions Political and Racial

World War Two and its aftermath changed Polk County in discernable ways, but the local political system rested unaltered within the constraints of old ways. As the disposition of Superintendent Brigham's educational proposals suggested, county government remained mostly ineffectual when it came to meeting real problems in a timely manner. Meanwhile, corruption continued to plague some aspects of its organization, especially law enforcement. In 1948, for example, Frank Williams won the office of sheriff to replace incumbent DeWitt Sinclair. As a county jury later determined, he did so at the urging of two illegal lottery operators, Emmett Caraker and Rhodes Boynton. "[They] took Williams out of a Federal Court bailiff's job in Tampa," a report declared, "and spent thousands of dollars to elect him sheriff of prosperous Polk County." The report added, "What they got for their money, [as] the State declared, was a promise from Williams that they could divide up the county and operate without fear of arrest by the sheriff's office and without competition from other racketeers."[30]

As occurred in other locations in Florida where governmental ineptitude and corruption ran large, many Polk veterans resented the situation and pledged to do something about it. One of the few signs that their efforts eventually might succeed came in 1948 with the election of navy veteran and Lakeland city attorney Albert Roy Surles, Jr., to the state legislature. During the 1949 legislative session, Surles worked with Frostproof's Perry E. Murray, then serving as speaker of the Florida house of representatives, to enact measures aimed at state government reform. Despite support from Governor Fuller Warren, their efforts fell short. Both men, though, pledged to stand for re-election and try again.[31]

The eagerness to effect change began by the decade's end to appear on the local, as well as the county, level. In 1949, for instance, twenty-eight-year old Archie McQuagge won a seat on Lakeland's city council. He assured the community of his firm belief "that Lakeland potentially is the finest city in the South." McQuagge offered a word of caution as well. "The time has come," he insisted, "for young people to take a more active part in the affairs of the municipal government."[32]

One reason for the difficulty in effecting change through elections concerned patterns formed before the 1937 repeal of the poll tax. That levy had suppressed voter registration tremendously, and, while its repeal prompted thousands to enter voting booths, registration totals remained arbitrarily low. By 1946 only one-half of those eligible in the state were registered. This left political control in the hands of the relatively small portion of the electorate that had permitted undesirable conditions to persist. Former governor Spessard L. Holland of Bartow, for one, continued to feel alarm at the poll tax's pernicious impact. Elected to the United States Senate in 1946, he soon pledged his best efforts to secure a constitutional amendment to ban the practice nationwide. Holland finally achieved his goal in 1963.[33]

African Americans organized the most important effort to boost Polk registration figures in the early postwar era. The 1944 United States Supreme Court ruling in *Smith* v. *Allwright* had opened the Democratic primary to black voters, and the statewide Progressive Voter League organized a few months later at Lake Wales. After Florida Democratic party officials dropped objections to implementation of the ruling in January 1946, the Negro Citizens Voter League quickly formed at Lakeland. Norris Woolfork presided, with Paul Diggs, H. L. Stephens, Elsie Dunbar, O. L. Williams, Louise W. Diggs, R. H. Mobley, and J. W. Whipper actively in support. Before the registration cutoff for May elections, they managed to register 1,894 black voters, about 7 percent of all those qualified to vote. Ongoing efforts led to further advances. By 1950 almost one-quarter of Polk's 37,000 registered voters were African American. At that point politicians had to begin considering the black vote as a factor in election strategies.[34]

Already, black voters had begun to exert greater influence on political affairs and, in rare cases, to participate as candidates. Just as white veterans wanted cleaner and better government, black veterans yearned for racial justice and an end to "Jim Crow" discrimination. Bartow insurance agent Robert D. Patterson, who had commanded white as well as black troops in the army, could be counted

31. *Bartow businessman and civic leader Robert D. Patterson.* POLK COUNTY HISTORICAL QUARTERLY.

as one among the many. By 1946 and with support of veterans such as Patterson, the National Association for the Advancement of Colored People had supplemented its Lake Wales branch with one at Bartow. A Haines City local formed the next year. Branches at Lakeland, Winter Haven, Bradley Junction, and Pierce followed. Soon, time arrived to test the desire and the will for change. An early effort came in December 1946, when Paul Diggs, J. W. Canady, E. F. Robinson, and Henry Silas challenged the county's all-white jury pool. This initial effort failed in Judge Roy H. Amidon's criminal court, however, and activists found it best temporarily to bide their time while nurturing their bases of support.[35]

Slowly, old practices began to alter. Harry S Truman in June 1947 became the first United States president to address the annual NAACP conference. On that occasion Truman, as one historian put it, "said forthrightly that full civil rights and freedom must be guaranteed to all Americans." Four months later a presidential commission urged an end to racial segregation and discrimination, following which in 1948 Truman ordered the desegregation of federal employment and the military. United States Supreme Court rulings meanwhile increasingly eroded authority for discriminatory practices. As a result, in March 1949 for the first time in memory an African American served on a Polk grand jury. That individual, fifty-nine-year-old James B. Welch, resided in Lakeland and worked as a fruit picker. Only six months then passed before T. J. Walker offered himself as a candidate for Lakeland city commissioner. The thirty-eight-year-old railroad worker lost the race, but by contesting it he broke a barrier nonetheless. Another barrier fell in 1953 when black jurors first sat in a county capital case. Among them were Namon Brown, Mrs. W. J. Allen, and Violet B. Pierce.[36]

A rise in anti-desegregation activism paralleled these advances for Polk's black community. Some politicians adopted rhetoric that blasted "outside organizers" for "coming into Polk County for the sole purpose of registering certain portions of the citizenry." Those efforts, at least one of the politicians insisted, "were designed to foment racial unrest." As the decade neared its close, the Ku Klux Klan emerged again to public attention. Reportedly, Polk Klan vigilantes helped to spark the 1949 attack on the black community at Groveland in nearby Lake County. Two days later, on July 19, Klan night riders fired into homes of several residents at Polk City. Not satisfied, they then burnt a cross on the grounds of the local black school.[37]

As had been the case for decades, some whites in Polk openly opposed Klan activity and, if quietly, supported selected civil rights ini-

32. *The small town atmosphere that persisted in Polk shines through in this 1949 photograph of the county courthouse and its environs in downtown Bartow.* FLORIDA STATE ARCHIVES.

tiatives. Many veterans, for instance, believed that—at least for men or women who had risked their lives on behalf of their country—the right to vote should not be interfered with or otherwise questioned. Likewise, when African Americans challenged all-white juries in 1946, white attorney E. E. Callaway of Lakeland represented them. Postwar optimism played its part, too. With good times at hand and better times expected, a measure of cooperation across racial lines encountered less resistance. Thus, when Lakeland's St. James Lodge No. 18, F&AM, announced plans for a new lodge building, whites joined blacks in raising necessary funds. Similarly, when Lakeland's Dr. David J. Simpson neared retirement age, Dr. Herman Watson and the white medical staff of Morrell Hospital gathered to honor their colleague. The *Lakeland Ledger* praised the step. "[He has] the confidence of the other members of the medical profession here," it declared of Simpson.[38]

The More Things Change

Emphasis on the changes touching Polk County in the mid-to-late 1940s easily can distort any true sense of daily life. For the most part, the area remained, in Scott Kelly's words, "a laid back place." Recalling one portion of Winter Haven as it appeared at the time, a frequent visitor underscored by exaggeration a larger point. "It was a wilderness then, and it was a long drive from Lake Cannon into town," she recorded. "The big excitement was the doctor who lived on the lake and had a seaplane," she continued. "We'd get to watch him take off." The woman added: "The area consisted mostly of woods and little swamp areas along the lake shore. I used to spend a lot of time trekking through the woods with my granddad."[39]

Most people, particularly children and teenagers, lived relatively uncomplicated lives. "Social life usually meant going to a high-school ball game on Friday, the Polk Theater on Saturday and church on Sunday," Lakeland's Neva Jane Langley recollected. "All of the teen-agers had favorite seats [at the Polk], where they would always sit to be near their friends." Lawton Chiles's memory ran along the same lines. "A really big night," he commented, "included a visit to the ice cream parlor after the show." For those whose parents permitted, outdoor movies became the craze. Lakeland's Silver Moon Drive-In Theatre welcomed is first patrons in 1948 with "Up Goes Maizie," starring Ann Southern and George Murphy, heading the bill. Winter Haven had its Havendale Drive-In, while Bartow, Mulberry, Haines City, and Lake Wales adopted the trend as well.[40]

It could not be denied, though, that change swirled in the air. The county stood on the brink of startling growth and unprecedented prosperity. Proof that things would no longer simply be the same awaited only the passage of a few years. First, however, international political forces and military confrontation would distract attention. And, before most could believe it was happening, Polk and the nation would find themselves again at war.

33. *The decade of the 1950s, as this photograph illustrates, brought growth to Polk communities such as Haines City, but urban congestion clearly remained a problem for the future.* FROM MCNEELY AND MCFADYEN, CENTURY IN THE SUN.

CHAPTER 4

උ~ා

The Building Tide, 1950-1955

*T*he decade of the 1950s launched the transformation of Florida toward its modern character and appearance, and, while the impact in Polk proved not quite so dramatic, change nonetheless touched the county profoundly. Newcomers sparked economic growth of immense proportions, pushing towns toward city status and setting in motion dynamics of lasting significance. Growth and the times begat other manifestations, as well. The nation's and the state's challenges came home to Polk, but they did so to a community mostly distracted by future possibilities rather than engaged in understanding past and present dilemmas. Meanwhile, war's sacrifice and loss once again confronted residents with sometimes painful consequences. Heady times to be sure, but crucial ones as well for what would come thereafter.

Census reports do not afford exact figures for growth in Florida and Polk County from 1950 to 1955, but they do allow a sense of the population boom that hit the region. The state at the decade's beginning contained slightly fewer than 2.8 million persons, a level that placed it twentieth among the states. Ten years later, nearly 5 million persons resided in the Sunshine State. This 79 percent jump elevated Florida to tenth on the list of states as ranked by population. Polk, meanwhile, experienced its own surge. In 1950, 124,000 persons called the county home. After ten years and a 55 percent gain, the total had risen to about 193,000. Not all of the increase came late in the decade, either. State estimates published in 1958 suggested Polk already had attained 176,000 residents, more than doubling its pre-World War Two high. By then the county stood eighth on the state's list of most-population subdivisions but failed to make a showing on the schedule of "most rapidly growing counties." That group included mostly peninsular coastal entities. By way of comparison with Polk, Dade in 1960 held 918,000 inhabitants, while nearby Hillsborough boasted almost 400,000.[1]

Distribution of population within Polk altered as immigration bolstered its residential totals. Relatively speaking, the county's southern sector—its historic heartland and power center—lost ground to the northern region. Bartow climbed during the 1950s from 8,694 to 12,858, but it lost its second-placed status to Winter Haven, a community that swelled to 16,069 from an earlier figure of 8,605. Tiny Haines City leapt 64 percent to 9,115, while Mulberry managed only to attain 2,901 from a previous report of 2,024. Lakeland, the county's largest town gained the greatest number of new residents, about 9,300 persons. Percentage-wise, though, the rate of change paled by comparison to that at Winter Haven and Haines City, with Lakeland tallying only a 30 percent gain. Despite the advances, Polk's communities remained of modest size compared to the state's large urban centers. Miami in 1960 held 282,000; Tampa, 271,000; and Jacksonville, 199,000. Hialeah and Miami Beach, among numerous others, also bested the Lakeland total.[2]

Polk's growth may have seemed modest in comparison to some other areas in the state, but it brought to the county thousands of new residents who found themselves thrilled at the opportunity and intrigued with the atmosphere. Tom and Willie Mae Taylor Ahl relocated in 1950 to Auburndale from Baxley, Georgia. During the war Tom had labored in a shipyard at Brunswick, but Georgia's postwar economy held little promise for an out-of-work shipbuilder otherwise trained only in farming. The family, daughter Betty "Plum" Taylor recalled, "rode down in the back of the semi-truck that was hauling their possessions." In Polk, a new world opened to the Ahl clan. "When we got there, there was no longer any need for us to take jobs other than to keep house," Plum commented. "I was in a strange land," she continued. "There were orange groves around us, and we'd never seen an orange tree. It had so many lakes everywhere. Suddenly we were with the elite." She added: "One thing that struck me there was that they had a drug store you could go in and get a sandwich and a soda. I mean you could get a spiced ham sandwich with lettuce on it."[3]

Significantly, too, the type of person moving to Florida began to change somewhat during the 1950s. In the years immediately following World War Two, most newly arrived residents tended to be younger, often veterans just starting postwar life while building a new family. Increasingly, though, older individuals and couples made the journey to Florida to spend their retirement years. Postwar prosperity, especially when coupled with the benefits of the New Deal's social security program, permitted those with modest means, as well as the wealthy, to enjoy the "golden years." To cite just one of a host of possible examples, Frederick Joseph Shilling, Sr., and wife Helen Shilling arrived at Lakeland from Washington, Pennsylvania, as the decade opened. Formerly, Shilling had worked as a federal mine inspector. Now, leisure time permitted him opportunity for other interests. In Shilling's case, serving as a founder of the Highlands Hills Presbyterian Church and later as a member of the Westminister Presbyterian Church numbered among the activities that he found most personally rewarding.[4]

It should not be forgotten when considering new arrivals that many longtime Polk families contributed to population inflation, as well. Veterans and their spouses naturally lent their support to the county's participation in the national postwar "baby boom" phenomenon, and their willingness to do so manifested itself into the 1950s. Fort Meade druggist Richard Fort and wife Mary Varn Fort, both Polk natives, deserve particular recognition for the part that they played. On September 27, 1953, they celebrated the birth of three daughters, believed to have been "Polk County's first healthy identical triplets." At the time Richard asked a nurse if such births were rare. When informed that "it happens once in a lifetime," he quickly responded, "Thank goodness." Betty, Barbara, and Beverly Fort joined a family that already included older brothers Dick, Bob, and Jim, plus sister Mary Anne. "Keeping everybody fed, clean and clothed was pretty rough going there for a while," Mary acknowledged.[5]

Legacies of Growth

With so many individuals and families opting to make new homes in Polk during the early 1950s, the county understandably experienced an enormous impact. Sometimes the changes proved easily anticipated and understood. Other times, surprises resulted that carried large and unexpected consequences.

The nature of how people lived, for instance, commenced to alter from previous patterns. Traditionally, single family homes planned and built as discrete entities and constructed of wood or brick had housed Polk's population. Plum Taylor discovered one change right away. "Our community," she explained, "was modern cinder block houses." Chances are that the Ahls did not have air conditioning in that home, but, as the years of the 1950s passed, more and more residents did enjoy that luxury. Very inexpensive electrical power permitted still-inefficient "window units" to come within the means of many more than a few. Open patios, too, became more common with enhanced mosquito control efforts. During the war, state chemists had come to see the use of the German chemical DDT as helpful to Floridians bothered by the insect's bloodthirsty proclivities. "Trucks and planes began spraying clouds of the toxin through neighborhoods and across the countryside," historian Mark Derr related. "Houses and lawns, farms and gardens, were treated monthly, with the residue building up not only in the homes and their residents but also in the environment." Discovery of the chemical's disastrous side effects awaited the 1960s.[6]

Many "modern" homes increasingly could be found as time passed in planned and affordable "suburban communities," a concept pioneered for veterans and their families at Levittown, New York. Winter Haven's Jan Phyl Village typified a statewide trend. Encompassing 1,200 acres and three lakes, the site contained more than 3,000 lots for homes. When disappointing follow through by the initial managers created instability and frustrations, though, Charles H. Race took control of the project. He turned it, in the words of a local historian, into "a thriving village."[7]

34. *As suggested in this image preserved of Bartow's Ritz Theater, the miracle of air conditioning delighted increasing numbers of Polk residents in the 1950s.* POLK COUNTY HISTORICAL ASSOCIATION.

If some housing initiatives could become "thriving villages," one in particular promised much more. "Large tract developments," such as Polk County's Indian Lake Estates, sought to create entire communities out of vacant land. Located east of Lake Wales off State Road 60 and commenced at mid-decade, it encompassed twelve square miles of property. Developer Leon Ackerman of Washington, D.C., offered purchasers only lots one-half acre in size or larger and promised a golf course, country club, wide streets, lake frontage, greenways, and recreational areas. Designed creatively to anticipate water-flow and drainage problems in a sometimes waterlogged region, Indian Lake Estates stood out among similar projects then under construction. "This development is so well engineered," the magazine *Florida Trend* reported a few years later, "that [our] reporter hardly found a puddle of water, though he visited it after a heavy rain." Investors flocked to snap up lots, with sales in the thousands quickly registered. Unfortunately, as will be seen, most held the property for speculation rather than for building residences.[8]

That left plenty of construction, nonetheless. Lakelanders in 1945 had thrilled at the issuance of $1.4 million in construction permits during a single year. That figure more than quadrupled in five years. By 1954, the city exulted in $9.1 million spent and experienced disappointment the next year when the total came only to $7.9 million. During 1954, the largest permit, which came to $700,000, reflected a growing population's need for greater sophistication in shopping. Tampa's Maas Brothers company built an imposing "department store" in the heart of the city's downtown area. Other towns' experiences echoed that at Lakeland. "A post-boom building record was assured for Winter Haven today," the *Lakeland Ledger* proclaimed as 1954 ended. The story detailed construction of ninety-nine new residences, ten duplexes, ten store buildings, two restaurants, and a motel, plus a hospital addition, Jewett High School for black students, and a $90,000 public library building. At Bartow, Crown Cork & Seal Co. erected a new can manufacturing plant while two proposed "subdivisions" seemed certain to attract a flood of new residents.[9]

Business activity at such levels led to higher payrolls and the need for improvements in banking operations. Employment rose at an encouraging 6 percent rate in 1954 to 40,400. The next year another 3 percent joined the work force, with prospects suggesting healthy increases for the foreseeable future. Meanwhile, county financial institutions that barely had managed to maintain themselves in business just a few years earlier now reported impressive deposit statistics. Additionally, the first new bank chartered for the county since 1929 opened. Backed by county tax collector Ray Clements, who assumed the post of chairman, the Citrus and Chemical Bank welcomed customers at Bartow beginning January 5, 1954. Four years later Clements sold his majority interest to citrusman Ben Hill Griffin, Jr. Then, in 1963 Griffin's twenty-nine-year-old son-in-law George Harris took over as chief executive officer. Griffin and Harris led the institution to become a power in regional banking circles.[10]

More people also meant more traffic and the need for more and better roads. The "grim toll" of traffic accidents had reached an annual high of thirty-nine by 1954. Even law enforcement agents were not spared as Bartow policeman Alvin G. "Babe" Bush fell victim in January when a truck with defective brakes struck his motorcycle. Traffic congestion on certain roads and at certain times accompanied and abetted the accident problem. As a result, "fourlaning" of roads became a battle cry in some vicinities. Lake Alfred city manager George T. Costello, for instance, demanded a survey of conditions on U.S. 92 within and near his community. The study found the highway "way too narrow" and mandated "some definite improvements" as essential. But, for the time being, progress stalled.[11]

Lakeland managed to accomplish more. Particularly, it planned a new "boulevard" as a truck bypass along the town's northern edges. Developed out of the former North Street and constructed during 1953-1954 by Ewell Construction Co., Memorial Boulevard provided what was considered for the times a high-speed urban artery. Business firms such as Waters Leasing Company seized upon the access it provided by erecting offices and operating facilities. "We went out there and bought ten acres of property," proprietor Robert Waters recalled. "It was all orange groves." Some, however, failed to appreciate the benefits of such progress. Grower Cecil F. Combee, for one, blamed the new road for flooding his strawberry and vegetable fields near Lake Parker. Demanding justice, Combee sued the county.[12]

The concept of "expressways" stirred even more interest than did Memorial Boulevard. Prior to World War Two, President Franklin D. Roosevelt's administration had proposed adapting Germany's *autobahn* limited-access highway system for the United States. President Harry S Truman revived this "interstate" system in the postwar years, and by 1947 Florida's highway planners had released a map that showed one of the multi-lane highways stretching from Daytona Beach through

Lakeland to Tampa. When Republican congressional leaders declined to fund the program, though, it languished. The state road board in 1951 breathed new life into the concept by postulating a toll road down the east coast with a cross-peninsular Daytona-to-Tampa link added. Governor LeRoy Collins's administration backed the Sunshine State Parkway scheme, and it met with the legislature's approval in April 1955. By year's end, however, no construction had commenced in or near Polk County and, for the time being, none would.[13]

Construction and plans for construction did result, in any event, in prosperity for construction and engineering companies. Likely the greatest success story involved James M. Wellman, a 1950 Florida Southern College graduate whose dream was "to find a need and fill it." Setting up in business as a housing contractor, he partnered the next year with Harvard alumnus William "Bill" Lord to build Lakeland's Southside Park subdivision. As the team gained experience and as one reporter described, "They perceived the need for an engineering and construction firm which could build the highly complex and specialized plants needed by the phosphate industry." Incorporated as Wellman-Lord Engineering in 1954, their firm had expanded operations outside the United States by 1958. Two years later, experts rated it one of the fastest growing such concerns in the nation.[14]

Moreover, the construction boom statewide supported countless ancillary businesses to service virtually insatiable building needs. Lakeland's troubled Florida Ceramic Tile Company counted as one of them when a youthful University of Florida graduate from West Palm Beach named James Wesley Sikes—together with his father Leon R. Sikes, Sr., and brother Leon Jr.—purchased it in 1954 for $8,000 and

35. *Businessmen Jim Wellman and Bill Lord partnered in the early 1950s to develop Lakeland's Southside Park subdivision before building Wellman-Lord Engineering into one of the nation's leading industrial engineering and construction firms. FLORIDA TREND.*

the assumption of $32,000 in debt. The business then ranked fifty-seventh out of fifty-seven tile manufacturers nationally. Reorganized by the Sikeses as Florida Tile Industries, Inc., the company stressed fast service and a willingness "to adopt modern manufacturing methods in an industry that has been notoriously slow to up-date itself." The first year, James W. Sikes reported $239,000 in sales. Eleven years later the annual figure came to $8.5 million, and a staff of sixteen had swelled to six hundred.[15]

An Economic Juggernaut

The health of Polk's traditional economic mainstays—citrus, tourism, phosphate, and cattle—provided the context within which these postwar innovations made their mark. As will be considered, each of them encountered problems during the period. Yet, each contributed gains to local pockets and black ink to business ledgers.

Citrus began the period on a high, as a California freeze drove prices upward. Already in 1950 Polk contained more orange trees than any county in the nation other than Orange County, California, and led all in fruit harvested. Some fresh fruit shippers resented being taxed to advertise citrus concentrate, but "baby boomers" literally cried out for their juice. Then, luck struck again when Texas groves suffered drought just as the concentrate business boomed and a Florida fresh fruit marketing program began producing results nationally. So many desired to take advantage that by 1954 oversupply depressed industry conditions to a degree. By no means, however, had prospects dimmed or spirits collapsed. Latimer "Latt" Maxcy of Frostproof learned that fact the easy way. He had merged his groves in 1949 with the Snow Crop division of Clinton Foods. In 1955 Snow Crop, in turn, sold out to Minute Maid and Standard Brands. "It was Maxcy's biggest break," a reporter concluded. *Look* magazine described his profit as "a bundle big enough to choke an alligator."[16]

Many businessmen managed to follow Latt Maxcy's example. Sam Killebrew, for example, made his share thanks to creative inspiration. "Sam set out in 1952—in a rickety old sawmill shed near Auburndale—to build equipment which would permit Florida's citrus growers to transport and spread chemical fertilizer untouched by human hands," an account of his activities detailed. "Sam planned and built a special semi-trailer that could take on a bulk cargo at a fertilizer manufacturing plant," it continued, "haul it to the spreading site and disgorge the cargo via a conveyor belt." A revised version, a "side-dump Bulk Hauler," followed, eventually to become standard equipment in many fertilizer plants. Diversification then brought millions to a man who had helped to revolutionize an industry.[17]

As Killebrew labored, tourists found their way to Polk in record numbers, just as they were doing at resorts throughout the peninsula. Cypress Gardens ranked high on most must-see lists. "Aquamaids," as owner Dick Pope called his attractive female skiers, proved a particularly popular attraction. One of them, Judy Miner, recalled the dangers faced by the women as they enchanted vacationers. "The bathing suits could be worn strapless," she explained, "but the skiers wore the straps after a fall nearly caused a calamity." Also at Winter Haven, the Florida Citrus Museum afforded visitors a "show window" of the industry beginning in 1952. Nearby at Lake Wales, Masterpiece Gardens debuted the Great Masterpiece the same year. A 300,000 piece mosaic of Leonardo da Vinci's "The Last Supper," the work of art came to Polk from Germany in the aftermath of the 1948 Berlin Airlift crisis. The Black Hills Passion Play premiered, also at Lake Wales, in January 1953. Josef Meier portrayed Christ during the final seven days of his life in an amphitheater especially constructed for the production. During the summer the troupe relocated to the Black Hills of South Dakota, where the play had been performed since the 1930s.[18]

One unusual attraction drew fans from near and far, and it did not cost them a dime. It came about beginning in 1948 when Swift and Co. phosphate operations began dumping sand washed from phosphate rock on a tract of land near its mine two miles south of Fort Meade. The pile mounted by 1951 to 200 feet, giving it a height of over 325 feet above sea level. Sand Mountain thus took honors as the highest point of land in peninsular Florida, a ranking previously held by Lake Wales's Iron Mountain. "It just stood up there, white," one longtime fan of its slopes recalled. Soon, children young and old

36. *Lake Wales's lovely Masterpiece Gardens.* POLK COUNTY HISTORICAL ASSOCIATION.

37. *Fort Meade's Sand Mountain offered free opportunity for fun in the sun, with Cypress Gardens magnate Dick Pope taking advantage of the attraction to spur interest in the new sport of sand skiing.* POLK COUNTY HISTORICAL ASSOCIATION.

frolicked there. "We'd just run up and down that thing," Loren Stokes related. "Just run all the way to the top and roll down," he added. "It was fun." Hugh Wright picked up the description from there. "Kids would take big pieces of cardboard and use them like sleds," he commented. "You'd see kids just tumble down and come out with five pounds of sand in their hair." Never one to miss out on an opportunity, Dick Pope soon captured the mountain as his own. He organized the International Sand Ski Tournament to take advantage of its powdery slopes. When the third annual event convened in late 1951, teams from Norway, Belgium, France, Holland, Denmark, and Switzerland competed.[19]

The fact that one phosphate plant could produce so much sand as a mere by-product of its operations suggests the enormity of the industry's continuing prosperity. Yet, it managed to take matters to a new level in 1953 with the opening by the International Minerals and Chemical Company of a $14 million plant for unprecedented commercial-scale production of triple superphosphate, a "high-powered refined phosphate" that sold "for a price ranging from 15 to 20 times that of raw phosphate rock." The Bonnie plant, situated between Mulberry and Bartow, included a conveyor ramp longer than two football fields. The experiment with production on such a scale proved so successful that, in 1955, the American Cyanamid Company announced it would erect a 200,000-ton triple superphosphate plant at Brewster. Given the "mushrooming growth" of the period and despite a violent strike that resulted in bomb destruction of a part of the Bonnie plant, by mid-decade local industry payrolls had neared an annual total of $17 million.[20]

Compared with other segments of Polk's economy such as the phosphate industry, the cattle business fared not so well. To the good, the Florida Southern College Bio-Research Laboratory under Dr. Boris Sokoloff furthered cattle feed research, finding possibilities in material such as mangrove leaves, wood, and bark. Still, by 1953 prices—and, consequently, profits—slumped due to drought and government pricing decisions. On the other hand, Polk's cowmen found reason to celebrate when it came to the subject of purebred cattle. The Imperial National Brahman Show opened for the first time east of the Mississippi River, at Bartow, in 1952. Eugene "Sonny" Griffin and his brother Bobby Griffin of Bartow stood among those who claimed top honors. Summerlin Institute sophomore Billy Stuart took the prize for showmanship. Meanwhile, Bartow's W. H. Stuart claimed recognition far and wide for his Brahman stock. At the 1954 Florida State Fair, for example, the Polk cattleman claimed thirty awards, including grand champion bull.[21]

It seemed as natural as could be, given the economic vitality surrounding Polk's residents, that the county—despite losing ground relatively speaking to faster-growing areas—maintained influence on a large scale. Fort Meade's J. R. Yearwood, for instance, contested a United States Senate race in 1950, with Bartowan Spessard Holland already holding a seat in that august body. One-time Winter Havenite Francis P. Whitehair served as undersecretary of the Navy during 1951-1952. Bartow attorney Bill McRae then headed the Florida Bar, pushing for reorganization of the state's judiciary. General James A. Van Fleet, as will be discussed shortly, commanded the Eighth Army in Korea. Meanwhile, Lakeland's Leonard "Preacher" Williams, a Washington Park High School graduate who had played for the Lakeland Tigers and the Indianapolis Clowns, in 1952 helped to racially integrate professional baseball by joining the Milwaukee Braves organization, later touring with the Jackie Robinson All-Stars. And, among the many other possible examples, in 1953 Lakeland's Neva Jane Langley reigned as Miss America.[22]

The county's re-emergence into prosperous prominence coincided with technological innovations that permitted easier and quicker communications. Telephone service, including long distance calling, had improved considerably thanks to World War Two advances. This resulted by 1953 in the introduction of "area codes"—Polk's was 813—compelling residents in many instances to dial as many as ten numbers where five or even four had sufficed until recently. More marvelously, television arrived, opening up the world to people whose lives often had seemed isolated and distant from larger concerns and happenings. Tampa provided the first broadcasting stations for Polk audiences. WTVT, Channel 13, carried CBS network programming, while WFLA, Channel 8, brought the NBC schedule into county living rooms.[23]

38. *Neva Jane Langley, seen here as 1949 Florida Azalea Queen, reigned in 1953 as Miss America.* FLORIDA STATE ARCHIVES.

Little wonder that Polk's people mostly missed the trouble signs that began appearing, problems that derived from the very prosperity in which they luxuriated. One of the first indications arose in 1950 when Kissengen Springs ceased to flow. "The bottom has dropped out of Kissengen Springs, so to speak," a county report described in April. "The underground stream that once boiled to the surface, discharging 22 million gallons of water per day, has completely subsided." Three years later the once-legendary gathering spot had "subside[d] into barren ruin." Florida Geological Survey experts noted "the alarming drop of the Polk County water table" and speculated that it resulted from "uncontrolled withdrawal of ground water by industries in the Bartow-Mulberry area." Tampa journalist Donald B. McKay already had put his finger on the problem in May 1950. "The lowering of the water table in peninsular Florida has been the subject of discussion and the cause of alarm for years," he argued. "The level of the our lakes is steadily lowering—I think the consensus of opinion is that the water table has dropped 25 feet in the past half century," he continued. "Conservation of our underground waters," McKay concluded, "and the rehabilitation of our once great forests are two of the paramount problems affecting Florida's future."[24]

McKay in 1950 could not foresee that air pollution soon would join his list of critical concerns. At the time he wrote, super-processing systems just had been introduced into the local phosphate industry. "The first real damage was found in 1950," local expert Edward Lightfoot later explained, "and it reached its maximum in 1955." Another report added further detail. "In the mid-1950s, half a dozen companies were manufacturing sulphuric acid by contact process in Central Florida," it commented. "For a distance of half a mile around each plant there was marked destruction of pine trees and lesser damage to vegetation." The report added, "People began giving attention to air pollution." The legislature realized that something had gone wrong and responded in 1955 with the creation of a special study committee to examine the situation. Pending the receipt of its report, the state board of health received authority "to control pollution of the air . . . in any place whatsoever." A federal official later commented on the result. "No substantial action," he noted, "resulted from adopting this law."[25]

The problem, accordingly, persisted with immediate impact on some county residents. By late 1955 owners had begun detecting large-scale damage to citrus groves located in proximity to phosphate plants. Dr. L. W. Wander of the Lake Alfred Citrus Experiment Station accepted responsibility to inquire as to the cause. His report, issued November 22, clearly defined the problem. "Phosphate plant fumes," Wander insisted, "harm citrus groves."[26]

Korean War

But, mostly, other matters commanded the attention of county residents in the early 1950s, and the Korean War stood very prominent among them. The conflict had commenced in summer 1950 when North Korean army elements under Communist leadership attacked South Korea across the 38th parallel. A small force of United States troops supported their South Korean allies, but the tide of battle soon pushed them into a besieged perimeter near the port of Pusan. While President Truman successfully sought the approval of the new United Nations for halting the aggression, his subordinates in the even-newer Defense Department desperately strove to mobilize sufficient forces and gather equipment and supplies. As they did, area commander General Douglas MacArthur planned counterattack. The general's brilliant stroke came in September at Inchon, port for South Korea's capital city Seoul. The successful landing led to an allied push toward and, ultimately, into North Korea. By November MacArthur's forces pressed toward the Yalu River, a natural barrier on the far side of which stood China, recently taken over by Communist forces and already called Red China by many. As the Americans approached the Yalu, vast numbers of Chinese soldiers flung themselves against the tide and overwhelmed lead elements of the allied force. Retreat ensued for the Americans. Truman relieved MacArthur in early spring for disobedience to his orders, and soon a bloody stalemate caught the opposing forces facing off roughly where they had stood when the conflict began.[27]

The war touched Polk County almost immediately upon its commencement. Elements of the Florida National Guard's 149th Field Artillery found themselves in the thick of the fighting in its opening stages. Private Clarence A. Tish, Jr., died July 25, 1950, with Corporal Bobbie J. Batte following on August thirty-first. Captain Johnnie M. Heirs and Major Henry W. House, Jr. also fell as casualties, respectively, on February 12, 1951, and October 7, 1952.[28]

The Chinese counterattack in November also drew Polk men into combat. As it turned out, luck held for Private John D. Polston of Winter Haven when he was captured with bullet wounds in both legs rather than killed. "I tried to run away but they ran me down," he explained after his release in 1953. Held at a camp near the Yalu River, Polston suffered from inattention to his wounds and the cold weather, but otherwise he fared well. "We did very little work in camp," he related. "We got books and magazines, they looked like propaganda to me," Polston added. "And for a year and a half we got lectures practically every day." He concluded, "I don't know if any American bought them but I didn't."[29]

Black Polk Countians naturally defended their nation's interests and honor alongside white residents in the newly integrated armed forces. The remarkable experiences of Lakeland's Corporal Roland Haynes help to make the point. "Haynes was captured when his integrated company was patrolling in a valley west of Wonju [in early 1951]," historian Hal Hubener has detailed. "After entering a village, the company was surprised by about 50 Chinese soldiers. When his gun jammed, Haynes threw a grenade into the approaching soldiers." Hubener continued: "He then was shot in the leg, fell to the ground, and was surrounded. After being forced to walk to another village, he was fed and the wound was dressed." Chinese officers thereupon issued Haynes, as an African American, a safe conduct pass—printed in Korean, Chinese, and English—that urged him to go "state side and enjoy apple sauce his mother makes and also caress his wife's brown hair." Haynes disliked apple sauce and was single, but he took the pass and headed for American lines with five others. Finding himself later separated from his party, the Lakelander then spent a nervous night faced off in a rural hut opposite a Korean guerilla with whom he was unable to communicate. "At dawn Haynes left," Hubener explained, "and found his way back to freedom."[30]

The toll of war continued to be felt in Polk for years. Families anguished when ill tidings came as, for example, when Fort Meade's Lillian Harper learned in summer 1951 that her husband First Lieutenant Lee A. Harper was missing in action. Loved ones at Winter Haven learned of the deaths of Private Carlton Rice and Lieutenant David C. Clements only in April 1953. Sadly, the remains of Clements, a jet pilot who crashed on duty in northern Japan, were not recovered and returned to Polk for burial until four decades later.[31]

Many were those who distinguished themselves. Machinist's Mate Second Class M. L. Compton of Bartow, for one, received his commendation for heroic action, as a local newspaper informed residents, "during the fire on the [flight] deck of the carrier U.S. Lake Champlain . . . which was engaged in launching strikes against the communists in North Korea." Officials awarded Colonel Raymond S. Holtzman, also of Bartow, the Legion of Merit for "meritorious service." Lieutenant Donald E. Brewer received the Navy Cross, second highest naval award for valor in combat, posthumously. The mention of these recognitions, though, should take nothing away from numerous others who served valiantly, whether they received awards or not.[32]

Some offered their service elsewhere than in combat but also contributed significantly to the war effort. To name one, Lakeland's Homer E. Hooks, a decorated World War Two combat veteran, found himself recalled to active duty in March 1951. "I suddenly got a notice from Uncle Sam that said 'Greetings' you are hereby called into active duty in the intelligence realm for the Korean War and report to the Pentagon," he recalled. "So, I reported to the Pentagon as a captain in intelligence . . . and served as a briefing officer for a year and a half." Hooks continued: "Every morning early I would go to the intelligence office in the Pentagon and get a telecom message from Tokyo on what happened in Korea the day before. This was top secret. I would plot this on my little portable map—where the lines were, what the enemy action was, what our response was, etc.—and then I would take that personally to the Secretary of Defense and give him a thorough briefing from my own notes and my own map." Auburndale's Donald Harvey "Bud" Corneal took a slightly different path. Also a World War Two veteran, he received new orders to report for service on January 21, 1951. Subsequently, he served until June 1952 as a captain with the national Air Defense Command.[33]

39. *One of Polk's greatest military heroes, Lieutenant General James A. Van Fleet, is seen here (left) at his 1953 Bartow homecoming celebration accompanied by wife Helen Moore Van Fleet and friend Major General A. H. Blanding.* LOUISE FRISBIE COLLECTION.

By far, Lieutenant General James A. Van Fleet took honors as the county's best-known Korean War participant. Distinguished for World War Two service in Europe and later for directing operations against Communist guerillas in Greece, Van Fleet in April 1951 succeeded General Matthew B. Ridgway as Eighth Army Commander, allowing Ridgway to take over for Douglas MacArthur as commander in chief, Far East Command. "The men in the front-line foxholes welcome a Communist offensive because that would give us our best opportunity to kill a maximum number of them," Van Fleet declared at the time. "He led large-scale military operations that twice threw back Communist attacks," a biographer noted. The writer added, "He was commander during difficult cease-fire negotiations." Meanwhile, on April 4, 1952, the fighting had cost the general his son Capt. James A. Van Fleet, Jr., an Air Force pilot lost in action on a night bombing mission. As the war neared its close in 1953, the general departed from active duty pursuant to mandatory retirement regulations. Van Fleet returned to Polk County. After toying briefly with the idea of running for governor of Florida in 1954 as a Republican, he pursued business and civic interests from his 2,000 acre ranch near Polk City. Among his many decorations for military valor were the Distinguished Service Medal with two oak leaf clusters, Distinguished Service Cross with two clusters, Silver Star with two clusters, Legion of Merit with cluster, Bronze Star Medal with two clusters, and Purple Heart with two clusters.[34]

Crime, Politics, and Social Discord

As General Van Fleet would have discovered upon his return to Polk, natural disasters, violence, crime, corruption, and growing racial tensions competed for attention with events such as those that beset Korea during 1950-1953. Visitations by three hurricanes between August 1949 and October 1950 seemed to set the stage for tumultuous times. Lightning in the meantime destroyed Winter Haven's Christian Science church, multiple fires ravaged valuable property, and cattleman grew apoplectic when a new state law effective June 30, 1950, banned their beeves from wandering the highways. As these events occurred,

40. *Sheriff Pat Gordon escorts convicted murderer Elwood North. He is accompanied by deputies Earl Carlton (front) and Floyd Ritchey (rear).* FLORIDA STATE ARCHIVES.

United States Senator Estes Kefauver toured Florida investigating government corruption and organized crime. The Kefauver report made its way into print on August 17, and six days later a grand jury indicted Polk County Sheriff Frank M. Williams for taking bribes from gamblers. Governor Fuller Warren suspended the law officer and replaced him with respected one-time chief deputy Hagan Parrish of Winter Haven. In March 1951 jurors convicted Williams and his alleged cohorts of conspiracy to take bribes, for which the former sheriff paid a $500 fine. County Solicitor Gunter Stephenson in October surprisingly dismissed other charges pending.[35]

By then residents fixed on a different crime, murder. Fort Meade's "young and dapper mortician" A. Elwood North stood accused during July 1951 in the death of his late cattle-ranch partner's widow, Betty Albritton. Tales of poisoning, quick embalming, and rapid burial captivated newspaper readers and purveyors of gossip. County residents divided in their opinions and loyalties. That North appeared to some as a "Tampa dandy" hurt his chances, as did the fact that Frostproof state representative Perry Murray, released from duties as speaker of the Florida house, represented the Albritton family as their attorney. "The trial was quite sensational," newspaperman Loyal Frisbie recollected. "The courtroom was packed every day," he added. "People brought their lunches in bags so they wouldn't lose their seats during the recess." Convicted by a Polk jury on September 12, North pursued controversial appeals that rent the county for three years. Their ultimate failure resulted in his execution by state authorities in late September 1954, but into the twenty-first century arguments flared about Elwood North's guilt or innocence.[36]

The North appeal headlines still had months to run when two other murder-related incidents shocked local citizens. In the first, Dr. Dodge D. Mentzer, a prominent Lakeland physician, shot and killed one of Florida's leading amateur golfers, Billy Leigh. The April 1954 crime came to light when Mentzer phoned police to report his deed. The physician soon informed Constable Monroe Brannen at the scene that "Leigh had been running around with his wife for three years and that he had told him to stop." Elizabeth Mentzer later corroborated the facts of the matter, suggesting that the murder occurred immediately after Leigh refused to leave their home without her. Dodge Mentzer quickly retrieved a gun from a nearby room, she testified. "Dodge, do you realize what you're doing?" Elizabeth asked. "I've told him to stay away from here," Dodge responded. "Now I'm going to shoot him."[37]

The second case concerned murder for hire, a plot foiled by Sheriff Pat Gordon who had taken office in January 1953 after defeating acting Sheriff Parrish. Lake Wales attorney Emmett Donnelly stood at the center of the scandal, aiming to profit from the deaths of several wealthy acquaintances including millionaire K. H. "King" Gerlach and socialite widow Mrs. J. L. Roach. Thanks to a few words overheard by a sharp-eared telephone operator, Gordon traced Donnelly's connections to Orlando attorney J. Willard Durden. That individual, interestingly enough, reached out to employ a Pensacola "hit man" who just happened to be a police informant. Staging a faked kidnaping of Mrs. Roach as bait,

Gordon and Deputy Jim Busbee utilized the hit man to flush out Durden for a supposed payoff. Caught in the act, Durden confessed, naming Donnelly as his co-conspirator. Shortly after Donnelly's release on bond, the Lake Wales lawyer killed himself with a shotgun blast. Durden, once convicted, received a one year sentence for conspiracy to commit murder and ten years for perjury.[38]

Through these years violence, particularly racial violence, wracked the state. It culminated on Christmas night 1951 in the not-very-distant Brevard County town of Mims with the bombing deaths of National Association for the Advancement of Colored People leader Harry T. Moore and his wife Harriette V. Moore. Suspected at the time and later confirmed, Ku Klux Klan members operating out of Orange and Lake Counties were behind the assassinations. In Polk, too, the Klan seemed to take on new life. The bombing of Bartow's John's Restaurant in December 1950 may have had nothing to do with the group, but the following July Klansmen burned two crosses at Lakeland, one at Lake Hollingsworth near Florida Southern College and the other in front of black civic leader Dr. John S. Jackson's Sixth Street home. The poor turnout at a Bartow Klan rally the same summer hinted that the organization enjoyed slight support in the county, but the membership persisted nonetheless in its hardline agenda. When in December 1952 the state's new NAACP field secretary Robert W. Saunders, Sr., of Tampa led a revitalized state conference to demand "complete and immediate integration," fuel poured onto the Klan flames.[39]

In such circumstances leaders within Polk's African American community understandably desired to reform law enforcement toward better protection of black citizens and greater sensitivity to their needs. As early as 1947 activists had petitioned the Lakeland city council, for instance, to employ black policemen, at least to patrol African American neighborhoods. Council members deferred action on the request, but, as the numbers of registered black voters rose, pressures built. Dr. David J. Simpson's ultimately unsuccessful 1951 run for a seat on the panel aimed to further the cause, but when white policemen shot John Robinson in the back and killed him on October 13, 1951, the drive for black policemen gained true momentum. "Concerned black and white leaders" demanded an investigation, while individuals such as H. L. Stephens, E. T. Pickett, Sr., J. W. Canady, W. J. Roy, and Andy Smith unified black community groups to demand council action. Political clout finally made the difference. In 1953 white candidate Scott Kelly, among others, responded to the demands with a commitment for change. As a result,

41. *Lakeland's first African American police officers. From left: Thomas Hodge, Edgar Pickett Jr., Samuel King, and Samuel Williams.* LAFRANCINE K. BURTON.

Lakeland employed its first four African American police officers the next year. Samuel L. King and Samuel L. Williams put on uniforms in January, with Thomas E. Hodge and Edward T. Pickett, Jr., following them in March.[40]

By then, African Americans had served in county law enforcement for almost one year. Sheriff's candidate Pat Gordon in 1952 already had learned to appreciate black voter strength and had given his promise to hire black deputies. Elected, thanks to that vote, he carried through after taking office in early 1953. "We had a meeting, and the group selected me," NAACP leader Jesse Nesbitt remembered. "Well, actually, [businessman and civic leader Jesse] Richardson, he kind of picked me, but the group voted." Nesbitt added, "I don't know who picked [army veteran] Percy Wilson." Gordon issued no uniforms at first to Nesbitt or Wilson nor did he permit them to arrest whites. After they seized a white man who was threatening his wife with a shotgun, though, no further mention was made of the limitation on arrests.[41]

A few communities besides Lakeland employed black policemen, although they placed strict limits on their authority. Haines City, for instance, found itself during 1952 in a fix. NAACP attorney Francisco Rodriguez had masqueraded as a prisoner in order to investigate charges of abuse, including forced labor of jail inmates in local citrus groves. As state field secretary Robert W. Saunders later put it, "We had real trouble there." The subsequent expose compelled city government in November to employ Frazier Neumon as a weekend policeman in the town's black section. Not until his second year on the job did Neumon receive full-time status, and for the first two years authorities refused to allow him to carry a weapon or make arrests. Winter Haven's turn came in August 1954 when Joel Wilburn, a veteran of South Pacific action during World War Two whose father pastored Williams Temple CME Church, agreed to patrol the Florence Villa section. Twenty years later, still on the job, Wilburn would enjoy the reputation of "a dedicated servant of the law."[42]

These pioneer black law enforcement agents certainly found themselves with work to do. Illegal gambling and liquor sales, together with associated crime, pervaded segments of the black community as they did the white. "Not only did officers battle local racketeers," community historian LaFrancine K. Burton explained, "but also those people who ran huge operations in Orlando, Daytona, Tampa, Jacksonville and Miami, and were trying to expand their 'businesses' to Polk County." Some local black entrepreneurs profited greatly from the criminal enterprise. Lakeland's Elijah "Shanghi" Jackson, for example, "made quite a bit of money" according to Burton. "He profited most from being the 'house-man,'" she related. "As such, he was the person who provided a place for the poker and 'skin' games, and got to 'cut the pot' (took a percentage of the bets)." Slaking customers' thirst for alcohol ranked high, as well, with the businessman. "Shanghi is remembered for having developed a unique rapport with local whites," Burton added. "He crossed certain racial barriers and won the cooperation of prominent citizens—especially during the 1950s and 1960s," she continued. "It was a well-known fact that some of our earlier officials, as well as white businessmen and businesswomen, were regular patrons of Shanghi's." Burton concluded, "It was speculated that he escaped many of the gambling raids because 'he had some of the cops in his back pocket.'"[43]

On another front of the racial divide, white officials in these years often strove to buttress segregation by creating or improving for African Americans facilities and services already available to white community members. Construction of Jewett High School and improvements at Bartow's Union Academy highlighted efforts to prove to federal judges that facilities might be separate but they also were equal. In other examples, Winter Haven in 1952 dedicated a "Negro Beach" on Lake Maude and Lakeland two years later constructed "a Negro recreation park and swimming pool." Yet, such initiatives inevitably proved too little, too late.[44]

Occasionally, a facility or institution actually ran against the tide to welcome black professionals on an equal footing with whites. Lakeland General Hospital in 1953 "swung wide the doors" to welcome Dr. John S. Jackson as an attending physician. Florida Southern College, too, attempted to eliminate barriers. When distinguished educator and businesswoman Mary McLeod Bethune addressed its Founders Week Conclave in 1953, she reminded the one thousand or so persons attending that President Ludd Spivey, having first invited her to speak in 1925, had been "advised not to ask her back." Instead, Spivey repeatedly had welcomed her to the campus. "The walls are crumbling and the doors opening [for African Americans in Florida]," she insisted. The audience responded with "a standing ovation."[45]

Mostly, though, segregation prevailed as African American resentment built. Future track great Robert Harris, son of First Baptist Institutional Church pastor James Harris, remembered Lakeland at the time as "a Southern city where blacks weren't welcome in some downtown stores and where the sports editor of The Ledger got in hot water for running a photo of black track stars on the sports page." Segregation only benefitted him, Harris argued, because it offered education at the hands of gifted black teachers. "I got all these great teachers because the system was bad," he observed. "The climate with the teachers was just absolutely wonderful, so supportive and reinforcing." James Denmark, the discovery of whose artistic genius remained years in the future, grew up at Winter Haven during the same period. He "taught blacks to dog paddle on the segregated beach at Lake Maude," a regional newspaper reported, while attending "segregated elementary and high schools, where cast-off books and equipment were as old as the instructors." Painfully, memories of the "lily-white city newspaper" and its refusal to publish stories about record-breaking black athletes haunted him. On the other hand, Denmark recalled one-half century later, "The sense of unity, family togetherness and the indefatigable spirit that the city's down-but-not-out black residents shared still burns like a blast furnace."[46]

Here was the time when Jim Crow traditions—longstanding patterns of racial discrimination—weighed in the balance. Federal courts increasingly had begun to chip away at their legal foundations. Most crucially, cases were moving through the system aimed at forcing desegregation of all public schools, an idea that shocked many but not necessarily all whites. In December 1953 a taste of what was to come touched Polk when local plaintiffs announced their intention to force teacher salary equalization. When filed in April 1954, the federal litigation involved 60 of the county's

105 black teachers. One month later the United States Supreme Court issued its first ruling on public school integration in the case of *Brown* v. *Board of Education of Topeka, Kansas*. In August and while local people awaited the second *Brown* decision concerning a timetable for enforcement, twenty-one petitioners represented by Francisco Rodriguez demanded the integration of Lakeland's Cleveland Heights Golf Course. Polk Countians found the ground rumbling beneath their feet and awaited anxiously important developments sure to come in the days ahead.[47]

42. *Polk County electoral politics in the 1950s for the most part still depended upon ballots counted individually by hand, as these precinct workers at Lakeland demonstrate. Agnes Dunway, at center, supports the process by stringing ballots together.* POLK COUNTY HISTORICAL QUARTERLY.

CHAPTER 5

∽

The Ordeal of Change, 1955-1960

*N*ot since the Civil War had Polk Countians faced as many questions of fundamental importance as they did from 1955 to 1960. They entered the period, though, with government in crisis and a society shaken by racial tensions and labor turmoil. Voices meanwhile had risen to offer guidance in forms and manners that aroused both passionate commitments and deep resentments. For some, distrust, alienation, and anger resulted; for others, hope. Well-meaning people all the while grappled with change and the impact of past decisions as they sped into the future atop a roaring economic tide that appeared to honor no boundaries. The world altered, and Polk teetered as it endeavored to regain a sense of balance.

At the decade's midpoint, county residents understandably wrestled with comprehending the nature and direction of the governments closest to them. The Democratic party kept local institutions firmly within its grasp, but African Americans such as T. J. Walker and Dr. David J. Simpson recently had defied convention to run for seats on the Lakeland city council. Rumors circulated of other individuals, backed by organizations such as the National Association for the Advancement of Colored People and the Progressive Voters League, intent upon following examples elsewhere. Politicians such as Lakeland's Scott Kelly and Sheriff H. P. "Pat" Gordon had appealed to black voters as decisive elements of their electoral coalitions, while Ku Klux Klansmen barked defiance and issued calls for militant resistance.[1]

While these dynamics played out, residents looked on as corruption continued to eat away at the fabric of local government, especially law enforcement. Only a few years earlier they had seen their sheriff hauled before the bar of justice for abetting illegal gambling. A United States Senate probe, having highlighted that situation, had embarrassed the county across the nation with its report. Then, the processes and personalities of local criminal prosecution had proved themselves incapable of dispensing exacting penalties in such a case.[2]

Meanwhile, other challenges to convention contributed, for some, to the troubling nature of the times. Women, for example, signaled new times aborning, as well as a building desire for the focus of attention to turn to their needs and concerns. The *Lakeland Ledger* during the period featured the work of prize-winning journalist Olive Stout Sykes, "a lady who has given much of her time 'over and beyond the call of duty' to her community in the presentation of news, and in the complete coverage of all news items of 'special interest' to women." Sykes and others could report women's farsighted initiatives, as well as the advance of women into employment roles previously denied to them. Women's clubs, frustrated at the reluctance of a male-dominated medical profession and of government to act, sponsored women's cancer clinics and support programs. At Auburndale, Ann Telford achieved the position of sales manager at Stewart Packing Company, only the second woman in the industry to do so. Even the doors of law enforcement cracked slightly open to women. Lakeland in 1954 had hired four women officers to check parking meters. Male supervisors followed general practice by referring to them as "meter maids."[3]

Although women had demonstrated business skills since the county's pioneer days, Gertrude Kuhn's career well illustrated they now were reaching further into the public sphere, offering the benefit of their talents ever more broadly to the community. "Trudy" Kuhn had arrived in Polk from Chicago before the 1920s boom times. Already working as a Florida State College for Women student, she edited the *Florida Flambeau* and wrote for the *Tampa Tribune*. By the 1950s Trudy owned and operated Bartow's Kuhn Plumbing Supply, but, as friend Barbara Lawn later commented, "She spent her time in the community." For forty years she served on Bartow's library board. She would share herself as well through the "Trudy's Musings" column in *The Shopper*. Beyond that, she played instrumental roles for the Bartow Crickette Club, Bartow Women's Club, Driftwood Circle of the Bartow Garden Club, Girls Villa Board Association, Augusta Bevis Music Club, Bartow's Art Guild and Beautification Board, Miss Bartow Scholarship Pageant Committee, and Lakeland's First Church of Christ Scientist. As Lawn insisted, "Her city was her life." An-

43. *As women emerged more into public life in the 1950s, civic clubs such as Winter Haven's Pilot Club offered a handy and effective institutional mechanism for service and contribution. Pilot Club members seen here included (from the left): bottom row, Kate McAnulty, Cloyce Thornton, Jacquelyn Staack, Ruby McKenney, Rotha Douglas, Harriett Owen, Clara Carpenter, Jo McDonald; middle row, Jo Burr, Marjorie Oglesby, Linnette Kennedy, Helen MacCalla, Ruby Snead, Elsie Laughlin, Madeline Ellsworth, Margaret Dana, Sally Abernathy, Sue Van Duyne, Irma Roubos; top row, Amelia Newland, Mimi Ross, Alice Thompson, Eleanor Smith, Florence Wilson, Florence Heimerdinger, Hazel Wilkerson, Elsie Kirk, Esther Smith, Leone Guy, Dorothy Ayers, and Helen Haines. FROM BURR, HISTORY OF WINTER HAVEN.*

other friend and beneficiary of Kuhn's generous spirit summed up her contributions and their implications regarding unrecognized women's achievements in the public sphere generally. "No one," Hazel Bowman declared, "did more for Bartow than she did."[4]

At least one woman had succeeded in cracking barriers to women themselves holding public office, as opposed to entreating male public servants to address their needs and concerns. Virginia Foley Miller came from one of Polk's premier political families, father James W. Foley having served on the county commission for three decades. In 1954 she had captured a seat on Winter Haven's city commission that she then held for twelve years. To do so, though, the League of Women Voters leader learned that she had to tread softly. "Earlier in her career, her platform did not have much political impact," *Tampa Tribune* writer Dolly Luhrs later noted of Foley. "She championed the reasonably non-controversial beautification theme." Luhrs continued: "Later, from time to time, she did tread on toes in her outspoken criticism of things which displeased her, and her fellow commissioners winced visibly. But she evidently carried it off well because she was always reelected."[5]

Voices besides those of African Americans and women challenged the political status quo, often drawing their context from the development of the "Cold War" internationally and a perceived threat from communism and communists at home. Among them, conservative Protestant ministers increasingly called for action on various fronts. "If God-fearing officials are not elected it will be the Baptists' fault," one visiting church leader typically declared. Not too familiar with local circumstances, he went on to praise Polk "where race tracks and dives are not at every cross roads."[6]

As it happened, many voters lost any sense of positive direction. Reflecting later upon circumstances in the early 1950s, then attorney general and afterward Florida supreme court justice Richard W. Ervin described the atmosphere that surrounded much political rhetoric of the times. "Our Florida people were not mature enough," he recorded, "to withstand the blandishments of the demagogues, the economic aristocrats of the era." Lakeland attorney and civic leader D. Burke Kibler expanded upon the theme. "Anyone could see that the world was changing," he explained. "What was important was the way you made things different," Kibler continued. "We made so many mistakes. No thinking person could possibly justify the old way." He added: "We lost the opportunity to do things much better than we did. We didn't do enough soon enough."[7]

Politics on the Edge, Part I

In such circumstances, it mattered considerably when the situation took a turn for the worse. This unfortunate evolution first began to manifest itself in June 1955 when phosphate industry workers struck for better wages and working conditions. The labor standoff lasted until late September, and, as one report put it, the bitter clash "was marked by many complaints of violence." The reporter explained further. "[The International Minerals and Chemical Company] reported a dynamite blast did at least $50,000 damage to its chemical plant at . . . Bonnie," he wrote, "a transformer was shot up at its phosphate mine near Bartow, a guard was shot at, roads were blockaded by pickets, nonstriking supervisory personnel were threatened and tires were slashed."[8]

At that critical juncture, death suddenly deprived the county of key leadership. Perry E. Murray of Frostproof, one of the state's most-influential political figures, died in a December 1955 automobile accident at his hometown. He had represented Polk County in the state legislature for fourteen years until his retirement earlier in the year he died. Murray had presided over the house of representatives as its speaker in 1949-1950; helped to lead 1945 and 1951 Polk delegations that were named most effective in the legislature; and in 1951 received the *St. Petersburg Times* award as the most valuable representative in the state. A memorial plaque placed with his bust in Lakeland's Florida Citrus Mutual Building reflected the sentiments of many county residents. It read simply, "Well he served his fellow man."[9]

Within less than two months following Murray's death, political scandal again enveloped the county. State representative Boone D. Tillett, Jr., of Lake Wales, who had been contesting a state senate seat against state senator Harry King of Winter Haven and former Lakeland mayor Scott Kelly, claimed that he had received a $10,000 payment from King to divert his energies to a different election. King, who had served in the senate since 1941, stood ready to assume its presidency in 1957. Governor LeRoy Collins appointed William B. Hopkins special prosecutor to investigate the matter. On March 20, 1956, a Polk grand jury indicted King for "perjury and violations of the state elections code," but the panel stunned residents by also indicting Sheriff Gordon and deputies Rollie Arnold, Sentell Monk, and James L. Busbee for "conspiring to commit perjury." The governor thereupon suspended Gordon and appointed respected Alturas citrus grower and cattleman Joel G. Garrard as interim sheriff.[10]

44. *Scott Kelly represented Polk County in the Florida Senate from 1957 to 1963. FLORIDA STATE ARCHIVES.*

Scott Kelly, who then easily won King's state senate seat, reflected on his memories of the affair. "What happened was that Tillett and King had served together [in the legislature]," he recollected. "They had a hostile relationship, they just didn't get along at all. And Tillett was intent on getting [King] one way or another." Kelly continued: "Anyhow, King tried to bribe Tillett to get out of the race. Well, I don't know the particulars. I didn't want to know the particulars, but I believe King went to Pat Gordon to see if Gordon couldn't get his deputies to set a trap for Tillett and the damn thing backfired on them and they got caught instead." Trials followed, but, as Kelly added: "In the meantime it was too late. The train had done left the station. I beat them all, I swamped all of them in the first primary, without a runoff."[11]

The Democratic party primary came on May 8, and shortly thereafter King, Gordon, and the deputies suffered convictions with Judge Roy H. Amidon sentencing King and Gordon each to five years imprisonment. Four days later former sheriff Hagan Parrish defeated Gordon in a primary runoff election. Appeals resulted by 1959 in reductions of sentences for King and the deputies. Gordon and King again appealed. Eventually Gordon served eleven months in prison before Governor Farris Bryant pardoned him in August 1961. The next year Boone Tillett died alone near Cocoa in a one-vehicle automobile accident, and Harry King won his appeal. On March 27, 1963, county solicitor Gordon Mac-Calla announced that the matter would end there. "MacCalla said that because the major witness in the case, which began in 1955, Boone D. Tillett, Jr., of Lake Wales, was dead," a newspaper related, "he did not feel justified in prosecuting a new trial."[12]

Political wounds opened by the scandal hardly had begun to close when MacCalla announced his decision. Many residents, especially African Americans, believed that Gordon had been prosecuted unfairly and for political reasons, sentiments that have persisted for almost half a century. Community historian LaFrancine K. Burton described the ties that Gordon had forged with blacks in Polk. "He is most remembered in the African American community for having assisted one young black man to escape an imminent lynching," she recorded. "In another case, he reportedly challenged the story of a married white woman who, after coming home very late, told her husband that she had been kidnapped and raped by a black man." Burton went on to relate, "And, in yet another volatile situation, it was said that Pat Gordon prevented certain bloodshed when he stopped Groveland's Ku Klux Klan from entering Lakeland's city limits where they planned to 'straighten out a few problems.'" As far as his trial and conviction were concerned, Burton found, "African Americans . . . believe that Gordon was 'framed and railroaded' out of office because of his unwavering stands on behalf of African Americans." She quoted Lakelander Ralph Laidler on the subject. "Pat Gordon tried to make sure that black folks were treated fairly," Laidler insisted. "And he sure was a friend to me."[13]

Back in 1956, more political turmoil brewed. Economic stresses brought about by the onset of a two-year period of severe drought as well by a widespread and potentially disastrous Mediterranean fruit fly outbreak during the summer had raised anxieties about jobs and security at the same time as civil rights demands stirred the region generally. The Ku Klux Klan decided to exploit the resulting discontent by flexing its muscle. Parades and rallies at Lakeland and Bartow heard speakers such as the Reverend R. D. Ingle of Jacksonville's Berea Baptist Church urge Klan membership and activism. Some Baptist preachers in the black community, as it turned out, decided to one up the robed knights when they prepared at Lakeland in July for a statewide rally at which 2,000 attendees were expected. The Reverend O. L. Williams of St. Luke's Free Will Baptist Church announced "a mass meeting to pray for the Ku Klux Klan." To an interviewer Williams explained his purpose, if somewhat wryly. "We believe," he declared, "that Christians should love one another for the good of our community." Many of Polk's citizens got the message, and a follow-up Lakeland KKK rally "fizzled."[14]

Republicans then entered the fray. This train of events had commenced back in 1953 when the legislative delegation, concerned about ongoing disputes within county government, successfully sought passage of a law reinstating the county budget commission, a body originally established in the 1930s by state senator Spessard Holland for the purpose of keeping close tabs on a leaky county treasury. Few residents paid much attention to the panel, even though positions on it were elective. In 1956, this created an opportunity for Republicans emboldened by recent electoral gains. These included Florida's and Polk County's 1952 support of Republican Dwight D. Eisenhower's bid for the presidency and William C. Cramer's 1954 congressional victory in nearby Hillsborough and Pinellas Counties.[15]

Lakeland's Wade M. Rhodes planned and guided subsequent events. As the electoral season developed, he realized that no candidates had qualified for three of the five budget commission seats and that, as expressed in a news report, "in the heat of the presidential campaign no one gave any thought to filling those positions." A precinct committeeman, Rhodes then quietly organized write-in campaigns for GOP candidates A. M. Pickard of Lakeland, Winter Haven's E. L. Jones, and Lakeland's Dr. James R. West. On election day President Eisenhower again took Polk, and, with about fifty votes each, so, too, did the Republican write-in candidates. "With Republicans peering over their shoulders," asked the *Lakeland Ledger*, "will it be a Happy New Year for the Polk Democrats?" The answer turned out to be "no." *Ledger* political writer Anthony Schiappa detailed what occurred. "One of the Republican-dominated commission's first acts was to call for detailed reports from all county officers regarding employees' salaries, their jobs, bonuses and vacation schedules," he explained. "That was in April 1957. Two months later, a suit was filed in circuit court which asked the court to declare the commission unconstitutional." Schiappa concluded: "Circuit Judge Don Register did just that, after hearing arguments on June 20, 1957. And the budget commission was no more—litigated out of existence." The Republicans' tenure thus proved short, but it served also as a harbinger of times to come.[16]

Given all of this, it had become evident to a growing number of Polk voters by 1956 that local politics required attention and adjustment. Scott Kelly's victory for the state senate seemed to point in that direction, as did Hagan Parrish's for sheriff. Youth, too, played a role. Lakeland's Aldine Combee captured a county commission seat, the youngest person ever to do so. World War Two veteran Ray Mattox of Winter Haven had seen only twenty-nine years when he secured a place in the state house of representatives. When Frostproof citrus man Ben Hill Griffin, Jr.—born in Fort Meade on October 20, 1910—won the right to sit beside Mattox, he stood out at thirty-six as the old man in the crowd.[17]

45. *When citrusman Ben Hill Griffin Jr. captured public office in the 1950s, he already held rank as one of Polk's leading businessmen. He is seen here (at far right) seated with (from left) Publix supermarkets head George W. Jenkins, Cypress Gardens founder Dick Pope Sr., and Florida Southern College president Ludd Spivey. LOUISE FRISBIE COLLECTION.*

Important to understanding dynamics then in motion, Ray Mattox in 1957 received the Jaycee "Man of the Year Award." The Junior Chamber of Commerce and its associated local groups by the mid-1950s had begun offering themselves as centers for political discussion and activism, especially among still-young veterans of World War Two and the Korean War. Their direction tended toward cleaning up corruption in government and reforming governmental processes in the interest of efficiency. They felt that they had fought for honest democracy during the wars and that the same should be available at home. "Polk County was active, really active," Scott Kelly remembered of the organization. "The Jaycees got a lot of people elected."[18]

A young man who once lost election to the presidency of the Lakeland Jaycees came forward in 1958 to typify their ideals and their activism. A Lakeland native, Lawton M. Chiles, Jr., then was twenty-eight years of age. At Lakeland High School he had immersed himself in politics, winning the senior class presidency after serving in 1946 as Senator Spessard Holland's campaign driver. Classmates remembered his winning personality and his boundless energy. As one phrased it, "He was always a go-getter." Later, he served for a time as an army artillery officer in Korea before completing his University of Florida law degree in 1955.[19]

Success at the law did not come quickly for the young attorney in Lakeland, and he sought employment teaching classes. Once again, Florida Southern College president Ludd Spivey influenced Polk County's future, this time by accepting the answer to a question that he had not asked or, more correctly, specifically asked. Chiles told the story in this manner:

> My clientele wasn't growing much, and I was about to starve. Hearing that there might be an opening for a part-time business law teacher at Florida Southern College, I went to the campus for an interview with President Spivey. Just before entering the president's office, Dean [Jean A.] Battle warned me that Dr. Spivey would ask me if I had used alcoholic beverages and that I should be very careful how I answered. Because of my financial straits at the time, I was hardly able to afford to eat, let alone purchase alcoholic beverages. Therefore, in answer to Dr. Spivey's anticipated question, I was able to answer that I had no liquor in my house. That answer, along with the fact that I was willing to accept the small salary Dr. Spivey offered, got me the job, and I began moonlighting as an instructor of business law.[20]

Chile's fortunes had rebounded sufficiently by 1958 to interest him in a more-active political role, but the opponent he picked hefted great political weight. Albert Roy Surles, Jr., first had achieved election to the Florida house of representatives in 1948 as a reformer closely allied with Speaker Perry E. Murray. With each reelection since, Surles had tended to distance himself from those early roots. The legislature then rested firmly within the grip of conservative north Florida legislators, a group that *Tampa Tribune* editor James A. Clendinen would label "the Pork Chop gang," and Surles accepted their leadership. "He sort of typified the old school, the pork chop school of politics," Homer Hooks recalled. Support for business loomed large for Surles, with Polk's phosphate, citrus, and cattle industries leading in importance. Yet, Surles seemed in the eyes of many to have lost interest in "the little man" or in reform. When in 1956 he defeated Lakeland attorney Walter W. Manley for re-election, rumors circulated that he had managed the deed only through generous donations of cash and other valuable considerations in certain precincts.[21]

So, the 1958 house race came down to the young versus the older, the little man versus the big interests, and the future against the past. Chiles bet on the future and won. The candidate and his wife Rhea walked door-to-door throughout the district, visiting all told some 14,000 homes. Then, friends got busy. "We came out with the idea of having the Jaycees throughout the county hand out fliers," Chiles supporter Jack Pridgen remembered. "Our goal was to have a flier on every doorstep on the day of the primary election." The strategy worked, and the challenger unseated the incumbent by a comfortable margin. "Chiles captured the imagination of the young people," Hooks explained, "the Jaycees, young lawyers and young professionals who were looking for change." Hooks added, "Lawton captured the imagination of the typical bright, young newcomer who was willing to take on new challenges. The world was changing, of course, as it does constantly and he was able to capitalize on that and he won."[22]

Civil Rights and Schools

It was against this social and political backdrop that Polk Countians learned of the United States Supreme Court's decisions in *Brown* v. *Board of Education of Topeka, Kansas* and numerous other rulings and actions that portended radical and, for many, unwelcome social change. The *Brown* decisions, given their profound significance, offer a good starting point for consideration of the subject. Coming in 1954 and 1955, they held unconstitutional the doctrine of "separate but equal" as applied to public schools. Even though the rulings could be construed as narrow ones, few believed that the court would not apply the same logic that "separate is inherently unequal" to other public programs, facilities, and services. The tribunal muddled its directive, though, in the second *Brown* ruling. This one, handed down May 31, 1955, failed to set a timetable for implementation of the first decision. Rather, the court merely ordered compliance "with all deliberate speed," an unfortunate selection of words that some southern politicians took as encouraging "massive resistance."[23]

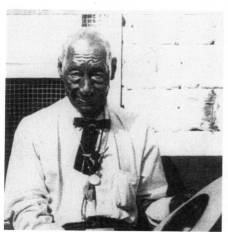

46. *One-time slave Charlie Smith remained alive in Polk County in the 1950s.* POLK COUNTY HISTORICAL ASSOCIATION.

Civil War memories yet persisted in Polk when the rulings were issued, and the county maintained a mostly segregated society that many saw as the normal order of things. Two Polk widows of Confederate veterans—Mrs. F. M. Armstead and Mrs. Mary C. Stuart—continued to receive state pensions. At Bartow, one-time slave Charlie Smith lived on. As to segregation, Joel Atkins recalled conditions when he arrived at Winter Haven in 1956. "Signs separating the races were everywhere," he observed. "They were at restaurant counters, business offices and bus stations." Of Winter Haven, the city that he came to love and to lead, Atkins added, "This was the most segregated place that I have ever recognized." Recently, white officials on the state and local levels

47. *Civil rights leader Joel Atkins stands in front of Winter Haven's Zion Hill Missionary Baptist Church, where he would pastor for forty-one years.* LAKELAND LEDGER.

had attempted to upgrade black schools to qualify them as "equal." In reality they remained substandard in many aspects, although few of Polk's schools white or black enjoyed a bounty of resources. Atkins's son William S. Atkins, who studied at Jewett High School, described conditions there. "We got books with other people's names in them . . . when we got them," he began. "The buses were really poor," Atkins continued. The football team used helmets passed down from Lakeland High School, and his classmates referred to their school's football field as "the Dust Bowl." Atkins added, "We knew what the field at Winter Haven High School looked like. There was no doubt that we did not have the best of things."[24]

Reaction to the *Brown* decisions initially varied within the white sector of Polk's population. Historian James V. Holton, who studied the question in depth, found "subtlety and ambiguity." He concluded, "The white mainstream in Polk County neither resisted nor embraced the cause of civil rights." Holton added, however, "The white majority certainly was not yet ready for even the hint of racially integrated education." Senator Holland urged "patience and moderation," while the *Lakeland Ledger* found "splendid idealism" in the court's actions but cautioned that "[desegregation] is of a broadly social nature that only the passage of time can take care of." The Florida Methodist Conference meeting at Florida Southern College in June 1954 proved more forthright. "We urge that our colleges, churches, universities, seminaries, hospitals and homes restudy their policies and practices as they relate to race," its statement proclaimed, "making certain that those policies and practices are Christian."[25]

The complexities of the situation revealed themselves in the *Polk County Democrat*'s multiple views and response to them. Sayer Loyal Frisbie, the publisher's father, condemned the first decision, insisting that it "will undo racial understanding contrary to the wishes of both sides." Publisher S. Lloyd Frisbie II urged "postponing the actual operation of their ruling for an indefinite period." The publisher's son Loyal Frisbie captured youthful optimism in support of the decision by use of Biblical analogy. "Well, it was bound to come," he began. "Although the ruling had been expected for some time, still it comes to many persons, both white and black, with something of a jolt that must have been felt by the people of Israel and Samaria when Jesus of Nazareth told them that they all, being alike children of God the Father, were brothers." Loyal Frisbie's son S. L. Frisbie, IV, explained his father's attitudes and what they produced. "Dad, who came home from World War II with an appreciation for the notion that all men are created equal—and suffer equally on the battlefield—wrote a column supporting the court's ruling," he observed. "Somebody called our house that night," Frisbie added, "and threatened to dynamite it."[26]

Florida officialdom unfortunately took its cue not from moderates such as Loyal Frisbie but from former governor Millard Caldwell who labeled the United States Supreme Court "Communist." In a chilling echo of the Frisbie experience, the *Miami Herald* editor's home was bombed when he voiced support for change. The Florida supreme court joined the rising chorus in November 1954. "I think the Brown Decision was a great mistake," Justice Glenn Terrell declared for the majority. "Whether or not the doctrine of 'separate but equal' has a place in the field of public education is a question of policy determinable by the Legislature. It is not a judicial question as I understand the canons of interpretation." Governor LeRoy Collins agreed. "The heavy hand of coercion whether by judicial or bayonets or otherwise should be taken off the South and allow Southerners to resolve our sins of racial discrimination, such as it may be, in our own time," he soon advised.[27]

Within the African American community bright hopes prevailed. Charles Coleman then taught students at Lakeland's Rochelle High School. When he heard the news of the first *Brown* decision he turned to his ninth grade mathematics class and exclaimed, "Some day Lakeland will have a black city commissioner." Many of his and other black students in the county meanwhile grew emboldened in defiance of traditional ways. "I never rode the buses," former Rochelle pupil Robert Harris recalled. "I didn't like the buses because you had to sit in a certain place and I didn't want to sit there." He added, "I would run everywhere I had to go."[28]

Hopes and expectations, as it turned out, met for the time being mostly with frustration. County leadership devolved into the chaos of scandal and a mire of indecision. School board attorney Clarence A. Boswell, Sr., emerged as perhaps the most influential voice in setting policy. At his urging the board on August 22, 1956, adopted a "Pupil Assignment Law" that effectively barred any African American pupil from attending any white school. Members of the black community understood the measure's intent perfectly. "From 1956 to 1963," historian Holton discovered, "not one Black officially requested a transfer to an all-white school in Polk County."[29]

A few advances altered some aspects of the county's racial divide, but only a few. Sheriff Parrish, for one, proved that he had learned from the past by assigning Percy E. Wilson as the first black deputy in the office's criminal department. Health care witnessed some change, as well. Late in the decade, Lakeland built a new hospital, subsequently called Lakeland General Hospital. City leaders promised to reserve a floor of the building for black patients but defaulted. Dr. John S. Jackson then tested the rules by admitting black volunteers for tests, but hospital staff referred them to nearby "colored" facilities. Led by N. C. Adderly and the Reverend John Jackson, black Lakelanders protested and, with NAACP support, sued in federal court to desegregate the hospital. "The city settled the case," Jesse Nesbitt remembered, "and integrated the hospital." Politicians occasionally attempted to assuage black concerns, as Lakeland's city government did by allowing construction of the Pinehurst Court subdivision. It did so by permitting conversion of a "white housing area" into a "Negro housing area." Realtor Ken Harris, who brokered the transactions, observed, "The transfer of property will provide for Negro expansion for the next 30 years."[30]

Diversions and Distractions

Troubling problems and nagging concerns notwithstanding, Polk Countians nonetheless focused their attention elsewhere most of the time, and, with the economy roaring ahead as it was, who wanted to argue with good times? "Polk Reaches Peak Prosperity in Late '59," a *Ledger* headline blared that December. "Farm employment is gaining, non-farm employment is rising, the factory work-week is lengthening and payrolls have set a new record," Florida State Employment Service manager Kenneth W. Ringdahl trumpeted. The same year the county's property appraisals jumped past the $1 billion mark, as bank deposits soared. Lakeland now hosted over one thousand businesses, with Winter Haven counting nearly five hundred. "A physical count of manufacturers, wholesalers and retailers in Polk County totaled 2,656," Dun and Bradstreet's Lakeland manager James W. Hill III had announced in January. Employment totals meantime reached record highs.[31]

Virtually every segment of the economy whistled along. "Here are all the natural facilities that breed wealthy men," one commentator explained to business leaders. "Polk has more citrus and cattle acreage than any other Florida county." Despite the fruit fly and severe freezes in December 1957 and January and December 1958, citrus growers and processors indeed counted high profits. Aiming to keep it so, experts labored intently in the comfort of the Florida Citrus Commission's new Lakeland headquarters, erected in 1956. Tourists all the while flooded by the groves on their way to Polk's attractions, with many opting to return and settle. As the decade closed Cypress Gardens alone was drawing one million visitors per year and expecting an upward trend for the future. Even small entrepreneurs, such as Carl Allen, recognized the opportunity their presence created. He first opened a bait and tackle shop at Auburndale before moving into the restaurant business in the early 1960s. At Winter Haven, William Shultz addressed opportunities of growth rather than tourism and did so on a large scale. His Polk Nursery Co. became the largest container nursery company in the state as well as the largest fernery in the United States.[32]

The phosphate industry particularly saw astounding advances. Its local operations achieved their biggest year in history during 1956, thanks in good part to the "mushrooming growth of [the] triple superphosphate fertilizer" business. Although another violent strike during the late spring and early summer of 1959 threatened to put a damper on production, the industry quickly rebounded given rising demand. A total of 5,400 workers earned $25 million in payroll during 1959, nearly exceeding 1956's record. The industry participated, as well, in the nation's crash program of scientific research that resulted from the Cold War and the Soviet Union's launch of the first man-made satellite into space on October 4, 1957. By way of example, the next year the International Minerals and Chemical Corporation opened a new mineralogical laboratory at its experimental research station at Mulberry, making that operation "the largest industrial research facility in the state."[33]

The "space race" generated by Sputnik's launch touched Polk in other ways, as well. The Congress in 1958 created the National Aeronautics and Space Administration, with missile testing and flight operations centered at Cape Canaveral on the Atlantic Ocean a little north of east from Polk. "East central Florida underwent a revolution in the late 1950s," according to historian Gordon Patterson, but Polk benefitted as well when local businessmen snapped up lucrative contracts. Frank M. Murphy, for instance, had begun his Bartow business in 1950 aiming to make heavy equipment for phosphate mine expansions. With the space race underway, Frank M. Murphy and Associates turned its attention to crafting launching pedestals and umbilical towers for the Saturn program. It accomplished most of the work at its steel fabricating plant at Pembroke, just north of Fort Meade.[34]

As fast transportation arrived in space, at least more-rapid transportation came to Polk. Thanks in good part to Senator Scott Kelly's influence as chairman of the state legislature's interim highway committee and Al Rogero's as a member of the state road board, Interstate 4 construction commenced within the county by 1959. By late in the year, the limited access expressway had opened from Lakeland west to U.S. 301 east of Tampa. Construction north and east of Lakeland to Orlando proceeded in 1960 with early completion expected. Soon television advertisements instructed residents in proper driving techniques on the unfamiliar highways. Especially, they warned motorists, in the event of a missed exit, not to back up.[35]

Growth, prosperity, and better transportation opened opportunities also for county towns that had struggled to survive during the bust and depression years and then staggered along thereafter beneath a crushing load of debt incurred as far back as the early 1920s boom. Haines City helped to lead the way. About 1956 local businessmen reorganized the chamber of commerce and installed a capable manager, Woodrow Todd. He encouraged adoption of "new and more ambitious ways of thinking." Drives ensued aimed at luring new industry to the community. Businessmen Clifford Swain and David Rogers III spearheaded efforts to organize an industrial development corporation, with stock to be subscribed by local people. Success soon came calling. First, the Addison, Illinois-based Nilsen Manufacturing Company opened a branch plant. Calco Corporation, another Addison manufacturer, followed with a precision oil field equipment facility. As optimism grew, in December 1960 area business leaders organized the Northeast Polk County Industrial Development Corporation to extend the developmental push throughout the area.[36]

"New and more ambitious ways of thinking" touched merchandising as well as industrial development. Large "shopping centers" became the rage with Lakeland-based Publix Super Markets, Inc., spurring construction of many. One that involved "a particularly extravagant outlay" rose at Winter Haven. Its opening in February 1956, the *Winter Haven Herald* asserted, was a "once-in-a-lifetime thrill." North Gate Shopping Center within one year contained fourteen establishments, anchored by a state-of-the-art Publix grocery store. "Not only are the business houses at North Gate about the last word in construction, equipment and utilitarianism," the *Herald* boasted on the first anniversary of its opening, "but the site itself has been so improved and beautified that it contributes greatly to the esthetic nature and appearance of our city." The newspaper added, "Now we have a million dollar shipping center conveniently located and with stores and shops that simply can't be excelled anywhere, including such metropolises as Tampa, Jacksonville and Miami."[37]

48. *Publix helped to pioneer the concept of "shopping centers" during the 1950s, adding as one of its showpieces the "particularly extravagant" North Gate Shopping Center at Winter Haven. Florida State Archives.*

Larger stores made their appearance, slowly cutting away at the claim small business owners traditionally had held on local trade. Publix helped to push the trend to the point that, by the early 1950s, the company already had found it necessary to construct at Lakeland a 125,000 square foot warehouse and headquarters complex. However, Publix was not alone when it came to the concept of price-cost efficiency through large scale operations. When an $85,000 Tip-Top TV and Appliance store debuted at Winter Haven in 1957, the event justified a fourteen-day celebration. "Each day since the modernistic building was opened on March 1," a reporter declared, "[corporate owners Marty and John Halabrin] and their staff have been hosts to hundreds of interested visitors, a majority of whom have become customers and given the firm a sales record that has exceeded fondest expectations." The reporter added, "The new store has many features hitherto unknown in this area and in size, equipment and arrangement compares with the largest merchandising marts in major cities throughout the country."[38]

The prosperity that justified construction of such "large merchandising marts" reached beyond Polk's white population and into the black community. Old-style lunch counters remained subject to racial restrictions, but not so most display rooms of new stores that depended upon impressive, steady, and dependable sales figures. One further manifestation of the warmth of better economic times appeared in church con-

49. *First Providence Missionary Baptist Church's new sanctuary at Bartow.* POLK COUNTY HISTORICAL ASSOCIATION.

struction. Bartow's First Providence Missionary Baptist Church erected a lovely new building that could seat more than six hundred members in comfort. Perhaps the county's oldest church in continual operation, First Providence's new facility sheltered fourth and fifth generation members such as Kathryn Northern and her daughter Gloria McCoy. Similarly, Beulah Missionary Baptist Church's new Fort Meade sanctuary first welcomed worshipers on February 2, 1957. On that special day, the Reverend Jocky Dupree preached on the theme "In the year King Uzziah died, I also saw the Lord."[39]

The ready availability of money unfortunately drew crooks as well as saints. Likely the era's most infamous Polk money episode involved the now-legendary "Great Fort Meade Bank Heist of 1957." In that instance Donald J. Thompson and Irvin U. Suits, well-fueled with alcohol, stole a plane in late October and headed for the riches awaiting at Fort Meade's First State Bank. Setting down in a cow pasture near Sand Mountain, the two would-be robbers hotfooted it into town and, thanks to *Esquire* magazine, the glare of national attention. Their various misadventures in grabbing $25,657 in loot paled by comparison with the mishaps of their attempt at flight. Police chief Glenn Baggett and associate Perry Johnson forced the pair to take to the air "with pistols blazing." This led to a quixotic flight to Plant City, a plane switch, a Boca Grande division of the theft proceeds, and a split in the partnership. Authorities grabbed one of the men when he accidentally landed at Tampa's airport next to the county sheriff and the Florida Sheriff's Association president.

The other suffered arrest after a drunken traffic accident on the road to Tampa. The entire episode lasted a mere eight hours, but the robbers' fame endured. Local historian Jeffrey N. Brown—whose grandmother Cleo Brown faced the bank robbers' guns that day—assures that, "at the annual Fort Meade Halloween parade a few days later, there were no less than four sets of 'bank robbers' mixed with the other creatures that go bump in the night."[40]

In retrospect the bank heist story brings a smile to the face, but not all consequences of Polk's prosperity could claim the same. Air and water pollution problems first noticed earlier in the decade now grew ever-more serious. Phosphate companies insisted that they had installed "pollution prevention stations . . . to stop trouble before it can begin," in addition to other cautionary actions. Complaints from Polk and Hillsborough nonetheless had reached such a level by 1957 that the state legislature created the Florida Air Pollution Control Commission to establish air pollution control districts. Florida Citrus Mutual, citing widespread damages to Polk crops, demanded early action on a Polk district. The commission's response in 1958 created for county Florida's first pollution control district. The commission and district subsequently enacted some regulations, but, as scholar Scott H. Dewey concluded, "Florida officials were reluctant to confront a powerful, polluting industry that increasingly dominated the economy of central Florida." As a result, little progress occurred even after respected plant pathologist C. Stafford Brandt determined "that industrial pollution was visible and serious."[41]

Water, its availability and its quality, too commanded increasing attention. The 1957 legislature addressed that concern, as well, by creating the Southwest Florida Water Conservation District to include Polk, Hardee, Highlands, DeSoto, Sarasota, and Manatee Counties. A six-member board appointed by the governor possessed "broad powers of control over the water in streams, lakes and underground sources." Despite that action, the water table continued to drop precipitously. Where Kissengen Springs had disappeared earlier in the decade, now another of Polk's longtime gathering spots suffered. Its waters receding by the late 1950s, Eagle Lake's dock within a few years stood on dry land. "As the water receded," one observer noted, "so did the number of people that used the pavilion." Some, such as Haines City's Forrest W. Rutherford, attempted to rouse the public to anger and action. "The public in general is seeing a few so-called big wheels of the state rob them blind," he declared in 1959, "and they do not have the nerve to stand on their own two feet and demand what is rightfully theirs." Few yet listened.[42]

Politics on the Edge, Part II

The era's advances sadly failed to extend to a desirable extent into politics and government, and, meanwhile, the taint of corruption lingered in the air. In September 1958 Sheriff Hagan Parrish revealed that former state legislator E. B. "Shorty" Jones had attempted to bribe him to permit Polk operation of bolita, the Cuban numbers game. Indicted by the grand jury, Jones's 1959 trial resulted in conviction. Sentenced to a five-year term in the state penitentiary, Jones appealed unsuccessfully and departed the county, presumably, for good.[43]

One month following Parrish's announcement, a group of businessmen reinforced concerns about governmental corruption by asking Governor LeRoy Collins for an investigation of county finances, including "actions of some county employees." The governor turned to State Attorney Murray W. Overstreet of Kissimmee who promised that the "mystery case" would go before a grand jury by early 1959. Informed sources hinted that matters of larceny, embezzlement, bribery, perjury, and more lay behind the complaints. When the grand jury finally reported in February, it contained "a scathing denouncement of a number of current practices" but found "no knowing or willful violation of the law." Its members added, though, certain qualifications. "On the extortion and malpractice count, the grand jurors said they first thought 'it might be applicable to some of the acts of the county commissioners about which we had received evidence,'" the *Polk County Democrat* reported, "but that a Florida supreme court interpretation of the statute convinced the jurors that 'we did not have before us sufficient evidence against any of the commissioners.'"[44]

Interestingly, these latest scandals may have produced an indirect but enduring result. Polk's judges traditionally had worn business suits when presiding in local courts. Now, the Polk County Bar Association, concerned for the appearance of professionalism and to lend dignity to proceedings, requested that circuit judges and the judge of the criminal court "don robes for courtroom procedures, when courtrooms are air-conditioned." Circuit judges William K. Love and Gunter Stephenson selected "the specific robes to be obtained," and the county commission approved their purchase in late February 1959.[45]

The contributions of women in public office might have helped to ameliorate the county's plight, but few candidates appeared and none other than Winter Haven's Virginia Foley Miller won positions. At Auburndale, though, Mayor Sam Newbern recommended Oveda

Caldwell's appointment to the city council in place of her late husband Walter Caldwell. The council approved and, further, designated Caldwell as mayor pro tempore. Notable milestones for women did come in a few areas other than politics. In 1956 following the death of her husband A. G. Hancock, Roberta Oxford Hancock succeeded to the presidency of Winter Haven's American National Bank. She distinguished herself in the position for five years. Not without significance, Lakeland's "meter maids" also scored a victory. In January 1959 local authorities permitted them, for the first time, to shed skirts and wear slacks on duty.[46]

On the question of race relations, matters simmered with occasional public eruptions. However, the potential for violence—something then occurring regularly elsewhere in the state—appeared vividly in June 1958 when Richard Ashe informed investigators at the state capital that the Ku Klux Klan operated Lakeland's United Gun Club "as a front in order to purchase and store large supplies of guns and ammunition." More heartening, Governor Collins experienced a change of heart regarding segregation and civil rights protections generally. "Our nation cannot survive without law," he declared to attorneys meeting at the University of Florida in 1958. "Law in turn must have the respect of the people," the governor continued. "The fundamental rule of the lawyer is to seek justice. The gardener, no matter how respectable in appearance, who plants seeds of disrespect for law can well expect a crop of disaster and violence." More directly, Collins also denounced racial segregation to the public as "morally wrong" and insisted that United States Supreme Court decisions "must be followed by Florida." His words, inspiring to African Americans and some whites in Polk and other parts of the state, offered a warm light to guide the very difficult journey that lay ahead.[47]

50. *Polk's impressive growth in the post-World War Two decades appears evident in this 1960s scene of Lakeland's downtown area.* LAKELAND PUBLIC LIBRARY.

"moving steadily into a richer future"

CHAPTER 6

༄

Surprises of Transformation, 1960-1965

*T*he 1950s had ended in Polk County as a whirlwind, and, as eyes turned toward the future, dreams of untold growth and bounty seemed grounded firmly in reality. Fading now were memories of the 1920s boom and bust and of the grim 1930s toll of unbending economic depression. The great victory that had brought World War Two to its close remained fixed as a source of pride and a guide for action; yet, residents looked mostly to eager possibilities as they greeted the years about to unfold. The expiring decade, though, had attempted to whisper a message of caution. Phenomenal increase, it had suggested softly, carried costs and required stressful change. Where that decade had offered its words of warning with a gentle touch, however, the county's people would discover to their surprise that the new era approached matters in a starkly different manner. The bill has come due, the 1960s now shouted, and demands for payment no longer can be ignored.

Without question the 1950s had pressed its imprint indelibly upon the county. Polk's population jumped during the period a breathtaking 55 percent to nearly 193,000. Small towns such as Winter Haven would almost double in size, and the county's largest municipality Lakeland would climb above the 40,000 mark. True, Polk's growth left the county trailing coastal areas where breathtaking increases leapt into the category of astounding. On the other hand, the rate of local growth had produced prosperity on so broad a scale that few paid attention when voices such as state senator Scott Kelly's expressed concern that Polk's traditional position of influence within the state had altered significantly. Such concerns, after all, could be dealt with later.[1]

That attitude appeared justified as the early years of the 1960s evolved. "Polk's Industrial Gains Set Records During 1961," a headline heralded. It added, "More in 1962." Haines City's venture into sponsorship of industrial development steamed along nicely, while Bartow seized upon unused assets of the past to address the future. "The Bartow Air Base, once used as a pilot training center, emerged in 1961 as the 'ideal' industrial park," the report detailed. "The base had dozens of buildings suited for industry and when the city of Bartow announced its plans for an industrial park, it had little trouble luring companies to the area." Winter Haven, too, shared in the good times, receiving "one of the biggest plums of the year when State Farm Mutual Insurance Co. announced it would locate its regional headquarters there." Meanwhile, phosphate companies invested another $60 million in new plants; the citrus industry prospered to the extent that the Florida Citrus Canners Cooperative at Lake Wales could enjoy a $1 million expansion of its facilities; and the years ahead promised more. "The county's newest industrial park—Lake Blue Industrial Park between Auburndale and Winter Haven—is expected to get its first plant," the report added.[2]

As they say, "you ain't seen nothin' yet." By 1963 advances came so rapidly that statistics keepers had problems keeping up. Manufacturing payrolls during 1952 had mounted to the then-impressive annual total of $17 million. Ten years later they topped $55 million. In the chemical and allied products industries, the figures ranged from $1.8 million in 1952 to $17 million in 1962. The food products industry, relatively speaking, had lagged behind. Its annual payroll had inflated only to $22.3 million from $10.5 million. The work force understandably had grown. In 1963 manufacturing employed 7,500 persons; mining 4,800; contract construction, 3,700; transportation, communications and public utilities, 2,100; wholesale trade, 2,900; retail trade, 9,400; finance, insurance and real estate, 2,800; services and miscellaneous, 6,900; and government, 6,400. As might be expected, average hourly wages varied according to nature of employment. Food-related concerns paid $1.61; chemical and allied products, $2.39; and non-metallic mining, $2.34.[3]

Other comparisons further illustrate the dynamic trends. All manufacturing had produced a payroll of $12.2 million in 1950. The 1962 results more than tripled that achievement. During 1954, 40,400 non-farm workers labored in Polk on a full-time basis. Five years later that figure stood at 49,300. Another half-decade pushed the total up to 60,100. In 1965, and despite a disastrous freeze in December 1962 and certain other setbacks, the county tax roll exceeded $1.15 billion dollars. A mere six years earlier it had encompassed only $347 million in taxable value.[4]

If any one development of the period highlighted for county residents the apparent surge in industrial growth, the opening at Lakeland in 1965 of a glass plant likely took the prize. "The growing demand for glass containers in the Florida citrus industry influenced Owens-Illinois' decision to erect the plant at Lakeland," a business publication explained. "Production of glass bottles is expected to be started at the new $6 million Lakeland plant . . . in September," it continued. "The highly-automated plant is described by the company as 'the most modern glass plant in the world.'" The report added, "More than 200 people will be employed at the plant, adding some $1 million annually to Lakeland's payroll." Local officials waxed euphoric at the news. "The selection of Lakeland by Owens-Illinois Glass Co.," the mayor exclaimed, "is the forerunner to more industry . . . as the city gains a reputation as one cooperative and anxious for good clean industry."[5]

So inspiring were outcomes such as this that leaders and news organs took great pride and expended great effort in touting them. "A big industrial break for Polk is overdue," the *Lakeland Ledger* had informed readers back in January 1963. "Now the civic and business leaders of the county are making a more concentrated effort to attract industry in much larger volume. However, regardless of whether any new industries of real magnitude are established in Polk during the present year, there will be a wide range of advances." The editorial continued: "People like to live here in the heart of Florida. The population increase will continue at a brisk rate. More people will be coming here from other states to establish residence. More business enterprises will be established here. . . . Polk's rich potential is rapidly being translated into productive, profitable reality." The *Ledger* concluded, "Polk unquestionably is moving steadily into a richer future."[6]

Signs of the Times

Every community in Polk evidenced the impact that growth and prosperity brought to the county, and the *Lakeland Ledger* editorial that praised the progress seen all around noted some of those changes. "The recent opening of the Fields and Kwik-Chek stores and the announcement that a huge shopping center that will include a Sears store, another Publix supermarket and 31 other stores," it observed, "mean that many level-headed business experts feel certain that the Lakeland area is an area of increasing opportunity." In 1962 alone Lakeland benefitted from just under $8 million in new construction. Florida Southern College's new John W. Branscomb Auditorium accounted for almost 10 percent of that figure, but the national discount "department store" J. M. Fields contributed more. Meanwhile, Sears, Roebuck & Co. shared plans for a "huge" new shopping center that eventually carried the name Searstown. Montgomery Ward quickly followed with its own $1 million store announcement. When the Peoples Bank mulled construction of a new home in 1963, it, too, chose to build at the $1 million level. The $200,000 spent that year for Lakeland's new and "ultra-modern" Grove Theater seemed paltry by comparison.[7]

Large and fancy definitely defined one trend, but so, too, did small and simple. The pace of life had quickened to the point that residents often craved "ease and convenience" when shopping. The "convenience store" resulted. "They all have open frontage where customers can help themselves quickly to last minute needs," Winter Haven historian Josephine Burr described, "paying at the check-out space in the center of each stop." The "Seven-Eleven" chain made early inroads in this regard, but "Li'l General" and "Shop & Go," among others, soon made their appearance as well.[8]

The yearning for ease and convenience lent itself, too, to the popularity of "fast food" restaurants. "Hang outs," on the order of Winter Haven's Hob Nob Tavern or Bartow's old John's Drive-In previously had met residents' needs for tasty but relatively quick meals. Now, A&W Root Beer "stands" and other chain eateries popped up across the county. No fast food restaurant enjoyed greater immediate popularity, though, than did the McDonald's Hamburger Drive-Ins. Extra-long and crispy french fried Idaho potatoes at 14 cents, simple hamburgers with mustard and catsup at 19 cents—plus thick shakes and Coca Cola to go—ranked high with consumers across the spectrum. Among the first such spots in Florida, Winter Haven's McDonald's opened for business in February 1963. The Hob Nob, "for years the most popular hangout for the swinging set," closed within three years.[9]

It became easier and quicker to get from place to place in the county in order to enjoy such innovations. Increasingly, four-laned highways made their appearance as traffic volume increased, although plans to enlarge U.S. 27 down the Ridge at least temporarily hit a roadblock in 1962 when Governor Farris Bryant opted to extend the Sunshine State Parkway instead. "[The] refusal of this administration to give the people some tangible evidence that it is not strangling free highways to build toll roads could bring a loss of public faith," state senator Kelly insisted. Bryant, he argued, "was selling out Florida." The big news came, however, with the opening of Interstate 4's final section to traffic on February 15, 1962. The discovery of "muck pockets" near Lake Alfred had slowed progress and required revised plans, but the availability of "high speed travel" pleased most despite the delays. The state road department also sweetened the pie by promising to survey the route for a bypass from I-4 through Lakeland by way of Dakota Avenue, Lake Wire Drive, and New York Avenue. The governor's ire at Senator Kelly might explain the lack of subsequent progress on fulfilling that promise.[10]

Many Polk communities spruced up to welcome the Sixties. Lakeland's efforts merit particular attention. In the late 1940s town fathers seriously had considered deeding downtown's Munn Park to the United States government for post office use but saw the plans crumble in the face of a Florida supreme court opinion that the property could not be disposed of and could be maintained only as "a park for public use." A decade later, a very different view prevailed and, with the dedication in November 1961 of the "Magic Fountain," the park now represented the centerpiece of downtown focus. City government also encouraged relocation of downtown railroad facilities and the opening of "major thoroughfares closed to through traffic for decades" because of railroad needs. "Now downtown Lakeland reflects a new spirit," the city's newspaper proclaimed. "In addition to the beautification of Munn Park, one major parking lot has been completed north of the railroad; and a second lot is to be improved in the future; Pine Street of the former blighted area is envisioned in future years as a modern business section in a progressible downtown district," the journal continued. "Indirectly, because of this major civic undertaking, a new financial institution north of the railroad is anticipated; the new postoffice and police building will be constructed on Lake Wire; [and] other business enterprises are in the planning stages." Talk even circulated—prematurely, as it turned out—that a Lakeland "coliseum" might arise at the old Lodwick Airport.[11]

The rush to beautify and modernize generated losses, then mostly unappreciated, that later produced regrets mixed with a sense of lost opportunity to preserve the best of the past. Doubtlessly many Havenites mourned the Hob Nob's demise, but sometimes the loss could be more subtle. In 1964, for example, Bartow's Craine's Feed Store closed when owner R. W. Craine retired. An establishment that obviously had catered to earlier Polk County lifestyles, it had operated for forty-one years. Perhaps Craine's enjoyed renown most generally from having served for

51. *For decades prior to the 1960s, residents and visitors alike had enjoyed pleasurable days and evenings at Eagle Lake's popular pavilion.* FLORIDA STATE ARCHIVES.

more than a decade as the site of Bartow's longest running checker game, an event described by one newspaperman as "a continuous attraction for both tourists and local citizens."[12]

Even some of the county's most-popular rendezvous points faded away, victims of changed times and trends. After Hurricane Donna smashed through Polk in September 1960, Eagle Lake's wrecked pavilion closed forever. At Fort Meade, Sand Mountain experienced a similar fate. Long gone were sand skiing championships and large happy throngs of fun seekers young and old. Meanwhile, by 1964 phosphate recovery techniques had grown efficient enough to justify mining the mountain. Operations soon commenced, and, within three years, "a huge hole" appeared where once had stood Polk County's highest elevation. "Well," Fort Meade's John E. Brown expressed, "it was fun while it lasted."[13]

Surprisingly, the planned destruction of yet another Fort Meade landmark at least stirred controversy, and it did so with meaningful implications for the future. By 1964 the seven-story Skeleton Hotel had loomed over one of Polk's key intersections for almost four decades. Given modern times, though, the city commission determined to rid itself of such a reminder of an inglorious past and purchased the site for $16,000 "with the avowed purpose of having the embarrassing structure torn down." The hotel's tenant, market operator Oscar Ford, cried foul.

"A majority of the people of Fort Meade do not want it torn down," Ford insisted. He agreed that some considered the building an embarrassment but, he argued, "others have looked upon it as an historic landmark." Historic landmarks of more-modest sorts did not yet command the respect that would accrue to them in future years, however. Ford's protest met with failure. The Skeleton Hotel came down, and a "service station" rose from the ruins.[14]

As historic or dilapidated structures (according to the eye of the beholder) increasingly disappeared from sight, communities continued to spring up to embrace and house the new Polk County. Of those originating in the early 1960s, Nalcrest likely claimed the most attention. Located east of Lake Wales, the project stemmed from William C. Doherty's presidency of the National Association of Letter Carriers, an organization whose initials lent to Nalcrest its name. A designed community for retired persons, it aimed to offer "low rental one and two bedroom apartments" and community amenities such as "a store, community center, complete recreation units, boating, fishing, swimming, and beach facilities." Postmaster General John A. Gronouski represented President Lyndon B. Johnson at dedication ceremonies held on January 20, 1964. After urging support for the president's proposed Medicare program, Gronouski expressed his pride "in this great project, the first of its kind in the nation." Jerome Keating, current president of the letter carriers union, then accepted the keys to Nalcrest on behalf of letters carriers throughout the United States.[15]

52. *Destruction of Fort Meade's Skeleton Hotel in the early 1960s signaled the end of an era that looked backward to the 1920s for signs of prosperity and, instead, looked forward to dynamic growth in the immediate future.* FLORIDA STATE ARCHIVES.

Problems that plagued another and grander development not far from Nalcrest meanwhile sounded alarm bells to the effect that, even in the warm climate of Polk prosperity, poorly conceived and managed projects might not prove viable. When opened in the mid-1950s, Indian Lake Estates promised large-scale development for the county's future. Investors purchased thousands of lots, but only 150 or so homes resulted. By April 1965 corporate president Anthony A. Maisano had announced the company's bankruptcy. A referee designated Tampa's Ernest L. Stewart as trustee to untangle its snarled affairs. The largest land foreclosure sale in Polk's history ensued in August when the Teamsters Union Pension Fund paid $1.9 million for control of the project, including 3,500 lots, a golf course, and other facilities. Lake Wales lawyer Clinton Curtis represented the Teamsters pension fund along with fund trustee Champ J. Madigan. "Neither Curtis nor Madigan would comment," a news report related, "on what will now be done with the property."[16]

Another dynamic that involved construction additionally touched many lives in Polk during the 1960s. The Cold War between the Soviet block and the United States and its allies never had cooled following the lowering of the "Iron Curtain" on eastern Europe and the eruption of the Korean War. The introduction of a Communist leadership in Cuba after the 1959 takeover of the island government by Fidel Castro heightened concerns for war, fears brought immediately home to county residents in October 1961 when the Cuban Missile Crisis routed convoys of military men and materiel along Polk highways. Schools began instructing students in "Americanism versus Communism," and classes in "civil defense" drew students and adults alike. In the circumstances and anxious about the possibilities of nuclear war, some families began constructing "fallout shelters." Local historian Freddie T. Wright

53. *Fears produced by the Cold War then being waged between the United States and its allies and the Communist bloc of nations headed by the Soviet Union led any number of Polk families to prepare for nuclear warfare by building fallout shelters such as the one illustrated here.* POLK COUNTY HISTORICAL ASSOCIATION.

recalled the era. "Many well-constructed buildings were designated as fallout shelters and stocked with a two-week supply of food," she recorded. "Families were encouraged to build and stock their own fallout shelters," Wright added. "Plans were published in magazines and stores sold prefab models."[17]

The numbers of fallout shelters constructed in Polk remained small, and some institutions preferred not to participate in the program. In November 1962 Lakeland General Hospital, for instance, declined county civil defense director G. Wes Gunn's request to designate it as a shelter. "The hospital's first duty [is] to its patients, doctors and staff who would be expected to care for persons injured in a disaster," administrator Sherwood Smith explained, "and . . . if other persons crowded into the hospital seeking shelter, the hospital would not be able to care for patients."[18]

Unanticipated Consequences

As growth, prosperity, and faster transportation arteries ushered in new approaches to shopping and dining in the faster-paced world of the early 1960s, they also produced revolutions of sorts in other areas. For county residents, the voters' 1963 approval of legalized liquor sales certainly stood out prominently. "Dry since 1887, Polk may have been the largest stronghold of prohibition in the United States outside of Mississippi," one state newspaper proclaimed. That, however, was not the end of it. "The wags," the paper asserted, "still call Polk the wettest dry county in the nation." Various purveyors of illegal spirits had prospered in the county for generations, subject to little interruption by law enforcement. In the situation, many adamantly opposed legalization. "Most people think the county is going to stay 'dry' for many years to come because of the strong opposition from the highly organized church groups, moonshiners, bootleggers, and their suppliers just across the county line in Hillsborough, Osceola, and Highlands counties," a reporter speculated prior to the election. "It's a strange alliance, with the church groups having sincere convictions and the moonshiners, bootleggers, and suppliers having a strong profit incentive with a captive market."[19]

The 1963 wet/dry election, as had the twelve similar referenda held during the previous seventy-six years, divided the county deeply. Credit or blame for the shift, according to one's perspective, devolved upon many but to none more so than to Publix Markets founder George Jenkins. He insisted to voters that "the county's economy is being retarded by being illegally wet." Jenkins pointed out that country clubs and other private organizations enjoyed exemptions from the sales ban, and that money paid to bootleggers escaped taxation and regulation as to quality. The Reverend Jack Eppes, who led the opposition, dismissed such arguments as nonsense. "It doesn't make any difference—$1 million or $10 million," he responded to the lost-tax argument, "it's still the devil's money." When it came time for voting, the addition of 4,517 names to the voter rolls pushed the county total to a record 76,739. About 65 percent of them turned out on a rainy day. A majority of nearly 26,000 backed Jenkins, and the remainder voted with Eppes.[20]

Varied reactions greeted the news. "The question being asked last night was 'When do they start selling liquor?'" the *Tampa Tribune* commented after results were announced. The Reverend Clare M. Cotton begged to differ. As chairman of the United Christian Action League, he saw no cause for celebration. Cotton likened the situation to being "on the losing end of a contest between good and evil where evil has been put on the throne and good on the scaffold." He concluded, "The day comes when judgment will run down as waters and righteousness as a mighty stream."[21]

It did not take long for changes in lifestyle to manifest themselves once authorities had issued alcoholic beverage licenses. "Until the county voted wet in 1963 [and] unless you happened to be an Elk or a yacht club member," *St. Petersburg Times* columnist Elizabeth Whitney reflected, "a big evening on the town probably meant dinner at Morrison's Cafeteria and a movie." Now, the definition of nightlife expanded dramatically for many, as suggested by the varied incarnations of Winter Haven's La-Mond's Restaurant. Purchased as a drive-in from Zack Glouser in 1953 by Robert and Marthalou LaMond, the Cypress Gardens Boulevard eatery originally "dished up 15-cent hamburgers, fries and shakes for a dime." When customers demanded air conditioning and inside seating, the LaMonds responded three years later with a dining room. By 1959, the "Frolic Room" had evolved for drinkers, as long as "anyone wanting to imbibe [brought] their own bottle." When Polk "cast off its shackles as a dry county," the LaMonds quickly grasped one of the first licenses issued and the Frolic Room transformed into LaMond's Steakhouse and Bikini Lounge. Exciting times followed. "We had go-go cages in the lounge, where [dancers] wore bikinis and sheer chiffon things," Robert LaMond remembered. Live music also punctuated nightly festivities. Local musicians such as Jim Stafford and Gram Parsons especially earned loyal followings. "It was more like a big den or playroom instead of a business," LaMond added. "It's been a really interesting ride."[22]

The type of lifestyle openly embraced by many of LaMond's customers drove a deeper religious wedge into the county's social fabric than had manifested itself since the 1930s. Numerous ministers and devout Christians found this behavior abhorrent, as they did other indications of the changing times. Signs of a backlash had surfaced well before the liquor vote. Among them, in 1963 ministers from throughout the county had combined in a "Sunday observance movement" to combat "the rapidly growing trend toward commercialization of Sunday." Even there, the waning authority of church fathers in an increasingly secular society seemed apparent. "It is not the aim of this movement to force anyone into church," Crystal Lake Baptist Church pastor John Doherty attempted to make clear, "but rather to protect the freedom of religion for those who are being forced to choose between their right to worship and their right to work." The problem at hand, the Reverend R. E. Rutland, Jr., explained, had reached "emergency proportions" in some areas of the state although he hoped "to be able to curtail the trend before it advances too extensively in Polk County." Mostly, the words went unheeded as Sunday business openings became ever-more common. Resentments such as the movement illustrated, on the other hand, remained a force that one day would command serious attention.[23]

Water on Tap and Air to Breathe

Issues of water conservation, control, and quality--as well as of pollution of the air—had appealed for attention from Polk residents by the 1950s, but, with one major exception, relatively little actual progress had resulted. The Kissimmee River valley constituted the exception. Following disastrous flooding in 1947, the United States Congress had approved a major plan for flood prevention there. The Florida legislature had furthered its implementation by creating the Central and Southern Florida Flood Control District. The U.S. Army Corps of Engineers then began in 1957 to straighten the river by relocating it, as local historian Alma Hetherington described, "in a new canal 58 miles long, 30 feet deep, and from 325 to 700 feet wide, at a cost of $25 million." The effort, backers claimed, "was the biggest earth moving project since the digging of the Panama Canal." As construction proceeded during the early 1960s, excitement about its completion sparked praise of the attempt to transform the Kissimmee "into a navigable stream to accommodate yachts."

Hetherington described the results. "When completed in 1965, the canal
... shorten[ed] the river by 55 miles and confine[d] it within dikes 15 feet
high, making it virtually floodproof."[24]

Flooding again provided the impetus for regional attention to water
flow in 1960, when Hurricane Donna swamped lowlands and thereby
altered the status quo at least insofar as government activism on water
issues elsewhere in the region was concerned. Stated simply, the flooding
produced by Donna made crystal clear the need for flood protection in
local basins beyond the Kissimmee. The Corps of Engineers thereafter
recommended the Four Rivers Basin Florida Project to include the Oklawaha, Peace, Hillsborough, and Withlacoochee Rivers, but the corps
did so with a condition. The federal government insisted that the plan's
implementation required a local partner.[25]

Other forces then converged to muddy the waters. The existing Peace
River Valley Water Conservation and Drainage District—including
board members Eugene Griffin of Bartow, James A. White of Haines
City, and Horace Jones of Lakeland and led by executive director Bo-
livar Hyde, Jr.—had found itself locked in battle with the Polk County
Property Owners League headed by its executive director Arthur Bissett.
The key issue concerned the district's attempt to secure "anti-pollution
controls for the Peace River." When the district asked the 1961 legislature

54. *Destruction derived in 1960 from Hurricane Donna's fierce winds and rain brought
about long-lasting results in Polk, including the eventual creation of the Southwest
Florida Water Management District.* POLK COUNTY HISTORICAL ASSOCIATION.

for taxing power, State representative Ben Hill Griffin stepped forward in opposition. Eventually compromise enabled the measure to move forward more or less with Griffin's blessing, but Bissett, the property owners league, two phosphate companies, the Polk County Farm Bureau, and the Polk County Cattleman's Association battled to halt its further progress. The county commission and "numerous conservation and water recreation groups" thereupon came to the district's defense. "Debate waxed hot and heavy from Bartow to Tallahassee over the controversial bill," the *Lakeland Ledger* reported.[26]

When stalemate resulted, the legislature decided to take a different course that also would address the federal government's insistence on a local partner for the Four Rivers Plan. It abolished the conservation and drainage district effective June 30, 1963, to be replaced by a new and larger organization, the Southwest Florida Water Management District. "Swiftmud," as it came to be known, encompassed fifteen central and southwest Florida counties that contained eleven river basins. Its original responsibilities centered mostly on flood control, but drought conditions compelled the district in 1965 to become a regulatory agency concerned with well permitting procedures, registration of well drillers, and regulation of well and lake levels within its boundaries.[27]

Swiftmud's exercise of regulatory authority might have come sooner and in a stronger form had it not been for Polk opposition. In late 1963 the district proposed establishment of a fifteen county underground water regulatory district. The Polk Property Owners League reacted with fury to the plan, Arthur Bissett labeling it "unnecessary, premature and wasteful of the taxpayers' money." The league's executive director then explained his position. "There is no proven need for limiting the right of a property holder to remove water from under his property, except possibly for very small areas of low elevation close to the Gulf Coast, and with heavy population concentration," Bissett asserted. "It is socialization of ownership of water for the sake of socialization and centralization of power, rather than to meet a real need of the public, the taxpayers, or the property owners."

Certain county commissioners jumped to support the league's position. "We object to the ignoring of the elected officials in Polk," Wilmer McCutcheon declared. "There is no present or future need for such control in Polk." On the other hand, not all of McCutcheon's fellow commissioners agreed with him. Aldine Combee, for one, voiced concerns about "some very critical problems, now in our lakes." He added, "Some lakes have dried up and water levels are low in others." In the end, a board resolution expressed "serious concerns and apprehension" about the Swiftmud plans, a statement that achieved its desired effect of slowing down regulatory implementation.[28]

The problem was that time proved Combee correct. Polk's lakes were suffering. Partly this resulted from a decade-long dry cycle that commenced early in the 1960s and that, at times, brought severe drought conditions. By 1962 municipalities such as Lakeland had imposed lawn sprinkling restrictions, a new and controversial step for county residents. Then, sinkholes began appearing with what seemed alarming frequency. On May 24, 1965, alone, eight sinkholes opened in Polk. That day, a "giant" hole "gobbled up" the intersection of Crystal Lake and Lake Hollingsworth Drives in Lakeland. It became "the object of thousands of curiosity seekers as the word traveled fast of the natural phenomenon."[29]

As such events occurred, residents began looking ever more closely at phosphate operations as a major culprit in the water crisis. Public pressures already had compelled eight companies to begin modest land reclamation efforts by 1961. American Cyanamid's Arthur Crago particularly pushed his fellow executives to understand the benefits of such initiatives. Advantageous publicity resulted for Crago's company, for example, with the creation of Saddle Creek Park northeast of Lakeland and its donation to the county. More practical advantages could accrue, as well. At Bartow, Armour Agricultural Chemical Co. anticipated the use of reclaimed land for "residential and commercial buildings." International Minerals and Chemical Corp. took matters a step further and developed the Haynesworth Heights residential subdivision north of Mulberry. These projects gained favorable attention, but there was a catch. As one report noted, "While all this suggests the phosphate industry is to be commended for its reclamation efforts, it should not be implied that the industry is embarking on a campaign to reclaim all mined-out land."[30]

55. *Phosphate industry executive Arthur Crago.* POLK COUNTY HISTORICAL ASSOCIATION.

The industry also remained capable of destroying whatever positive image its reclamation and early anti-pollution efforts achieved. American Cyanamid blundered, for instance, when it proposed to mine Lakeland's Lake Parker in 1962 with the promise of compensating for the intrusion by building a causeway and recreation area across its northern end. After threatened lawsuits brought the plan to a halt, Arthur Crago nonetheless declared: "We are very sorry about it. We thought that the mining and causeway would be something nice for everyone concerned." A series of dam breaks undermined the industry's image further. Especially, in late 1964 American Cyanamid and the Virginia-Carolina Chemical Company received blame for a number of such incidents, ones that led to large kills of fish and aquatic life in the Peace and Alafia Rivers.[31]

Air pollution charges confronted the industry, as well. In places bird life virtually had disappeared, while citrus groves, cattle herds, and vegetable crops deteriorated when exposed to noxious fumes and other discharges. Finally, in February 1963 the Florida Air Pollution Control Commission acted against Armour's Fort Meade plant for "knowingly polluting the air with acid fumes and endangering public health." The panel also set deadlines for emission reductions at four other county plants.[32]

Pressure such as this produced some results, but not always those that were expected. To cite an example, in December 1963 IMC announced its intentions, never implemented, to close the Prairie phosphate plant at Mulberry. "Company officials said that the closing was necessary because of demands from the State Board of Health brought about by non-residents concerning the level of dust emitted from the plant," a report observed. "Shutting down the Mulberry operation is the first industry closing in the state caused by air pollution," it continued. Then came a statement fraught with meaning for the county's future. "The Prairie plant will be replaced," the report detailed, "with a larger and completely modern facility in an area outside Polk County."[33]

This signaled the beginnings of the movement of the phosphate industry elsewhere than Polk, although decades would pass before its implications truly were felt. For the time being, in fact, it seemed ridiculous even to think that the industry might one day disappear. In the quarter-century following 1940, fertilizer usage tripled, a fact that spurred enormous industry growth. "Upwards of $100 million is currently being spent on construction and expansion of Florida phosphate facilities—the biggest building spree in the history of the industry," an April 1965 study discovered. Oil companies, realizing the potential, had begun to enter the field, bringing large reservoirs of surplus cash and world-wide distribution systems. Continental Oil bought American Agricultural Chemical Co. (Agrico); Socony Mobil took over Virginia-

Carolina; and Cities Service co-opted U.S. Phosphoric Products. "Vast new plants are being erected, older ones expanded," the study added. Its author may have had in mind W. R. Grace and Co.'s Ridgewood chemical complex. Planners designed the $10 million facility, constructed by Lakeland's Wellman-Lord Engineering, to incorporate the world's largest phosphoric acid plant. Company experts promised anxious residents that the new plants "will be virtually air and stream pollution free."[34]

Polk County's heyday as the phosphate industry's great home nonetheless had begun to pass. Symbolic of that fact, the last of Polk's many phosphate company towns closed. Brewster once had served as home to 3,000 persons who, one way or another, maintained ties to the American Cyanamid Company. "The key to living there was working for the company," journalist Leland Hawes reported, "and most employees qualified for frame houses that were considered comfortable and inexpensive." Environmental problems, though, eventually grew substantial. "So often, when the plant would get out of control, the dust from the dry-rock plant would cover the houses," one-time resident Leo Borders added. Trees were dying, and people were getting sick. "And they knew that if it was killing the trees, it would kill the people," Borders continued. "That's the reason we had to move." Ray Albritton, another former resident, picked up the story. "After the village left in 1960, the drying plant, shops, main office and chemical plant remained for awhile," he wrote. "There was a recession in the phosphate industry in the early 1970s," Albritton concluded, "and the chemical plant was shut down."[35]

Steps Forward in Civil Rights

The early 1960s produced circumstances that compelled Polk Countians to begin contending with long-delayed questions about civil rights and racial discrimination, and local activists legitimately could claim credit for that development. Up until that time, the civil rights movement generally had disappointed supporters with the advances made. Florida particularly stood out as one state that had achieved few positive results when it came to racial segregation and the destruction of other racial barriers. Dedicated but tired workers yearned for progress. Then, on February 1, 1960, four students from the North Carolina Agricultural and Technical School sat down at a segregated Greensboro lunch counter and demanded to be served. This event launched a new era in civil rights history, infusing the movement with the energy and vitality of untold numbers of young people determined to force change. Sit-ins, wade-ins, swim-ins and all manner of similar protests thereafter shook the South, while "freedom riders" bussed from state to state seeking to break down traditional bars restricting transportation and accommodations.[36]

Word of the first sit-in ironically arrived in the county almost coincidentally with news that one of America's great civil rights heroes—and a one-time Polk resident—had died. Henry and Dora Sweet's son Ossian Sweet had grown up at Bartow in the late 1890s and early 1900s. Desirous that he have opportunities for life on a larger scale, the Sweets sent their son to Wilberforce University, after which he studied at Howard University's School of Medicine. In 1925, then living in Detroit, Sweet purchased a lovely home in a white neighborhood. A threatening white mob gathered, stones were thrown, and gunfire from the Sweet house subsequently killed a white man. Authorities prosecuted Ossian Sweet, his brother Henry, and others for murder, but the National Association for the Advancement of Colored People arranged for their defense by famed criminal lawyers Clarence Darrow and Arthur Garfield Hays. Tumultuous proceedings eventually resulted in acquittals despite "irreparable damage" to the Sweet family and to race relations generally. Remaining in Detroit following the ordeal, Dr. Ossian Sweet lived until March 19, 1960. He directed that, upon his death, his remains be returned to Bartow for burial.[37]

Ossian Sweet had meant more to African Americans in Polk than the fact that he once had lived there. Much of his family remained in Bartow, and he made it his practice to visit every year, usually around Thanksgiving. "If Detroit disappointed Ossian Sweet, sabotaged his dreams, broke his heart," biographer Phyllis Vine insisted, "Bartow did not." To local people he had become "a symbol of success in the urban North." He bought land and an "enormous" home. He hunted, fished, played cards, and enjoyed music and family. The visits grew longer as he aged, and his impact grew as well. He became, a friend related, "the image everybody wanted to set their standards by." The friend added, "That which we didn't see, we imagined."[38]

With such an image before them of an individual willing to risk death in the defense of his home and civil rights, many others pursued the cause in Polk following Sweet's death. LaFrancine K. Burton described one such person for *Lakeland Ledger* readers in words that illustrate the commitment and the courage required. "Madalynne Brooks is best remembered as a civil rights warrior," she wrote. "She was the first African American matron hired by the Polk County Sheriff's Department. She openly voiced her disgust with the racial injustices that blacks endured in Lakeland and, as a result, she and her family lived with constant death threats that were meant to stop her fight for equality." Burton continued: "She ignored those threats and was responsible for black youths who staged sit-ins at segregated lunch counters at the Kress Store and the McCrory's Store that were downtown. She was also one of the organizers who led the protest movement to integrate the Polk Theatre."[39]

The desegregation of the S. H. Kress store lunch counter at Lakeland marked an early milestone for the movement and the era. In March 1961 the store had shut it doors to the public as rumors told of a planned sit-in that did not materialize. In April, though, two African Americans appeared, ordered hamburgers and soft drinks, and received service. The young people then left, and the manager declined to call police. In that manner, the first of thousands of barriers fell.[40]

Some communities resisted, with tensions elevating accordingly. At Haines City in January 1962 a "riot" resulted in the arrest of scores of black youths. At Frostproof the next month twenty arrests ensued when sheriff's deputies confronted an angry crowd, and bricks and stones "heavily damaged" the lawmen's patrol car. Similarly, Lakelanders witnessed what city manager Robert V. Youkey optimistically described as "minor problems" in 1965. He credited "the gradual and non-violent approach to racial integration" as allowing the community to avoid "the demonstrations, violence and bloodshed that clouded many communities."[41]

Winter Haven tried to take a better path as early as 1961 with the creation of a bi-racial human relations commission similar to one that Governor LeRoy Collins earlier had implemented for the state. Mayor Tom Turnbull appointed the seven white and three black members. They included Chairman W. E. Rynerson, J. Hall Connor, Mrs. Lamar Beauchamp, George Dorman, J. M. Berry, Don Newell, and Hagan Parrish. Original representatives of the African American community were Joel E. Atkins, Simmie McNeal, and Florida Marie Thomas. Lemuel Geathers, another activist who also worked closely with the commission, remembered the experience. "The integrated Human Relations Committee met many times out of the public view for 'safety reasons,'" he commented, "because some people didn't approve of the group." Nonetheless, Geathers credited the panel with finessing a number of advances, including the integration of the municipal golf course. "For years I've thought that we were one of the better towns because of factions in both the communities who got together to work things out," Geathers concluded.[42]

56. *Lemuel Geathers helped to transform the racial climate at Winter Haven in the early 1960s and went on to serve as the community's first African American mayor. Lakeland Ledger.*

As Joel Atkins's experience illustrates, though, even in a community such as Winter Haven old ways died hard. Pastor of the Zion Hill Missionary Baptist Church, Atkins found himself called upon time and again to exercise leadership. "He led marches at Lake Silver where blacks were not allowed to use the beach; marches at the public library; and at Morrison's cafeteria," reporter Deborah Circelli explained. Friend Ernestine Davis, who later headed the local NAACP branch, remembered that "Atkins led a demonstration in Florence Villa to get Henley Grocery to hire [her]." Another friend, Althea Mills summed up Atkins's contribution. "He was always right there leading the way regardless of what it was," she declared. "There was nothing to stop him or discourage him. His course seemed to have been charted."[43]

One initiative in which Atkins, Mills, and others cooperated resulted in cracking the segregated walls of Polk's public school system. Having attempted to further integration by administrative means and finding only frustration, they decided, after sixteen other Florida counties had accepted the inevitable, to sue. On September 1, 1963, their attorney—NAACP counsel Fernando Rodriguez—filed the action in the United States District Court for the Middle District of Florida at Tampa with Mills's son Herman Mills, Jr., as the lead plaintiff. The proceedings in *Herman H. Mills et al* v. *Board of Public Instruction, Polk County, Florida* thereafter consumed sixteen months and included Superintendent Shelley Boone's curious testimonial insistence that Polk already operated an integrated system. The case culminated on January 15, 1965, when Judge Joseph P. Lieb held that Polk was "operating a compulsory bi-racial school system" and directed the school board within six weeks to submit a plan "for the removal of dual attendance zones and for the opening of all public schools . . . on a non-racial basis, including the elimination of the assignment of teachers, principals, and other personnel of the defendant on a racial basis." As will be seen, complete implementation of the judge's order would require thirty-five years.[44]

Integration of the county courthouse fortunately had not taken so great an effort. During 1962 a coalition of NAACP branches within the county had protested segregated conditions at the courthouse in a letter sent to the county commission. Reportedly, Chairman L. W. "Les" Dunson responded quietly but decisively. According to NAACP state field director Robert W. Saunders, "The board chairman apologized and ordered the immediate end to segregation in the courthouse." Saunders noted, though, that Dunson's response left individual judges with authority to assign seats in their courtrooms.[45]

Matters of Government and Politics

With so many hot-button issues and so much growth facing the county and its governmental components, the early 1960s necessarily involved any number of interesting developments related to government and politics. Women particularly scored notable successes. In 1961, to offer an example, Lakeland's Dora Cox Phillips assumed a position on the county school board, the first woman elected to that panel. At Lakeland two years later Lois Searle took a seat as the first female member of the city commission. In February 1965 she rose to the position of mayor, marking Lakeland as the first major Florida city to extend that honor to a woman. Marianne Boyd of Winter Haven accepted a position of the first Polk County planning board in 1963, as did Lake Wales's Charlotte Tomlinson on the Florida Milk Com-

57. *Lakeland's Lois Searle, seen here with husband William Searle and Publix Markets founder George W. Jenkins, broke barriers for women during the 1960s as a Lakeland city council member and as mayor.*
LAKELAND PUBLIC LIBRARY.

mission. Notably, Blanche M. Work, a former teacher who served as chief deputy supervisor of registration under Hugh E. Carlton, in 1964 accepted appointment as supervisor upon his retirement, an act that made her Polk's first female constitutional officer. "I think we might have a woman president someday," she declared upon taking her oath, "but probably not for the next couple of administrations." Work added, "As more women get into government, there will be a better choice for women in the higher elective offices." Polk voters thereafter elected her to the job as soon as they got the chance.[46]

Blanche Work went on to enjoy a long and happy career as an elected official in Polk, but that end did not result for everyone. Lakeland mayor William H. Loftin, for instance, bet his electoral future in 1963 on resentments against federal government intrusion into local affairs, including the exercise of power by activist judges who were enforcing civil rights directives. Loftin chose federal aid for local works projects as the specific focus of his condemnation. "It breeds apathy, destroys initiative and opens the doors to invasion of individual rights," he insisted. Loftin and several other mayors attempted to turn the anti-federal aid position into a grass roots political movement. The small communities of Fort Meade, Mulberry, and Haines City objected, however, slowing momentum. National news organs nonetheless featured Loftin and his allies, especially after United States Chamber of Commerce president Wedin P. Neilan praised them in a major address. Lakeland voters had the final say, however. In November they ousted Loftin "by commanding margins in all four districts" in favor of political newcomer and appliance dealer W. J. "Pete" Peterson. The anti-federal aid movement thereupon collapsed.[47]

State senator Scott Kelley also misread the signs of the times. He launched a gubernatorial candidacy in 1964 aimed at cornering the conservative wing of the Democratic party. "My biggest supporters of course were Polk County and west Florida, because I was from out there," Kelly recalled. "I had bet on the fact that I had played football with so many of those guys who later on were in city government and county government and prominent businessmen." One student of the election described Kelly's approach to the contest. "He designated himself as the 'symbol of opposition to civil rights in Florida,'" he wrote, "and promised to ignore the civil rights measure [just enacted by the Congress] if he were elected." The scholar added, "Kelly also opposed further desegregation of the state's public schools." On primary election day in May, hometown favorite Kelly easily carried Polk but managed only a third place finish statewide.[48]

State representative Ben Hill Griffin's fortunes rose as Kelly's fell, allowing him to take Kelly's seat in the state senate in 1965. Interestingly, Griffin projected positive stances rather than expressions of antagonism and resentment. His special cause at the time concerned education. He had articulated his feelings on the subject earlier in the election cycle when he, too, had considered a run for governor. "The state has got to provide the best in services," Griffin insisted. "Especially in the field of education." He added: "Florida must not scrimp to the point it gives people second rate things. It's not necessary. There's plenty of money."[49]

As it happened, educational spending then held ground as one of the county's most-heatedly argued political issues. Administrators anticipated not less than 45,000 students would attend classes by fall 1964. School board chairman Austin Race, Jr., attempted to raise awareness of the problems entailed by arguing that "the system is just falling behind." Race added, "We have got to get more money from some source to continue to grow." With few new sources coming available, Superintendent Shelley Boone turned to a temporary solution. "It now appears necessary," he advised the board and the public, "to build a limited number of portables (movable classrooms) in order to house the children in September."[50]

Not only were the public schools chronically underfunded, but in 1963 embarrassment resulted when it became known that Polk's percentage of high school graduates going on to college ranked second lowest in the state. This buttressed support for creation within the county of a junior college. The legislative delegation arranged authority and start-up funding, but the law required property owners to authorize ad valorem taxation to support the institution. The debate turned sharp, and final approval came "in a squeaker" with Lakeland-area precincts rejecting the notion handily. Infighting among municipalities then followed as to which one would host the new institution. Winter Haven ultimately won, although classes first convened in September 1964 in vacant buildings at the old Bartow Air Base. Tampa native Dr. Fred T. Lenfestey served as the school's first president and to him goes much credit for its early successes. Quietly, Polk Junior College opened without racial restrictions placed upon admission.[51]

The question of planning for the future likewise stirred controversy and no small amount of turmoil. With growth seeming about to overwhelm the county, many informed persons believed that the situation required early and organized preparation and, possibly, the adoption of a county zoning scheme. The county commission, responding to this

input, in October 1963 named a seven-member planning board that included R. D. "Dick" Baggett, Bruce Fullerton, Wallace Storey, Earnest
L. Glass, Charles E. Whitten, E. J. "Ed" Sanders, Jr., and Marianne Boyd.
Bartow attorney Storey emerged as chairman. The commission studied
the issues, held hearings, and in summer 1965 issued recommendations
for the adoption of a planning program that included comprehensive
countywide zoning. Reflecting a growing trend, it noted particularly that
"trailer or mobile homes" had become "a major problem." When afforded the chance in November to approve or disapprove a tax to fund
the plan, property owners condemned it. In words that carried a chilling message for the future, county commissioner Wilmer McCutcheon
reacted to the results. "They proved it was too radical a change," he
declared. "In the future it will be more practical to solve the county's
problems one at a time."[52]

58. *Walt Disney's vision of a Disney World rising from former swampland and cattle range just north of the Polk County line was to produce changes so enormous that their reverberations would continue to be felt in the twenty-first century.* POLK COUNTY HISTORICAL ASSOCIATION.

CHAPTER 7

೧

Waiting for the Mouse, 1965-1970

*T*he late 1960s came to Polk County filled with paradox. The range of prosperity reached out further and higher than would have been thought possible a few years earlier; yet, as time passed many of the county's people found themselves increasingly divided and, in some cases, embittered. Shockingly, Polk failed to grow as expected; nonetheless, urban problems touched the lives of more persons than ever before. Delight in Polk living meanwhile competed with proliferating restrictions on where that life could be enjoyed. The English novelist Charles Dickens spoke to the best of times and the worst of times, and so it seemed in Polk as the decade of the 1960s passed away. Undeniably a new era had dawned. Many preferred to deny that it was so.

The decade's last half commenced with county voters refusing to plan for the future. Residents traditionally had defied anyone and everyone who tried to tell them how to live their lives, and by a margin of three to one they now rejected a well-prepared proposal for comprehensive planning and countywide zoning. The decision left Polk as the only county in Florida without some county zoning scheme. The sense of the thing seemed to boil down to a *Tampa Tribune* headline regarding Lakeland's future. "Nothing," it declared, "can stop progress."[1]

The failure of the November 1965 planning and zoning vote took on particular significance when weighed against the backdrop of events unfolding in Polk's northern reaches and in Orange and Osceola Counties. "Will Walt Disney do it again?" the *Miami Herald* questioned that month. "Just about every Florida freeholder with as little as a quarter of an acre within 50 miles of Orlando is holding his financial breath pending pin-pointing of the location of a reported 32,000 acre tract 'near Orlando' destined for a Disneyland East," it continued. Columnist George Burke added, "The air is filled with conjecture on what a Disneyland project could mean to the already booming Florida." In those heady days the possibility of a 1969 grand opening for Walt Disney World appeared plausible. Although in actuality it would take until October 1, 1971, to prepare the entertainment mecca for a flood of patrons, its arrival loomed directly ahead and in the immediate future.[2]

That context permits appreciation of the governmental tragedy that struck Polk in 1965, the county commission's failure to exercise a leadership role when it came to anticipating and preparing for large-scale growth. To their credit commissioners Wilmer McCutcheon and Les Dunson individually backed the proposed plan. Floyd Woods opposed it. Commission chairman Alan Trask and commissioner Aldine Combee declined to take any position. As a result, in one reporter's words, "[The county commission] never did give official approval to the plan." What the commission did do was require that it be submitted to a referendum rather than simply to adopt the proposal. Trask later acknowledged that he had been "surprised to learn that no other Florida county acquired its zoning through referendum such as Polk has attempted."[3]

The impact of the county commission's inaction and of the voters' subsequent negative decision alarmed not only many Polk residents but experts and leaders statewide who were focused on Disney World's coming influence on Florida. "Polk Countians are not facing facts," urban planning consultant Dr. E. R. Bartley insisted to members of the county's builders' association. "You are ten years behind schedule," he added. "If you started right now, it would take you ten years to catch up to where you should be today." What could residents expect? "[They] will pay dearly in the future to drain flooded subdivisions, put in storm drainage, repave pot-holed streets and try to screen the ugliness of the monotonous architectural repetition of the construction," a developer commented. Former Governor LeRoy Collins attempted to signal his concerns. "We must seek new industry here," he informed a Lake Wales audience, "but more than that, we must attract new industry on a well-planned basis." Expressing a similar tone, one respected Florida magazine quoted the opinions of professional planners. "They fear that Polk, closest unzoned county to the heart of the Disney impact area," its report read, "is in danger of becoming the 'back street' for the glamour set."[4]

Even some leaders of the opposition to the planning and zoning plan soon realized their mistake. "We did not understand it," they acknowledged. "It's not difficult to defeat any program as vast as zoning through misconceptions and emotionalism," the men continued. "If we had to do it again we would work for some sort of a sound zoning plan."[5]

The Prosperity Party

Although its impact cannot be ascertained with certainty, the zoning vote likely contributed to the fact that, for a time, Polk essentially stopped growing. Some of its principal cities and towns actually lost population. These facts, however, did not appear clear to those witnessing first hand the local economy's vitality. As late as January 1970 census experts estimated that Polk, by 1968, had grown to hold 239,500 residents, a 22.75 increase over 1960. Preliminary returns of the actual 1970 census, released in July, therefore proved stunning. Polk, according to the new estimates, contained only 222,143 persons. As a result, it had dropped to ninth in population among Florida's counties where thirty years previously it had claimed a fifth-place ranking, a fact still reflected in the county's "5" numerical designation on motor vehicle license plates.[6]

Final census tabulations showed Polk's situation slightly better than previously reported, but not by much. The county held 227,222 persons, and most of the 16.4 percent increase over the 1960 total could be attributed to the decade's first half. Lakelanders had believed that their municipality might break the 50,000 mark. They discovered that it had slipped below the 40,169 reported ten years before. Bartow and Winter Haven, as a newspaper put it, "showed similar trends." Arguments naturally ensued to the effect that it just could not be so, but the facts remained. The county simply took what comfort it could from the census bureau's designation of a standard metropolitan statistical area for the Lakeland-Winter Haven region. The new SMSA tied for 127th in size nationally and in Florida came in eighth, behind Pensacola but ahead of Daytona.[7]

Residents could be forgiven for believing in these fast-paced times that more and more people were appearing around the county despite what turned out to be population dips in some areas. For one thing, increasing numbers of winter visitors called Polk home on a seasonal basis. Baseball factored in this. Several teams maintained spring practice in Polk and had done so for decades. Among them, the Detroit Tigers had become a familiar institution at Lakeland. Winter Haven rejoiced in 1965 when it convinced the Boston Red Sox to adopt it as a spring home beginning the following year. Banker Andrew Ireland's leadership produced a new $400,000 stadium, courtesy of the city government, as well as the Red Sox team. "They found no difficulty in obtaining living quarters," Josephine Burr recorded of the team's members, "and entered wholeheartedly into city living."[8]

Beyond the seasonal residents, the number of tourists mushroomed too. By 1966 an estimated two million persons per year were enjoying the attractions and delights of the Polk Ridge area, a vicinity promoted as the Holiday Highlands. "The top tourist getter in the state year after year," a feature article observed, "[Cypress] Gardens has lured many of the aforementioned people to our sunny clime." The new Florida Citrus Showcase Dome constructed in 1965, Winter Haven's Slocum Water Gardens, Taylor's Candy Factory in Davenport, Minute Maid's Auburndale citrus processing plant, and Winter Haven's Howell Glass Blowers contributed as well. Other popular sights included Lake Wales attractions such as the Singing Tower at Mountain Lake Sanctuary (Bok Tower), the Great Masterpiece, the Black Hills Passion Play, the Chalet Suzanne, and the Casa de Josefina. Frostproof meanwhile drew guests who appreci-

59. *Winter Haven's Chain of Lakes Stadium hosted baseball fans delirious at the prospect of watching the favorite Boston Red Sox at play.* POLK COUNTY HISTORICAL ASSOCIATION.

60. *The Florida Citrus Showcase Dome rose at Winter Haven during the mid-1960s, reflecting Polk's continuing and dominant role in the state's citrus industry. FLORIDA STATE ARCHIVES.*

61. *The award-winning Chalet Suzanne Restaurant and Country Inn. AHL, LAKE WALES.*

ated that at "the Friendly City of the Highlands" they could count on "the sun shin[ing] 360 days or more per year."[9]

Fine dining offered its allure as well. A county used to good food now furnished the state some of its best restaurants. When *Florida Trend* magazine first conferred its "Golden Spoon Awards" in 1967, Winter Haven's Sundown Restaurant stood seventh on the list of twelve honorees. Auburndale's Lombardi's, Bartow's John's, Lake Alfred's Rodenhaver's, Lakeland's Farmer John's Red Barn, and Lake Wales's Chalet Suzanne received mention for their "top quality." One judge begged to differ about the top award. He insisted that "the Chalet Suzanne in Lake Wales in my opinion is unequalled in the world." After a fire damaged the Sundown that year, other Polk restaurants stepped up to claim the main prize. In 1969 two of the state's top six restaurants, according to the magazine, operated in Polk. The Chalet Suzanne naturally received the coveted golden spoon as did Lakeland's Fox Fire Inn.[10]

The excitement about Disney World and other developments also masked from view the possibility of decline in Polk growth, although the intense focus that shifted to Orange and Osceola Counties certainly contributed to that decline. What residents could see however, were visions of the "megalopolis" that planners believed eventually would stretch along the Interstate 4 corridor from Daytona to Tampa. "In this area in the 1960-64 period industrial concerns financed new plants and major expansions constituting 81 percent of all such developments in the state," a business journal revealed. Its reporter spoke of the coming of "pretty" industrial plants and of a "country club" atmosphere for work and play. "The growth of industry, the concentration of city dwellers, the development of the Florida megalopolis, does this mean that Florida will change?" the journal asked. The answer: "Yes, of course it does."[11]

Polk Countians—those who were paying attention, at least—perceived their county as about to play a vital role in the development of the megalopolis and as reaping directly the benefits of the Disney World phenomenon. "Polk County" Powerhouse of Progress," the *St. Petersburg Times* proclaimed in summer 1966. "No other county on the Suncoast can even come close to Polk in several significant categories," it argued. "Polk is a powerhouse of both potential and progress." The report noted the record-breaking growth of Polk's phosphate industry, together with the county's number one rankings in Florida for cattle raising and citrus production. The article quoted Lakeland's planning director George A. Sanford as arguing that "on a percentage basis Disneyland will mean more to Lakeland than to Orlando since it's the same distance in miles from Disneyland to Orlando and to Lakeland." Illustrating present and anticipated growth trends, the piece noted: "In 1965 and so far in 1966 just one Lakeland engineering firm, Wellman-Lord, has imported engineers at the rate of 40 a month. Two other firms, Gulf Design and Lakeland Engineering Associates, are bringing them in almost as fast." The article concluded, "That's a lot of engineers—and they're not coming to pick oranges."[12]

Even Orlando's principal newspaper conceded Polk's place in the order of things. "Changing Scene Expected in Osceola, Polk," an *Orlando Sentinel* headline expressed on January 1, 1967. It added, "Prosperity to Enhance '67 Progress." Haines City's Bill Holt pointed out in the same newspaper's columns that "the Sunshine Parkway and the development of Disneyland could have a great deal to do with the improvement of our local economy." At Winter Haven, "a full scale building program" progressed, the *Sentinel* reported, one that included a new municipal golf course, Polk Junior College, a hospital addition, two new shopping centers, and a public safety building. "Most of the cities in Polk have reported more growth than in the previous year," its story explained further. "Chambers of commerce throughout the county are constantly seeking new businesses, new industries." Summing up, the report disclosed, "Most are optimistic about landing one or more during the coming year."[13]

Even though a flood tide of new businesses, industries, and residents failed to inundate the county in the years that followed, optimism remained the common theme. Spirits leapt when employment reached an all-time high in 1967, for instance, and kept growing modestly. The Florida State Employment Service that year designated Polk as "a leading industrial center in the state," outranked only by Dade, Hillsborough, and Duval. When the year proved a tough one for the citrus, phosphate, and construction industries, forecasters simply saw "a brighter New Year" ahead. Haines City's chamber of commerce manager John Keirsey struck a similar chord. "Am I optimistic?" he asked metaphorically. "I sure am. I'm optimistic." Banker Jim White's perspective typified that of many. Things might not be everything we thought that they would be at this point, he admitted, but Disney World was about to serve as a "springboard" that "would only accelerate Polk's growth."[14]

Outsiders sensed the same thing. That factor propelled Bill Watkins to relocate his business's headquarters to Lakeland in 1966. By the time he decided upon the move, Watkins Motor Lines had grown into "one of the largest carriers of perishables in the country." Numerous other examples can be cited. Auburndale, for instance, drew companies looking toward future growth, as well. During 1968 the United Container Corporation and U. S. Mobile Homes erected new plants in the town's industrial park. Back at Lakeland, to cite another, Piper Aircraft opted in 1968 to establish a huge production plant. The 162,000 square foot facility opened in early 1970. Meanwhile the world-ranging Bechtel Corporation of San Francisco entered the Polk picture, too, and did so the easy way. It simply bought Wellman-Lord Engineering, wisely leaving James M. Wellman in charge.[15]

One type of business concern outshone all others that ventured into the county during the period. "The impact of the Disney development is not expected to have any effect [in Polk] during the year of 1967," a newspaper had informed its readers early that year, but it had added, "However, there is some trading in land in the area." Companies intent upon land speculation suddenly seemed to crop up everywhere. "They came in droves in the mid-60s, when Polk Countians still found it impossible to believe the growth and tourist and money projections being thrown at them by the Disney people," the *Lakeland Ledger*'s Ed Domaingue reported. "The speculators went to the ranchers with thousands of acres of pasture and swampland," he explained. "And the owners of the pastureland and ranchland sold and sold, secretly chuckling at the 'huge' profits they were making on their undeveloped, unimproved land miles from any signs of civilization." Domaingue added: "They thought back to the $20, $30, $50 an acre they had paid for the property. The speculators were paying $200, $300, and $400 an acre." He concluded, "By the end of the sixties, however, the speculators were the ones who were laughing."[16]

None of the speculators or developers surpassed the Gulf American Corporation. Baltimore appliance salesmen Leonard and Jack Rosen had established the company late in the 1950s and had launched its Florida activities by building a community southwest of Fort Myers that they called Cape Coral. Other large-scale developments followed, but so, too, did scandals associated with their business and development practices. General Acceptance Corporation eventually bought out the Rosens, in any event, and the company by the mid-1960s had begun to buy up Polk land. By decade's end its holdings, located mostly in the county's eastern hinterlands and facing Osceola and Highlands Counties, amounted to 7 percent of Polk's total land mass.[17]

Not only did GAC intend to own a good part of Polk, it planned to reap huge profits from developing the property. By 1967 the company prepared to dot the county with large-scale projects. The first came east and south of Lake Wales and carried the name River Ranch Acres. Tracts totaling 57,000 acres comprised the site, for which the company paid approximately $11 million. In two-and-one-half years purchasers grasped 27,000 parcels there for an estimated $80 million. "River Ranch Acres will keep a bit of the flavor of the area's past," a magazine writer explained. "It is an old style western resort," the piece continued. "The property will not be developed in the traditional sense. Instead, it has a modern hunting lodge, trap and skeet ranges, riding stables, a rodeo arena, campgrounds and barbecue sites, tennis courts, swimming pools, and a fishing marina. It even has a lighted airstrip for the conveniences of its visitors." The writer added: "The camping haven is not being subdivided for development. Instead, it is being sold in its natural state for hunting, fishing and other outdoor activities for those susceptible to the call of the outdoors."[18]

Given this climate of optimism and investment, business and professional interests already established in the county prepared to slice their own pieces of prosperity's pie. Symbolizing this fact, in 1966 Senator Spessard Holland's Bartow law firm, known as Holland, Bevis, Smith, Kibler & Hall, relocated most of its personnel to a $200,000 office complex at Lakeland. Partners included W. F. Bevis, Chesterfield Smith, D. Burke Kibler III, and Warren Hall, although Smith's time during much of the period mostly was spent elsewhere in his capacity as chairman of the Florida Constitutional Revision Commission. Shortly, Kibler, too, would accept state office, becoming first a member, and then chairman, of the Florida Board of Regents. When in 1968 the partnership merged with Tampa's Knight, Jones, Whitaker & Germany to form Holland & Knight, it became the state's largest law firm. Broadcaster and journalist Tom Brokaw would call it "a veritable colossus of the law."[19]

Political Affairs

As the 1960s moved from their midpoint to their conclusion, Florida underwent a political renaissance of the first order. The state's legislature had become the most unrepresentative of such bodies in the nation, with the Pork Chop Gang of north Florida Democrats and their small county allies tenaciously clinging to power. That situation ended abruptly after the United States Supreme Court in 1966 voided the state's legislative reapportionment scheme and directed a redrawing of lines based upon the principal of "one man, one vote." Five years earlier President John F. Kennedy's first judicial appointment had placed Bartow attorney William A. McRae, Jr., in office as a judge of the United States District Court. Now, Judge McRae took the Florida legislative question under his jurisdiction and in 1967 mandated a fair redistricting plan.[20]

Judge McRae's reapportionment decision carried immense significance for the state and its government. First, it transferred political power over budget and legislation from north Florida to central and south Florida. Most onlookers interpreted this as a tilt in favor of moderate-to-liberal, sometimes referred to as progressive, thinking. "Florida was enjoying a peaceful revolution of earthquake proportions," political columnist Martin Dyckman explained. "In 1967, most Florida politicians saw government as a basic good that could—and should—be made better." One individual who embraced that philosophy was state senator Lawton Chiles. He belonged, for instance, to a small group of veteran legislators who believed that goals of good government could not be realized unless its workings were opened to the public. With that motivation Chiles, who had been elevated from the house of representatives to the senate by Polk voters only in 1966, joined Pensacola's Senator Reuben Askew and others to push for passage of a "Government in the Sunshine" law. The success of their efforts in 1967 set the stage for Florida to pioneer the "open government" concept in state and nation.[21]

Another aspect of the peaceful revolution concerned a Republican challenge to Democratic rule in Florida, with the details of the challenge hinting at political revolution in Polk's own future. Even before Judge

McRae's reapportionment order, Floridians in 1966 had rejected south Florida Democrat Robert King High in order to elect Claude R. Kirk, Jr., as the first Republican governor to preside over the state since 1877. Kirk's triumph had resulted, partly, from the support of Polk Democrats. The county had been voting Republican in presidential elections since 1952, and now some of its conserva-

62. *Numerous prominent Polk County businessmen including James W. Sikes, seen here second from left, joined to support Florida's Republican gubernatorial candidate Claude R. Kirk Jr. in 1966. Sikes is pictured with other mid-1960s executives of Florida Tile Industries, Inc., including (at left) Jobie Watson, Leon R. Sikes Sr. (second from right) and Leon R. Sikes Jr. (at right). FLORIDA TREND.*

tive residents opted to extend that trend to state elections. "There weren't many Republicans as such then," D. Burke Kibler observed. "There were conservatives and there were liberals." He continued, "The ones that were significant in [Kirk's] election were Democrats that were conservative and did not want a South Florida liberal as [High] was, and from Miami, that made him even more liberal." Kibler added, "A south Floridian was something we didn't want."[22]

These Polk conservatives, in the circumstances, networked to Kirk's financial and electoral benefit. "[Florida Citrus Commission member] Keith Scales [of Leesburg] called me and said that a group of people that I knew in Leesburg, Orlando, and Ocala, and that kind of area, were impressed with Claude Kirk and wanted to know if I would arrange for him to meet some people in the Lakeland area," Kibler explained. "I had never met Claude at the time, but I agreed to do that. One of my closest friends, Jim Wellman . . . was a very active citizen [and] a big conservative. He later was on the National Republican Finance Committee," Kibler commented further. "Jim, when I called him, and I called several others, Scott Linder, I think was one and Jimmy Sikes perhaps . . . Jim immediately offered a place he had out at his Wellman-Lord engineering complex for parties and all." Kibler concluded: "Jim was so enamored with him that he probably became Claude Kirk's closest supporter, strongest supporter, and one of his closest friends. We all became friendly with Claude." Given such support, Kirk easily swept Polk in November 1966 with 56 percent of the vote and a plurality of nearly six thousand.[23]

The Kirk victory, following on the heels of presidential candidate Barry Goldwater's 1964 Polk win, emboldened some local Republicans to begin challenging Democrats in local contests. "The political scene in Polk County in 1967 was dominated by Gov. Claude Kirk Jr.," the *Lakeland Ledger* informed its readers. "In Polk, there were quiet stirrings at the grass roots level of citizens moving to challenge the ever-ruling hierarchy of Democratic officeholders who have dominated public affairs in the county since pioneer times," its story noted. "The stirrings were real and from a sea of changing political sentiment will come, almost surely, a challenge to Polk Democrat chieftains from Republican candidates in county elections in the new year." Republicans gleefully spread rumors that former state senator Scott Kelly was about to join their party. That desertion from Democratic ranks failed to occur, but others did. After the GOP pledged an all-out assault on the county commission, Lakeland's Charles Whitten, for one, announced that he had switched to the Republicans to oppose Commissioner Aldine Combee.[24]

The county commission offered a particularly ripe target since it once again wallowed in turmoil. Having three times been investigated by grand juries since 1959, the panel had taken to fighting against itself. This fact emerged into public view in January 1966 when "an explosive, tension-charged meeting" resulted in Commissioner Alan Trask ousting Chairman Les Dunson from his position. Dunson had gained the chairmanship a mere six days previously. Trask justified his participation in the embarrassing episode by insisting that Dunson had promised to step down once selected. "This is about the bloodiest thing I have ever seen," Dunson remarked afterward. "I'll tell you one thing. This isn't the end of it," he added. "Everything this board does from now on better be accomplished on top of the table."[25]

The very fact that the board's activities might not "be accomplished on top of the table" served to open a path for Republicans, and it then turned out that Governor Kirk enjoyed an opportunity to further their goals before 1968 elections could occur. During February and March 1968 approximately one-half of Florida's teachers walked off their jobs when the governor and legislative leaders failed to respond to Florida State Teacher Association demands for greater support. In Polk 500 educators reportedly resigned in sympathy with the ultimately unsuccessful teacher strike. This trial for school superintendent Shelley Boone happened just as the county system experienced renewed challenges regarding racial integration. Boone's health gave way, and he opted to resign. This permitted Governor Kirk to name a replacement. He selected Florida Southern College education professor Merle Dimbath. As of June 1968, the twenty-nine year old Republican ran the county's school system, having breached the wall of Democrat dominance in county government.[26]

Republican dreams of further progress crashed in disappointment, however, when the November elections came around. County voters were not yet prepared to abandon their traditional Democrat leanings. Some races did come in close. Particularly, twenty-seven year old Lakeland real estate man Joe Sargeant, who the previous year had run unsuccessfully for the legislature, narrowly lost a county commission race to incumbent Democrat Floyd Woods. Democrat W. W. (Bill) Read meanwhile dispatched school superintendent Dimbath. Read's task had been made easier when the Republican's lack of presumed educational credits became public knowledge.[27]

All was not lost for the Republicans, though. At the November election commission chairman Trask had achieved a victory in his race to succeed retiring state senator Ben Hill Griffin, Jr. Trask resigned his place on the commission in order to accept the new position, and Governor Kirk in December designated Joe Sargeant to hold the commission seat. Officially sworn into office on December 17, Sargeant thus became Polk's first Republican county commissioner. His tenure proved brief and unpleasant. The Republican never achieved a working rapport with his Democrat colleagues, and, when he announced in April 1970 that he would not seek election "for personal reasons," he blasted county government generally as "archaic." As Sargeant departed the panel in December, though, he strove to strike a positive tone. "Certainly we have had our differences," he informed his colleagues. "Overall, I have enjoyed the

63. *This swearing-in session for Polk area legislators took place in 1970. Facing the camera (from the left) are Quillian S. Yancey, Ray Mattox (face obscured), C. Fred Jones, Larry Libertore, John R. Clark, and R. Ed Blackburn Jr.* FLORIDA STATE ARCHIVES.

experience [and] in a way I am sorry I am leaving." Former deputy circuit court clerk Frank "Bubba" Smith, a Democrat, thereupon replaced Sargeant and ended the Republican advance on county government for the time being.[28]

For the lessons they taught as to why the Republicans were not more successful in Polk during the late 1960s and early 1970s, the circumstances of the Sargeant appointment deserve scrutiny. The fact of the matter was that Republicans were divided by personality and interest, just as were the Democrats. The commission district to which Sargeant received appointment lay in the county's southern and southeastern extremes; yet, the appointee resided in Lakeland. Longtime Republicans who did reside in the district strongly resented the imposition of a man whom they considered essentially an upstart carpetbagger. Wesley B. Craig, secretary of the Lake Wales GOP organization, denounced the Sargeant appointment as an "injustice to the voters of Lake Wales, Frostproof, and Fort Meade." He added, "Since this young man has been twice rejected by the voters, it is hardly satisfactory to find ourselves represented, or perhaps we should say mis-represented [by him]." The Lake Wales group had pushed former Polk County Farm Bureau president Bruce Fullerton for the job, revealing an additional weakness in the Republican armor. Fullerton himself had switched parties only in 1968, leaving Sargeant the senior GOP man in consideration.[29]

Disenchantments

The intra-party Democratic and Republican spats, when combined with feuding between the parties and echoes from tales of government corruption, began to disenchant more residents about local government's viability and credibility. Mulberry's police scandal particularly offered one of the era's harrowing tales of local corruption. This affair erupted in 1965 thanks to *Tampa Tribune* journalist John Frasca's inspired investigative reporting regarding a wave of robberies and burglaries. A Sanford man, Robert L. Watson, unfairly had been convicted of one of the robberies, the reporter discovered. The true culprits, he reasoned, were several local policemen operating as a crime ring. The crusade launched by Frasca's stories ultimately achieved Watson's release and revealed the police complicity. Frasca, who won the Pulitzer Prize for his efforts, took care to point out that Mulberry residents, as opposed to county officialdom, had fostered neither the crime nor the unfair conviction. "It wasn't the people of Mulberry who sent Watson away," he quoted café owner

Johnny Mitchell as insisting. "If it wasn't for them, the way they came forward to help that boy, he'd still be in prison." Frasca's 1968 book *The Mulberry Tree* subsequently shared the story and Polk's embarrassment with the nation.[30]

As Frasca's publisher prepared to release his book, other scandals appeared to further undermine local government claims to honesty and credibility. Amid rumors of county planning fraud, for instance, Governor Kirk ordered an investigation that included focus on "higher ups in local government." Perhaps more importantly, in 1968 a petit jury convicted criminal court clerk Robert J. Haslett, "the most unbeatable office holder in Polk County," of embezzlement and perjury. Thousands of dollars in confiscated "bolita money" had disappeared from Haslett's custody. The accused doggedly maintained his innocence, charging County Solicitor Gordon MacCalla with "vindictiveness." MacCalla's assistant Monte Campbell came in for more-personal attack. "You're just a lackey for the county solicitor," Haslett charged in court. "You're a Charlie McCarthy and you're enjoying every minute of this." Responsibility for restoring the office's credibility following Haslett's removal devolved to Lakeland industrial arts teacher E. D. "Bud" Dixon, whom voters in 1968 chose to fill the criminal court clerk position. Statewide judicial reform in 1972 thereafter unified Polk's criminal and civil court clerk jobs, with Dixon holding the new clerk of courts office for the next quarter century.[31]

Crime generally seemed to fly out of control, and, while the same situation prevailed in much of the country, local government nonetheless appeared to some as incapable of doing anything about it. Gun battles between police and suspected evildoers underscored the sentiment, such as when police officers J. C. Entzminger, N. R. Lacopoulos, and E. T. Pickett ended up shot after a 1965 confrontation in the Lakeland J. M. Fields service station parking lot. Memories remained fresh at the time of the murder two years earlier of Deputy Sheriff Leon A. Bernard who, although off duty, courageously pursued a robber fleeing from Bartow's Sun Finance Company.[32]

Each year that passed heightened fears of the rise in violent crime. An example of the worst occurring concerned Roy Lee Waldon. In 1968, he methodically killed his mother, his brother, a young girl, and an unborn child—plus, he wounded two other persons—in a thirty-five minute "trail of death" at Lakeland. Waldon then turned his pistol upon himself and committed suicide. Given such incidents, murder totals climbed to record levels. Also, new approaches to crime literally brought the problem home to some residents as illustrated by another Lakeland incident that happened late in the period. Comfortably ensconced watching television at their Lake Hollingsworth Drive home, Mr. and Mrs. James L. Ewell were stunned when a "pistol waving" man "crashed through a plate glass window and held them at bay in their living room." Threatening to kill the couple if they tried to chase him, the malefactor soon made away with $800 in cash.[33]

Two murders especially drew interest and served to stoke flames of concern. In the first, citrus magnate Charles Von Maxcy fell victim at his Sebring home to a plot that involved the hiring of "two Boston underworld characters" to kill him. Although widow Irene Maxcy agreed to testify—in return for immunity from prosecution—that her "stocky, balding, ex-bookie" boyfriend John J. Sweet had arranged matters on her behalf, a first and sensational trial at Bartow nonetheless resulted in a hung jury. State Attorney Glen Darty refused to let the case drop. A second trial followed in late 1968 that saw Sweet convicted and sentenced to life imprisonment. County Solicitor MacCalla later prosecuted a remarried Irene Maxcy Wells for perjury.[34]

The second murder drew attention across the county's racial divide. On February 28, 1969, the body of Carrie Lee Williams, the thirty-eight year old wife of Lakeland National Association for the Advancement of Colored People chapter president Otis Williams, was discovered in her car parked on a gravel driveway in north Lakeland. Police soon arrested family friend Sidney Wilson, who had purchased a life insurance policy on the deceased. The case went to trial in July. Circuit Judge J. H. Willson, however, granted a directed verdict of acquittal for Wilson after finding the prosecution's case insufficient. The case grew more controversial thereafter as unsubstantiated stories spread quietly in local power circles linking Carrie Lee Williams romantically with a major pillar of the county's white political establishment. Whether from that or some other cause, the murder thereafter remained unsolved and the perpetrator unprosecuted.[35]

The Vietnam War doubtlessly contributed, as well, to residents' growing sense that matters generally were spinning out of control. Whether an individual supported or opposed the United States's role in the conflict, the departure of young men and women from the county to participate in it personalized the fighting, sometimes very painfully. As early as 1963 friends and loved ones of Lt. James E. Johnson of Winter Haven feared his loss when his B26 bomber was shot down. Fortunately, Johnson survived a two-day jungle ordeal to reunite with his wife of one month Margaret Johnson and his mother Mrs. Aaron Johnson.[36]

Soon, though, the news turned more dire. In 1965, Lake Alfred's Thomas Clifford Edwards died in Vietnam, as did Lakeland's Dorse Riggs. The next year claimed Fort Meade's Harlon Harris, Jr., Eloise's Ronnie Hankins Rintliff, Bartow's Donald Coles Woodruff, and Lakeland's James Ray Pearson, Donald Frederick Weinman, and Kenneth Ray Temples. The toll grew heavier as time passed, including both those who died and those who suffered capture. Marine PFC James W. Spivey of Fort Meade, killed in 1969, numbered as just one of what by then amounted to many casualties. It came almost as a relief to many at Eagle Lake when the name of a still-alive Bradley Smith appeared on a March 1970 list of fourteen persons held in a North Vietnam prisoner of war camp.[37]

Word of losses, as true in all wars, sometimes could stagger entire communities. To cite a single example, Lt. Richard E. Hood, Jr., who was killed in an ambush during July 1967, literally had been Winter Haven's pride. A 1966 graduate of the United States Military Academy, Hood had served as president of the Winter Haven High School student body, vice president of the National Honor Society, president of the Junior Honor Society, vice president of the Key Club, and delegate to Boys' Nation in Washington, D.C. Active in the Boy Scouts and youth affairs at Beymer Memorial Methodist Church, Hood also had won two years running the Science Award given by Winter Haven's medical association. Hood's death, as with the sacrifices of others, left a deep and empty place at Winter Haven that his life had filled with honor and achievement.[38]

As in previous conflicts, young men and women from Polk who served in Vietnam distinguished themselves and honored the county by their courageous service beyond the call of duty. Lt. Hood, for example, earned the Silver Star medal for his heroism, as did numerous others including Lakeland's Captain Arthur J. Wacaster. Marine Lt. Col. William Finch received the Legion of Merit as well as the Silver Star for his bravery, while Bruce A. Rhoden claimed the Distinguished Flying Cross and the Air Medal with a V device for heroism in two separate combat actions. The names of others deserve notice, but that of First Lieutenant Ronald Ray requires mention. On June 19, 1966, in Vietnam's Ia Drang Valley, "without hesitation or regard for his own safety, he dove between [a] grenade and [his] men, thus shielding them from the explosion while receiving wounds in his exposed feet and legs." Viet Cong machine gun fire then hit Ray several times before the lieutenant could silence the weapon with another grenade. "While suf-

64. *Captain Arthur Joel Wacaster of Lakeland numbered as one of many Polk Countians to earn commendations for valor, including in his case multiple awards of the Silver Star medal, during combat operations in Vietnam. He is pictured here in his office near Hue and Phu Bie as commanding officer, Headquarters Company, First Battalion, 501st Airborne Infantry Regiment, 101st Airborne Division. ARTHUR J. WACASTER.*

fering great pain from his wounds," his award citation read, "Ray continued to direct his men until they were no longer in immediate danger before allowing himself to be evacuated for medical treatment." A grateful nation conferred upon the Auburndale hero the Medal of Honor.[39]

As the Vietnam War persisted abroad, another unsettling dynamic further stirred local concerns that the world had swirled off its axis. Specifically, the generations began to clash at home. A "generation gap" opened within so many families that the outfall split society generally. College students particularly sought to alter institutions and society, sometimes by direct and controversial methods. Webber College offers an example. The women's school in fall 1970 had decided to adopt coeducation. Yet, by October administrators found themselves confronted by unexpected demands. "Webber College students went on strike Thursday," a report noted, "and were granted more changes than requested."[40]

Under new leadership, Florida Southern College did not prove so tractable. President Ludd Spivey had retired in 1957 to be replaced by Dr. Charles Thrift, who reflected a more conservative approach than had his predecessor. "At the height of the student uprising all over the country in the sixties, the issues of open dormitories and liquor on campus were being pushed upon the administrators and trustees of universities and colleges," Cushman S. Radebaugh recollected. "Many of the colleges and universities, including most of our large ones, acceded to the student demands," he continued. "These issues became red hot at Florida Southern, too, and the student body threatened to walk out en masse if their demands were not met." Radebaugh concluded:

"However, its administrators, under the very able leadership of its president, Dr. Charles T. Thrift, Jr., backed by all its trustees, said that Florida Southern College would be a Christian college or none at all. Remaining staunch, the administrators, trustees, and faculty withstood the pressures and refused to be swayed by the student demands."[41]

A newer institution, but one that would become a mainstay of higher education in the county, adopted a similar conservative stance. Warner Southern College traced its origins to a 1964 decision by the Southeastern Association of the Church of God to sponsor a four-year college in Florida. After Babson Park businessman J. W. Holland donated 350 acres along Crooked Lake for the project, the association brought its plans to Polk. Dr. Leslie Ratzlaff raised funds and oversaw the building process in the mid-to-late 1960s, benefitting substantially from the generosity of mobile home manufacturer Hersel Studebaker and his wife Eula Studebaker. Groundbreaking ceremonies followed in December 1967, with the first freshman class of seventeen students commencing studies in September 1968. At Ratzlaff's suggestion, trustees named the new college in honor of Daniel S. Warner, founder of the Church of God movement. Historian James V. Holton explained the school's mission. "Warner officials," he recorded, "worked hard to establish the college as a liberal arts institution as well as a training institution for church ministries." Accreditation came to Warner Southern in 1977, with state approval of the college's teacher education programs arriving with one year thereafter.[42]

A very negative aspect of youthful rebellion increasingly concerned use of illegal stimulants and depressants of various sorts. By the late 1960s, more than a few of Polk's young people had advanced from beer and liquor to marijuana and LSD. This evolution had progressed to the point by 1970 that some parents had begun to fear the possible impact on their children of innocent holidays such as Halloween. "In October, everything was normal until about a week before Halloween, when several calls from different areas of the county warned deputies that somebody might coat the trick or treat candy with the hallucinogenic drug LSD," a year-end law enforcement report related. "[Sheriff Monroe] Brannen called a press conference and warned parents to keep their children in the neighborhood on Halloween night, and many did," it added. The situation concluded, fortunately, on a happy note. "As it turned out," the report observed in closing, "there were no reports of LSD-effected children after the trick or treating was over."[43]

All manner of other issues raised passions and provoked unease, with the desirability of sex education in the schools taking center stage by 1970. The public tiff originated in January when a ministerial group approached School Superintendent W. W. Read for "an official commitment that sex education would not be taught in the Polk County Public Schools." The "Polk Citizens for Moral Education" thereafter convened public meetings to discuss "the uncontrolled teaching of sex and showing of sex films in Polk County schools" and launched a petition drive that eventually gained two thousand signatures. When Reed opted not to offer the requested commitment, the Lakeland Ministerial Association jumped to his defense. Neither side of the controversy proved willing to back down, and so the matter simmered unresolved.[44]

Also unresolved and serving additionally to generate controversy, unease, and disenchantment with local government were growing environmental problems. Beginning in 1965 with Lakeland's popular swimming spot Crystal Lake, waters previously taken for granted began to test as unsafe for recreational use due to high bacteria counts. Concerns had reached such a stage by 1967 that Lake Marion property owners formed the Central Florida Anti-Pollution League to block Haines City's plans to pump sewage effluent into that water body. The year 1969 brought national exposure of phosphate industry pollution when *Life* magazine ran a photograph purporting to show "a Polk County fertilizer plant emitting pollutants and ruining the citrus and cattle industries." Florida Phosphate Council executive director Homer E. Hooks labeled the photo "phony" and accused the magazine of maligning the county "for the sake of sensational journalism," but the counteroffensive rang hollow for many who saw pollution's toll first hand. By the time toxic "bluegreen scum" began washing up on the shores of Lake Bonny in 1970, it had become apparent to most residents that pollution had reached, as the Mountain Lake Sanctuary's director put it, "an alarming stage."[45]

Some individuals, yearning to return to what they remembered as a simpler and better time, fretted even about the march of women toward greater involvement within the public sphere. Where many had applauded Lois Searle in 1965 as she took over as Lakeland's mayor, others held their cheers until 1969 when a male, Dwight Goleman, defeated her bid for reelection to the city commission. Annie Leigh Sessions's rise by 1967 to the presidency of Lakeland's First Federal Savings and Loan Association similarly had helped to break barriers and offer a role model for others. Still, voices could be heard expressing resentments that she had taken a job away from a man.[46]

Civil Rights and Uncivil Clashes

Polk County's world of paradox during the mid-to-late 1960s likely found its most vivid expression in the realm of race relations. Surprising some, remarkable advances arrived with the era. Every step forward, though, seemed to provoke resentments on the parts of others. Ultimately, as governmental institutions again proved either unable or unwilling to offer positive leadership, disagreements tragically evolved toward civil discord.

The advances commenced in 1965 when the county school system, pursuant to federal court order, began the process of desegregation. That fall 170 African American juniors and seniors entered nine previously all-white schools. Mostly the transformation occurred peacefully. "If we consider the level of violence that erupted across the south against school integration," transfer student LaFrancine Jackson Burton later explained, "Lakeland's residents are to be commended for having accepted the inevitable with relative calm." Fears among and forecasts by some whites that black students could not compete at the level of white schools quickly proved fallacious. Valorie Davis Montgomery, for one, discovered Fort Meade High School to be "just as easy as all-black Union Academy." Robert Ervin Montgomery agreed. Starring in football, basketball, and track, he managed nonetheless and with ease to graduate as salutatorian of his class.[47]

Many of the students who made this transition possible did so partly from their love of the county and their desire to seek the best future possible for it. Charles Richardson, to name one, opted to become one of the first to relocate from Union Academy to Bartow High School. "He loved to tell stories about growing up in Bartow and Polk

65a & 65b. *Volunteers such as Fort Meade's Valorie Ann Davis and Robert Ervin Montgomery pioneered the desegregation of Polk's public schools in the mid-1960s.* COLLECTION OF THE AUTHOR.

County," a friend later recalled. "He really loved his childhood in Polk County." Richardson's future life would prove the truth of that statement. Following graduation in 1967 he went on to college at the University of Maryland where he earned bachelor's and master's degrees. A career as a college administrator followed, but his ties to Polk remained strong. After a twenty-year absence Richardson returned to the county in 1993. Within five years he had achieved election to the Winter Haven city commission, eventually serving the municipality twice as its mayor. In November 2002 Polk voters turned to him to serve on the county commission. Charles Richardson by then had evolved from a student breaking segregation barriers to the first African American county commissioner in Polk's history.[48]

Charles Richardson's ability to claim a county commission seat rested upon a foundation laid by others beginning in 1968. That year Fort Meade's Walter Jones narrowly missed election to that town's commission, but the candidacies of two other African Americans resulted more happily. At Lakeland, Dr. John S. Jackson bested W. J. "Jack" Day to win a commission seat. The city-wide vote that made Jackson Lakeland's first black elected official included white, as well as black, support. Similarly, at Bartow mortician and civic leader George H. Gause dispatched two white opponents in a city commission race and without a runoff. His strength in white and black precincts allowed him the next year to cruise to reelection without an opponent. Also in 1969 Herbert J. Menchan, who then served as principal of Fort Meade's middle school, attempted to usher Winter Haven into the new era, as well. The attempt fell short "only by a few hundred votes," but Menchan, too, had helped to lay the groundwork for Charles Richardson's subsequent career.[49]

County civil rights activists meanwhile reached out to offer leadership to the state. The Reverend Joel Atkins particularly did so by moving in 1967 from the vice presidency to the presidency of the NAACP's Florida State Conference of Branches. He inspired and rewarded local workers by bringing the conference's annual meeting to the county in 1968. Atkins soon was endeavoring with others to relocate the state NAACP headquarters to Lakeland. Organization officials had received a deed to the proposed building site by early August 1970.[50]

An event that occurred three days following delivery of the NAACP headquarters deed pointed out the residual and even enhanced resentment of some residents to advances such as those mentioned. "A cross was burned in a Lakeland man's front yard Sunday morning," the *Lakeland Ledger* reported, "after he participated in a motorcade for the

NAACP." Never far from the surface of county affairs, the Ku Klux Klan seemingly enjoyed a resurgence in support during the late 1960s. A rally south of Lakeland in 1967, for instance, drew three hundred persons to hear a Klan officer claim connections between communism and civil rights.[51]

66. *African Americans, thanks in part to the power of new federal laws, gained increasing clout in Polk County elections during the late 1960s. Here, a deputy voter registrar guides 94-year old Mrs. Donnie Cummings through the process that will permit her to vote for the first time.* LAKELAND PUBLIC LIBRARY.

Former Florida A&M University president Walter L. Smith gained firsthand knowledge of the secret organization's shadow in Polk when he led a 1968 workshop at Bartow in his capacity as director of the state center for human relations. The session, intended to bring together black educators and civil rights advocates to plan for school integration, attracted individuals such as C. C. Corbett, Gordon Foster, and Dr. James Beck. "While the meeting was progressing, a group of imposing looking white men entered and, without speaking, stood against the walls of the room," Smith remembered. "The men were stern faced," he continued. "They looked like they could kill an elephant with a toothpick." The dozen or so white men, by their very presence, "interrupted" the workshop. "After thirty minutes, they walked out in a line," Smith explained further. "But, when the workshop adjourned, we discovered that Ku Klux Klan literature had been left on automobiles in the parking lot." The civil rights activist added, "Their literature accused the committee of being communists, trying to destroy the community."[52]

Klan agitation drew strength from the school system's inability to implement student integration effectively and the problems that developed as a result. Frustrated at the slow pace of progress and angered by what they considered foot dragging by school officials, Joel Atkins, Otis Williams, and other leaders criticized a proposed "freedom of choice plan" and demanded full integration. On October 14, 1968, United States District Court judge Joseph Patrick Lieb agreed. He ordered the school district "to formulate and adopt a comprehensive plan which shall deal with the use of school facilities at all grade levels and with the assignment of students to those facilities in such a way as to effectuate a transition to a racially non-discriminatory school system in Polk County." Superintendent Merle Dimbath interpreted the order as requiring the closing of all previously black schools. That mandate infuriated many African Americans. "They were being absorbed, losing schools vital to the identity of the black community," one journalist commented. She added, "Black families often picketed outside the schools in protest."[53]

Far-greater problems quickly followed. Historian James V. Holton described the situation that evolved. "Angry white parents organized grass-roots efforts to stop integration, citing cultural and legal objections," he wrote. "Some white parents carried out personal acts of defiance by subverting school assignment policies. Black parents angrily condemned the closing of traditional black schools and the dispersal of black teachers and administrators." Holton added: "Without black school board members to represent their interests, black citizens in Polk County turned to community leaders to speak for them. Black students endured years of hostility and increasing bitterness, occasionally lashing out and lashing back at their tormentors, as they adapted to predominantly white schools."[54]

Lynda Johnson witnessed at close range the experience of those years. "The first year was terrifying," she recalled of her experience as a ninth grader transferred from Rochelle to Lakeland High School. "When you walk outside and see paddy wagons and dogs on the campus, it's frightening," Johnson explained. "You never knew what to expect." She added: "I would never go to the bathroom, I would just hold it all day. That's how bad it was the first two years." When "huge fights broke out," Johnson concluded, "you kind of took off and ran for your life."[55]

The school system continued to operate and students black and white benefitted from the experience much of the time, but the county paradox ruled their dilemma. White voters in some circumstances would support black candidates for local office and otherwise buttress civil rights advances, but given a court order to change more quickly something approaching rebellion flared with children left to pay the price. Polk thus departed the 1960s and entered the 1970s with Ku Klux Klansmen distributing literature calling for a boycott of public schools to protest integration, the inevitability of which most residents had accepted five years earlier. And, all the while, events elsewhere set the stage for change almost beyond belief and eyes anxiously cast glances northward to where a mouse and his friends prepared to make a new home.[56]

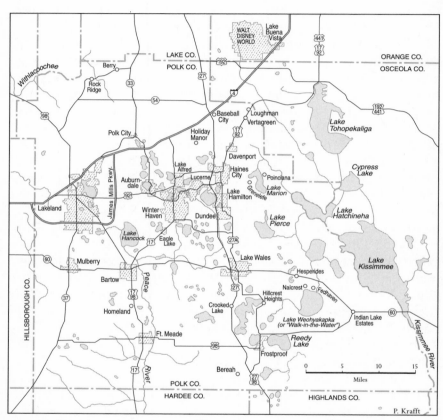

67. *As illustrated by this map, Polk County's historic core of settlement expanded to the north and to the east during the final decades of the twentieth century.* Polk County Historical Association.

"a prophetic glimpse into the future"

CHAPTER 8

Ⴍ

Taking Our Breath Away, 1970-1975

Although it occurred in another county, the opening of Walt Disney World set in motion chains of events that reverberated in Polk County for the remainder of the twentieth century and into the twenty-first. Few truly had imagined that the mouse could roar quite so loudly or that Mickey's influence would be felt so profoundly. The development that ensued from his Florida debut altered settlement patterns in place for generations and initiated shifts that eventually would remold local social, business, and political institutions. As always, though, change's price tag demanded attention. Precious resources taken for granted, almost forgotten at times in their familiarity, suddenly appeared jeopardized or else lost. A united people with gifted leadership could have withstood the demands of the times, but the past hung heavily upon Polk in the early 1970s. Division typified the scene rather than unity, and tests of leadership produced mostly disappointing results.

Amid gala celebrations Walt Disney World revealed itself to the public on October 1, 1971, and, naturally, a Polk family claimed the right to pass first through its gates. William Windsor, Jr., his wife Marty, and their children Jay and Lee had spent the previous night "parked [in their Volkswagen] at a Texaco service station just off Interstate 4." Friends back at Lakeland had questioned their dream of becoming Disney's "first family," but, in true Polk fashion, they persisted. "Their eyes were bright with excitement when they learned they had won," the *Orlando Sentinel* detailed the next morning. Dozens of reporters and photographers followed the family as its members toured the fascinating new resort. Bands serenaded the Windsors, and "Mickey Mouse spent much of the day with them." William, as excited as his sons, repeatedly pointed out surprises and attractions. "See that over there, Jaybird," he would call. "Look at that." In the end Disney officials sweetened an already happy day by refunding the $9.50 the family had spent for ticket books. "I don't care," a grinning William Windsor declared. "If they don't refund my money, I won't care."[1]

Countless others agreed with the Windsors, and Walt Disney World soon become the world's favorite tourist destination. Ten thousand persons shared the occasion on opening day, but twenty million were passing through its portals every year by 1980. The billionth visitor, according to one account, crossed Mickey's threshold by 1994. New attractions, their owners yearning to profit from the tide of money flowing into the state, seemingly sprung up at every hand. Meanwhile, settlers flooded in as well. Florida's population swelled by nearly three million to almost ten million during the decade. Polk's 1970 total of 227,222 meanwhile ballooned to 321,652.[2]

It took several years for Disney's impact to hit Polk with full force, but excitement nonetheless filled the air. The *Lakeland Ledger* conveyed a sense of the times in its 1971 year-end roundup of local news. "1971 was the year of Disney and as the year drew to a close Disney World dominated the news," the paper observed. "Attendance records were broken, and 70,000 were estimated to be in the Magic Kingdom Dec. 30. Traffic filled the highways, people spilled over into motel lobbies in attempts to find a place to stay." The summary concluded, "Polk County had a prophetic glimpse into the future as the year ended."[3]

Business at Every Hand

Even with the full impact of Disney delayed for a while, developments of various sorts promised good times in the near future. One magazine by February 1972 was trumpeting "East Polk: Where Disney World's Cup Runneth Over." The article noted nine major developments announced for the U.S. 27 corridor through the county but stressed that land speculation still dominated activity. "Where U.S. 27 crosses Interstate 4 in the rolling citrus and cattle land southeast of Orlando, there is an acre of land," it noted. "It has changed hands four times in recent years. The first time it sold for $870. The last time, it brought $130,000." Inflation of values on such a scale could not help but capture imaginations. "Perhaps more than anywhere else in the state, East Polk is feeling—and showing—the effects of Disney World," the article continued.

"It is booming, is bracing for even bigger booms, and is trying hard to face the changes, good and bad, that the boom is expected to bring."[4]

As far as tangible progress mattered, construction activity mostly awaited the future. As to exceptions, the Gulf American Corporation had expanded its area activities considerably. Particularly, it had announced and commenced construction on River Ranch Shores, a development situated "side by side" with its River Ranch Acres project. Located "in southeastern Polk" and "hugging the shores of the Kissimmee River east of Lake Wales," River Ranch Shores included about 16,000 homesites that eventually, so the company argued, would house 50,000 persons. Its designers envisioned "a vacation-second home type community that Everyman dreams of living in." As writer Majorie Green noted, "Long-range plans call for the construction of several churches, townhouses, condominiums, neighborhood shopping centers and a man-made string of lakes." She added, "Naturally, it wouldn't be complete without a golf course."[5]

As ambitious a project as River Ranch Shores appeared to many county residents, it could not hold a candle to GAC's next announcement. The city of Poinciana, GAC promised when unveiling plans in November 1971, would be the "City of Tomorrow." Constructed on 47,300 acres, it would grow, project designers insisted, to hold 250,000 to 300,000 inhabitants within thirty years. Located at its nearest point "within a quarter of a mile from Disney World," the development's "western edge" stretched "to within three miles of Haines City" and to the east across the Osceola County line. "Contractors are merrily building the project's first houses and streets," a February 1972 report advised. Adding to the initiative's allure, the developer established a Scout camp there the next year. GAC Properties, Inc., named the facility for its president S. H. Wills.[6]

The rising economic tide floated most Polk boats. "The boom philosophy is contagious," an onlooker exclaimed. "Local businessmen are jumping on the prosperity bandwagon." Florida's Department of Commerce proclaimed, "Disney World has had a tremendous impact on the hotel and restaurant business in Polk County." Its Lakeland office added, "There is a big demand for labor openings in the construction business." Through late 1974 and despite a severe national economic slowdown, the good times continued to prevail. "For most of these past 12 months, the business community has been determined to compare 1974 with the banner years of 1972 and 1973," *Lakeland Ledger* business writer Peter Fiero discovered. Scott Linder, president of the Florida Chamber of

Commerce as well as of Lakeland's Linder Industrial Machine Co., felt the same way. "I think Lakeland is in better condition than many other places in the U.S.," he informed Fiero. "We have a lot to be thankful for in this area."[7]

The prosperity found its reflection in most of Polk's municipalities. Bartow treated itself to a new city hall, for instance, while Auburndale launched a downtown redevelopment program. Lake Wales similarly looked to reviving its urban core. As its municipal "facelift" neared completion in 1973 residents beheld that it had "changed downtown Lake Wales from a depressing, deteriorating area to a vital economic and aesthetic unit." *Ledger* reporter Larry Thornberry provided details. "The package includes four blocks of new pavement and sidewalks with curbs and gutters along with planters, landscaping, modernistic lighting, a mall with a fountain, an all-weather pavilion, and more than 5,000 trees, plants, and shrubs," he related. "Aesthetically," Thornberry observed, "it probably is the trees and shrubs more than anything else that has transformed a grubby shopping district into a pleasant shopping park." He added, "If the project has created no individual windfalls, it certainly has breathed new economic life into the downtown area as a whole."[8]

The breath of new economic life that invigorated most of the county perhaps energized Lakeland more than any other Polk community. Well before Disney World welcomed the Windsor family, the city's pulse already had begun beating at a far faster rate. "This has been the year that changed the look of downtown Lakeland," one news source reported at year's end 1970. "And several other parts of the city too." A Maas Brothers department store and a $1.6 million public parking garage highlighted improvements, together with a J. C. Penney outlet and the First Federal Savings and Loan's new headquarters. Among other innovations Grove Park Shopping Center expanded, a "four-plex" motion picture theater rose, a "huge" Woolco department store opened for business, and a Kwik-Chek "supermarket" awaited customers. The boom's commercial centerpiece was the Lake Parker Mall. When dignitaries broke ground for the $7 million forty-five store mall on May 21, it promised the county not only its first "mall" but also its largest shopping center. Then, in April 1971 George Jones and Tammy Wynette opened their Old Plantation Music Park, establishing the city as a pulsing center of country and western music. Taken together, the improvements earned Lakeland designation in 1972 as "an All-American city."[9]

The next several years continued the trend. Lakeland in 1972, for example, broke all previous records for construction. Figures for

68. *Lakeland's Old Plantation Music Park.* POLK COUNTY
HISTORICAL ASSOCIATION.

residential building neared $5 million, while twenty-seven commercial projects involved almost $2 million more. To meet increasing needs, Lakeland General Hospital committed over $10 million for improvements. And, the City of Lakeland contributed about the same for the erection of a regional civic center.

The story of the next year played out much the same but on a larger scale. "Nine new housing projects with costs ranging from $1 million to $8 million are primarily responsible for nearly 2,200 new housing units covered by building permits so far this year," city building superintendent Emery Davis reported. So expansive had development become by then that city leaders imposed a planned unit development ordinance "which restricts development on a piece of property to the plans originally approved by the planning and zoning board."[10]

The U.S. 27 corridor, as would be expected, fared well during this period although development in its upper reaches lagged unexpectedly at first. To the good and after fifteen years of planning, in 1971 the state finally moved ahead with four-laning the overcrowded roadway. Then, in 1972 Ringling Bros. and Barnum & Bailey cast its sights on 135 acres of orange groves located just below the Interstate 4 intersection. In October the company employed circus historian Chappell P. "Chappie" Fox to help realize a theme park that was "a sawdust place of death-defying feats on a daily basis." Circus World, Fox informed local residents, "will be educational, entertaining and will bring the era of the circus back to the hearts and minds of the people." Construction on the project began in April 1973, and one year later it opened to the delight of fans. Not everything proceeded according to plan, however, and the proprietors soon closed the park for renovation and expansion. It reopened in 1976 with high hopes and a new entertainment format that stressed "singers, musicians, and specialty acts."[11]

69. *Circus World offered Polk one of numerous tourist attractions that opened gates in the aftermath of Disney World's debut.* POLK COUNTY HISTORICAL ASSOCIATION.

Whatever its format, Circus World's presence sparked further development at the I-4/U.S. 27 intersection or, as it came to be called, "Barnum City." All of the services and facilities that might be expected in the vicinity of a major attraction emerged into view. "By 1977, five motels with a total capacity of 800 rooms had been built," journalist Cinnamon Bair commented. "A campground, several gas stations and a Horne's Restaurant also shared a one-mile strip along U.S. 27." Three years later as many as 24,000 vehicles passed the site every day.[12]

Increased traffic on U.S. 27 symbolized not only the tourism boom but also sustained growth. "We call it the '27 syndrome,' Central Florida Regional Planning Council executive director Jim Duane explained. "People come down from Disney World off Interstate-4 and like the beauty and small-town atmosphere so much, they end up staying." Estimates for 1973 accordingly placed the county's population already at 258,515, suggesting a three-year increase of over 30,000. Forecasters projected trends for a 92 percent jump over that number by the year 2000, a development that, if realized, would give Polk one-half million residents by the century's end. In 1973 alone, the *Lakeland Ledger* asserted, the county had gained "about 10 per cent." University of Florida experts confirmed the paper's claim, adding that the following year the total mounted to 268,300. Yet another 10,000 arrived in 1975.[13]

The level of increase demanded the expansion of towns and cities, plus the building of new communities. Even tiny Eagle Lake took advantage of the times to transform itself from a town into a "city" with a proper city manager. Lake Alfred delved into growth control measures, requiring developers to submit project impact plans. All the while, builders announced new subdivisions and developments with numbing regularity. "Bok Woods" graced Lake Wales, for instance, while "Highland Lakes" opened at Bartow. The county commission meanwhile signaled approval of "major" developments, such as Arrowhead southeast of Haines City. Taking precedence as one of the most "major" of the developments, Grenelefe took life off the western shore of Lake Marion, east of Haines City, beginning in March 1974. "Grenelefe (an alias used by Little John, one of Robin Hood's legendary band when he entered the Sheriff of Nottingham's service in disguise) will eventually cover close to 1,000 acres and include two golf courses; a 22-court tennis complex; and country club; convention center; marina; 1,000 rental condominiums; 100 country homes and 88 estate homes," a promotional article informed the public. The $65 million venture's "main thrust" involved "rental condominiums operated like a resort hotel by Radisson."[14]

The building up of post-Disney Polk brought with it tendencies away from traditional county patterns in several respects, ones that were to carry significance in the coming years. Many new arrivals were retirees,

70. *Dozens of residential developments, often including a golf course, sprang up during the 1970s. Many of them were located on or near flood-prone or otherwise environmentally sensitive lands. The new buildings surrounding a landscaped golf course seen here at Grenelefe near Haines City and Lake Hamilton suggest the enormous impact of this intensity of development upon water and sewage-disposal resources.* POSH GOLF TRAVEL

for instance, and not infrequently Republican in their political orientation. Among younger arrivals, modest means and even poverty often marked their lives. Unable to find work and without skills or training, they kept county unemployment totals high. Thanks partly to the national economic recession then underway, the Polk unemployment rate crested for the period at 12.1 percent in June 1975.[15]

Also, many of the new residents opted otherwise than to live in detached single-family dwellings or even in apartments, townhouses, or condominiums. Rather, they chose—based upon convenience, modest cost, and relative freedom of movement and action—to occupy "mobile" and prefabricated "modular" homes. Formerly called "trailers" by residents, mobile homes especially drew interest. "Trailer facilities" had proliferated in Polk during the mid-to-late 1960s, with the county standing alongside Duval, Palm Beach, Lake, and Leon Counties in that regard. The absence of county zoning regulations had encouraged proliferation of what increasingly came to be called mobile home parks and mobile home estates during the next decade. In one instance, the Florando Investment Corp. announced plans in 1970 for a 3,000 acre park in the county's northeastern corner. By 1973, 10,000 to 15,000 mobile homes dotted the county landscape, and those numbers rapidly grew. "Mobile homes were permitted in greater numbers than single family conventional homes," county development coordinator George Stahlman reported in late 1975, "as has been the case for quite a while."[16]

Planning and Zoning

The magnitude of growth that Polk anticipated during the early 1970s finally forced the county commission to reconsider its responsibility for zoning and the planning efforts required for such an exercise in governmental regulation. As recently as 1965, thanks in good part to the commission's default in leadership, voters had rejected a county zoning plan. Within three years, local governments at Lakeland, Winter Haven, and Haines City had urged immediate action without voter approval. The county commission first hired a consulting firm to suggest necessary action but then caved into anti-zoning pressures and abrogated the contract. "Polk County, other than some of its municipalities, is growing without a plan," the *Orlando Sentinel* lamented. "With a population of at least 235,000, the county has 13 cities, the largest of which is Lakeland," it continued. "Between these communities reside enough people to twice defeat proposed county zoning when put to a vote." The *Sentinel* delved even deeper into the meaning of rural refusal to plan and zone: "Outside some of the municipalities, where planning and zoning [does] exist, an uncontrolled growth goes on. Some call it 'progress,' but some city officials, such as William Pierce of Haines City, fear the progress—which includes junkyards, beer joints, and in many areas almost a shanty-type residential area—may ruin the image of those inside the city limits."[17]

Still, as the decade of the 1970s opened, officials temporized. Commissioner J. B. Thornhill, for one, promised in January 1970 that the commission would act "as quickly as possible on an interim zoning plan." Thornhill added, however, that "before enacting it, the board wants to make sure it is right." When rebuked by Haines City Citrus Growers Association president R. V. Phillips for the reluctance to act quickly, Thornhill conceded, "The county is far behind on zoning and we realize it."[18]

The almost irresistible pressures stemming from the approach of Walt Disney World's opening ultimately produced action, prompting the *Tampa Tribune* to describe the zoning decision as "THE happening of Polk's introduction to the surging 1970s." Florida's revised 1968 constitution conferred "home rule" powers upon counties, and the Polk Association of Chambers of Commerce, among others, argued that its provisions offered the commission all the authority it needed to act

71. *Disney World magic produced profound changes in Polk County.* WALT DISNEY PRODUCTIONS.

without a vote. A newly designated county planner worked quietly on a zoning scheme as anticipation mounted. In May an "interim protective development regulation of 1970" circulated, offering a plan that barely regulated land use and carefully avoided the term "zoning." The plan's modest reach notwithstanding, public hearings produced "loud vocal opposition" to the point that in August a narrow commission majority dropped the idea of zoning altogether. Intense pro-zoning reaction to that decision brought about a reversal, with the commission opting to accept a revised plan "that would cover the entire county with zoning protection." But, it did so subject to voter approval. City people thereafter battled country people for support at the polls. In November 1970 came "the revolution." Many voters declined to take a stance; of those who did, most unexpectedly sided with the city folk.[19]

The revised interim zoning plan of 1970 thus became Polk's basic regulatory framework for growth for the next dozen years, although effective implementation came slowly. As if to highlight the snail's pace of tighter growth control, County Planner George Stahlman attempted in September 1972 to caution potential buyers against many as-yet-unregulated land developments. They constituted, Stahlman insisted, "a scandalous flim-flam without conscience being conducted on a grand scale." The county commission itself slowed the pace of planning in 1973 when it refused federal aid to assist the process because attached conditions required efforts more stringent than the commissioners were willing to approve.[20]

What the commission did do, at Commissioner Floyd Woods's suggestion, was to establish a "blue ribbon" growth study committee in summer 1973 to "come back within a relatively short time with broad recommendations as to how we can best address ourselves to the specific (growth) problems." The committee, including three members from each of five commission districts and chaired by Haines City attorney Andrew R. Reilly, evidenced a distinctly pro-growth and pro-industry cast. James M. Taylor, Douglas E. Bark, and Paul D. McDonald represented district one; Edd Dean, Jr., Ken Morrison, and Bill R. Delph, district two; Dwight DeVane, Tom Turnbull, and Jack D. Simmons, district three; Wade Rees, Jack W. McKay, and Reilly, district four; and Max Barnett, David J. Partin, and Dwight Goleman, district five. The panel's first recommendation, adopted by the commission in late 1973, called for creation of a zoning advisory board "to hear petitions in zoning cases." Named to that body were Paul McDonald, Edd Dean, Jr., Dwight DeVane, Martin Halabrin, Jr., Jay Merkel, Bobby Lee, and Nelson Futch.[21]

The blue ribbon planning committee's final report reached commissioners' desks in 1974. The four volume compilation, as one reporter expressed, "gave the county a list of recommendations and priorities for orderly growth." Given the mild nature of the recommendations, many were accepted "and put into practice." Only at that point did Polk commence a serious planning and zoning effort, the last county in the state to do so.[22]

Actually, pressure emanating from recently enacted state laws had resulted in some concrete steps toward regional planning even before Polk's county plan took effect. After initially objecting in late 1972 to a planning district that "would reach from the north edge of Polk to the south edge of St. Lucie and Okeechobee counties," the commission soon allowed an interim "areawide planning organization" to begin establishing links. The coordinating body dropped "interim" from its title by January 1973 and commenced to "tackle problems involving planning regions, Green Swamp and sewerage systems." Renamed the Polk County Planning Council in February 1973, the group expanded in July to include Polk, Highlands, Hardee, and DeSoto Counties. Approval of the creation of the Central Florida Regional Planning Council followed in December, with Okeechobee County added to the mix. In 1974 the council located its headquarters at Bartow and expanded its purview to include "a recycling effort" for waste.[23]

Environmental Consequences

While residents and officials grappled with the question of expanding government's powers to control growth, the seventies immediately reminded Polk Countians of the vulnerable condition into which man had placed the local environment. On January 14, 1970, the Southwest Florida Water Management District (SWFWMD) received "a startling report indicating a sizeable loss of water in the Florida aquifer covering in Polk County." With time's passage concerns focused in part on the phosphate mining locale south of Bartow where a "big red hole" had appeared. "The 'big red hole,' explained one newspaperman, "is a common term for the area of water table drawdown, as much as 60 feet over the past 20 years, due principally to heavy phosphate industry use." By 1973 SWFWMD would take pains to caution the public of dire consequences to be expected if dropping aquifer levels countywide caused the "hole" to suffer further deprivation.[24]

Calamity played its part in raising public awareness of environmental problems. On December 3, 1971, an earthen dam maintained by the Cities Service Co. phosphate operations near Fort Meade collapsed. One billion gallons of phosphate slime poured into Peace River and its tributaries. "The slime spill killed countless fish and temporarily destroyed the Peace River," Attorney General Robert Shevin concluded. Litigation that followed resulted in a momentous decision by Florida's Second District Court of Appeals. "The impounding of billions of gallons of phosphoric slimes behind earthen walls which are subject to breaking even with the exercise of the best of care strikes us as being both 'ultrahazardous' and 'abnormally dangerous,'" the court declared. Faced with the judicial declaration, phosphate companies weighed their options, finding it difficult, if not impossible, to turn away from dependence on earthen dams and clay settling ponds. Meanwhile, another industry innovation marked the landscape. Companies increasing constructed gypsum stacks. According to engineer O. H. Wright, the huge piles of the fertilizer manufacturing byproduct—one easily might reach fifteen stories in height—resulted from an additional processing step necessary to make phosphate rock usable for the manufacture of certain chemical products.[25]

The return of dry conditions furthered the rapid widening of the environmental quagmire. Although plentiful rainfall had released the county from a decade-long low-rainfall cycle in 1968, the new decade brought a reversal, with some experts considering "the drought of 1971" to be "the worst in Florida history." Typifying the impact on local water bodies, Lake Hamilton's level struck recorded lows in 1972, 1973, and 1974. SWFWMD, eyeing Peace River's decline, in spring 1972 declared that stream's drainage area a "water-use caution area." As it did, wild fires gripped the region. One 1971 blaze consumed ten thousand acres and required Interstate 4's closure.[26]

One aspect of the low water levels involved intensified water pollution, especially in Polk's lakes. With federal, state, and local regulators not yet pursuing the subject with the vehemence that would mark their efforts in later years, Kathleen High School teacher Ed Vetter found himself the responsible party for protecting the county and alerting its citizens to growing problems. In the early 1970s and on his own volition, Vetter charged his junior and senior science students with monitoring water quality levels in eleven Lakeland area lakes. They documented, as *Tampa Tribune* reporter Bill King described, "the slow deaths of the area's namesakes." By decade's end Vetter's efforts had brought both bad news and national acclaim. "I think the lakes are unsafe for swimming and skiing," he advised in 1979. "If you can ski without ever falling into the water," he added, "it would be all right." That year President Jimmy Carter singled out Vetter and three of his students—Randy Barber, Jimmy Skinner, and Cynthia Jo Parker—for their extraordinary contributions to environmental protection.[27]

Coming hand in hand with news of water pollution in lakes came word of radium contamination of ground water. A federal study released in September 1974 concluded that Polk water samples contained twenty-five times the limit of radium recommended by the United States Public Health Service. Federal officials pointed to the gypsum slurry stored in holding ponds for phosphate mining operations as the culprit, arguing that an acid contained in the slurry seeped into the underlying limestone aquifer. State health guardians downplayed the report, insisting that the radium level was "probably not dangerous" and noting that "higher death or cancer rates" had not yet been observed. Still, state and federal officials combined to form a task force to study the problem. Other than for noting that the radium isotope 226 found in Polk County lost only half its radioactivity over a 1,500 year period, the panel accomplished little for the time being.[28]

Enforcement of environmental laws and regulations, mostly enacted by federal and state governments in the early 1970s, generally lagged far behind need given the sensitivity and opposition of some businesses and industries. Although isolated initiatives helped to stir public demands for greater protection, in Polk the efforts stood out for their relatively infrequent occurrence. In 1970, to offer an example of one early attempt, the Florida Game and Fresh Water Fish Commission announced that it would file criminal charges against Ben Hill Griffin, Inc. for "pumping raw sewage into Lake Reedy in Frostproof." In that instance, though, the county solicitor later ruled the dumping accidental. The state's Department of Air and Water Pollution Control also cited ten local companies for violation of air and water quality control laws, but the actions apparently produced little positive result.[29]

Unfortunately, these developments did not encompass one of Polk's greatest environmental challenges. Where the Green Swamp region's significance and fragility previously had received little attention, circumstances now combined to threaten its ecological balance and to compel governments at all levels to consider, if not address, its problems. The years 1971 and 1972 proved crucial. Drought temporarily drained the swamp of much of its surface water, with Green Pond running completely dry. Meanwhile, developmental frenzy virtually engulfed portions of the vicinity as Disney World's opening drew closer and then passed. By summer 1972, as one report observed, "There are more than 18 major developments in the Green Swamp area where land is being sold for housing." Ken Morrison of the Coalition for the Environment warned officials and county residents that the swamp constituted "the most environmentally endangered land in Polk County." Chairman Don Williams of the Lake Wales Chamber of Commerce Conservation Committee heard Morrison's call and urged the county commission to bar development and to stop all road building within its bounds. "It looks bad up there," Williams declared. "They are building houses and roads and are ruining the water recharge area there." Responding to the entreaty, the commission imposed a construction permit moratorium. Chairman Frank "Bubba" Smith announced in July that "the action was taken to prevent possible damage to the Green Swamp which is a prime water storage and recharge site for central Florida."[30]

The commission maintained its stance against developmental pressures only for a short while, as counter arguments arose to the effect that the swamp was not, in fact, "a major recharge area." Ignoring the spurious nature of the claim, some commissioners and community leaders pushed for early go-ahead for over a dozen projects. SWFWMD attempted to slow the trend. "Green Swamp is a fine recharge area," its geo-hydrologist Gerald Parker explained. "Like a bucket of water, of course, when it is full it will not take more water, but every gallon that is drained off is not available for recharge or drinking." Governor Reuben O'D. Askew heeded the warnings and in September 1973 designated the swamp as a "first priority" for protection. The United States Soil and Water Conservation Service joined "the move to preserve Green Swamp from land speculators" in November. Having studied a number of developments, it concluded that "not one of the proposed seven had any appreciable amount of dry soil, and [that] it is questionable whether they have any means to provide for proper draining or sewage effluent disposal." Attorney General Robert Shevin meanwhile sought a temporary injunction in Circuit Judge Oliver L. Green's court to halt several projects but had to settle for an agreement with one developer to abide by certain limitations as it pursued announced plans.[31]

The debate accelerated in 1974 with announcement of a huge new development, a response by the governor and cabinet, and a frustrating stalemate. The announcement came in January by Land and Leisure, Inc. The company planned a $70 million residential and commercial project that would cover two thousand acres surrounding the intersection of I-4 and State Road 557A, a site located approximately five miles east of Polk City. Architects estimated that almost ten thousand persons would reside in the community within about five years. Governor Askew and the state cabinet decided in consequence that circumstances required them to act. They declared the Green Swamp an Area of Critical State Concern and designated it as one of the state's top four regions for protection. Then came the frustration. Charged with authority to enforce the mandate, the state's Department of Community Affairs proved timid in moving ahead. As one reporter would comment as late as 1991, "DCA has spent that last 17 years sitting on its bureaucratic behind."[32]

Widening Divides

Given so many distractions, it appears understandable that Polk Countians mostly failed to understand the severity of the environmental problems the county faced. The Disney-born economic boom naturally consumed a great deal of energy and required considerable attention, but so, too, did rifts within society at large. Whether the divide came between young and old, black and white, or those of one religious disposition and another, the chasms widened in the early 1970s and presaged mounting troubles to come.

To begin with, the Vietnam War—already so painfully etched into the county's experience—persisted as casualties mounted and the country tore itself in frustration. Finally in 1972 negotiations ensued that resulted on March 29, 1973, with the withdrawal of the last United States combat troops from that nation. "The longest and most controversial war in American history was over," one historian observed, "leaving in its wake a bitter legacy." As a part of that legacy, the toll of death continued as injuries eventuated into fatal consequences or else other circumstances produced equally deadly results. Major Gerald R. Olson of the 149th Field Artillery of the Florida National Guard, for example, paid with his life on October 9, 1973. Meanwhile, survivors and their loved ones coped with the conflict's continuing price, as terms such as Agent Orange (a toxic agent used during the war) slowly crept into the nation's vocabulary.[33]

Violence at home, in Polk and nationally, paralleled conflict abroad. Headlines repeatedly blared such declarations as "Polk Crime Figures Rise Dramatically." Estimates for 1973 alone saw murders up 140 percent; robberies increasing 33 percent; and assaults up 198 percent. Matters thereafter seemed only to grow worse. "In 1974," as the *Lakeland Ledger* noted, "the increase [in crimes] was faster than the population growth."

Illegal drug use contributed to the alarming state of affairs. Marijuana and cocaine suppliers constituted the principal targets of law enforcement activity, and record "busts" grabbed headlines and filled courtrooms. Other "controlled substances" commanded attention, too. "Police raided a laboratory in Mulberry [during October 1974] capable of producing one million methamphetamine (speed) pills a week," the *Ledger* reported. "Supplies covered by the raid were worth $1.7 million."[34]

For various reasons some criminal incidents naturally commanded greater attention than did others. Such was the case in 1971 when two armed men attempted to rob Florida Board of Regents Chairman D. Burke Kibler's Lake Hollingsworth home at Lakeland. Alerted to the situation by a family member, police soon found themselves in a gun battle that left one officer wounded. A gunman thereafter escaped temporarily with neighbor June Royal as a hostage. Fortunately, both assailants eventually were captured and Royal was released unharmed.[35]

By no means did the Kibler incident stand out for the intensity of its violence. On January 6, 1974—a day that would come to be called "Bloody Sunday"—three separate murders occurred within two hours at Lakeland, Wahneta, and Haines City. The greatest notoriety, though, likely stemmed from the September 1973 slaying during an attempted robbery of Lakeland furniture dealer James Carl Turman by furloughed state prisoner Willie Jasper Darden, who nearly murdered sixteen year old Philip Arnold as well. Darden's appeals of his January 1974 conviction reached the United States Supreme Court and extended until his 1988 execution. The *Orlando Sentinel* insisted that Darden's was "the most litigated death-row case in Florida history."[36]

One murder that occurred outside the county's bounds brought pause, as well, to those both appreciative of heroism and weary of crime. During World War Two, Fort Meade's James Henry Mills had earned the Medal of Honor for valor during combat in Italy. Now, on November 9, 1973, wrenching tragedy ended his life. "Mills and a friend stopped to help three men with car trouble near Gainesville, Florida," biographer Joe Spann explained. "The men robbed and savagely beat them, leaving them for dead inside Mills's car," he continued. "Badly injured, Mills crawled nearly half a mile to a nearby house for help." Spann concluded: "James Henry Mills died two days later in a Veterans Administration Hospital from the wounds he suffered at the hands of three unknown thugs. He was buried in Lakeland's Oak Hill Cemetery."[37]

Nonviolent crime seemed to proliferate along with its violent counterpart. William Reno's actions well illustrated the fact. The Miami man in 1974 leased Auburndale's unused "speedway property" on State Road 542. After Reno renovated the facility amid high expectations, residents then looked on as the entrepreneur pled guilty, as one report explained, "to charges that he was connected with an east coast auto and truck theft ring." Soon bankrupted, Reno left the speedway idle thereafter for nearly half a decade.[38]

More than a few citizens perceived crime in relaxed moral standards and in the service industries the evolution had spawned. The saga of Lakeland's "X-rated" theater typifies the point. Adult Cinemas, Inc. and operator Lee Hall announced in 1971 intentions to open the new establishment. Mayor Joe P. Ruthven thereupon declared that he "would not allow such a movie house in the 'All-American' city" and attempted to block the event, including the shutting off of electricity to the building. A circuit court injunction against the mayor followed in late December, and Hall promised a grand opening "in two weeks." Perhaps significantly, when Judge J. H. Willson issued his ruling, the only Lakeland official present was Ruthven.[39]

Innovations such as an X-rated theater and "adult" book stores deeply offended the religious and moral sentiments of numerous residents and did so at a time when, as explained in Chapter Seven, passionate debate over sex education in the public schools already sparked controversy. By summer 1972 at least one minister had approached the county commission, showing and describing "obscene pictures" and urging action "against the decline of the moral climate of the community." The next year the commission adopted a new obscenity ordinance, one that Sheriff Monroe Brannen quickly attempted to execute by raids "on two adult book stores and a theater in Lakeland." The results of

72. *Lakeland's mayor Joe P. Ruthven battled the spread of the "X-rated" movie industry at Lakeland during the early 1970s. He is seen here (seated at center) flanked by Commissioner Charles Whitten on the left and Commissioner Marvin Henderson on the right. Standing are (from left) Commissioners Charles Lake, Dwight Goleman, John S. Jackson, and James West.* LAKELAND PUBLIC LIBRARY.

prosecution, however, communicated mixed signals. In the first case to come to trial, jurors who reflected the county's diversity of opinion found themselves unable to reach a decision. The court thereupon declared a mistrial, and the public clamor continued for the time unsatisfied.[40]

The county's racial divide similarly experienced diversity of perspective, passionate debate, and lasting impact from events of the early 1970s. Significant milestones passed to the good. August 1970, for example, brought Polk its first African American attorney. Lakeland native Arthenia L. Joyner had graduated from the Florida A&M University School of Law in 1968 and achieved admission to the Florida Bar the next year. Joyner soon concentrated her practice at Tampa, but by 1973 Columbia University graduate Larry Jackson had arrived to fill the void created by her departure. Born at Fort Lauderdale, Jackson chose Lakeland because "I wanted to be in a small town like Lauderdale was when I was growing up there." Testing the Polk city on a personal visit, he found a surprise. "I talked to people in the community about how they'd feel about having a black lawyer in town," he recorded. "The feelings I got were very positive." An advocate for civil rights, Jackson later launched a newspaper and became the first black man to run for a Polk County judgeship. He served, as well, as the first African American to sit on the Lakeland Area Chamber of Commerce's board of directors.[41]

Other recognitions came to members of Polk's African American community. High on that list of honor came the name of James E. Stephens. Principal at Bartow's Union Academy from 1938 to 1968, Stephens in 1974 assumed the chairmanship of the Polk Community College board of trustees. Although no longer a Polk resident, Dr. James J. Gardener in 1971 received appointment by Governor Reuben Askew to the Florida Board of Regents. Raised at Pierce, Gardener in 1977 became the board's first black chairman. Advances came, as well, in the business world. To cite an example, in 1975 Mary E. Jones of Fort Meade, the daughter of Albert and Gladys L. Tucker,

73. *Attorney and activist Larry R. Jackson launched his Polk County legal practice in the early 1970s.* LAKELAND PUBLIC LIBRARY.

74. *Bartow's George H. Gause broke racial barriers through service as city councilman and mayor.* POLK COUNTY HISTORICAL *Association.*

emerged as Polk's first African American banker by accepting employment with Bartow's Citrus and Chemical Bank. Suggesting the promise of the rising generation, the preceding year Lakeland's Brenda Freeman had claimed the honor of Queen of Orange and Green at Florida A&M University. The same city's Nat Adderly meanwhile received well-deserved praise for founding the Child of the Sun Jazz Festival.[42]

Representation in local governments advanced for members of the black community beyond previous attainments. Of particular importance, Bartow's George H. Gause in 1971 enjoyed election by his fellow city commissioners (all of whom were white) to the position of mayor. The action made Gause Florida's first African American mayor of a majority-white town since the 1870s. "I have always looked upon human beings as human beings, not by race," he commented at the time. "And people have done the same for me." Lakeland's Dr. J. S. Jackson also won re-election to Lakeland's city commission in 1971. Early the next year he rose to the position of mayor when Charles Whitten resigned to take office as a county commissioner.[43]

Others soon found their ways into elective public service, and George Gause, for one, believed that by then barriers had begun to fall quickly. "Beginning in January," he insisted in December 1973, "[Polk will have] more black elected officials than any other county in the state, setting the pace for Florida." Gause cited not only himself and Jackson but also Haines City commissioner Claude E. Holmes, Lake Alfred's Harry Adamson, and Lakeland's Charles Coleman. Had Gause waited only a short while to make his statement, he could have added the name of Lemuel Geathers, elected in 1974 to Winter Haven's city commission.[44]

These advances unfortunately prompted groups such as the Ku Klux Klan to reinforce and expand their hate-based agendas. Cross burnings and threats against civil rights leaders such as Otis Williams and Willie Speed during 1970 evolved to KKK grand dragon John Paul Rogers's run for the Polk school board in 1972. Falling short in that effort, Rogers's supporters thereafter pushed their man unsuccessfully for selection as Lake Wales's police chief. In the years immediately following, Lakeland took on the guise in some eyes of a Klan haven. And, as *Florida Trend* magazine explained in 1979, "Some local political candidates during this decade have considered it the vogue to include the Klan in their advertised list of community memberships and civic activities." In 1975 the city's Ramada Inn hosted the United Klans of America's statewide convention, a function that attracted three hundred attendees. Meanwhile, Lakeland's black residents, now a potent force in municipal politics, shrugged off "the annoyance of Klan demonstrations."[45]

What could not be denied, though, was that Klan activity reflected a continuing rise in racial tensions. The school integration crisis, already creating havoc by 1970, escalated for several years. A walkout by black Lakeland High School students in 1971, for instance, developed into a boycott. Additional walkouts at Kathleen High School and Lakeland Junior High School came thereafter, as did the opening of a "freedom school" at Alex Harper's Greater St. Paul's Missionary Baptist Church. Mayor Joe Ruthven and Commissioner John S. Jackson helped to mediate the dispute with Harper, Joel E. Atkins, Otis Williams, and others playing crucial roles. Then, Mulberry High School troubles led National Association for the Advancement of Colored People leaders to promote a boycott of all Polk public schools. The turmoil had reached Lake Wales by year's end, resulting in the call of "a state of civil emergency." The unrest revived at many schools in 1972. At Bartow fights, firebombs, and fear highlighted a deteriorating scene. Felicitously, an interracial parents' group named TEMPO (Teens, Educators, Mommas, and Poppas Organization) formed at Lakeland and endeavored with some success to "seek solutions to the problems." Tensions eased slowly, but the school system remained in tumult at mid-decade as monetary shortages produced fiscal crises and a hiring freeze. School Superintendent W. W. "Bill" Read by then had paid the price for the problems. Voters in 1972 had ousted him in favor of North Central Area Superintendent Homer Addair.[46]

Even eventualities that seemed marks of genuine progress on one side of the racial divide by the early 1970s could appear starkly different on the other. Lakeland's Civic Center offers an example. Hailed as "the finest public indoor mass facility in Central Florida," the complex first welcomed patrons in November 1974. The gala opening celebration, on the other hand, witnessed black community protests that the historic Moorehead neighborhood had been destroyed to make room for the center. The resentments lingered. "I have very fond memories of the neighborhood," Carolynne Mather recollected almost three decades later. "I remember the togetherness, the way neighbors were close-knit."

Some politicians involved in the decision quickly came to understand just how deeply those lingering resentments were felt. "George Trask and I both ran for state Senate seats," Joe Ruthven commented, "and both of us lost." He added, "It was a big, big controversy and the city was divided right down the middle."[47]

Leadership

Although the decade commenced with a Polk leader projecting himself upon the national stage, county government's credibility suffered new reverses during its first half. Stirring pride, state senator Lawton Chiles walked across the state and into Florida voters' hearts on the way to his 1970 election to the United States Senate. In doing so Chiles replaced the county's retiring United States Senator, Spessard Holland of Bartow. Representative Bob Brannen in the meantime captured Chiles's state senate seat, and state representative William H. "Bill" Bevis of Fort Meade earned the first of two terms on the Florida Public Service Commission. Heralding another—a very different county political tradition—a grand

jury in 1971 indicted Brannen on eight counts of income tax evasion and conspiracy. His ultimate conviction, though, involved obstructing justice by indirectly seeking to influence a prospective juror during the tax evasion trial. Brannen received a sentence of four years in prison, but federal judge Gerald B. Tjoflat later reduced the term to less than six months. Lakeland's N. Curtis Peterson, Jr., succeeded to the senate seat and served with distinction until 1991.[48]

75. *Portrayed here about 1990, Lawton Chiles carried on Polk's tradition of state and national leadership forged by Park Trammell and Spessard L. Holland through service as United States Senator from 1971 to 1989 and as governor of Florida from 1991 to 1998. With Chiles is his "confidant and most powerful aide" Rhea Grafton Chiles. FLORIDA TREND.*

Problems with voting and recounts gave rise to concerns in these years, a circumstance that also had occurred previously. Officials acting during the September 1970 Democratic primary election simply turned voters away from a polling place where "all three machines were reported inoperable." At the same election Frank Wesley demanded a recount in his state legislative race with former University of Florida football great Larry Libertore after workers discovered a "1,000-vote error" that made Libertore "the clear winner." Wesley's pleas failed to accomplish their purpose, and Libertore went on to represent Polk in the Florida House of Representatives from 1970 through 1974.[49]

Politicians' surprising actions also reminded residents of old Polk traditions. State representative Ray Mattox of Winter Haven, for example, announced in 1974 that he "wanted to be the Ralph Nader of the right" and launched a fundraising campaign aimed at accumulating $250,000 "to spread the gospel of free enterprise." Frustrated by the response, Mattox acknowledged that "it's been hard to stir up interest." One-time state senator Ben Hill Griffin, Jr., two years earlier had leapt into the governor's race as qualifying closed. "Some of my friends can't understand why I'm doing this and others have even snickered at me," Griffin admitted, "but I was born during a hurricane and some people say I've been living in a hurricane ever since. I'm not going to stop now." One newspaper labeled the run as "eccentric—and unsuccessful," adding that "the voters gave him a mandate to stay in Frostproof."[50]

The Republican party showed growing strength but could not manage to gain a permanent toehold in government. In 1970 former Polk County Democratic Executive Committee Chairman Wallace Storey bolstered GOP ranks when he joined the party. On the other hand, County Commissioner Joe Sargeant, appointed by Governor Claude R. Kirk, announced his retirement during the same year in the face of certain loss. After the governor placed C. C. "Doc" Dockery on the school board to replace the late Seth McKeel, Dr. Robert A. Buccino recaptured the seat for Democrats. His party swept all other county offices that year. The scene had changed little by mid-decade. Declaring party preference in 1975, 73,001 voters proclaimed Democratic loyalty while only 19,335 opted for the Republican banner.[51]

Advances by women anticipated the immediate future far more so than did Republican political fortunes. In June 1972 Jan Mann assumed office as Lake Wales's first female commissioner. Marjorie L. Jaeger joined the Polk County Board of Zoning Adjustment in August as its first female member. Republican activist Alice Faye Redd achieved distinction by her selection as one of the nation's "10 outstanding women," and Vastie Lyle became Winter Haven's pioneering woman city clerk. Louise Bennett meanwhile directed municipal affairs at Dundee as city manager. During 1973, Lillie Judy took up the mayor's gavel at Davenport; Frances Hancock claimed a seat on the city commission at Auburndale; Barbara Periman won a place on the Bartow commission; and Peggy Brown did the same at Lakeland.[52]

The advance of women into leadership positions persisted and grew in 1974 and 1975. As reporter Kai Wallace observed when the first of the years closed and the second commenced, "It's been a good year for women in Polk County." During the period, attorney Susan Roberts received appointment to the Lakeland municipal court bench and Sylvia Eason joined the Mulberry commission as the town's first female officer. Beverly B. Burnsed narrowly lost a state house of representatives race but became Polk Community College's first female trustee. Winter Haven police chief Hamp Rogers broke new ground by placing female police officers Mary Mariani and Judy Ryder in uniform, giving each a gun and a squad car,

and assigning them on shift "with the same responsibilities as a man." Sandra Woodard emerged as the county's first female detective. Charla Mercer headed negotiations for the Polk Education Association, and Barbara Costello took the oath as Haines City's first women commissioner. Jane Eden became Dundee's second female city manager. And, among other achievements, Winter Haven's Mrs. Gabe Stewart III presided as vice chair of the state Republican party.[53]

It was a good thing, too, that women increasingly claimed a leadership role. Stormier times lay ahead for Polk's residents, and effective leadership otherwise would prove difficult to find. The county's post-Disney roller coaster ride promised adventures ahead; yet, national and local problems left the county yearning for some sense of peace. The status quo might manage to maintain itself for a while, but serious crises lay not too distant on the horizon.

76. *Lakeland city commissioner Peggy Brown's election to office typified the growing influence of women in public service during the 1970s.* LAKELAND PUBLIC LIBRARY.

77. *Civic Center construction destroyed Lakeland's historic neighborhood of Moorehead, the core of African American settlement in the city from the early 1880s to 1971. Recognition came only belatedly that such urban renewal projects brought loss as well as gain. Not until the 2002 ceremony shown here did the community properly mark the site and reflect officially on the area's rich heritage.* LAKELAND LEDGER.

"what matters has happened"

CHAPTER 9

Unsettling Progress, 1975-1980

The gift of growth and prosperity, yearned for and promoted by government and business interests alike, began to stir concerns in Polk County as the decade of the 1970s neared its end. At home, mostly unhurried life experienced within a beautiful environment of rural and small town pleasures continued on a day-to-day basis. Yet, the world seemed at times to have gone mad. Crime, racial tensions, a divide that had opened between generations, moral challenges, and other developments of the era pressed their weight ever more heavily upon the collective conscience. Coming as it did atop that foundation, the pace of local change increasingly stirred anxieties and a softly aching sense of loss. Now, greater numbers of residents felt the need to scrutinize the price that Polk was paying for the realization of earlier dreams. Questions as to direction and leadership emerged as crucial ones, while the county's people searched for the proper guide to follow as they made their way into an uncertain and vaguely ominous future.

Although that future turned out somewhat differently than expected, the experts agreed in the late 1970s that Polk stood on the brink of phenomenal growth. The national economy might suffer anemia and the ravages of inflation, but more so than not, as one headline writer expressed it, "In Polk, The Boom Signs Are Intensifying." The *Tampa Tribune* summed up the situation as it then appeared. "Polk County," it informed readers in 1979, "lies in what economic officials say is the fastest growing part of the state," The state Division of Economic Development agreed. "Polk's economy is ripe for growth," its report asserted. County Planner George Stahlman, dismissing more modest projections, insisted in 1979 that 1990 would see one-half million residents competing for Polk's bounty, up from an estimated 284,000 when he spoke. Land availability seemed the major problem. "Urban sprawl still has room to spread in Polk," one study proclaimed, "before it encroaches on the resource base for citrus, phosphate and cattle." Still, it noted further, "considerable land is already tied up in phosphate, citrus and cattle [and] the county needs to insure suitable and efficient space designated for industrial use." Another report issued in 1980 stated the matter more succinctly. "Polk County," it declared, "is expected to shuck off its cowboy and cracker image for suburban city life."[1]

Many residents perceived such forecasts as threatening, preferring not to lose the quality of life that they loved and to which they had grown accustomed. "Life here is not quite so urban, but we do have the advantage of being close to the cities," LaCona Raines Padgett explained. "We are able to be acquainted with people, to have more of a personal, one-to-one dealing with people," she continued. "We were discussing this last night. It's a beautiful climate, handy to things, yet the traffic is not so bad that we dread going anywhere." Padgett added: "To me, this is the real Florida. It's full of the old southern hospitality. The people are warm. We all stick together, especially in time of trouble. People here are very neighborly." She concluded: "Polk County and the style of life in Polk County, now that's the real Florida."[2]

Although residents generally appreciated what the county offered— despite continuing problems of pollution, political leadership, crime, and what have you—they increasingly split in their opinions about how the future might change the equation. "It's such a great place to live that more and more people are coming here," Al Bellotto commented. "All of a sudden, we're not being able to be as free as we were. I was born and raised here, and I love it, but this people-problem really bothers me." Somewhat to the contrary, Gene Robson shared Bellotto's love for the place but saw few problems ahead. "I don't think the angels could make it no better," he informed an interviewer. "Actually, I don't see anything for the future except life being better. I don't have nothing but love for the county and the life it's given me and my family."[3]

The growing sense that essential elements of Polk's heritage and social fabric stood in jeopardy helped to work a small but meaningful change in perspective for many residents. The change involved a question of loss. "The world was changing faster than people could grasp," Fort Meade's Lawrence Sthreshley remembered, "and very few people were paying attention to what we were letting go of without thinking." Development and urban renewal of the 1950s, 1960s, and early 1970s had produced many results, including the slow acceleration of life's pace. In the process, the thinking of the times had permitted venerable structures that recalled the county's past to be cast away in the interest of what most believed to be progress. In the case of Lakeland's Civic Center, the entire neighborhood of Moorehead had suffered destruction as a result. Now, historical preservation began to command a priority, at least in some instances.[4]

Two incidents, while isolated and of direct significance only to local communities, help to point out the nature of this dynamic. At Lake Alfred, supermarkets long had rendered obsolete the 1923 "cash grocery store" operated by Q. W. Brian and son Van Brian. "The weeds grew and nobody cut them, the paint peeled and nobody repainted," an onlooker recorded, "and Van and his boy Bobby passed the derelict daily and remembered with some pain how it had looked when granddaddy had it." At the time, one abandoned structure mattered little. "The pain was shared even by the townspeople who really didn't care much about the building either way," the onlooker continued. "It was condemned and pronounced an eyesore, but enforcing clean-up ordinances was a problem since they couldn't catch the owner." As late as 1973 the razing of the structure appeared assured. Then, Brian family members decided to take matters into their own hands. They repurchased and rehabilitated the building "like granddaddy had it," for themselves to operate as an antique store and for their community to enjoy. "Van just shudders a bit when asked about the cost of the purchase, restoration and the likelihood of the antique shop ever paying off the investment," a reporter noted, "but the building and the 'fooling with antiques is in our blood so I guess it doesn't matter.'" The reporter added, "What matters has happened."[5]

Saving the Brian grocery store depended upon a single family's initiative, but enough of a shift had occurred in public perception of the importance of local heritage by 1975 that the community of Frostproof could join together to save one of its landmarks. The story unfolded after the Polk County School Board announced plans to demolish the town's 1926 high school building. Preservation advocates organized and protested the decision, convincing the school board in 1978 to sell the building to the town for one dollar. A fundraising campaign then produced $30,000 for renovations of the first floor, and Frostproof thereby created for itself a new city hall. "That building," alumna June Felt would exclaim two decades after the high school's original demolition announcement, "is the greatest thing we have in Frostproof."[6]

More than minimal credit for the increasing sensitivity to historical preservation and greater appreciation of Polk's past must be afforded to the Polk County Historical Association. That group organized in 1974 specifically to preserve "our rapidly vanishing historical heritage." Representatives of every area of the county gathered under Chairman Glenn Hooker's leadership to provide a continuing organizational framework for advocacy and collective interest. "In order to band together, local historians from each community, about 50 in number, assembled in Bartow on Sunday afternoon, June 23, 1974, and the PCHA was born," Hooker recalled. "The common bond of these volunteer people was a love for Polk County's past, coupled with an intense desire to see it perpetuated." By popular acclaim Hooker received the association's presidency, with Elizabeth Brown as secretary and Mrs. Robert E. Powell as treasurer. Founding directors included Carl Allen, Auburndale; Elizabeth Cody Moore, Babson Park; Mary Holland, Bartow; Louie D. Berry, Davenport; Walter Crutchfield, Fort Meade; James H. Gardner, Lakeland; Dr. and Mrs. E. C. Burns, Lake Wales; Louise Garrett, Lake Alfred; Mrs.

78. *Early in the existence the Polk County Historical Association moved to construct a historical and genealogical library at Bartow, a project ultimately redirected when the availability of the 1909 courthouse for library and museum purposes rose as a possibility. Here, association and community leaders gathered in late 1980 to break ground for the proposed library. Present were (left to right) Bartow City Manager James R. O'Connor, Bartow Chamber of Commerce Executive Director Mayme Burdin, Bartow chamber president Tim Murphy, banker Laura Barnhill of Winter Haven, historical librarian LaCona Raines, PCHA members Lawrence F. Sthreshley Jr., county commissioner Ernie Caldwell, Polk County Historical Commission member Wilbur Purcell, county judge Randall McDonald, Polk County Historical Quarterly editor and PCHC member Louise K. Frisbie, state representative C. Fred Jones, PCHA president Glenn Hooker, clerk of courts E. D. "Bud" Dixon, unidentified, and Bartow city commissioner William R. Goddard.* POLK COUNTY HISTORICAL QUARTERLY.

Henri Sparkman, Mulberry; Mrs. Myron Miller, Winter Haven; Carroll Yawn, Winter Haven; and Mrs. H. L. Reeves, Frostproof. Getting right to its task, the association immediately commenced publication and dissemination of the well-illustrated and smartly written *Polk County Historical Quarterly* under Louise K. Frisbie's farsighted editorship.[7]

The national bicentennial in 1976 offered the PCHA and other historically minded organizations, individuals, and communities a handy focus for raising public awareness of local history and its importance. On its part, the association held local history seminars, as well as launching an oral taping program and a campaign to collect historic photographs. Meanwhile, several local histories reached publication as did the county's first photographic history, Louise Frisbie's *Yesterday's Polk County*. Municipalities naturally sought to commemorate the national celebration with initiatives of local importance. Mulberry, for instance, developed a bicentennial park, while Bartow reconstructed Fort Blount to commemorate its original 1851 settlement. Sometimes programs evolved with time into far more than originally planned. At Lake Wales, to cite an example, Mimi Hardman chaired the local bicentennial commission. From the experience she conceived the idea of a Lake Wales Depot Museum based at the city's longtime train station. Over time the concept grew to encompass multiple structures and to inspire other preservation endeavors of importance to Lake Wales residents.[8]

79. *Civic activist Mimi Hardman and fellow volunteers transformed an abandoned train station into the Lake Wales Depot Museum.* POLK COUNTY HISTORICAL ASSOCIATION.

Finding Guidance

Looking to the past for answers to questions of the present and future offered a plausible alternative to other options as Polk Countians perceived them in 1975 and 1976. All around concerns of previous years appeared to be growing in severity and in resistance to resolution. Crime, to name one sore spot, jumped from the pages of newspapers and from television screens during local news broadcasts to assault wary residents. The "Ski Mask Gang," one of many criminal combinations, long would be remembered for launching a nine-month crime wave throughout the region. As the *Lakeland Ledger* reported, "The gang . . . pillaged, raped and murdered their way through terror-filled nights for many Central Florida families." Another newspaper added detail. "The masked [black] men preyed on white victims, robbing at least 16 homes, killing two men and raping five women," it related. "The robbers poured Liquid Plumber in one victim's eyes, burning away her eyesight," the story continued. "Frightened homeowners bought guns and barred their doors," the account added. Law enforcement officers eventually caught four individuals, including one woman and one juvenile. A jury in 1976 sentenced the two adult men, Daniel Morris Thomas and Lee Otis Martin, to one hundred years each in prison. In a separate trial Thomas received a death sentence and met with execution in 1986.[9]

The Ski Mask Gang barely had been disposed of before other sensational crimes burst to attention. February 1976 saw officers crushing "a Lakeland-based state auto-truck-airplane theft conspiracy." The arrests covered thirty persons, and, reportedly, the ring's take amounted to "the largest ever in dollar value in the United States." The next year matters grew worse. "Polk County's reputation for crime is no secret, but even law enforcement officers were shocked at 1977's crop of arson slayings, child killings and rapes at gunpoint," *Lakeland Ledger* reported Bob Weiss asserted. "It's been a year of sex crimes," Weiss added. "One brutal crime tended to run into the next." From there, the trend continued through the decade.[10]

Law enforcement, in line with voter demands, meanwhile concentrated a good bit of its attention on crime related to the sale and use of illegal drugs. Manifesting their zeal, Lakeland police took to attending rock concerts at the Lakeland Civic Center. They did so, according to one report, "not to hear the music, but to arrest those smoking marijuana." Even when police seized drugs, the final word on the subject had not yet been spoken. In January 1977, 600 pounds of marijuana disappeared from Circuit Court Clerk Bud Dixon's evidence locker. Five months later authorities arrested two former sheriff's deputies for the crime. When other deputies legally seized four tons of marijuana near Indian Lake Estates in April 1979, it was said to be "the largest haul of marijuana on record." Then, when the deputies grabbed more than 500,000 methaqualone tablets from a Polk County-based drug smuggling operation the next year, authorities termed that event "the biggest such bust in the country."[11]

80. *Multi-talented Clerk of Courts E. D. "Bud" Dixon administered Polk's courts for nearly three decades, guided the county's historical community, pushed for dedication of the 1909 courthouse as the Polk County Historical Museum, and managed to find time to cheer local gatherings with country tunes that he sang while accompanying himself on the guitar. LAKELAND LEDGER.*

Law enforcement's ability to address drug or any other crimes unfortunately met with renewed testing in the decade's second half. The period commenced in 1975 with two sheriff's department officials finding themselves indicted either for perjury or for other criminal charges. Convicted, a captain was banned from law enforcement as part of his sentence. Later that year a deputy similarly endured prosecution and conviction, in his case for petty larceny of a Lake Wales grocery store. In the meantime, the department's reputation for leaks, as least as rumor had it, had prompted a law enforcement organization that shared information on a statewide basis to suspend Polk from membership. Not long thereafter Sheriff Monroe Brannen learned that the Florida Department of Law Enforcement had arrested forty-five persons connected with a Lakeland gambling ring and had done so without notifying his department in advance.[12]

Even the sheriff soon found himself in trouble. Published reports circulated in late 1975 alleging that Brannon had instructed deputies Melton Godwin and John Baggett "to look into rumors" about one of the sheriff's potential electoral opponents, former Bartow police chief Marvin Pittman. The reports also disclosed that two private detectives had conspired to discredit Pittman. The matter simmered as the election season unfolded. Then, in August 1976 a grand jury indicted Brannen, Godwin, Baggett, and investigator James A. McCall. Charges included perjury and criminal conspiracy to expose Pittman "to hatred, contempt and ridicule." The sheriff blamed "a politically motivated grand jury" for the prosecution. An October trial appeared to support his contention when a jury took a mere twenty-five minutes to acquit Brannen of perjury. Defense attorney Wallace Storey declared, "It was a just decision," and Judge Gunter Stephenson subsequently quashed the indictment that had charged the sheriff and others with conspiracy.[13]

Sheriff Brannen's precedent-setting sixteen-year career, despite the verdict, had reached its conclusion. In September primaries former Florida Highway Patrol trooper Louie Mims had defeated the veteran lawman. Returned with his acquittal to the office from which Governor Reuben O'D. Askew had suspended him in favor of Lakeland attorney Quillian S. Yancey, Brannen quickly resigned. The governor thereupon appointed Mims to fill out the term. Even then the sheriff's office contended with questions as to its credibility. In early 1978 three ex-deputies charged "that several current deputies were involved in a beef theft ring; that an assistant state attorney took a bribe not to prosecute a marijuana case; that guns seized as evidence and lent to deputies had not been recovered when the deputies left the department; and that members of the state attorney's staff used marijuana." A grand jury found "no evidence to support the charges."[14]

Indicative of the times, the intensity of moral outrage voiced at crime, drug use, and law enforcement corruption found expression almost as profoundly when it came to "dirty" dancing. The matter centered on an announcement in January 1976 that Lakeland's Peek-a-Boo Lounge would begin to feature "topless" entertainment. Ministers and church members rose in protest under the Reverend J. B. Buffington's leadership. They demanded a county "anti-topless law" at the earliest possible moment. So strident did the campaign become that it generated 1,500 letters to the *Lakeland Ledger*'s editor in February alone, and by March the county commission had obliged the protesters with an ordinance. Since a similar regulation enacted in Lee County then faced court challenge, enforcement awaited a Florida supreme court decision. That panel upheld Lee's position in 1978, Sheriff Mims attempted to enforce the ban, and more court battles ensued. Meanwhile, tempers flared and outrage explored new bounds.[15]

Long before then, the county's capacity for such outrage had come to the attention of music promoter Richard Bichler. He naively had proposed in 1977 to stage "The Labor of Love Musical Festival" near the Lakeland Airport on a Labor Day weekend. Bichler's temerity immediately drew Reverend Buffington's response. The minister published a two-page advertisement in the *Ledger* warning of "the moral degradation that could occur at such an event." Fur flew. By the time Sheriff Mims announced that he "just didn't have the manpower to police the 50,000 persons expected," Bichler prepared to throw in the towel and go

elsewhere. "I'm not gonna stir up a hornet's nest," he informed reporters. "I learned my lesson. There will be a concert, we've already got the
property," he added. "There are other people who are more receptive
than those in Polk County."16

Even with the clamor arising from all of these controversial aspects
of Polk life, news of the environment and its problems gained ground
in public awareness and contributed to anxieties and frustration. Admittedly, some of the news was good. In 1971 the state legislature had
approved a severance tax on phosphate in a deal cemented on a quiet
visit to the county by Governor Askew. The agreement came thanks to
the labors of industry attorney Chesterfield Smith. "The severance tax
clearly was inevitable," Smith's partner Burke Kibler explained, "and
the industry wanted to get the best deal that could be gotten." The arrangement permitted the industry to use a portion of the tax revenues for
voluntary reclamation of mined land. Four years later 20,000 acres had
been reclaimed, with 29 percent of the property devoted to residential
use. Developments such as The Bluffs at Christina, located south of
Lakeland, highlighted the possibilities for further accommodation of a
growing population.17

The legislature revisited the severance tax in 1975 and amended the
law in a substantial manner. It first required that companies reclaim all
land mined thereafter and, in the case of 83,000 acres of unreclaimed
land mined previously, conferred responsibility on the state to determine
how best to move ahead. The law doubled the severance tax and created
a Phosphate Land Reclamation Commission appointed by the governor
and chaired by Charles Hendry to plan future action. This raised local
hopes that the "moonscape" evident in many portions of the county
soon might be transformed into lovely vistas.18

At that point a snag developed. Earlier warnings of radium contamination of local ground water resulting from phosphate mining briefly
had captured attention and then had faded. In October 1975, the Office
of Radiation Programs of the federal Environmental Protection Agency
sounded renewed alarms when it concluded that "radioactive gas coming out of the ground at reclaimed mine sites could be hazardous to the
health of anyone living in a house built on that land." Independent experts
confirmed the problem. As the Southern States Energy Board's Kenneth J.
Nemeth noted, "This is a crucial matter that should not be taken lightly."
Yet, local officials and industry spokesmen downplayed its importance.
County Commission Chairman Charles Whitten, speaking for the board,
telegraphed a "wait-and-see attitude." As one newspaper characterized

Whitten's words, "The Polk County Commission will take no stand on this one." The state, too, opted not to grant the EPA's request that building on reclaimed sites be discontinued, and not for another decade would the term "radon gas" become one of common usage among residents.[19]

The "big red hole" proved less easy to ignore. The area south of Bartow that in previous years had experienced dramatic drops in the water table seemed to be growing. At the midpoint of the 1970s the hole measured thirteen miles in length and seven in width. Water table levels had reached within twenty-five feet of sea level where the average stood one hundred feet or more just twenty miles to the north. No one yet could project with any assurance of accuracy the future implications of the environmental dilemma, but when Lake Garfield, one of the county's largest lakes, "dried up and vanished, as if its plug had been pulled" in May 1976, the signs appeared none too good.[20]

One problem thought to have been resolved, at least partially, suddenly moved back to the front burner. In November 1977 the Florida supreme court struck down state restrictions on building in the Green Swamp, finding the underlying law "unconstitutionally vague." Developers swarmed to realize opportunities. It turned out, though, that some unscrupulous land dealers already had been mass marketing "useless" lots within the swamp's bounds to unsuspecting Puerto Ricans using "brilliant color photographs of Walt Disney World" in promotional brochures. Prices for homesites ranged up to ten times assessed values.[21]

Nature, too, proved capricious. Normal rain beginning in 1976 appeared to lift the decade's dry cycle, but icy conditions then lashed the county in January 1977, lowering temperatures into the upper 10s and raining snow down up residents. The freeze, calculated as the worse since 1962, destroyed 30 percent of fruit ripening on trees. In May 1978 a different natural phenomenon produced devastation, as well. A tornado touched down first at Old Lakeland Road and Thornhill Road before spinning northeast. At Auburndale the twister heavily damaged the middle school before dissipating itself. Fortunately no children were present at the school, but the tornado had claimed one victim in Margaret Schnaare, who had sought shelter in a storage shed.[22]

Political Consequences

In an environment that more and more seemed so contrary to peaceful pursuits, government's inability to address problems meaningfully reached a crisis point. At mid-decade reports described trouble at every hand. "Political turmoil and unrest touched nearly every Polk County municipality in 1975," the *Orlando Sentinel* advised at year's end. Recall efforts aimed to oust mayors at Bartow and Lake Wales, nepotism claims split Eagle Lake, Dundee's mayor blasted the local police for operating a speed trap, two Lake Wales commissioners found themselves indicted, and so forth. By contrast some concerns seemed less urgent. "Lakeland and Winter Haven, among the least controversial cities in the county, had problems," the *Sentinel* acknowledged, "but not of the same proportion as the other cities." Subsequent experience reflected the same tone. In 1977, for instance, Eagle Lake appointed its twelfth police chief in eight years. Winter Haven that year drew unwanted attention when published reports disclosed that its police department had hired newspaper reporter Barbara Eidson as an undercover police officer. Bartow commissioners resigned to protest financial disclosure requirements; Mulberry's administrative problems left it beleaguered; Auburndale grappled with overflowing sewage; Lake Alfred coped with water pollution; and, among other examples, Dundee's administration "found itself under nearly continuous attack."[23]

Rancor and confusion elevated to such a level foreshadowed political upheaval, and Polk voters proved more than willing to play their part. Upsets and turnovers dotted the political landscape. Women especially demanded and received a greater role in public affairs, a development not too surprising given the fact that for much of the late 1970s the county's Lois Cowles Harrison served as state president of Florida's League of Women Voters. Suggesting the general trend, at Lakeland in 1976 Peggy Brown took charge as the city's first female mayor since Lois Searle a decade earlier. One year later, after Mayor Charles A. Coleman passed away, Carrie Roberts Oldham accepted an appointment to fill the vacancy. Quickly elected to a term in her own right, Oldham went on during 1980-1981 to serve as Lakeland's first African American female mayor.[24]

As illustrated by Lakeland's example, African Americans too made gains in elective local office. Notably, and in addition to Coleman's and Oldham's achievements, former Bartow mayor George H. Gause created precedent in 1977 by becoming the first black member of the Polk County school board. Albert Kirkland did the same the next year by breaking the racial barrier on Lake Wales's city commission. By 1980 Lemuel Geathers presided as Winter Haven's mayor. Each of these individuals sensed that real change had begun to occur, given time's passage and the challenges faced by county residents. Geathers recalled a white man during the period telling him that "I think you're the best qualified person for the job, but I can't vote for you because it's against everything I've believed in all my life." The now-veteran politician responded simply, "Go back and tell others that I [am] the most qualified for the job." Oldham offered a more philosophical overview. "We had entered a new era when minorities were more accepted," she reflected. "People now don't look at the color but at the quality of the individual."[25]

Changeover seemed the rule in every direction. In 1976 Winter Haven banker Andrew Ireland, for instance, defeated state representative Ray Mattox and others in a contest to succeed James Haley as Polk's delegate to the United States House of Representatives. Hitting the ground running, in only a short time the freshman congressman was said to be especially popular with Democratic House Speaker Thomas P. "Tip" O'Neill. State legislative contests also involved turnovers and precedent-setting results. The delegation remained entirely Democrat, but Beverly B. Burnsed defeated Gene Roberts to become its first female member. At the same time state representative Wendell Watson suffered defeat at the hands of Gene Ready. Young Bob Crawford took a third house seat in a runoff with Les Dunson.[26]

Women managed breakthroughs in county offices, as well, with change there reflecting the ongoing political revolution generally. Susan Wadsworth Roberts, recently appointed to a county judgship, experienced little difficulty in her first electoral foray. Helen Gienau bested Eloy Delgado to replace Blanche Work as supervisor of elections, and Nancy Simmons won Robert Buccino's school board seat in a race with Joan Buccino. Woman power also fueled Bernadine Spanjers's triumph over Democrat Royce Beasley for a second seat on the school panel, earning her honors as the first Republican ever elected to countywide office. Completing that board's transforma-

81. *One of numerous women to emerge victorious in Polk County politics during the mid-1970s, Helen Gienau (seen here at right) succeeded longtime supervisor of elections Blanche M. Work (at left) in January 1977. HELEN GIENAU.*

tion, Fort Meade's Dan Moody claimed an additional seat from Robert Estes.[27]

Voters reserved a healthy measure of their ire for the county commission. The major race on the ballot in 1976 pitted political novice Brenda Taylor against veteran commissioner Floyd Woods. "I was listening to the radio as the returns started to come in," Taylor remembered. "I elevated from a 'lowly housewife' to a 'business executive' before the evening was over." The changes had not yet played out fully. In December twenty-two year commission veteran J. B. Thornhill announced his resignation for health reasons, and Governor Askew designated Ralph Stalnaker to sit in his stead. Voters again had their say in 1978, when another "upstart political novice" who relied upon a "grassroots campaign" and a frustration-fueled "taxpayers revolt" ousted Stalnaker. In the process Ernie Caldwell climbed over Delgado and Thornhill to reach the runoff with the incumbent.[28]

When combined with the impact of the untimely death of commission chairman Aldine Combee in an 1971 automobile accident, the electoral revolutions of 1976 and 1978 infused county government with youthful energy and reoriented the county commission toward new perspectives and approaches. "It was a year of transition for the county commission," political writer Keith Moyer explained of 1977. He added, "The board took several progressive steps." Among them, the new commission attempted to organize county government more professionally. The board stepped away from traditional "good old boy" politics by implementing a workable affirmative action policy. It also redesignated its administrative assistant Cecil Lewis as "county administrator," conferring upon him supervisory responsibility for all employees working for the commission as well as authority for hiring and firing. Soon, the members also tackled growth management. Their decision, given the flood of newcomers expected to pour into the county, was to adopt guidelines for regional development that exceeded the restrictions mandated by the state.[29]

Not all of Polk's governmental bodies, whatever new blood they might have contained, reacted as sensitively to African American concerns as did the county commission in adopting and enforcing its affirmative action guidelines. Mulberry, Fort Meade, and Lake Wales found their municipal authorities subjected to suits for racial discrimination in 1978 and 1979. The litigation—brought by a Washington, D.C., law firm on behalf of local plaintiffs—mostly charged biased allocation of services and improvements, especially in the area of recreation. Bartow found a happier path to resolving similar questions. There, a Concerned

Citizens Civic Council led by C. C. Corbett agreed to forego a suit "if communications lines could be kept open." City officials responded by "stepping up their campaign to improve city services in Bartow's black sections."[30]

The school board came in for its share of problems, as well. The relatively inexperienced panel found itself operating beginning in January 1977 under the leadership of Lakeland's Ted Aggelis. Benefitting himself from only three years' experience, Aggelis brought to the job of chairman what appeared to many to be a deeply held opposition to racial integration and a lack of finesse in discourse and the conduct of sensitive negotiations. Only months were required before tempers flared despite board member George Gause's well-intentioned attempts at mediation. Debates concerning "cross-busing," "cluster schools," and "the neighborhood school concept" drew crowds and headlines. Given Aggelis's rhetoric, white backlash at integration jumped to a new level. "Within a couple of weeks," system historian James V. Holton discovered, "enrollments at local private schools soared." Florida's Ku Klux Klan grand dragon John Paul Rogers, an unsuccessful school board candidate five years earlier, joined hundreds of parents in demanding an end to busing. Aggelis then led the board in 1978 in an attempt to bill the federal government for desegregation costs. The empty gesture availed nothing. As historian Holton concluded, "Polk County learned to accept the costs of integration."[31]

Doubtlessly the school board experience frustrated George Gause severely, although many of the women who assumed office or else pioneered in jobs traditionally reserved for men could have felt compassion and understanding. Brenda Taylor, for one, credited her fellow county commission members for their acceptance but noted gender-based problems nonetheless. "After the [first] board meeting, I sat down at a totally empty desk in a chair that was way too big for me," she recalled. "It only took me five years," Taylor added, "to get my own chair to fit." While male commissioners accommodated their female colleague in the panel's deliberations and activities, the same did not prove true for all. "Developers and other businessmen seemed to have trouble," Taylor explained. "I felt at first that they weren't comfortable discussing big-time business with me."[32]

Women venturing into law enforcement particularly found the going tough. Lawrence Crow, then a supervisor on the Lakeland police force, recalled the situation when that city hired its first two female officers in 1978. "[Women cops] were tolerated but not accepted," he commented.

"Initially, I think there was a distrust by male officers," Crow continued. "They didn't feel they would back them up or feel they could protect them." Accordingly, "Schedules were made so women always worked in zones adjoining areas where men patrolled." Crow added, "That just goes to show how much their ability was doubted." One of those new hires, Debra Henson, determined not to let the situation get the best of her. In time, her persistence paid off. "The guys realized they could count on me," she informed an interviewer. "I jumped right in. I could also run under clotheslines—my short little legs can really move." Henson moved up in the department almost as quickly as she moved under clotheslines. Within two decades she occupied the position of deputy chief.[33]

82. *Judge Susaan Wadsworth Roberts being sworn into office during January 1977 by Judge Clifton M. Kelly, while Randall McDonald and Dennis Maloney await their turns.* BARTOW POLK COUNTY DEMOCRAT.

Other women found circumstances more conducive to professional advancement than did Debra Henson in her early law enforcement years. Judge Susan Roberts, to cite an example, recalled a warm reception upon her arrival in the early 1970s and remembered that some competitors even lent her a hand. "To me people hadn't been inhospitable [and] at that time it was very, very difficult to get a job, for a woman to practice law," she reflected. "Walter Manley, for instance, befriended me even though we competed for family law clients." Roberts continued: "Polk County's always been good to me. It had this bad reputation so far as women in public life are concerned, but they gave me a job! They then promoted me—they made me a judge. There was one [female judge] in Dade County and one in Jacksonville, and that was about it." She added, "It always tickled me that Polk County was ahead of Tampa and Orlando."[34]

One politically minded young woman with Polk roots turned away from a prestigious national position that her efforts had earned but did so in a manner that residents easily understood. The daughter of Lakeland's Eric and Regina Berg, Connie Berg Plunkett had jumped on presidential candidate Jimmy Carter's campaign bandwagon as early as December 1974. A "tall, beautiful blonde, obviously very intelligent," Plunkett soon discovered that sex scandals then dominating the news converted some of her apparent assets into drawbacks. Nonetheless she worked hard, often directly with the candidate, and emerged, according to a feature article in the *Ladies Home Journal*, as one of Carter's "top aides." Following his election she served as chief liaison between the Carter-Mondale campaign and the Democratic National Committee, but she turned down a permanent job working in the new administration. "She's missed her private life and that's the biggest reason," *Lakeland Ledger* reporter Dave Joachim related. "But she also has plans for herself in politics."[35]

Having explored Connie Plunkett's reluctance to accept a position with the Carter administration, note should be taken that other residents more willingly stepped up to answer President Carter's call. Particularly, in 1977 the president appointed George Carter Carr of Lakeland as a United States District Judge for the Middle District of Florida. A former law partner of United States Senator Lawton Chiles, Carr then was serving as Polk County attorney. His reaction to word of the appointment was "I'm elated." The judge went on to serve with distinction, eventually as chief judge of the district, until his death in 1990. "[George] was a jurist who loved the law," Chiles related, "and won the respect of lawyers and defendants with even-handed control of a courtroom."[36]

Happenings and Passages

The decade of the 1970s came filled with a human richness, poignancy, and meaning that a brief review of that era's advances, challenges, lapses, and frailties unfortunately glosses over. Consequently, it properly serves any attempt to convey a true sense of the times to offer recognition of some of the otherwise unmentioned events and personalities, happenings and passages, that marked that era of transformation.

For one thing there were the inspiring acts of heroes and heroines. In 1970 Amos W. Hill placed his own life at risk and suffered burns to pull Betty Grace Strauss from the flaming wreckage of her automobile near Mulberry. The Carnegie Hero Fund Commission awarded him their bronze medal for his selfless act. Three years later Fort Meade policeman Lamar Barefoot nearly lost his life when shot in the line of duty by an assailant. In 1974 Deputy Sheriff Sollie Walter "Wally" Rabun, Jr., paid the ultimate price. Answering a call from the Eloise community, he was killed instantly when his car was struck by a train.[37]

Many Americans in 1973 came to view Chesterfield Smith as a hero. Having already completed a term as president of the Florida Bar, Smith

83. *Bartow's Chesterfield Smith emerged into national prominence as president of the American Bar Association during the Watergate crisis that eventually resulted in President Richard Nixon's resignation from office.* St. Petersburg Times.

then presided over the American Bar Association. At the time the nation reeled from the Watergate affair that had embroiled President Richard Nixon and his White House staff. As political chaos ensued and the future of constitutional government came into question, eyes looked to Smith for leadership. In December, having agonized over the matter, Smith issued a public call for the president's impeachment. His statement commenced with the now-famous phrase, "No man is above the law." Although highly controversial at the time, Smith's willingness to place his own reputation and career on the line found itself justified by subsequent disclosures and President Nixon's eventual resignation. "We, the people, at the end of the day had the final voice in what happened," former U.S. Attorney General Elliot Richardson declared. "We were given that voice by the leadership of the Bar, which itself was embodied in Chesterfield Smith."[38]

Heroines also offered themselves in sometimes surprising ways. Lakeland's Sherry Rene Barnett, despite deafness since birth, matured into a multi-talented and gifted athlete while also scoring high academically and securing election as president of her freshman and sophomore classes at the Florida School for the Deaf and Blind. In 1976 Polk Countians delighted in her qualification for participation in the XIII World Games for the Deaf at Bucharest, Romania. "Track is very dear to my heart," Sherry declared. "I love to run and I like working hard so I can be good." She had developed plans for the future, as well. "I would like to coach other children, especially deaf children," she stated, "because I know how it feels to be deaf and I would like to help them learn that we are just like other people."[39]

In a similar vein, Ethyle Fackler earned respect for her courage. Coping with the results of polio that afflicted her at age four, she lived paralized from the waist down and confined to a wheel chair. Notwithstanding the limitations, by 1979 she had earned an associate degree from Polk Community College and was completing work for a bachelor's degree at Florida Technological University. Employed by the United Way of Greater Lakeland as a secretary, Fackler had served as president and secretary-treasurer of the Big Wheels Bowling League, secretary of the Mid- Florida Chapter of the Muscular Dystrophy Association, secretary-treasurer of the Lakeland Committee on Employment of the Handicapped, and president of the Lakeland Physically Handicapped Club. Little wonder that in 1979 the Lakeland Pilot Club selected her as Handicapped Professional Woman of the Year.[40]

Some people achieved public acclaim for actions that could be described as highly unusual if not bizarre but that also resounded deeply with human implications. At mid-decade, for example, rumors spread of a "wild man of the Green Swamp" who had been spotted over a period of eight months or so. Given the violent nature of crime then prevalent, fears escalated for the safety of those living and working nearby. When authorities apprehended the "wild man," though, they discovered him to be a terrified Taiwanese sailor who somehow had gotten to the swamp in an effort to avoid deportation. Tragically, two days after his detention, the man hanged himself in his cell at the Sumter County jail.[41]

Acclaim came to others more harmoniously. A native of Ittabena, Mississippi, Moses "Doorman" Williams breathed the magic of Delta blues as a child. By age nine he had left home to travel with the all-black Silas Green Minstrel Show, a company that once stopped over in Haines City. Numerous odd jobs thereafter led Williams to employment with Ringling Bros. Barnum & Bailey Circus, and perhaps that connection drew him back to Polk when Circus World opened its doors. However he came to settle at Waverly and Lake Hamilton, he brought to the county a remarkable instrument and skill: Doorman Williams stood out as a virtuoso on the one-stringed door. *Winter Haven Herald* reporter Tom Palmer described the invention. "At each end of the door is a nail, with broom wire strung from the top end, over a tin can, down over a whiskey bottle and around the second nail," he wrote. "It is played by strumming it with one finger from the left hand while moving a bottle up and down the string to produce different tones." Featured at the Florida Folk Festival, Williams drew enthusiastic applause and fans aplenty, but the reality of the entertainment business compelled him to make his living as a grove worker for the Haines City Citrus Growers Association.[42]

On the subject of music and festivals, Polk inaugurated several during the decade that became revered traditions. In 1976 restauranteur and folk music lover Carl Allen launched what became the annual Florida State Bluegrass Festival in downtown Auburndale. The first event drew 150 or so of the curious, but within two decades hosted upwards of 200,000. It was said that Allen dreamed up the festival so that "even folks without money could hear some real music." Two years after the Bluegrass Festival premiered, another music-related gathering drew as many as 120,000. The Lakeland Civic Center, having hosted Elvis Presley and Frank Sinatra already, offered the Florida Stampede. The "rodeo-rock show-soul show-midway festival," as center director Mike McGee hoped, would become an annual event.[43]

Polk communities enjoyed various new facilities and amenities during the decade, as well as the annual shows. They ranged from Bartow's new city hall and Florida Department of Transportation building to Haines City's community center. Given generous federal aid programs and a necessity for action, modern sewage and waste treatment systems proliferated and even rural residents were required to connect with sewer lines in an expanded county system. Recreation centers of a nature far more elaborate than those previously available appeared in many municipalities. The county's people even came close to watching a new courthouse rise, but angry voters turned thumbs down on the proposal by a ratio of three to two in 1976. On a more positive note and thanks to Sheriff Monroe Brannen's leadership, the Florida Sheriffs Association decided in 1971 to locate its Girls Villa for troubled youths near Peace River Park east of

84. *Lake Kissimmee State Park, Polk's first such state facility, opened in the early 1970s.* POLK COUNTY HISTORICAL ASSOCIATION.

Bartow. The facility's first phase opened August 27, 1972.[44]

Some of the new amenities even graced the environment at a time when environmental degradation seemed to prevail. For one thing, Polk managed to acquire its first state park in 1970. The ball rolled into motion in January when state authorities deeded 5,027 acres located fifteen miles east of Lake Wales on Lake Kissimmee's northwestern corner for Lake Kissimmee State Park. One year later another designation recognized the beauty of Polk's waters. In January 1971 authorities named Peace River's sixty-three mile run from Fort Meade to Arcadia as a State Canoe Trail. "It was magnificent," one canoe enthusiast recorded. "The only sound we heard was the screeching of a red-shouldered hawk above us," she added. "I wanted to relish every sound and delay moving on as long as I could."[45]

The times naturally brought to Polk the echoes of happenings regionally and nationally. To name just a few, direct long-distance telephone dialing arrived in 1970, as did eighteen-year-old voting. Less desirably, the energy crisis of 1973-1974 brought the 55 mile per hour speed limit and "hard headed truckers" intent upon violating it. That dilemma resulted, as well, in a temporary county gas rationing program and long lines of frustrated drivers waiting not so patiently at gas pumps.[46]

Important passages, too numerous to attempt to enumerate, must be illustrated by a few examples. Dr. Charles Thrift, the president of Florida Southern College, retired in 1976. Dr. Robert A. Davis replaced him. Sadly, in 1971 Senator Spessard L. Holland passed away. U.S. Highway 17 received his name as a memorial. The same year the death of citrus magnate Latt Maxcy signaled the end of one era and the opening of another for that industry and for the county. Less prominently, Sam Wiley died in 1979 at the age of 109. Hailing from Richmond, Virginia, "Uncle Sam" had settled at Lake Wales during the boom years of the early 1920s. His life had seen remarkable transformations, and he left as his legacies a host of descendants and the First Institutional Baptist Church to which he was devoted. His wife Fannie had predeceased him by fifteen years. The oldest living Polk Countian, also the oldest living American, had gone before Sam on October 5, 1979. Born in slavery, Charlie Smith had lived adventures enough to fill many lives. With his death an era truly ended for all.[47]

It would be remiss, given all of the decade's vicissitudes, not to recognize that, in an important manner, the 1970s ended on a note of optimism. For all of the racial turmoil that racked county, state, region, and nation, most thoughtful persons black and white believed that matters were improving even if they had not yet reached full resolution and acceptance. Lakeland attorney Larry Jackson touched on the point in late 1979. "I don't think that racial violence is something that worries people here that much anymore," he asserted. "The question for white and non-

85. *Mayor Carrie Oldham and other officials greet President Jimmy Carter upon his arrival at Lakeland Municipal Airport for a campaign swing during 1980.* LAKELAND PUBLIC LIBRARY.

whites is not one of how bad things can get," he continued. "What the races have to figure out . . . is what they can make that is good from the potential that is here." Carrie Oldham sensed something of the same type. "The late 1970s, early 80s were a crucial turning time," she remembered. "People began to feel: 'Let's get it all together.'"[48]

86. *Refugees from Cuba and, later, Haiti flooded into Florida during the 1960s and afterward, fleeing turmoil and repression while seeking freedom and opportunity. Significant numbers of these persons soon found their way to Polk County. Historical Association of Southern Florida.*

CHAPTER 10

ᘓ

Spiraling Down, 1980-1985

*E*very generation of Floridians, it seems, must relearn the lessons of the boom and bust cycle. For Polk Countians, experience drove home that point beginning in the early 1980s. What had appeared to be unassailable growth and economic promise turned virtually in the wink of an eye to desperate crisis. Scenes reminiscent of the Great Depression returned to punctuate the county scene as leaders scrambled to discover any source of relief. Life most certainly did not end, but its tone reverted to a harsher reality. Cynicism replaced optimism for many, and the price to be paid for the future swelled with the desire to re-establish wistfully remembered good times.

Viewed from a distance, matters logically should have taken a different course. More than three million people moved into Florida during the 1980s, a fact that pushed it past Pennsylvania, Ohio, and Illinois to fourth place among the states in population. Overall the state grew by 26 percent, with central Florida claiming more than its share of the gain. Every seven and one-half minutes a new arrival took up residence in the region that encompassed the nearby counties of Orange, Seminole, Lake, Osceola, Brevard, and Volusia. By 1990 one of three inhabitants there had arrived within the past ten years. As the *Orlando Sentinel* calculated, the totals meant that 181 people per day had opted for a central Florida home. The figure multiplied to 65,700 per year or 657,000 during the decade.[1]

Polk, too, saw population totals rise, although—as will be discussed—the growth sometimes contributed to the problems rather than to aiding their solution. The year 1980 found the county with 321,652 residents. A decade's passage witnessed that number climb to 405,382. Thus, where the six-county region mentioned above swelled by one-third, Polk could boast a mere 19.4 percent increase. Virtually all of the gain centered in the county's northern and northeastern reaches in proximity to attractions such as Walt Disney World and Sea World. Polk City, located close to the environmentally endangered Green Swamp, jumped by 150 percent to 1,439. Auburndale registered a respectable surge of 36 percent to 8,858. Lakeland meanwhile charted an enhancement of 30 percent to 70,576; Hillcrest Heights, 24 percent (221); Winter Haven, 17 percent (24,725); Lake Wales, 14 percent (9,670); Lake Alfred, 14 percent (3,622); and Haines City, 8 percent (11,683). Davenport, Dundee, Eagle Lake, and Mulberry tallied positive figures but less than 5 percent growth. Of Polk's seventeen incorporated municipalities, five lost population. Bartow dropped 0.5 percent to 14,716; Fort Meade, 10 percent to 4,976; Frostproof, 6 percent to 2,808; Highland Park, 16 percent to 155; and Lake Hamilton 27 percent to 1,128.[2]

An understanding of the types of persons who were arriving in those years helps to explain what the growth meant to the county. First, many of Polk's new residents were retirees, often living on limited incomes. This fact sparked resentments on the part of some leaders and longtime residents who perceived the newcomers as either unable or unwilling to contribute financially and personally to solution of the county's problems. John M. Hamilton of the Lakeland Area Chamber of Commerce summed up the attitude. "I'd hate to see this become a retirement town," he declared. "Retirees don't pay their own way." Nonetheless, a virtual deluge of retirees flooded into certain neighborhoods and communities, especially at Lakeland and Winter Haven. Sixty-four year old Jack Sarvey, recently settled in Polk, told the story in 1985. "From what I've seen, Lakeland's not a real lively city," he related, "but if you want to pass yourself off as a senior citizen you can do most anything." City planner Jim Verplanck commented upon the local reaction to the presence of Sarvey and his peers. "That doesn't please a lot of people here who want Lakeland to build its industrial base and attract working people." Office manager Bill Wilson reached further with his comments. "The whole town," he insisted, "is being geared for retirees."[3]

The resentments focused increasingly on where and how a large proportion of the retirees tended to live, that is to say against mobile homes, mobile home parks, and mobile home living. For one thing, mobile homes seemed to be appearing everywhere, and not by mirage. By 1982, more new mobile homes were being sold in Polk than in any other

87. *Although this photograph was taken after the decade of the 1980s, it well illustrates a trend then underway in Polk that led to greater numbers of residents living in mobile and modular homes.* TAMPA TRIBUNE.

Florida county. "Residents resent the mobile home parks and prefabricated communities that attract senior citizens," Verplanck explained of the consequences. Accordingly, when John Hamilton addressed his concerns about retirees not paying their own way, he particularly referred to "those who live in mobile homes."[4]

The mobile home parks housed another large segment of the newly arriving population who were not retirees but whose presence also stirred resentments, the low-income unemployed. The nation by 1980 had entered tough economic times that were to persist for years. As had occurred during the Great Depression, good numbers of those unable to find employment elsewhere looked to the Sunshine State where golden harvests were perceived as ripe for the taking. Publicity early in the decade had highlighted Polk as a spot where those opportunities could be reaped. In one example, the *Tampa Tribune* had boasted that "Polk Plans to Keep Growing Despite Problems of the '80s." Its article observed, "Even with a gloomy housing market predicted for 1980 and $3-a-gallon gasoline by 1982, Polk County is expected to continue to [enjoy economic expansion because its] lakes, groves and laid-back lifestyle are attracting more and more year-round residents." The piece quoted county commissioner Frank "Bubba" Smith to the effect that "once sleepy towns such as Davenport, Lake Wales, and Haines City will start booming like Lakeland." The *Tribune* added, "Polk is also expected to continue to dominate the citrus and phosphate markets, although some are predicting groves will turn to gold for developers." A year later the same newspaper insisted that "a population explosion lies just over the horizon" for the county's Ridge area. "Primary reasons," it quoted county planners as observing, "are people tiring of crowded coastal areas and the [attractiveness of the] higher ground of the region."[5]

The racial and ethnic origins of some of these low-income arrivals complicated matters further. Economic and political crises in Cuba and Haiti had launched waves of refugees upon Florida's shores. Thousands found their way to Polk. The Haitian population at Winter Haven alone was fluctuating somewhere between 800 and 3,500 by year's end 1981, and totals mounted thereafter. So severe was the plight of many that the state funded a Polk County refugee center to aid in meeting needs. Some officials' tempers flared at the action, seeing it as enhancing Polk's attraction for these unemployed and poor persons, many of whom could not speak English. "I am not in favor of setting up a refugee center in Winter Haven, " Mayor Bruce Parker said. "It's time for everybody to sit down and say, 'Let's have an immigration policy.'" State representative Gene Ready "vowed to stop the funds," but, as state supervisor Lynda Sommers explained, "We're set up now."[6]

Economic Depression

Perhaps the enlarged presence of elderly, low-income, and poor people would have spawned resentments in ordinary times, but circumstances through the early years of the 1980s proved anything but ordinary. By mid-decade thousands of unemployed persons from elsewhere had joined with thousands of residents who had lost their jobs to suffer together the consequences of depression-era conditions. The local economy earlier had produced tough times when it came to low-skill job availability despite booming conditions, so the fact of unemployment was not the surprise. In 1979, for instance, Florida reported a 7 percent unemployment rate. Polk, the same year, dealt with a level three percentage points higher.[7]

The problem came with the dramatic rise in unemployment levels beginning in 1980. The national recession coupled with local reverses sent the rate soaring to 17.9 percent in September 1981. One month later, with an additional 0.2 percent tacked on to the total, Polk claimed position as the county with the second highest unemployment rate in the nation. By April of the following year forecasters anticipated a 20 percent level within months. In August the rate crested for the time being at 19.1 percent, a plateau at which 28,000 individuals found themselves in want of work. After unemployment dipped to 17.2 percent at year's end, officials still referred to the situation as "staggering." September 1983's 18.7 percent left Polk third in the country in jobless levels. It seemed almost a miracle when the rate plummeted to 11.8 percent in 1984, but the trend calamitously reversed itself in 1985.[8]

The magnitude of the economic doldrums appeared clearly and early. In 1981 owners found themselves compelled to sell Lake Wales's Masterpiece Gardens at auction, and the Great Masterpiece itself closed. Bok Tower required extensive advertising to combat dwindling attendance, and Cypress Gardens saw the turnstiles register only 1.3 million visitors where 2 million or more routinely had cleared the gate a few years earlier. "Polk County, for all practical purposes, is in a depression," an economist declared the following year. Lakeland Mayor Frank O'Reilly agreed, at least to a degree. "I can't say the situation is desperate," the politician cautioned. "But it is serious. It's very serious." By the time O'Reilly spoke, "long lines of laborers [wound] around Lake Mirror near the unemployment office." Affluence still prevailed in many areas, but homeless missions "swelled with hundreds of jobless vagrants huddled in soup lines." Among those lining up, according to social workers, were "modern-day equivalents of dustbowl Oakies, laid off workers from Michigan, Alabama, Georgia, Kentucky and elsewhere."[9]

Lakeland's condition during 1983 and years following suggests the broader picture. "It was depression-style unemployment," one report advised, "and it reverberated through Lakeland's economy in odd ways." Piper Aircraft, the city's third largest employer, reeled from cutbacks and layoffs. When the company finally shut its doors in 1985, a $17 million payroll and 875 jobs had disappeared. Opened in 1973, the plant at its peak had provided work for 2,200. Once thriving businessmen and more than a few proud professionals "left the area." Symbolic of their flight, "vast sections" of Lake Parker Mall lay vacant. City commissioner Larry Durrence discovered just how bad things were at home when he visited the nation's capital to plead for assistance from a not-very-sympathetic Reagan Administration. As Durrence looked around, he saw "the mayors of Flint, Michigan, and Rockford, Illinois, and a scattering of other cities in the Rust Bowl." The Lakeland officials, it turned out, were the only ones from the Sunbelt. "The national press was very amazed to find someone from Florida in that delegation," Durrence recalled. "They asked us what in the world we were doing there."[10]

Causes for the economic malaise appeared just as clearly as did its impact. In Piper Aircraft's case, the national recession coupled high jobless figures with monetary inflation to produce "sluggish demand and rising product prices." These "marketplace pressures" forced consolidation. Polk suffered accordingly. The same conditions struck other local industries, especially tourism. Cypress Gardens's founder Dick Pope had earned fame for snappy credos such as "Give tourists a fair show for their buck." Another of his sayings now echoed the tolling of depression's bell. "Without friends," he argued, "Florida's dead." So, too, was the Pope family's control of what in pre-Disney World days had been the state's largest tourist attraction. In April 1985 the Popes disposed of Cypress Gardens to the book publishing company Harcourt Brace Jovanovich in a stock swap valued, according to some sources, at $23 million. That firm promised to pump in sufficient funds to "rejuvenate the gardens."[11]

No local industry felt the weight of national recession more than did the phosphate industry. Dwindling reserves of recoverable ore had prompted business concerns to begin expanding to adjacent counties as early as the mid-1970s, but in 1979 Polk still produced 80 percent of the country's mined phosphate. The new decade's first year found Florida production totals climbing to the record high of 43 million tons, with 15,000 persons employed in the process. Most of them labored in Polk. The soft economy in 1981 forced some cutbacks and layoffs, though. Then came a "historic collapse." An area newspaper reported the details. "More than a dozen mines and fertilizer plants were closed temporarily during 1982," its article commented, "and by June there were 3,500 phosphate employees out of work around the state." The report continued, "[At year's end] four separate phosphate companies announced new cuts, which could idle nearly 700 more miners and chemical workers by sometime [in February 1983]."[12]

Cautious expressions of optimism for the future came tempered with fears that more depressing news was yet to come. "I wish the trauma were over," the Florida Phosphate Council's Tim Clarke admitted, "but 1983 does not look like it's going to be a particularly good year." Clarke added insightfully, "It could be as bad or even worse than last year." It was worse. When industry unemployment numbers reached 25 percent or 2,300 Polk jobs in spring 1983, council spokesman Bob Bonnell warned: "We could see 30 per cent unemployment. We don't see any improvement until the second half of 1984." That year—1984—witnessed pronounced industry shifts to sites outside the county as production prices climbed past sales receipts. Gardinier declared bankruptcy only to be rescued by the agricultural conglomerate

Cargill, Inc. Other companies went searching for buyers as well. At the decade's midpoint conditions stagnated even as the nation's economy improved. "It looks like 1985 is going to be very close to 1984," an industry executive announced late in the year. "There's nothing on the horizon to give us any more hope."[13]

With the tourism and phosphate industries depressed from unfavorable national and international conditions, the citrus industry loomed ever greater in importance until it, too, ran headlong into adverse circumstances. They arrived in a variety of forms and fashions. Drought and water restrictions in 1981 naturally caused concerns, as did a Mediterranean fruit fly scare. More significantly, a hard freeze produced real damage. "Many growers," the *Lakeland Ledger* advised, "said the Jan. 13 and 14 freeze was the worst in years as oranges froze solid on the trees." Polk groves, it was stated, were "nailed by the cold." Some industry titans reined in their investments. Ben Hill Griffin, Jr., for instance, sold his packing houses and a large juice processing plant to Procter & Gamble Co., which launched the Citrus Hill brand name. Others retained their faith in the future, however, and comforted themselves with the hope that better times awaited just over the horizon.[14]

The optimism proved ill founded. Severe freezing conditions returned in January 1982. "Polk County's orange crop dropped 24 percent from projections; the grapefruit crop fell off 12 percent," one report enumerated. "In all, the January freeze cost growers an estimated $100 million." Compared to the subsequent Christmas Day 1983 freeze, it meant little. The later event, as the *Miami Herald* reported it, "cut a swath through one-third of the state's groves, crippling the economy in 11 citrus-dependent counties." For fifty straight hours sub-freezing temperatures beset the heart of the citrus region. "More than 100,000 acres of trees are dead," the *Herald* described. "An additional 150,000 acres will not bear fruit next year." It added, "Growers say it could take a decade for the region to recover." Statewide losses ranged well over $1 billion. Of groves affected, an estimated 30 percent would never return to production.[15]

Even though the Christmas Day freeze delivered its icy havoc with greatest intensity to the north, Polk staggered along with other counties. "Almost all citrus in Polk County, plus large portions of the county's strawberry and tomato crops," the local emergency board proclaimed, "were hit hard." More than half of late season Valencia oranges were lost, along with one-third of the early and mid-season varieties. The timing of the event especially harmed farm workers and fruit pickers, leaving many "penniless, homeless and unable to find work elsewhere."

At gathering spots such as Lakeland's Little Lost Diner, the laborers quietly assessed their fate. "This freeze's gonna hurt a lot of people, yes it will," picker Alvin Killette acknowledged. John Holbrook agreed. "It's been rough," he sighed, "all the way around."[16]

It was going to get rougher. A three-day January 1985 freeze took temperatures down into the teens and removed between 10 and 15 percent of Polk's 130,000 acres of groves from production. As owners and workers persevered at attempts to minimize the damage, the futility of the efforts quickly became apparent. "These people are out trying to save what they no longer have," Babson Park grocer Erin McCallister commented ruefully. Unemployed workers thereafter "flooded" unemployment offices with claims for relief. That December another freeze struck but mostly spared remaining citrus groves. It inflicted its painful grip instead on vegetable crops.[17]

The apparent return of citrus canker added its own destruction. That eventuality leapt to public attention when Franklyn Ward feared that he had discovered the destructive bacteria at his Avon Park nursery in 1984. "The word that canker had shown up in one of Florida's biggest citrus nurseries struck fear and confusion into the hearts of thousands of Floridians who make their living growing citrus," one newspaperman explained. "State agriculture officials," he continued, "ordered a mammoth eradication program on citrus stock thought to be potentially infected." They also temporarily embargoed shipments of fruit out of state and helped to generate a compensation program from losses growing out of the burning of trees. By early 1985 more than seven million nursery trees had been destroyed at nine commercial nurseries. During that year nine more nurseries, three of them in Polk, lost their stock as well. Haines City's Bill Adams, who operated Florida's largest citrus nursery, alone lost three million trees.[18]

88. *A citrus canker scare beginning in 1984 resulted in widespread destruction of nurseries and trees, dealing a further blow to Polk's teetering economy.* FLORIDA STATE ARCHIVES.

Consequences

Dynamics of the magnitude that shook the county in the early 1980s could not help but usher in profound consequences. By way of example, the freezes dramatically reoriented the Florida citrus industry with short and long term implications in Polk. In the short term, they produced sudden and sizeable drops in land values. Surviving groves slipped about 2 percent in value during the first eight months of 1985, but frozen-over citrus acreage plummeted about 22 percent. In dollar terms value slid during that short period from about $4,462 an acre to $3,494. That presumed, of course, that an owner could find a willing buyer with the means to consummate a purchase.[19]

Of long-term consequence, the geography of the citrus industry shifted irrevocably. "Unless there is some drastic change in the climate or the demand for oranges, never again will citrus be more than an agricultural footnote in most of North Central Florida," an authority pronounced. "And never again will Lake County, once the number two citrus producer in the state behind Polk County, be a leader in Florida citrus," he continued. "Its prominent place is being taken by counties to the south, such as Indian River, St. Lucie, and Hardee." Given Lake's proximity, citrus men in northern Polk could not have rested easily or in comfort at the change.[20]

Actually, many groves in northern Polk were destroyed beyond re-habilitation, giving rise to yet more consequences. "The freezes of the early 80s killed off groves in the Green Swamp," Bartow's Pat Huff re-membered. "That left cheap land for development." A good bit of what did become available for development found itself transformed from citrus to mobile home park use. Dry conditions permitted such habitations by rendering forests underlain with muck and water into dry land. Drought, though, bred forest fires. When the state's Division of Forestry proclaimed 1985 as "the most destructive fire season on record," it speci-fied that the district including Polk, Hillsborough, and Pinellas led the state. Not surprisingly, mobile homes often stood in the paths of the flames. "A fire in a swampy area north of Lakeland several years ago covered several thousand acres, but virtually no property damage oc-curred because so few people lived in the area," an official observed. By 1985, however, the situation had changed. "That swamp," forestry officer Mark Hebb noted, "is now slam full of mobile homes."[21]

Demographic changes touched the schools as well. Through most of the 1960s and 1970s Polk's education system had rocked through crises of racial integration, a teacher strike, budget shortfalls, poor planning for rapidly escalating school populations, taxpayer revolts, and a host of other concerns. Now a different set of challenges arose. The district student population began dropping. "We just haven't had anything happening to bring in families with young children," the board's finance director Tony Telleck lamented in 1980. That might seem the kind of good news that would offer a respite from problems, but such did not turn out to be the case. Where schools abounded, populations dwindled. Where they did not, populations swelled, creating demand for new construction. To handle the burden, tax rates inched upward as did taxpayers' tempers. Fractious times, as a result, continued to mark the education landscape.[22]

As they did, the system's leadership underwent key changes that contributed at least temporarily to instability. Scarred from the battles of the late 1970s discussed in Chapter 9, Superintendent Homer Addair turned over his position in 1981 to Southwest Area Superintendent Clem Churchwell, an advocate of racial integration. Known as "a strict disciplinarian," Churchwell particularly targeted drug use by students for attack as a part of his program. At a meeting on the subject held in Bartow during October 1983, he collapsed and soon died of a heart attack. Governor Bob Graham replaced him with Winter Haven High School principal John Stewart. The new superintendent achieved his own election with ease the following year.[23]

Even though some positive-appearing consequences turned out to be something else entirely, one major and positive result of the dynamic changes of the early 1980s deserves mention. It concerned the nature and future of the economy. County commissioner Royce Ready helped to get the bandwagon going when he suggested late in 1982 the need to diversify Polk's dependency on phosphate, citrus, and tourism. His solution aimed at attracting new businesses and industry to the county through the creation of an Economic Development Division. Others soon echoed Ready's call. When Winter Haven developer Buddy LeRoux emphasized Polk's advantages in a respected business magazine at year's end, for example, he underscored his belief that "If some light industry comes into this area, it's just going to fly." State senator Curtis Peterson, then serving as senate president, used his authority to highlight similar themes. Concerned about finding jobs for idle workers, he convened a meeting of community representatives in January 1983 to discuss matters openly. "The group said a priority to putting people back to work permanently," a report detailed, "should be to try to lure new business."[24]

The cause of economic diversification, once it had come to the fore, developed as time passed into something akin to a mantra for those who embraced it. The Lakeland Area Chamber of Commerce especially took up the chant, with John Hamilton aiding the process at every turn. "We need diversity," he insisted repeatedly to whoever would listen. "The more we can counterbalance the phosphate and citrus industries, the more stable our economy will be." As Hamilton and his allies envisioned their cause, its outcome involved "the development of new industrial parks and the attraction of light industry."[25]

The cause proved a hard sell within a county historically wedded to an economy founded upon citrus, tourism, and phosphate. *Florida Trend* magazine in July 1984 stressed that fact in focusing on Lakeland and its "Detroit-style afflictions." "Lakeland's leaders haven't the vaguest idea of what they want their city to be, except that they don't want it to change too much," the journal observed. It quoted People's Bank president Alton B. Bennett on the point. "We want more industry and more jobs," Bennett acknowledged, "but most people are satisfied with our role." The article went on to notice the virtual absence of "high-technology firms" in the county's business community. Instead, manufacturers were "meat-and-potatoes companies one would expect to find in, say, Dubuque or Kokomo: mobile-home manufacturers, steel fabricators, glass-container plants and small-aircraft companies." *Florida Trend* perceived an unwillingness to face cold reality. "Lakeland is facing . . . a period of decision," it concluded. "The economic pillars of Polk County's economy, citrus and phosphate, will not recover their strength."[26]

In the face of such publicity and such cold reality, the Lakeland Chamber of Commerce redoubled its efforts. Particularly, it conceived the "Second Century Lakeland" program. That initiative anticipated "a special fund-raising project" aimed at restoring the downtown area, setting aside land for industrial parks, and recruiting new industry. "We prefer small- to medium-size industries," John Hamilton explained, "just in case something does happen, thousands of people aren't involved." About two hundred local businesses quickly contributed $2 million to the effort. What excited many was a transportation improvement envisioned for the long term to stir the city's economic revival. "The region's central location has been enhanced by a plan to encircle Lakeland with a highway that ties into Interstate 4," a business writer commented. "The project, scheduled to be completed in the 1990s, will make corporate recruiting easier and may open the floodgate of growth." While the chamber's attack on the city's economic afflictions barely had gotten underway at the decade's midpoint, positive results already could be identified. In 1984 fourteen new companies, averaging fifty employees each, had moved into the community. At the least, their coming stood out within a grim economic picture as a very promising development.[27]

Another promising development saw Commissioner Royce Ready's dream of a county office of economic development come to realization in 1983. Polk's Economic Development Department soon launched several initiatives designed to help position the county as "a central location for warehouse and distribution operations, and tourism-related activities." This included cooperation with the Second Century Lakeland backers and independent efforts to attract "industrial prospects" to the county. A voluntary Economic Development Council of Polk County and its president Dave Ellsworth complemented the county department's work. In 1985 it associated with the public/private Central Florida Development Council.[28]

Political Afflictions

If Polk's economy suffered from afflictions, its political scene ailed as well, although careful note should be taken before delving into the details that some political leaders did strive meaningfully and successfully on the county's behalf in its times of trouble. State senator N. Curtis Peterson stood out most importantly in that regard. First elected to the senate in 1972, he had risen within one decade, as mentioned earlier, to assume the body's presidency. Meanwhile, the senator had mastered the intricacies of the budget

89. *The leadership of State Senator Curtis Peterson, who served as president of the Florida Senate during 1982-1984, proved crucial for Polk County during the 1980s.* FLORIDA STATE ARCHIVES.

process, specializing in transportation and education issues. Folksy and evidencing a sharp political acumen, he pressed for a variety of benefits for his home county. Among the accomplishments, he arranged legislative approval for a branch campus of the University of South Florida to be located at Lakeland and he urged authorization of the Polk County Parkway, as the proposed Interstate 4 loop around Lakeland came to be called. In the field of education, Peterson furthered legislation to increase scholastic standards, extend the school year, and raise the number of credits needed for graduation. Beyond that, as state representative C. Fred Jones recalled, "If it was good for Polk County, he saw it was done." Son Pete Peterson remembered, as well, his father's favorite quote. Taken from the Reverend Peter Marshall, it expressed Curtis Peterson's personal philosophy. "The service we give," Marshall had insisted, "is the rent we pay while here on Earth."[29]

Then, there was the other side of the political coin, the one that reflected less well on the county. Take the example of Peterson's senatorial colleague Alan Trask, who, as the *Lakeland Ledger* related, "came to rue what his lawyer called his carelessness with his finances." The newspaper explained the circumstances that led up to the Winter Haven Democrat's resignation "under fire" in June 1982 "to avoid possible ouster from the Senate." The charges related to "unusual accounting and reporting practices that made him seem wealthy and made it easy for him to borrow money when he was actually $600,000 in debt." For some reason Trask felt so strongly about his opposition to the Equal Rights Amendment then up for ratification that he delayed his resignation until he could vote against it. Voters subsequently elevated state representative Robert B. "Bob" Crawford to the upper chamber to fill the vacancy.[30]

The sheriff's department bore responsibility, as well, for creating its share of embarrassment for the county. This occurred primarily as a result of the 1984 sheriff's race and its outcome. That contest had pitted incumbent Louie Mims against several opponents. One of them, former military policeman Dan Daniels, may have been the first Polk political candidate to truly understand the demographic revolution then overwhelming the county. Realizing the growing political importance of retirees and the elderly generally, Daniels had spent several years organizing Crime Watch programs for senior citizens. The bitter electoral rivalry then saw Mims initially best Daniels only to lose to the challenger in a runoff thanks to massive support from elderly voters. By December Mims had become convinced that Daniels also had bought support by offering jobs to several defeated sheriff candidates. He so informed the governor's office, state authorities launched an investigation, and the matter quickly emerged into the public light as harsh and personal accusations bounced back and forth between Mims and Daniels. By July, though, state investigators acknowledged that they could find no credible evidence that Daniels had committed any such crime.[31]

By no means did that relieve Sheriff Daniels from the glare of negative publicity. As the investigation had heated up, Daniels had announced the receipt of threats against his life as a result of a promised crackdown on the drug trade. "You folks can go straight to hell," he declared of the never-identified culprits in a press statement, "and take with you the poison that you spread among our young people in Polk County." A week later Daniels changed tack, insisting that the drug traffickers had dropped their threats in favor of "possible" bribe offers. In the meantime the sheriff had appointed a "Minority Action Group" of eight blacks and one Hispanic, headed by Charles Hinson, "to help him recruit blacks, women and Hispanics as deputies." Suddenly, in May he dismissed the panel, arguing that it "didn't do very well." Member Dee Van Pelt, editor of the county's black community newspaper the *Polk County Banner*, spoke to the mess. "There was quite a bit of friction and not enough cooperation," she observed. "It very definitely was not productive. We just couldn't gel." On his part Daniels promised designation of a replacement advisory panel, stressing that "retirees will make up a large part of the new group."[32]

Where others might have sought to avoid stirring additional controversy, Daniels paused only long enough to catch his breath. In July, for instance, the sheriff allocated a significant portion of his scarce resources for "a new crime prevention program aimed at educating the public and the business community about the threat of terrorism." Daniels took pains to point out that his target was "not the kind of terrorists that hijack airplanes, but people who use force and violence to gain control over an area." He explained the vague reference to include "drug dealers trying to 'move' into an area, or radicals who bomb buildings for political reasons." As residents scratched their heads in bewilderment, their sheriff went on to reassure them that "This is not aimed at any specific problem or threat in the county."[33]

That set the stage for the employment of deputies with ties to the Ku Klux Klan. The two former Lakeland police officers involved in the mini-scandal had supported Daniels's election bid and had emerged as sergeants in the new administration. As explained to the public by the *Lakeland Ledger*, routine lie detector tests had revealed the men's Klan ties as well as the fact that they had "committed what was termed in polygraph exams as 'warrantless entries'—searching private residences or vehicles without a court order." Daniels—who had known of the Klan links--responded by attacking the *Ledger*, branding it "inhumane and blood-thirsty." The deputies told several versions of their story, at one time denying any Klan ties and at others admitting membership but insisting that "they had no philosophical ties" to the organization. The resulting public outcry at least prompted Daniels to draft a policy "barring active members of the Klan from employment with his department." One student of the Florida Klan later commented on the irony that Daniels's department "seemed unable to identify nocturnal cross burners" even when some of its members were so familiar with the group committing the crimes.[34]

Matters also sizzled at the county commission and on the school board. In the former case, Commissioner Charles Whitten found himself embroiled in controversy when he accepted lucrative employment with a realty firm associated with Springtree, a 12,000-unit housing development proposed for the Lakeland Municipal Airport vicinity. Serious questions arose about the project's impact, leading the Central Florida Regional Planning Council to ask Polk's commissioners to deny approval of needed permits. Political opponents quickly pointed to Whitten's conflict of interest, as a result of which he eventually succumbed to demands that he resign from the realty job. Voters remembered the indiscretion, however, and ousted Whitten in 1980 in favor of Royce Ready.[35]

Meanwhile, events involving school board member Jim Rehberg reflected not only controversy but also the increasing role that conservative religious groups intended to play in county affairs. Rehberg had joined the school panel in January 1981 after member Ted Aggelis temporarily had departed to run unsuccessfully for a state senate seat. Described by one local newspaper as "a high school dropout not given to reading novels much," Rehberg had drawn much of his electoral support from fundamentalist Christians associated with the Moral Majority. That body, in turn, received considerable encouragement from the First Assembly of God which, in 1980, had moved ahead with plans to develop the former Carpenter's Home property on Lake Gibson with residential and commercial innovations as well as the construction of a 10,000-seat church. In any event, the Reverend J. B. Buffington, who headed the Moral Majority, prompted Rehberg to demand the removal of Kurt Vonegut's novel *Slaughterhouse Five* from the Lake Gibson High School library's shelves and elsewhere because of "all those cuss words and all

90. *During the 1980s the First Assembly of God Church purchased and renovated the Carpenters and Joiners Home located north of Lakeland on Lake Gibson, adding to the facility a beautiful church designed to blend easily with the existing historic architecture.* LAKELAND PUBLIC LIBRARY.

that filth" in the book. Review committees split in their opinion about the matter, although Lakeland's refused to eliminate "an honest piece of literature." With the religious influence not yet organized to the extent that it would be in the future, voters proved less ambivalent and ousted Rehberg from his seat in 1982.[36]

During these years of the early 1980s, Polk's evolving demographics, plus state and national trends and local controversies surrounding Democrat officials, served to enhance the local strength of the Republican party as well as that of fundamentalist Christian organizations. Importantly, Democrats continued to win virtually all elections in Polk, a fact that may have contributed to the decision of the county's lone Republican official, school board member Bernadine Spanjers, to vacate her position in 1980. Still, Polk that year gave Republican presidential candidate Ronald Reagan "a solid majority" over President Jimmy Carter despite the president's visit to Lakeland that October. The county also backed Republican United States Senate candidate Paula Hawkins over her Democrat opponent. When its electors considered Reagan's bid for re-election in 1984, they increased his local margin from 57 percent to 70 percent.[37]

Within that four-year span changes of major political significance had occurred even though they came as an uphill battle for the Republicans. "When I came in," GOP county chair Jean Burt recalled, "I had virtually no candidates, and there had been a real absence of campaign expertise." Then, the party managed a major coup. United States Congressman Andy Ireland in 1984 decided to switch his registration from Democrat to Republican. The move appeared to carry some risk at the time, but concerns evaporated as election day neared. Ireland took 63 percent of Polk's vote as he cruised to easy re-election. Meanwhile, his coattails proved strong enough to carry Republican school board candidate Rubie Wilcox into office and only narrowly missed doing the same for another school board candidate. Voters noticed, in the process, the manner in which the Republican victors had managed their campaigns. The contrast to traditional Democrat intra-party feuding could not have been more vivid, and many one-time Democrats came away impressed.[38]

Criminal Conduct in a Deadly Environment

Republicans managed in the early 1980s and through Ronald Reagan's presidency to capture to their political advantage the issue of crime control, and it should not be forgotten that crime in fact posed immediate and far-ranging problems. A *Lakeland Ledger* headline for an article summing up important events of 1985 well illustrated the point. "Disaster, Unemployment, and Murder Marked Polk," it shouted. Three years earlier the *Orlando Sentinel* had ventured into the same territory. "Tidal Wave of Crime Hits State," that journal had declared. "In many ways it was a dreary year," the article observed. "A year of crime careening out of control, of personal tragedies, of the federal government thrusting national problems on state shoulders, of social cracks in the floor." The *Sentinel* continued, "Neighborhood crime-watch groups and the sale of home-security devices and pistols flourished."[39]

The range and nature of violent crime staggered local imaginations. In 1980, to cite an example, babysitter Christine Falling killed five children left in her care, including two Lakeland boys, and managed to avoid detection until she confessed during a psychiatric hospital stay. The next year Lakeland's Phillip Atkins sexually violated and brutally murdered his six-year-old neighbor Antonio Castillo. Also in 1981 Paul Beasley Johnson of Eagle Lake slew Deputy Theron A. Burnham and two others, while bank robbers took the life of Frostproof police officer Henry

McCall. One-time cook Gerald Eugene Stano may have ended the lives of almost forty women in Florida and two other states, three of them from Polk, before his one-man crime wave ended in 1982.[40]

As the carnage continued, residents armed themselves in light of the seeming incapacity of law enforcement to control the onslaught. In just one community, sixty-three women in 1983 signed up for a crime prevention firearm training program. "With the amount of problems that we're having in the country today," Bartow police officer Dennis Hoecherl explained, "people have purchased firearms. They want to be familiar with them." An account of the program's progress noted that "participants are expected to bring their own weapon, ammunition, holster, earplugs and sunglasses." Hoecherl added, "I'm excited about what we have to offer."[41]

Illegal drug trafficking and the effects of drug abuse helped to stoke the violence and push crime statistics higher. Where huge marijuana seizures typified the 1970s, however, cocaine now emerged into greater prominence. "Record quantities of cocaine are piling up in evidence bins throughout Florida," one newspaper alerted readers in early 1985. "You can ask yourself, does this mean there's more coming in or does this mean we're getting better at catching them?" rhetorically asked South Florida Task Force on Drugs spokesman Jim Dingfelder. "I'd love to say we're getting better," he continued, "but I couldn't really tell you what's happening." Sheriff's deputies cooperated with customs service agents in 1981 to grab 528 pounds of the substance near Lake Wales. "It was the largest cocaine seizure in Florida," the *Tampa Tribune* reported, "and the second largest in the country." Three and one-half years later flying smugglers jettisoned 988 pounds over Polk, Pasco, and Hillsborough Counties. Subsequent arrests brought "the largest aircraft cocaine seizure in the Tampa District."[42]

Drug-related concerns grew so pervasive that residents and officials resorted to extraordinary measures. In 1985 Frostproof voters, for example, approved a tax to fund drug investigations. "We ought to do it all over the state," barber Johnny North opined. On another front, in 1981 School Superintendent Clem Churchwell backed the use of drug-sniffing dogs in school halls and locker rooms. "We need to take [the dog] through the classes just to scare them," Lakeland police officer Gary Gross argued in urging a greater effort. "Let them know there is a good chance they are going to get caught if they bring drugs to school." Lakeland High School student president Susan Harrell generally backed the sniff tests but expressed disapproval of more-general searches "unless there was reason to believe individuals had drugs on them." State Attorney Quillian Yancey feared that matters might be taken too far. "How can anyone have privacy from a dog?" he queried. School board member Dan Moody likely spoke for many when he supported anti-drug abuse programs "as long as it is within the legal limits." Moody added, "We recognize that we do have a problem among students and, being adults, we want to put the reins on this activity." Moody then struck a cautionary tone. "Whether the police could stop at random and search individuals is open to legal interpretation," he observed. "[Yet,] the need for probable cause should follow through." Moody continued, "Students have the same rights as adults, even though they are minors."[43]

As the dogs prowled school campuses, con artists and white collar crooks stole the spotlight from petty thieves and burglars. Two examples suggest the greater problem. Earl Hopkins operated a "Ponzi scheme" that bilked seventeen Polk doctors and others out of millions. "A Winter Haven orthopedic surgeon who helped Hopkins convince others to invest and previously was convicted for beating Hopkins," a published report mentioned, "was awarded a more than $50,000 judgement against [the con man]." A Winter Haven "do gooder" named Michael O'Shea, who worked as a General Foods accounting manager, turned out to be "three-time ex-convict" Herbert DeGreve. He disappeared in early 1984 just before discovery that almost $4 million was missing from the General Foods treasury. "It seemed unbelievable to those who knew DeGreve (O'Shea)," a crime writer observed, "that he could regularly attend church, sit on the board of a local bank and spend leisure time as a Little League official and still be accused of embezzling."[44]

It even appeared at times that the environment had entered into some sort of criminal conspiracy. In 1983 the Environmental Protection Agency discovered that the pesticide EDB had contaminated drinking water supplies "along the Ridge" and banned use of the substance. Two years afterward

91. *A worker at the Burns Avenue water plant in Lake Wales endeavors to assure quality drinking water for local residents and visitors despite EDB contamination.* LAKE WALES PUBLIC LIBRARY. •

the prestigious *Journal of the American Medical Association* disclosed that ground water contamination in Polk had been linked to higher rates of leukemia. The next month state Health and Human Services secretary David Pingree added another blow when he warned that "up to 1,000 Floridians a year" were dying of radon gas exposure, with the problem centering "in Hillsborough and Polk counties, where many people live on uranium-bearing land which produces the gas."[45]

Kudos

The news ran so bleak during the early 1980s that word of notable accomplishments itself fell victim to the times. So that it will not be thought that Polk passed those years without instances of remarkable achievement or occurrences of a notably positive nature, the several mentions that follow aim to cement the record by way of example.

As a beginning, in 1981 acclaim greeted announcement of the well-earned retirement of Thomas B. Mack from Florida Southern College. "He had come to the college's citrus department in 1951," respected historian James M. Denham commented, "alive to the industry's importance and to the need to preserve materials relevant to its development and impact upon the state." To further his passion, Mack created on the FSC campus the Florida Citrus Archives, an institution that eventually became, as Denham explained, "the largest single repository in the world of citrus and related photography, books, films, business records, documents, artifacts, and memorabilia." On July 1, 2002, the state of Florida would declare Mack's remarkable achievement as the official archives of the Florida citrus industry.[46]

Acclaim directed itself as well to individuals and teams outstanding for their athletic accomplishments, although Polk by that time had offered the state and nation countless champions and prizewinners. To cite only a few examples, golfers Bob Nichols and Andy Bean had captured international acclaim for their prowess on the links. In the water, Bartow native Annie Lett had set state records in high school before moving on to All-American honors at Auburn University. Meanwhile, Winter Haven's Ken Riley had numbered as one of many Polk high school football standouts who went on to collegiate fame and professional careers. The long list of stellar Polk athletes stretched on from there.[47]

The early 1980s witnessed a proud extension of the county's legacy of achievement. Florida Southern College Moccasin basketball team, for instance, grabbed the 1981 NCAA Division II national basketball championship. Coached by Hal Wissel, the squad included All American center John Ebeling, as well as Brian Radon, Felix Tertullen, Clide Roberson, Mike Hayes, Mark King, and Cesar Odio. Winter Haven swimmer Rowdy Gaines, on the other hand, claimed renown on the world level. At age 25 the oldest member of the United States Olympic Team, Gaines captured 3 gold medals at the 1984 Summer Olympics, in the process setting an Olympic record in the 100-meter freestyle competition. Also not to be forgotten, in 1983-1984 Bartow High School Yellow Jackets coach Paul Quinn claimed distinction as the most successful active coach in Florida high school football. At the conclusion of the 1983 season, his record boasted 238 wins against 61 losses and 8 ties in 28 years of coaching.[48]

92. *Polk Countians owed credit for many civil rights advances, especially in the Lake Wales vicinity, to James and Jeresa Austin. LAKE WALES PUBLIC LIBRARY.*

Distinction also continued to come during the early 1980s to women and African Americans who desired to serve the county. Longtime civil rights leader James Austin, to offer an example, won election in 1981 to the Lake Wales city commission. Eight years later he sat as mayor. During 1982 Maryly VanLeer Peck took over as Polk Community College's first woman president. So successful was she in the position that she ran the institution for the next fifteen years. In yet another instance of a woman expertly handling the responsibilities of office, County Judge Susan Roberts rose to the circuit bench in 1984 by appointment of Governor Bob Graham. Voters repeatedly re-elected her thereafter into the twenty-first century.[49]

Women, of course, were contributing to the county's welfare in capacities well beyond the limits of public office. Westwood Junior High School librarian Mary Coe certainly was one of them. Concerned that children with emotional and physical handicaps were not receiving the attention that they needed, Coe set about the task with determination.

Various projects, including special classes in how to make holiday pot-holders, produced excellent positive results. "I think she's fantastic," teacher Rosalind Moore declared. "She reads them stories, reads them poems, she's just been so kind to them. She's really interested in children, she's so special." For her money, Coe saw it all as "a lot of fun."[50]

The local environment, specifically that of the Kissimmee River valley, found a friend, too. In 1984 and at the urging of environmentalists outraged at the damage caused by the Army Corps of Engineers's earlier "straightening" of the river, Governor Bob Graham appointed a thirty-three member river resource planning and management commission to chart the region's future. Some expressed concern about any action that might mandate the environmentalists' dream—restoration—arguing that such an undertaking might further hurt the weak economy. "Restoration, coupled with public purchases of riverfront land, is going to kill some condo development plans and take land off the tax rolls," one observer forecast. By mid-decade, the commission's report neared completed and Polk's residents awaited its recommendations.[51]

In an era when a prized county attraction such as the Masterpiece Gardens could close as a casualty of economic decline, it brightened spirits when Louis and Jean Louwsma purchased the Casa de Josefina and set about to restore the once-glorious mansion that had stood empty for years only to be seized upon as a clubhouse for a condominium complex. The Louwsmas by mid-decade had filled the Casa's rooms

93. *The lovely Case de Josefina, built during the boom times of the 1920s and located near Lake Wales.* POLK COUNTY HISTORICAL ASSOCIATION.

"with lovely Victorian furnishings" and were delighting in its wonders. "I've had nothing but good happen to me while we've lived in the house," Jean Louwsma observed. "I think that it was meant to be mine for a while."[52]

The good news about the Case de Josefina contrasted woefully with that from Lakeland's exotic Polk Theatre. In December 1984 that cherished forum for entertainment closed its doors, already evidencing a state of disrepair. "It definitely could not compete with the more popular big-screen theaters throughout the area's shopping malls," its chronicler Hazel L. Bowman detailed. Fortunately, preservation-minded residents, organized as the Polk County Landmarks, Inc., purchased the facility with the intention to raise funds to restore the Polk to its former glory. By the decade's midpoint little had been accomplished, though, a fact that left the Polk standing almost as a metaphor for the county's status. Would Polk find a path toward restoration of its fortunes or would it decline further into a relic of past glory? Time certainly would tell.

94. *By the late 1980s, Lakeland's Sun'n Fun Fly-In drew crowds numbered in the hundreds of thousands.* POLK COUNTY HISTORICAL ASSOCIATION.

"promoting our strengths and working on our weaknesses"

CHAPTER 11
~
Breaking Old Ties, 1985-1990

*T*he half decade that ran from 1985 to 1990 saw forces that already had dominated the earlier years of the 1980s push Polk toward new orientations as the century's final decade prepared to open. Where some hopes might have existed previously that the county's mainstays of economic progress could revive and sustain it indefinitely, events soon proved the facts otherwise to most onlookers. New days were dawning, but they, too, involved difficult questions and the strain of lingering past dilemmas. Admittedly, moments of exciting optimism gave birth to dreams that the decade might end with a signal of all's well. Then, an icy nightmare shook residents awake to the reality of a changed and changing world.

Economic calamity had greeted Polk's people as the 1980s commenced, and in many respects the brutal conditions persisted as the years passed one to another. Unemployment rates, which had dropped briefly to less than 10 percent in 1984, stood at nearly 13 percent in late summer 1990. That level just about doubled the state average. In the latter year Fleetwood Homes shut down its manufactured housing plant at Lakeland due to "sluggish sales"; Florida Tile Industries and the Pepperidge Farm bakery idled workers; and the Estech, Inc. (formerly Swift and Co.) Silver City phosphate operations near Fort Meade closed permanently, laying off an additional 200 wage earners. Where one year previously county development officials had celebrated securing a huge Wal-Mart distribution center, they now mourned its loss to Hernando County. The fact was that, as tough economic conditions again gripped the nation, many Polk Countians felt the pain. "People really aren't spending money now," Lake Wales appliance repairman

C. Wilson lamented insightfully. His employer had just cut him from eight to five-and-one-half hours per day.[1]

There had been days, on the other hand, when it appeared that the county finally had weathered the various economic storms that it had faced. One student of the subject had addressed that question in 1988. "Pity Polk County no more," he wrote. "These days, Polk has problems of the opposite nature," the man continued. "Development is moving in so rapidly that officials are scrambling to raise funds for highways, police and other needs." Former Lakeland mayor Larry Durrence agreed. "We've made considerable progress," he asserted. Since 1984, twenty-five companies had arrived or expanded in Polk, bringing 3,000 new jobs. In 1987 alone four developments of regional impact in Polk had achieved Central Florida Regional Planning Council approval. They promised 11 million square feet of industrial space, 4.6 million square feet of commercial space, 2,000 hotel rooms, and 12,000 residential units. If completed, experts expected the four projects to generate a $1 billion annual payroll.[2]

Economic diversification efforts ongoing at Lakeland especially seemed to be justifying their costs. The slogan "Lakeland: Florida's Distribution Center" illustrated the city's plan to promote itself as a "strategic center for trade and commerce in Florida." Aiding its revival, the Edward J. DeBartolo Corp.'s $60 million Lakeland Square Mall rose north of Interstate 4; a $78 million Pepperidge Farm plant, the same that idled workers in 1990, had opened to employ 400; and Publix Supermarkets had completed a 220,000-square-foot warehouse while the company planned to add a new regional headquarters. Proposed residential and commercial developments and ones under construction nearby included Oakbridge ($500 million) in southwest Lakeland; West Lakeland ($1.9 billion); and Green Valley "on an eight-square-mile site in the environmentally sensitive Green Swamp area." Even tourism seemed on the upswing. In 1988 the annual Sun'n Fun Fly-In, an aviation event held at the municipal airport, drew 197,000 spectators. Suddenly, it appeared literally that the sky was the limit. "High unemployment was one of the best things that ever happened to Polk County," real estate broker Gene Engle insisted. "We started promoting our strengths and working on our weaknesses."[3]

It might perhaps be more correct to assert that the Interstate 4 corridor reflected the county's progress toward prosperity rather than limiting the statement to Lakeland. "Squeezed between Orlando and Tampa, Polk now offers Central Florida abundant, inexpensive land for development," the *St. Petersburg Times* reported in 1988. "Indeed," its article continued, "as the community seeks a new identity, promoters concede that new growth on the I-4 corridor is blurring boundaries." Economist Thomas Powers amplified the comments. "It's almost like a suburb between two mega-stars, Tampa and Orlando," he argued. Lakeland Chamber of Commerce president Bill Loftin felt the same way. "We've made a lot of strides," he noted.[4]

One stride that touched the Interstate 4 corridor involved the attraction previously known as Circus World, and its experience highlighted both the potential for the region and nagging problems connected with Polk's efforts to realize that potential. As had those responsible for other attractions, Circus World owner Jim Monaghan struggled with the tourism slump of the early 1980s and a scarcity of the financial resources necessary to maintain his business's competitive edge. In April 1986 he sold it to the publisher Harcourt Brace Jovanovich. That conglomerate closed the amusement center, transforming the I-4/U.S. 27 property from Barnum City to Baseball City as of April 1987. The new theme park, officially designated Boardwalk and Baseball, hosted spring training for the Kansas City Royals baseball team and other baseball activities. Additionally, a large shopping center housed ten retail outlets, including a bar called The Dugout. The Ted Williams Best Western Motel graced its vicinity, while a four-lane road—they called it Homerun Boulevard—paved the way for future growth near the attraction's entrance.[5]

95. *Although its opening raised high expectations in Polk, Baseball City soon succumbed to economic problems and poor attendance.* POLK COUNTY HISTORICAL ASSOCIATION.

But, given the volatile economic times, happy celebrations at Boardwalk and Baseball's opening unfortunately soon took on a different coloring. As it happened, the corporate owner assumed a large debt in resisting a takeover attempt and, in order to solidify its financial position, sold its amusement parks—also including Cypress Gardens and Sea World—to Anheuser Busch in November 1989. Six weeks later, having decided that the new property was losing too much money, Busch suddenly closed the entire show. Nearly 900 workers found themselves out of jobs, while 900 visitors then on the grounds found themselves summarily escorted out. "It's unfortunate," Florida Southern College economist Carl Brown observed by way of an obituary for the attraction, "that there were such high expectations for that location."[6]

That was the problem in a sense, high expectations. People desired the return of good times and growth to even better times so fervently that they perceived relatively small signs of progress as large and permanent ones. Had all other things turned out well, perhaps a little luck might have produced enough movement in a desirable direction. Mostly, the luck was not forthcoming. One survey of the situation noted some of the problems faced merely in coping with the growth that Polk already was experiencing. "Even with its recent change in fortunes, Polk still faces some tough economic challenges," a business writer observed in 1988. "For one thing, many of the high-paying jobs lost prior to the region's economic collapse have been replaced with low-paying service jobs," he continued. "That has held per capita income to about 80 percent of the statewide average." The challenge of how to pay for "new public works to accommodate the thousands of residents moving into the area" loomed large, as well. Roads appeared the most obvious of the concerns as traffic began to clog many arteries in the county's northern and northeastern sectors, but law enforcement, fire protection, and recreation needs demanded attention too.[7]

Turns of Economic Fate

Beyond the challenge of meeting the minimum infrastructure requirements of ongoing growth, questions regarding the county's historic but deteriorating economic base complicated movement toward resolving the economic quagmire. Citrus, tourism, and phosphate had spawned wealth and security for many over the passage of generations; yet, each of those vital segments of the economy now fought either for stability or else to stem further losses. Tourism, for instance, remained open to question—as seen with Boardwalk and Broadway's experience—as a reliable basis for large-scale investment. Local communities, unwilling under the circumstances to commit sufficient public resources to maintain or create tourism-related amenities, felt the sting as crowds went elsewhere. Winter Haven discovered that fact in 1988 when the Boston Red Sox announced future cancellation of its agreement with the city based upon complaints about the condition of the stadium and field. The team played its last game there four years later. Compounding the loss, as city manager Carl Cheatham noted, was the fact that the city was "full of retired New Englanders who moved there to watch their beloved Red Sox." Now, their continued commitment to the community weighed in the balance. Even when tourists could be attracted, an infrastructure problem undercut progress. As one review concluded in 1988, "Polk does not have an adequate stock of hotel rooms to support a strong tourism industry."[8]

The tourism industry's late 1980s trials withered by comparison to those of the phosphate industry. Although in 1986 India and the People's Republic of China had begun large-scale purchases locally, industry fortunes changed for the worse, not the better. "The phosphate industry is in dire straits," Florida Phosphate Council spokesman Elin Oak acknowledged in 1987. The previous year had proven the worst of a decade filled with bad years. Total employment, 60 percent of which centered in Polk, had dropped to 11,666 in 1985. One year later, only 9,702 kept their jobs. Layoffs, mine closings, mergers, and sales of operations marked the day. Mulberry, the self-proclaimed "Phosphate Capital of the World," lay mired in depression. "I never once dreamed I would live to see this happen to the phosphate industry," Mayor Carl M. "Kid" Ellis admitted. "Former phosphate workers drive trucks today," a reporter discovered. He added: "They pick oranges. When things get desperate, they ask the community service center for emergency food and rent money." Even in such circumstances, many refused to ask for help. "They have pride," businessman James Jackson explained. "People will sit there and lose their house before they ask for help."[9]

Over the remainder of the decade the depression-like conditions fortunately eased slightly as phosphate and fertilizer production demands increased modestly. For the most part, a weakened national economy that produced a weakened dollar could be thanked for buttressing export orders. The weakened dollar also brought into the local industry ownership picture an unlikely new partner. In 1989 the People's Republic of China, through the Sinochem American Holdings subsidiary of the China National Chemicals Import & Export Corp., purchased U.S. Agri-Chemicals Corp. and its Bartow and Fort Meade fertilizer plants.

Further investments followed from the same source, and luckily so. Old mines continued to close as the industry moved inexorably away from Polk to adjacent counties. When Estech shut down its fifty-year-old Watson Mine south of Fort Meade in late 1988, Central Florida lost one of only two high-grade phosphate mines remaining. The industry lost, as well, another 120 jobs.[10]

With Polk's phosphate empire nearing its extinction and the industry seeking better fields for endeavor elsewhere, many eyes naturally turned to the citrus industry for the county's salvation. The freezes of 1983 and 1985 had decimated local groves; still, optimism ruled the day. Even though acreage dedicated to the industry had dropped from 129,912 to 106,993 in two years, Polk remained in 1986 the number one citrus county in the state. A world-wide crop shortage that resulted partially from shortfalls in Brazilian production aided recovery efforts. Production levels increased to 32 million boxes in the 1986-1987 season. The next season saw them mount to 44 million, with higher totals anticipated in 1988-1989. Experts concluded as a result that "citrus production—a mainstay of Polk's economy—has returned to full vigor."[11]

Good, if bittersweet, news additionally supported the recovery. In 1989 reports revealed that the citrus canker scare that had beset the industry for half the decade had constituted nothing more that "a big lie." In what was described by analyst Phillip Longman as "a most bizarre series of events," 32 million nursery trees had been destroyed without substantive cause. "The canker eradication program, as more and more ruined nurserymen are beginning to realize, was in reality a cynical government cover-up designed to benefit Florida's largest agribusinesses," Longman explained. He continued, "As key government scientists and regulators have known all along, most of the trees the state burned were perfectly healthy; none was infected with canker, nor with any other serious disease." The furor that ensued following such disclosures shocked the industry and likely contributed to Florida Agriculture Commissioner Doyle Conner's decision not to seek re-election in 1990. Voters, faced with a choice as to who should take over as head regulator of the state's agricultural sector, turned to Polk's Democrat state senator Bob Crawford over Republican candidate Charles Bronson.[12]

The good news ended there, at least for the time being. At Christmas 1989 a killer freeze "as cold as Scrooge's heart" attacked Florida groves mercilessly. "We had heavy losses all the way to Homestead," one authority observed. Officials declared that "the freeze reduced Florida's citrus crop 30 percent." That left usable production at the lowest point seen for twenty-five years. In Polk, 75,000 acres of citrus trees were "severely damaged." Grower James E. Allen, Jr., of Lakeland later summed up the resulting situation. "A lot of trees died," he reported, "and growers are getting out of the business." The jolts continued, as additional assessments revealed startling aspects to the damage. "Polk growers," one industry expert commented in an important example, "face losing their century-old standing as the state's largest citrus producer."[13]

Sad to say, the process that placed Polk on the path to losing its standing in state production had been operating for several years as selected growers had decided following the decade's earlier freezes to seek safer environs for their investments. "Many of the large citrus corporations and cooperatives have opted to move their operations south, to warmer areas," a 1988 report had disclosed. "Buying up former cattle lands, these large growers are putting in huge groves," the article continued. "For instance, Ben Hill Griffin Inc. recently planted 1,450 acres of trees in Charlotte County, and Alico Inc., the publicly held company founded by Ben Hill Griffin Jr., just planted a 1,500-acre grove in Hendry County." It added, "Citrus World, the Lake Wales cooperative, also has planted 3,000 acres of citrus trees in Hendry."[14]

96. *The 1989 freeze devastated the citrus crop and further dampened already depressed spirits.* POLK COUNTY HISTORICAL ASSOCIATION.

It might well be argued that areas heavily invested in citrus and phosphate could reorient themselves to light industry and other non-agricultural pursuits. For some locations, which is to say ones in the I-4 corridor or else in easy proximity to it, that brand of thinking merited real consideration. For the county's southern half, its historic heartland, a very different situation prevailed. No limited access highways reached into those regions, nor did a landscape pocked with phosphate mining scars endear itself to those yearning for a comfortable retirement amid semi-tropical splendor.

As Mulberry's example illustrates, these conditions left many local communities hustling in the late 1980s to find some reliable and lucrative route to the future. Faced with the misery left in the phosphate industry's wake, it proved no easy task. "Mulberry's dependence on the phosphate industry is almost complete," Central Florida Regional Planning Council planner Brian Sodt observed in 1987. "It is a community that developed in par with the industry, and it's always been in sync with the peaks and valleys of the industry." Given those circumstances, it took some time for local leaders to realize the need for change. Early hopes that extending the town limits to include two nearby mobile home parks built on reclaimed phosphate land might improve matters by doubling the population and adding to the tax base proved less than helpful.[15]

At that point Sam Whitney's Vindicator of Florida Inc. entered the picture with the idea of erecting near Mulberry a $6-7 million food irradiation plant to disinfect and extend the shelf life of various foods. The highly controversial process of food irradiation sparked quick response, as opponents organized to block the innovation. They achieved an early victory in October 1989 when the city commission agreed to annex the industrial park in which the plant was to rise so that Mulberry, rather than the county, would decide whether and how the facility would be permitted to operate. Four months later the commission agreed to a one-year moratorium on construction, pleasing the Polk County Commission to Stop Food Irradiation and others. Seven months afterward, and to the surprise of many, the Mulberry commission reversed itself and approved the plant. Commissioner Johnnie B. Smith, an early opponent, explained that prayer and a call from local Methodist minister Danny Davis had helped to change his mind. An outraged Jan Privett of the county's chapter of the Concerned Citizens League of America served notice that her group would "keep trying to prevent the plant from being built." Construction activities commenced, but the timing of the plant's opening could not be forecast because the state, too, held permitting authority.[16]

The decade thus closed at Mulberry with the town's future remaining uncertain and the community still dependent almost totally upon the phosphate industry. "You can't get by without the mine," retired worker Motis Duffey remarked in December 1990. "That's where the money's at," he added. "If it wasn't for that, we'd be pitiful around here." It was too late, though, to block the industry's inevitable departure. "This was real pretty country around here once," lifelong resident Wilbert Lancaster insisted wistfully. "It was all big pine timber [before] the companies came through here and used it up and played it out." Lancaster concluded: "We're just like red-headed stepchildren now. We're thrown away. But look what they left us. A big mess."[17]

As the Florida Department of Environmental Regulation had reminded residents in early 1989, the mess produced by the phosphate industry or, at least, existing within proximity to it extended well beyond Mulberry's town limits. That agency had concluded that "waste from Central Florida phosphate plants—some of it accumulating for 60 years—is threatening the aquifer that supplies 90 percent of the state's drinking water." Many of the plants cited lay within Polk. One newspaper explained the problem in this manner. "Most of the waste created comes from the manufacturing

97. *Questions about the danger of phosphate waste products stored in gypsum stacks troubled many county residents, likely including the persons living in these homes near Mulberry.* POLK COUNTY HISTORICAL ASSOCIATION.

of phosphate, an agricultural fertilizer," it began. "The waste products are placed in huge gypsum stacks and contain sulfuric and phosphoric acids that work down through the soil to the aquifer," the article continued. "The acids eat holes under the piles and actually dissolve the aquifer below." Under questioning, DER officials acknowledged that "there never has been a state standard for dealing with phosphate pollution and they are trying to formulate one, rather than deal with contamination problems on a case-by-case basis."[18]

This disclosure came only a few years after a separate state report had revived the question of radon gas danger. That controversy had stemmed from a 1986 attempt by state health officials to map Central Florida areas "believed to be at high risk for radon gas." They had undertaken the task as part of efforts to enforce rules requiring special construction standards and warnings where large concentrations of the potentially deadly gas were found. When the map revealed "a large chunk of southwest Polk" as high-risk land, developers urged the county commission to seek a permanent injunction by "charging the map is unconstitutional and that [the state] singled out Polk County in a feeble attempt to comply with its own rules." The county sued, and, in response, the legislature—at the request of state representative Beverly Burnsed and state senator Curtis Peterson—funded a statewide re-study of the problem. State representative Larry Libertore, who headed the study commission, extended the effort into 1988. "For many, many years, we've been getting along with radon," he explained. "For us to have to make a decision now, we're just not ready."[19]

The long-awaited commission report arrived in 1988 but generated little steam to propel protective efforts. It announced discovery of high radon levels in eighteen counties. The study, as conducted by the Florida Institute of Phosphate Research, also "showed lower levels than expected" in Polk even though the county led the state. The panel called for state radon resistant building codes but accepted that five or more years of additional study would be required first. "How can you enforce something you're not sure will work," Libertore queried. "It's just too big an issue to address in a hodgepodge fashion," he observed. "It's a sensitive issue that no one really has a handle on yet." Representative C. Fred Jones of Auburndale, who chaired the House Community Affairs Committee, vowed to enforce a minimum four-year delay and to bar counties from adopting their own radon safety building codes. Environmentalists countered by pointing out Jones's "attachment to the phosphate industry and his known record for stalling any radon protective measures statewide." Builders and real estate brokers mostly shrugged off the matter. "There's developments all over town that have been built on reclaimed lands," Polk County Builders Association president Pat Kelly declared. "We need some scientific studies with enough data to come up with some building codes the builders can use," he continued. "As builders, you've got to have some responsibility about it," Kelly commented further. "How would you like to be responsible for somebody's health?" he concluded. "We—all of us—could be walking on thin ice."[20]

Criminal Distractions

As was traditional for the county, Polk's residents tended to afford warnings about radon gas dangers about as much attention as did the real estate industry. They simply had too many other concerns—and more easily understandable ones—that demanded their attention, with crime continuing to hold a place near the top of that list. A virtual plague of criminal behavior had raged in the first half of the 1980s, and the decade's second half brought little relief. By 1987 the total number of crimes known to have been committed in Florida during the year soared past the one million mark. The chances of becoming a victim stood at about one in twelve, with Polk Countians enjoying somewhat less favorable odds. Prison populations ballooned to the point that one wit suggested the rise might offer a solid investment opportunity in hard times. "It's too bad you can't buy stock in the prison population," he joked, "it shows nice increases every year."[21]

Violent crime and offenses connected with illegal sale and use of drugs continued to highlight the criminal scene in Polk. Two examples help to offer a sense of the times. During 1985, forty-five murders served to set a new annual record for Polk, up from thirty-seven in 1984 and thirty-two in 1983. "In the eight years I've been here," Assistant Public Defender Larry Shearer exclaimed, "it's never been this [bad]." Another record fell in 1986 when agents arrested five people, seized five planes, and confiscated 1,100 pounds of cocaine at a remote Green Swamp airstrip north of Lakeland. The additional 135 pounds of marijuana taken in the raid were not needed to make the event "Polk's biggest drug bust."[22]

Heartless cruelty punctuated many offenses. Millionaire Durward Faulk of Polk tried to murder his wife by pushing her from their boat in an attempt at drowning her. Unable to swim, she screamed for help as Faulk casually circled the boat, waiting for his wife to die. An Osceola County jury found little problem convicting him of attempted murder in

1990. The same year another jury convicted Lakeland's Thomas Coe of murder for killing his two-year-old stepson Bradley McGee by dunking "the baby head-first into a toilet to discipline him." The case thereafter served as a catalyst for passage of stronger state child abuse laws.[23]

Civil crime, meanwhile, broke records, hearts, and pocketbooks. In the era's most spotlighted incident, prosecutors in the closing days of 1987 accused Winter Haven businessman Stephen L. Smith and his SH Oil & Gas Exploration of massive fraud. Those who knew the "up and coming entrepreneur" from one of the region's old families expressed disbelief that he could have operated a securities scam. "I just don't think that Steve would do anything wrong," one friend insisted. "I believe there must be some mistake." There was not. Initial estimates of the magnitude of Smith's crimes suggested that he bilked up to 270 investors of $85 to $100 million. When he ultimately pled guilty to federal charges in April 1989, the figures had risen to 712 investors and $125 million. The human cost rose far higher. "People who worked all their lives lost their homes, their cars," Haines City's John Coffay observed. "It was devastating."[24]

Utter disrespect for the law and its processes appeared to have reached records highs for the modern era, as well. This fact found telling illustration in 1987. "A 19-year-old man in Polk County Circuit Court, seeking a hearing on whether he was competent to stand trial on drug charges, peeled down his bright orange prison pants and mooned the courtroom, including the judge and a dozen attorneys, other defendants and spectators," a news item detailed. It added, "He was granted the hearing."[25]

The antics of a nineteen-year-old drug user seemed inconsequential next to the acts of Ku Klux Klan grand dragon Donald Lloyd Spivey, although their contempt for the law manifested itself equally. One week after the Kathleen man made headlines in 1990 by offering to assist Eagle Lake police to "battle drug dealers on the street," Polk law enforcement officers arrested him for the rape of a sixteen-year-old girl he had recruited for the organization. Spivey fled to Canada, only to be apprehended and deported to face the charges. Convicted, he foreswore repentance and instead satisfied his own emotional needs by accusing the judge of being a colleague's homosexual lover.[26]

Polk even witnessed unlawful attempts to secure Stinger anti-aircraft missiles and other military weaponry, ostensibly for use against Columbian government helicopters operating against local drug lords. The two men involved in the affair actually approached Polk sheriff's detectives, presumably unaware of their identities, about their plans. Months of pa-

98. *Sheriff Dan Daniels stirred controversy that led to his early departure from office.*
LAKELAND LEDGER.

tient handling, investigation, and coordination paid off in May 1990 arrests. Department spokeswoman Lynne Breidenbach beamed with pride. "This is no hick operation," she boasted. "People have the wrong impression of this agency," Breidenbach went on to assert. "We've got some special agents who play in the big leagues and can do just about anything."[27]

If a certain defensiveness appears to exude from Breidenbach's comments, that posture might have arisen from a series of events that occurred with respect to the sheriff's department during the decade's final half. Sheriff Dan Daniels had faced controversy since his earliest days in office, but nothing prepared residents for the happenings of 1986 and early 1987. First, committing himself to a running battle with the *Lakeland Ledger*, Daniels forbade his staff to respond verbally to any inquiry from the newspaper, claiming that it "has abused me and your sheriff's department to an excessive degree." Then, State Attorney Jerry Hill launched an investigation amid allegations that Daniels had diverted funds from a nonprofit golf tournament to buy sheriff's decals for his supporters. Hill's inquiry ranged out from that point to address old and several new accusations. They included inconsistencies in the department's bidding policy; Daniels's alleged acceptance of unreported cash campaign contributions in violation of state law; misuse of the Sheriff's Department Junior Deputy Golf League Classic fund; and promising jobs in return for campaign support.[28]

The political crisis reached its breaking point in January 1987 when the Polk grand jury called for Daniels's resignation or else his removal by Governor Bob Martinez. "We base this recommendation on overwhelming evidence of misconduct and incompetence on the part of Sheriff Daniels and many of the people he has put in positions of leadership," the report stated. "The fact that the sheriff's office has become a joke to many is no laughing matter for the citizens of Polk County." The grand jury report named, as well, Sheriff's Captain Maines Waters and one-time Major Marvin Pittman in connection with the issue of Daniels's promising of jobs in return for campaign support.[29]

The sheriff soon resigned. "I have never learned to be a politician per se and that is quite clear," he expressed at the time. "In fact, I have tried hard not to be one." A conciliatory tone evidenced in Daniels's resignation letter later changed to one sharply critical of Hill and Chief Circuit Judge William A. Norris, Jr., with allegations that county politics had rendered him a victim. Back home in Winter Haven, Daniels eventually published a newspaper, *The Eagle*, that in time offered, in one reporter's words, "biting criticism of those he viewed as his enemies, and of the liberal wing of politics." The former sheriff frequently aired criticisms of African Americans and of black aspirations, as well, especially after he became a regional officer of the National Association for the Advancement of White People. He passed away, still a resident of Polk and certainly remembered as one of the county's most colorful and controversial figures, in July 2003.[30]

Daniels's departure from office created an opportunity for Governor Martinez, a Republican, to work a second political revolution in Polk by the designation of a Republican as sheriff. Martinez's man proved to be Lakeland Chief of Police Lawrence Crow, who had switched from Democrat to Republican "a few months" before his appointment. The new sheriff could boast a career in law enforcement and a bachelor's degree in police administration. Married, with two children, and only in his mid-40s, Crow appeared a more-than-acceptable replacement for his predecessor. Polk's voters agreed and elected him to the office with 63 percent of the vote over Democrat Tom Wheeler in 1988. Crow thereafter maintained the position into the twenty-first century.[31]

Which is the not same thing as saying that Crow brought no controversy to his new job. An early instance occurred in 1989 when reports revealed that, under Crow's direction, county jail officials required homosexual inmates to wear red bands around their wrists "for the inmates' own protection." The practice came to be referred to as the "pink tag" system. "The bracelets don't come in pink, they're really 'insignia red,'" Captain Dale Tray explained. "If they did, we'd buy them in pink." Civil rights advocates condemned the practice, as did some newspapers. "Bigotry in any form is offensive," one editorial argued, "but the Polk County policy is particularly heinous, masked superficially as something in the inmates' best interest."[32]

Attention to Government

As events touching on the sheriff's office suggest, government and politics during the last half of the 1980s proved a subject far from dull. The school board particularly found itself at the center of any number of interesting situations and dilemmas. News that the dropout rate had reached 11 percent during the 1985-1986 school year failed to stir any considerable publicity, but, when school officials, following a "mooning" incident, ordered a Bartow High School student sent for ten days to a county school for problem children, the spotlight shone brightly. Eventually the Second District Court of Appeal intervened to encourage settlement of the dispute, although not before the incident came to statewide attention. One Miami television personality, appalled at the Polk action, even mooned his audience in solidarity with the young man. "I wanted people to see how innocent it can be," the Miami man commented. "A lot of us have 'mooned' people. It's a harmless prank."[33]

Less humor attached itself to the issue of student lie detector tests, although that matter also brought the school system a generous measure of unwelcome attention. It arose in 1986 with revelations by the *Winter Haven News Chief* that the Polk system had utilized polygraph tests on up to 200 students per year for the previous five years without board authorization. In Florida only Duval County did the same, but it did so to twenty or fewer students annually. With the exposure, the school board—at member Ted Aggelis's urging—ratified the practice by a four-to-zero vote. School Superintendent John Stewart then suspended the examinations, an action that the board overrode by a margin of three-to-two after Aggelis expressed dismay. "What bothers me," the feisty board veteran declared, "is when the liberal news media and the [American Civil Liberties Union] come in and try to set policy."[34]

Months of controversy ensued, with a debate on the NBC-TV show "Today" bringing the policy and policymakers to national attention. The Associated Press aired the experience of Lakeland High School student body president Steve Misencik, an honors graduate on standby to attend the United States Air Force Academy. Forced to prove his innocence of grade changing, he endured "the most nerve-wracking experience of my life." Jo Misencik, Steve's mother, expressed her own frustration. "We were trapped—judged without proof on somebody's word," she asserted. "That children have to prove themselves innocent, isn't that a horrible thing to be taught in school." Other parents warned that Polk faced becoming "the Salem of the South." In time, the ACLU sued for $5.5 million, with its lawyer raising the question of "Ouija board justice." Board attorney C. A. "Bubba" Boswell, who earlier had supported the practice, by then advised its discontinuance. Only Aggelis objected. Voters subsequently had their say in November elections by ousting Aggelis. Board member Dan Moody correctly summed up prevailing sentiments. He called the whole affair "an embarrassment for the school system."[35]

As those events unfolded, the nature of county politics experienced subtle change, with Republicans gaining strength although not yet decisive strength. In doing so, the GOP benefitted from disenchantment with Democrats, a growing population of retirees living within the county, the authority of the Reagan presidential administration, and the presence of a Republican governor in Tallahassee. Increasingly, Republicans found themselves able to contest most local races. In 1986, for example, Representatives Beverly Burnsed and Charles Canady, Jr., both Democrats, endured serious—though unsuccessful—contests from Republicans Kent Harrison and Joe Wilkerson. Quite a few of the GOP candidates shared one trait in common, their recent switch from the Democratic party. Thus, when school board member J. J. Corbett found his seat contested, he discovered his Republican challenger David Hallock to be the man he had defeated four years earlier in the Democratic primary.[36]

One additional factor benefitted the Republican ascendancy significantly. Fundamentalist, "born again," or otherwise conservative Christian groups had learned important lessons about politics and the organizational skills required for success at election time. Whether in the form of the Moral Majority or some other individual group or denomination, they brought to the political table a passion and commitment unrivaled by their opponents. Of special importance in this regard, the Carpenter's Home Church determined to make a political difference. By 1988, for instance, its leaders even encouraged students from the church's Evangel School to campaign for GOP candidates such as John Reaves, who was contesting a state house seat against Democrat Tom Mims. The church fell short of its goal as Mims defeated Reaves, but blame for the loss might have rested more properly with Ku Klux Klan leader Donald Lloyd Spivey who campaigned in his Klan robes for the Republican. "He would probably disapprove of this," Spivey declared of candidate Reaves. "I want to make that clear," the grand dragon continued. "But he is a Christian, an honest man." Spivey added: "Mims has his black supporters here. It's only fair Reaves gets the white people out here."[37]

As Reaves's candidacy illustrated, Republicans entered the 1988 elections with high hopes. Mostly, they failed of victory, although George H. W. Bush carried Polk in the presidential contest with two-thirds of the vote and Sheriff Crow easily achieved election. Democrats, including United States senatorial candidate Buddy McKay, managed wins. Significantly, though, McKay's margin against statewide winner Connie Mack amounted only to three-tenths of 1 percent. County Republican chair Jean Burt and other GOP leaders found much to celebrate in the results. "It was historic," Burt exclaimed. "We know a Republican can win in Polk County." She added, "Polk County has come around to being a true two-party county."[38]

The 1988 contests set the stage for lasting GOP gains. Furthering that end, Republican activist Bill Siegel had grown so enthusiastic in 1988 that he organized the Men's Republican Club of Winter Haven, a group that by summer 1989 could claim "about 100" members. "Eight years ago," Siegel commented, "this group no more would have flown than me going to the moon." Some Democrat officeholders got the message. In March 1989 two-term county commissioner Lee Draper changed his affiliation to Republican, becoming the only GOP member of that body. Although Polk Democrat Bob Crawford then presided over the state senate, even the legislative delegate saw an important defection. Already conservative and stung by House Speaker John Mills's earlier action in removing him as majority whip for refusing to support a tax on services, Charles Canady, Jr., opted to join Republican ranks in June. Canady thus emerged as the first member of that party ever to represent Polk in the state legislature.[39]

Republicans could be forgiven for looking forward expectantly to the 1990 elections, but a surprise entrant into the governor's race turned the dynamics of the season upside down. Lawton Chiles had retired from the United States Senate in 1989 tired and frustrated. Friends believed that Florida required his services, though, and encouraged the veteran Democrat to run for governor the next year against incumbent Bob Martinez. Chiles's late entry into the contest caught the Democratic field unprepared, and the former senator and his running mate Buddy McKay captured nearly 70 percent of the vote and the nomination. In November, the team repeated their victory, upsetting and ousting the sitting Republican governor. Polk, as it had done every time it had been asked, backed Chiles. In Polk and in the state at large, 56 percent of ballots cast favored the Chiles-McKay ticket.[40]

Chiles's candidacy provided coattails for Democrats to ride in local elections. It especially produced a high voter turnout that brought many Democrats to the polls who might, otherwise, have declined to vote. The Republican party had targeted several Polk races for special assistance, and its strategists had expected their candidates to fare well generally. The GOP stressed opposition to abortion rights as a theme statewide and in Polk. This emphasis may have hurt the party's prospects, however, as women voters backed the Democrats by large margins. State representative Canady likely felt the political sting of this factor in his narrow loss to Democrat Quillian Yancey in a state senate election to replace state senator Curtis Peterson. Rick Dantzler's win over Republican crossover Ernie Caldwell in a second state senate race evidenced a similar turn of events. A Democrat, Joe Viscusi, even managed to take Canady's house seat.[41]

The near-Democrat sweep of Polk contests brought other happy party candidates into office or else returned them there. Among them, Bob Connors and Dan Costello joined the county commission. Given that two years earlier former Winter Haven Mayor Marlene Duffy Young had won a seat vacated by longtime member Jack Simmons at the same time that Neil Combee had defeated incumbent Royce Ready, new winds definitely were sweeping through the county courthouse. Anne Kaylor's win in a county judgeship race signaled, as well, that women's involvements in local politics continued to thrive.[42]

At first blush the results seemed to spell trouble for the Republicans, but all was not what it appeared. For one thing, the GOP won its first election for a legislative seat from Polk when Bartow's John Laurent bested Ben Fredericks in a south-county district heavily Democratic in registration. When party switchers were taken into account, dramatic change had occurred in a few short years. As GOP chair Jean Burt turned her position over to Jack Turner late in the year, she mused on the progress made. "The Republican Party now offers candidates on the ballot," she commented. "Prior to the last few elections, all of our elections were determined in the Democratic primary, and now we have two-party elections." Burt continued: "We've brought the registration up from being outnumbered by the Democrats 4-1. Now there are 1.62 Democrats for every Republican registered in the county." Burt then ticked off an accumulation of accomplishments. "Republicans in office," she detailed, "in-

99. *Congressman Andy Ireland's switch from Democrat to Republican helped to fuel GOP hopes in Polk during the late 1980s. Lakeland Ledger.*

clude Sheriff Lawrence Crow, School Superintendent John Stewart, School Board member Rubie Wilcox, County Commissioner Neil Combee, and John Laurent." Burt concluded, "In the Sheriff Crow era, we have proved that good Republican candidates can be elected to office here. It proved that Congressman Andy Ireland was not a fluke."[43]

Not to be Forgotten

100. *Fort Meade's Mary E. Jones helped to break political and professional barriers for women and for African Americans. Seen here with Citrus and Chemical Bank head George Harris, Jones in the late 1980s became Polk's first African American bank officer. MARY E. JONES.*

Counted among those individuals and accomplishments that should not be overlooked for the years 1985-1990 were several additional milestones passed by women and by African Americans. At Fort Meade, for example, Mary E. Jones in 1986 became the city's first African American commissioner. Two years later she claimed precedence as the town's first female and first African American mayor. Nonplused, Jones went on to become in 1989 the county's first black bank officer and, in 1990, its first black candidate for the county commission. Another woman of outstanding ability, Lucy DuCharme, in 1988 took over the reins of the Polk County Democratic party from the capable hands of one-time civil rights activist Lemuel Geathers. DuCharme went on to serve as party chair until 1992. Meanwhile, Lakeland's Gow B. Fields made headlines as the first African American Republican to join the Polk Community College board of trustees. His designation came in 1989 from Governor Bob Martinez upon the recommendation of party leader C. C. "Doc" Dockery.[44]

101. *Polk County civic leader and Democratic party executive Lucy DuCharme.* POLK COUNTY HISTORICAL ASSOCIATION.

Gubernatorial appointment in early 1987 also placed a county resident, Stephen H. Grimes, on the Florida supreme court. A longtime friend of then United States Senator Lawton Chiles, Grimes had launched his legal career at Bartow, following service in the Navy during 1951-1953, with what would become the Holland & Knight law firm. He had received appointment to the second district court of appeal in 1973. On the supreme court Grimes took a leadership role, serving from 1994 to 1996 as chief justice. He retired from the bench in 1997. "Justice Grimes," Governor Lawton Chiles remarked at the time, "you leave some big shoes to fill."[45]

Cultural affairs within Polk took a solid step forward in September 1988 with the opening of the new Polk Museum of Art at Lakeland. The $5 million facility immediately drew plaudits as "a shining example of how to build a museum." The superb art center could trace its origins, though, to humbler beginnings. It had originated in 1966 as a children's museum in one room of a church, and in the following decade it had relocated to a one- time Publix Super Market. Planning for its grander home had commenced in 1981 under executive director Ken Rollins's supervision. "This, we feel is going to be the next growth area in the state of Florida," Rollins commented when his project came to fruition. "And the museum is poised to grow with it."[46]

Historical affairs, too, witnessed advances through the period. Court clerk E. D. "Bud" Dixon as chairman of the Polk County Historical Commission combined with other commission members such as William T. Ruster and Dwight DeVane to create a "Heritage Park" at Homeland. Upon land donated by the school board, historical structures such as the county's oldest school house, Homeland's pioneer Bethel Methodist Church, authentic log cabins, and other early homes and structures found safe and permanent homes. In the meantime, residents found a delightful site for gatherings, community functions, and the celebration of Polk's rich past. Lake Wales's historic heart commanded attention, as well. Civic leader and Depot Museum director Mimi Hardman spearheaded efforts in 1988 to establish that city's first historic district and architectural review board. Preservation expert Bill Adams assisted the initiative, while a new group, Historic Lake Wales, planned historic tours to complement the plans.[47]

Finally, Polk treated itself to a gift during the decade's second half when county government acted to erect a new courthouse. First authorized by the county commission in 1982, the nine-story, $37 million Bartow edifice first welcomed 570 county employees and countless residents in July 1987. "It's a beautiful building," the *Lakeland Ledger* proclaimed. The structure boasted an opulence previously unknown to county government, including "marble walls and floors, seamless oak paneling, and expensive furnishings." Troubles soon developed, however, with cracked walls, slippery floors, and a leaking roof. Increasingly, workers also seemed to be missing time from the job, having found themselves feeling ill since moving into the county government's new headquarters. Unhappy with these problems and fearful that they might have a "sick building" on their hands, county commissioners ended the decade with suits pending against the contractor and architect. It appeared as though the 1990s probably would see further complications, as such indeed turned out to be the case.[48]

102. *Builders and developers such as Sam Rodgers, seen here looking over plans at Sandpiper Golf and Country Club on Socrum Loop Road in north Lakeland, attempted to meet and to encourage Polk's impressive growth in the 1990s.* LAKELAND PUBLIC LIBRARY.

"we made it before phosphate, and we'll make it after phosphate"

CHAPTER 12

୬

Glimpses Over the Horizon, 1990-1995

*P*olk Countians anticipated the decade of the 1990s not only as a respite from difficult times but also for the promise of permanent advances and warm prosperity such as that reflected elsewhere in the Florida peninsula. Old mainstays—whether ones influencing the economy or politics or society as a whole—in the previous ten years seemingly had disintegrated without notice or hope for second chance. Now, a confused picture greeted residents, a scene that telegraphed messages strikingly negative and undeniably positive in an endless stream as the pace of life quickened with change. Meanwhile, residents found themselves divided starkly in their approaches to resolving the crises of life that confronted them within the increasingly frenetic atmosphere. Occasionally, decisions made actually led to happy solutions. Many times, though, they appeared merely to sharpen edges and widen the divide.

The 1990s would bring lasting change to Polk, a substantial part of it fueled by growth and the nature of subsequent development. At the decade's commencement, the county held 405,382 persons; at its end, 483,924. The addition of so many new residents could not help but carry an impact, although careful attention to the figures told a story that differed considerably from the apparent one of substantial growth. Florida during the 1980s had swelled in population by nearly 33 percent. Polk had increased by 26 percent. In the 1990s, the state's rate of increase slowed to 23.5 percent, but Polk's registered only at 19.4 percent. These comparisons meant something important in the real world. Polk, for instance, had claimed a place of major significance in Florida politics through the twentieth century. Three governors, three United States senators, and innumerable state cabinet officers, presiding officers of legislative chambers, judges, and justices had wielded power to the county's benefit for nearly a century. As the 1990s opened, Polk's Lawton Chiles captured the governor's office on the way to two terms as the state's chief executive. But would the county's ability to exert that magnitude of influence continue?[1]

103. *Democrat Rick Dantzler earned respect while representing Polk County in the Florida House of Representative and Florida Senate during the 1980s and 1990s.* LAKELAND LEDGER.

A 1992 political survey questioned whether it would, particularly when mandated legislative redistricting and reapportionment were considered. "Polk County, once a power in state politics, has lost a major force with the announcement that state Rep. C. Fred Jones, the dean of the House of Representatives, is not seeking re-election," the report began. "The county's power base now lies in the Senate, where state Sens. Rick Dantzler and Quillian Yancey are finishing their first two terms," it continued. "But redistricting leaves Yancey's position in doubt. He now lives in the same district as Dantzler, and Yancey said last week he will not oppose his fellow Democrat." The survey went on to recall different times. "It's a far cry from the halcyon days of the mid-1980s when state Rep. Beverly Burnsed ran the House Transportation Committee, Jones headed the Community Affairs Committee, Rep. Charles T. Canady, then a Democrat, was House Majority Whip, and Dantzler was considered a bright up-and-comer. In the Senate, Curtis Peterson was just coming off a term as senate president, and Sen. Bob Crawford was chairing the Natural Resources and Conservation committee." Senator Peterson described what that level of clout had meant. "We were among the top influential delegations," he insisted. "We didn't have the votes that Dade County had, but we had as much influence." County Democratic executive committee member Greg Ruthven summed up the situation. "Seniority means getting things done," he declared. "Our seniority is gone."[2]

Just who made up Polk's citizenry was changing, as well. For one thing, the county's base was growing older. By 1990, the population of persons sixty-five or older ranked as "one of the fastest growing in Florida," having jumped almost 64 percent in ten years. That meant nearly 20 percent of residents qualified as elderly as the decade began. Approximately the same figure applied as it ended. This represented a significant change from the immediate post-World War Two era when a more-youthful population set about building prosperity and ushering Polk into modern times based, in good part, upon the support of an activist government. A half-century later, older voters tended in local elections to vote for Republican candidates who opposed government growth and the taxation required to pay for it. At the same time, governmental responsibilities in caring for the elderly had blossomed enormously.[3]

While perhaps not offering so great a change, the county's racial and ethnic base, too, had shifted. African Americans in 1990 contributed 12.9 percent of Polk's total. By 2000, the figure had reached 13.5 percent. More dramatically, Hispanics saw their numbers rise markedly. At the decade's beginning, 4.1 percent of the county pool represented that classification. At its end, the percentage stood at 9.5, which is to say, about one in ten.[4]

Linked to the increase in elderly, African American, and Hispanic populations—as well as to the county's economic problems generally—was the persistence of chronic poverty. With the start of the 1990s, over one-tenth of Polk's residents were unemployed. Per capita income then amounted to $15,160 annually, as opposed to a Florida total of $18,539. In excess of 51,000 individuals lived below the poverty level. Monetary inflation appeared to make wages increase as the years passed, but, in fact, the gap in earnings widened as money purchased less. In 1995, Polk Countians achieved per capita wages of $17,446. At that point, state residents counted on $21,890. By 1997, just under 75,000 of Polk's inhabitants subsisted below the poverty level. Two years later, as the decade neared its close, in Lakeland alone over 11,000 persons qualified as poverty stricken; the Winter Haven-Auburndale vicinity counted above 14,000; and the Lake Wales area housed 5,000 such needy persons.[5]

Interestingly, though, most newcomers—including the needy—opted not to live within one of Polk's numerous incorporated municipalities, a fact that placed an increasingly heavy burden on a county government already stressed by demands of various kinds. Where the county's population mounted by slightly under 79,000 during the 1990s, less than one in four of the newcomers claimed a home in town. Polk's largest city, Lakeland, enjoyed only an 11 percent increase to 78,162 in spite of the county's 19.4 percent rise. The second largest, Winter Haven, expanded but 5 percent to 25,944. Bartow counted only a 4 percent increase (to 15,341), while Haines City added 12 percent to 13, 131. Auburndale and Lake Wales managed to climb over the 10,000 mark, although not by much. Fort Meade claimed sole rights to edging above 5,000. Only six of the communities experienced growth above the level recorded for the county. They were Auburndale, Davenport, Dundee, Highland Park, Hillcrest Heights, and Eagle Lake. None except Auburndale contained in excess of 3,000 persons, with Highland Park and Hillcrest Heights boasting less than 300.[6]

Home Siting

As the song asked, where have all the people gone? In line with earlier trends, they focused in the county's northern and northeastern reaches, with the Interstate 4 corridor offering the region its backbone. New un-incorporated communities debuted with regularity or else older ones saw revised plans expanding their scope. Poinciana offers an excellent example. First announced in the 1970s for the "rural fringes of eastern Polk," it had gained some 3,600 homes and 9,000 to 10,000 occupants by 1991. A dozen or so miles to the north, the Disney corporation by then aimed at construction of its planned community Celebration. Hoping to take advantage of the attraction of that internationally advertised project, developers in 1991 announced three new communities to supplement Poinciana. Envisioned to cover 6,500 acres, the proposals reached across the county line from Polk's northeastern corner into western Osceola. They offered sites for 10,000 homes and, within two decades, expected to draw 30,000 new residents. "This is not as [far] off the beaten path as you would think," developer Roy Flack commented. "It was off the beaten path 20 years ago, but there's been a lot of growth in there since." As was increasingly customary, shopping centers and golf courses competed with residential areas where homes priced from $60,000 to $125,000 would rise.[7]

Celebration's creation touched Polk so intensely that, before 1992's close, thirteen residential developments either were announced or un-der construction between U.S. Highways 27 and 17-92. County Road 54 particularly guided the line of new building, with the historic timber and marine stores community of Loughman serving as an anchor for the growth. As one newspaper reported, "The present rural flavor of the Loughman area—where the biggest building spurt in recent years has been a new post office, is about to change." Residents already in place, fearful of unbridled and unplanned growth, successfully appealed to the Polk county commission to slow the pace of development by temporarily banning new projects involving more than two homes per acre until the county's comprehensive plan could be adjusted to protect the area.[8]

If longtime residents believed that they could hold back development's tide where it wanted to pour, they mostly were mistaken. Happenings along U.S. 27 illustrate the point. "A little more than a decade ago, anyone venturing down U.S. Highway 27 through south Lake and northeast Polk was headed somewhere else," an *Orlando Sentinel* reporter observed in 1994. "There was no place to stop; citrus groves covered the landscape from the highway to the horizon." He continued: "But in the past four years, U.S. Highway 27 has gone from being a thoroughfare to a destination. More than a dozen subdivisions have popped up along the highway and one of its feeder roads—Polk County Road 54—and they are attracting home buyers by the hundreds." A consultant explained the dynamics at play behind construction of developments such as Davenport Lakes and Ridgewood Lakes. "It's one of the hottest markets in metropolitan Orlando," he noted. "And it really is part of the metro Orlando market." The man added: "It used to be that we thought of Polk County as a kind of suburb to Tampa. But this market has nothing to do with Tampa. It's all being driven by what's happening in metro Orlando."[9]

The immediate problem that confronted builders, residents, county and state regulators, and environmentalist groups such as the Sierra Club concerned the proximity of this growth to the Green Swamp. Polk and Lake County boards of county commissioners had shown generosity in approving projects in the swamp. Twenty-seven of them had surfaced by May 1990 when the state Department of Community Affairs decided finally that it had to act to restrain runaway development. These proposed communities often represented far more than modest mobile home parks. Scandinavia USA, for instance, anticipated 1,061 residential units, 54,000 square feet of commercial space, and an 18-hole golf course on 1,020 acres.[10]

A closer look at one proposed Green Swamp development, Lexington Park, helps to shed light on the problems. On 9,850 acres that straddled U.S. 98 where it met the Hillsborough line, backers intended to place 20,000 residential units, five golf courses, and nearly 9 million square feet of commercial and industrial space. The *St. Petersburg Times* described its impact. "Imagine the filth of 50,000 people washing right

104. *This tranquil image of Green Swamp as viewed from Rick Ridge Bridge, drawn by Tom Freeman, belied the reality of area development in the late twentieth century. Polk County Historical Quarterly.*

into your water glass," it suggested. "If supporters of a proposed development called Lexington Park get their way, that is precisely what will happen: A big sewer will be built right on top of Florida's water supply. And the concept of growth management in Florida will go right down the drain." Jim Studiale, a Lakeland development official, explained how such a proposal could achieve approval. "We planners suffer sometimes from not being able to see the forest for the trees," he commented. "Any lay person or an eighth grade class would look at this and say, you would never put a city there." Studiale continued: "Yet as we analyze all the details we lose sight of those basic facts and say, how can we make it work? I'm distressed that it seems such a debatable issue when it's not in the best interest of Polk County." The Southwest Florida Water Management District (SWFWMD), the *Times* added, rated Lexington Park as likely to cause a "widespread damaging effect" in "four of five [water and wetlands] categories." In the words of development review coordinator Ellen Hemmert, "That's about as strong a statement as we can make."[11]

Members of the Polk County commission, led by Chair Marlene Young and Commissioner Robert Connors, realized under the circumstances the need for greater county action to regulate development, particularly in the Green Swamp. Publicity such as one newspaper's comment that "Polk County has yet to see a development it didn't like" stung even those who prized sensitivity to creating a strong business climate, especially when opinion surveys found that "protecting the environment" ranked as "the key issue facing the state" to county voters. In the circumstances, Young and Connors urged creation of a task force to "work on a range of topics from improving development regulations to lobbying state officials to buy more of the swamp." The board's action approving the suggestion seemed, for the first time, to commit the panel to accepting responsibility for taking environmental concerns seriously or, as Connors's original proposal had stated, "As commissioners of Polk County, we also have the considerable responsibility to act as stewards of the varied and impressive natural resources of that area."[12]

The task force might have seemed a simple idea at the time, but matters did not work quite that way. In April 1992 the panel issued a preliminary report that called for greater protections for Green Swamp lands. "It's apparent," task force member Doug Morrison acknowledged, "that current development controls aren't sufficient." Among suggestions made were "increased public ownership of some lands, prohibiting industry and other intensive land uses in some areas, strictly regulating septic tanks and creating buffer zones to protect lakes and wetlands." The report further called for limitation of land use within the Green Swamp core to between one home per 40 acres and one home per 100 acres, with outlying areas permitted one home per 5 acres to one home per 20 acres. Property owners within the swamp's limits—or, at least, many of them—reacted in outrage. "It has a lot of people riled up," a minister opined. Another man offered, "[Landowners] had better take this seriously, because the impact to them would be devastating."[13]

As progress slowed locally, the state stepped up pressure on Polk to act. In summer 1993 Governor Chiles and the Cabinet refused to grant Polk more time, insisting that a Department of Community Affairs standard of not more than one home per 20 acres in Green Swamp be mandated. Within weeks, the state's Department of Environmental Regulation turned up the heat on developers further by filing felony charges against one firm and certain of its officers for "knowingly destroying wetland without permission" in an area "along Interstate 4, west of Haines City." Department spokeswoman Nan Baggett made clear that the action was intended to send a louder signal. "You are going to see developers facing charges a lot more frequently because [a new and more severe] statute is beginning to be enforced." Dan Costello, then chair of the county commission, stressed that Polk desired to act. "There's no argument about protecting the resource," he argued. "It's just the means of protecting it." Still, 1994 arrived without approval of Polk plans, leaving regulation in state hands and property owners spewing about lost or potential profits.[14]

Concerned that emotions had reached a critical point, state representative Dean Saunders, a Lakeland Democrat and real estate agent, proposed a compromise that might cool tempers and lessen the anti-regulatory sentiment among owners. His plan called for the state to purchase development rights for lands in the Green Swamp and to establish an authority composed of local people to negotiate the purchases. Participation by land owners remained strictly voluntary. "I want to protect the area," Saunders explained, "but not by breaking the backs of the people who happen to live there." The Polk County commission embraced the idea, as did many environmental groups. How much money the state would appropriate caused the greatest problem, with $30 million eventually getting approval. Governor Chiles signed the measure in May 1994, and the Green Swamp Land Authority organized at the Bartow offices of SWFWMD in August. Polk representatives on the authority included former state representative C. Fred Jones, Lakeland tax consultant Judy Raney, Lake Alfred citrus grower and cattleman James Shinn, and acting county administrator Jim Rhoden.[15]

SWFWMD also reinforced its own commitment to preserving Green Swamp wetlands and those in nearby areas. Utilizing funds from the state's Save Our Rivers program, it signaled its stance in September 1994 by purchasing 1,234 acres northeast of U.S. 98 where the highway cuts through the swamp "en route to Pasco County." The transaction complemented SWFWMD's pre-existing holdings of 118,000 acres along the Withlacoochee River. "We're hoping we can buy all those lands in that area," land resources director Fritz Musselmann asserted. To emphasize the district's intentions, he pointed to a 7,000 to 8,000 acre tract where "the district is [already] training its land purchase sights."[16]

Away from the Flow of Traffic

Conditions did not appear the same for all county residents as they did for those facing a traffic deluge on U.S. 27 or County Road 54. As will be discussed, depressed economic conditions maintained a hold in several areas while, in others, reminders of development dreams from times past served as warnings for those investing in newer schemes. In the former case, River Ranch Acres stands out prominently. Launched with excitement and amid high expectations in the 1960s, the development subdivided seventy square miles west of the Kissimmee River into 1.25 acre lots. Purchasers all over the country grabbed up parcels before the project filed for bankruptcy. In 1982 hunters who owned less than 10 percent of the property organized and claimed access control. Over time, as a reporter discovered, "a small town [came to be] erected without building permits." The reporter offered more detail. "There, hundreds of shanties, campers, mobile homes and even houses have been erected on other people's property," he wrote. "Dirt roads wind through pine forests to mobile homes served by 55-gallon water barrels on roofs and an occasional television antenna. Beyond, swamp buddy tracks wind like skeins of yarn through grassy wetlands." By the mid-1990s, officials agreed that the community violated county ordinances but declined to take any action against the hunters' group or the squatters. "It's a wild, wild West," county development officer Ron Borchers declared. "None of this is permitted." He added, "We really don't have the manpower . . . to go out and sweep the area."[17]

The county's southwestern quarter meanwhile tumbled along painfully in the wake of citrus and phosphate industry calamities. Citrus, for example, had suffered a deadly blow with the Christmas 1989 freeze. A combination of oversupply, foreign competition, and high prices thereafter drove many consumers away as the groves migrated deeper into the southern peninsula where warmer temperatures were guaranteed. In 1992, St. Lucie County temporarily ousted Polk from its position as the state's center of citrus production. Modest gains restored the title the next year, but, by then, Brazil supplied a substantial portion of the orange juice that reached customers in the United States. Well-established trends then wrote the final word on Polk's standing in the industry. In 1995, St. Lucie again claimed the premier rank as citrus producer. To make matters worse, Hendry County moved into second position, with Polk trailing at third. Hendry actually bested St. Lucie when it came to oranges.[18]

Phosphate fared less well for most of the decade's first half. Already in the doldrums, the industry greeted the early 1990s with closings and bankruptcies. Then more problems developed. Nations in Eastern Europe, including Russia (the former Soviet Union), witnessed demand for fertilizer plummet in 1992-1993, extending to three years a decline in world phosphate use. Reports at the time described the industry as "in a tailspin," "battered," and "in a state of turmoil." The next two years fortunately brought modest export increases, thanks partly to orders from Vietnam. Some reports by late 1995 even spoke of a returning boom, as global demand swelled and China and India handed in large orders.[19]

The industry had altered significantly, though, with long-term implications for Polk. For one thing, consolidations had changed the face of the business. In 1993 fourteen fertilizer companies had remained in operation in Florida. With the purchase of Mobil Mining and Mineral Co.'s central Florida phosphate plant by Cargill Fertilizer Inc. in 1995, that number dropped to eight. "It's a capital-intensive business," Cargill spokesman Gray Gordon explained, "and you have to be pretty well committed to the business to be in it." Further, a migration of phosphate mining out of the county continued as finite resources diminished. Even those elated by the mid-decade boomlet knew that mining's days in Polk were numbered. "Phosphate mining is a temporary use of the land," League of Environmental Organizations executive director John Ryan observed in words that mirrored the thoughts of many. "Eventually they will leave . . . and what they will leave behind is gyp stacks, sulphur ponds and clay settling ponds." He added, "The face of southwest Polk County will be forever changed."[20]

The concerns that Ryan expressed unfortunately translated themselves into harsh environmental reality in the early 1990s. Floridians generally grasped that fact in summer 1994 when a "monster hole" 180 feet deep and 125 feet wide opened in a fifteen-story gypsum mound near Mulberry, causing officials to speculate openly on the effects of the hole on groundwater contamination and of human exposure to low levels of radioactive materials found in gypsum. One university professor, apparently under the impression that he offered reassurance, insisted that "consumers shouldn't feel any ill effects—for the time being" even though "there is some increased risk of cancer during their lifetime." The man amazingly went on to state: "You saw what happened [with the nuclear reactor meltdown] at Chernobyl. That's not going to happen in Polk County." Environmental activist Gloria Rains gave what she considered practical advice. "I wouldn't drink the water from there," she admonished. "Polk County is the pits because it has so many polluting factors."[21]

Only months later two large phosphate spills emptied tainted water into Peace River. In one of the incidents, according to report, "a wall of water" was "released from Cargill Fertilizer's Fort Meade Mine when an earthen dam gave way. The twenty million gallons or so of mud and sand contained, an expert avowed, "high levels of acidity, turbidity, calcium and possibly fluoride." Little wonder that, the following week, county voters stunned pundits by approving a tax on real property to fund a bond issue to purchase environmentally sensitive lands.[22]

The question of whether communities dependent upon citrus and, especially, phosphate could survive occupied center stage in many local debates. The county's oldest town, Fort Meade, numbered as one of those places. Mayor Ernest Peavey by 1991 could note, "We [have] lost 900 to 1,000 jobs [and] that has had a shock on Fort Meade." City Commissioner Garrett Cagiano asked the county commission to waive the collection of impact fees to help jump start the local economy. "For the first time in Fort Meade's history," he insisted, "we are not secure in our role as an agro-industrial community." Chamber of Commerce director Beverly Ferris agreed. "The picture they are painting is not a bright picture," she said, "it is a realistic picture." Some residents anticipated the worse. "I think Fort Meade's very much headed downhill and will continue to head downhill," William "Buddy" Keen, Jr., argued, but others saw matters differently. "I disagree with the doom and the gloom, and I don't think we're drying up," Commissioner and former Mayor Bill Joe Loadholtes observed. "We made it before phosphate, and we'll make it after phosphate."[23]

105. *Optimist Bill Joe Loadholtes, a Fort Meade public official, believed that his vicinity would survive economically despite the foreseeable end of local phosphate mining operations.* POLK COUNTY HISTORICAL ASSOCIATION.

Commissioner Loadholtes, as it turned out, had it right about Fort Meade for the community gained 20 percent in population during the decade, but at Mulberry, with 2 percent growth, circumstances not so favorable prevailed. As mentioned in Chapter 11, by the late 1980s the town strove to find alternative avenues for obtaining economic stability, with the operation of a food irradiation plant seeming a viable option to some. As construction completion neared in fall 1991, "scores of food companies," according to a published account, "announced a ban on irradiated foods." In air-ing his company's stance, Publix Markets chairman Howard Jenkins bluntly stated, "We have a lot of customers tell us that they don't want irradiated foods." When operator Vindicator received a state permit in December to commence operations, opponents called for a boycott "of all Florida fruits and vegetables." Yet, the nation's first food irradiation plant proceeded with its work.[24]

As if that were not controversial enough, in 1992 eyes and ears turned to the announcement that the community, surrounded as it was by several of Florida's major toxic polluters, would host the state's first hazardous waste incinerator. "Everything is fine here as far as I am concerned," city manager Floyd Woods observed. "There is probably less pollution here than in a lot of other places." Actually planned by a Westinghouse Electric subsidiary for a site eleven miles south of Mulberry on land surrounded by phosphate mines, the facility incorporated a 200-foot-tall smokestack for presumably non-toxic emissions. The Greenpeace environmental organization helped to rally spirited opposition, with 600 passionate protesters filing in at one hearing. The air grew so heated that, when a federal Environmental Protection Agency official seemed to be defending the proposal, one individual blared, "You pig, this is just a joke to you." He added, "The least you could do is keep a straight face."[25]

The public concerns drew the attention of powerful persons, however, and the incinerator project soon ran into trouble. Governor Lawton Chiles, for one, called for further study, and state senator Rick Dantzler asked for a three-year moratorium on construction. The 1994 legislature agreed but extended the delay only for eighteen months. It soon became clear to the plant's backers that their proposal suffered from terminal unpopularity. In July, Westinghouse announced that it had dropped the

106. *The controversial Vindicator food irradiation plant at Mulberry.* POLK COUNTY HISTORICAL ASSOCIATION.

$75 million plan. Polk County Commissioner Robert Connors, who had labeled the incinerator a "pandora's box" that would lead to massive shipments of hazardous waste into the county and entice industries "to continue to pump out waste," cheered the decision. "It was never needed," he declared. "We don't generate enough hazardous waste in Florida to justify it. Our goal should be reducing what we produce."[26]

Besides irradiation plants and incinerators, distressed southwest Polk also drew serious attention as offering sites for new electric power plants. Tampa Electric Co., for example, in 1990 announced that it would locate a large facility in the region after controversy compelled the utility to abandon plans to construct it near a south Hillsborough aquatic preserve. Persons sensitive to environmental considerations reacted strongly. "Polk County has been a dumping ground," Concerned Citizens League of American president Grady Whitaker exclaimed. "If you've got anything you don't want, and you don't have nowhere else to put it, you put it in Polk County." No sooner had TECO's foot edged in the door than other utilities followed in haste. By 1993 no fewer than twelve power plant projects had been proposed for the vicinity. If constructed, they would place Polk in position as having "the highest concentration of power plants in one county in the Southeast, possibly the nation."[27]

One community, Frostproof, decided to apply salve to its economic malaise with a sense of humor. Anxious to draw tourists and other visitors in greater numbers, the town government reacted positively to George Houghtaling's suggestion of a "Buffalo Attraction and Chip Throwing Contest." Basically, the plan called for people to visit a site at Houghtaling's farm where they could pay to throw dried buffalo chips. The visionary ran into problems with the county zoning board, though, when he "actually passed a chip sample around." Flabbergasted, board member Jim Watkins found himself inquiring, "People really do pay to do this?"[28]

Even those towns and cities that avoided the severe conditions experienced at Fort Meade, Mulberry, and Frostproof realized the need to make themselves more interesting and attractive to tourists and potential residents alike. History and heritage repeatedly offered an avenue of approach. In the case of Haines City, for instance, the "Heritage Days Celebration," originally staged in the mid-1980s, grew ever greater in significance. "It's our heritage," chamber of commerce executive director Ouida Gray answered when asked what set her community apart from others. "Some cities are blessed with major tourist attractions, others with natural wonders, and those who have neither often create their own." Gray added: "Since local residents are fiercely proud of their heritage, history became the perfect choice for a celebration." The annual event honored a "Pioneer of the Year." In 1993 the choice centered on businessman and civic leader Owen Flowers, whose family had arrived at the tail end of the 1920s boom and had contributed to the community ever since. Flowers proudly received the award as the first African American to be so honored, although he pointed with equal pride to the fact that his son Reggie Flowers took precedence as the first black youth to graduate from Haines City High School.[29]

Preservation impulses naturally flourished as history took on greater and greater significance in challenging and fast-changing circumstances. Whether to destroy or rehabilitate derelict structures such as Lakeland's Terrace Hotel, the same city's venerable high school building, Haines City's Palm Crest Hotel, or any number of other edifices harkening to Polk's past occupied communal attention. Other developments additionally reinforced a growing sense of dependence upon the past as an aid to finding a path to the future. The county's Homeland Heritage Park opened on a regular basis during this period, for instance, and the county decided, given the availability of its new courthouse, to turn over the 1909 structure at Bartow for use as a historical library and museum. Court clerk E. D. "Bud" Dixon accepted responsibility for overseeing the courthouse's evolution to history center. Also reinforcing a strong sense of heritage, several designations on the National Register of Historic Places recognized historic Polk legacies, including Lakeland High School and the Mountain Lake Sanctuary. Columnist Bill Maxwell helped to put into words a sense of the meaning of such historic places. "I was looking at humanity's past," he wrote of Bok Tower and its gardens. "I felt small, yet significant at the same time," Maxwell added. "I felt alive."[30]

The call to history found itself, perhaps not surprisingly, accompanied by tense differences of opinion. Martha Kareen Jackson, to cite an example, spoke to the ordering of priorities in a time of economic hardship. "Fort Meade is feeling the need to expand and grow and our parents' generation

107. *Frostproof's historic high school building.* POLK COUNTY HISTORICAL ASSOCIATION.

must let us move forward and not backward," she expressed. "To be able to preserve our heritage and our history is wonderful," Jackson continued, "but to move forward is our survival." At Frostproof, in another example, termites, bad weather, and neglect again had besieged the 1926 high school building, renovated earlier but now threatened anew. Some residents saw the landmark's continued presence in the community as vital, but others demurred in light of the costs of preservation. "I'm one of the first ones to stand outside and wave a flag and say, 'I love this building,'" City Manager Roger Hook insisted, "but from a business standpoint, can we afford to maintain this?" Patricia Wilson added, "I think the money could be spent in a lot of better places.[31]

Republican Ascendancy

The decade of the 1990s not only stirred a powerful wind of restoration spirit, it also ushered in a political revolution with the step-by-step rise of the Republican party toward local power. Numerous factors weighed heavily into the equation. Among them could be counted increased Republican strength on the state and national levels, demographic changes within the county, a courthouse scandal that seemed to highlight Democratic ineptitude, the emergence of a dedicated and well-organized "religious right," party switches, more-effective party organization and fundraising, a political backlash arising from official actions appearing to favor environmental over business concerns, and the personal qualities of individual party leaders.

Many of these factors have been considered in previous chapters or else require little explanation, but the courthouse scandal certainly merits additional attention. It will be recalled that, in the mid-1980s, the county treated itself to a large, opulent, and striking new courthouse at Bartow. Problems quickly developed, though, with construction and design quality. Perhaps more significantly, employees soon began to sense a relationship between the new facility and illnesses they had acquired. After 110 employees filed worker's compensation claims during 1991 that listed building-related illnesses, the county commission agreed in January 1992 to relocate over half the structure's occupants pending repairs. Court clerk Bud Dixon demanded more. "I'm suggesting to you this minute," Dixon emphasized, "I want to move the offices of the clerk." In early February, Dixon raised the ante by contending that a "state of emergency existed." The commission majority temporized. "As far as I know," Marlene Young responded, "there is no emergency."

108. *Polk County's new and troubled courthouse, opened in July 1987.* POLK COUNTY HISTORICAL ASSOCIATION.

Noting that a move would "cost taxpayers thousands of dollars," Dan Costello added, "I'm not going to be panicked into making a decision." As Circuit Judge Randall McDonald later informed the board members, "[Courthouse employees] have a very real sense that you people don't care about them."[32]

Matters proceeded from there. Late in February a health expert informed the county that the courthouse suffered from "sick building syndrome" and declared that it "should not be occupied while the remedial work is under way." Finally pressed to action, the commission discovered that, as to relocating employees, "all but one of the proposed buildings would not provide any better environmental conditions than the courthouse." By April, no alternatives remained. The commissioners opted to transfer all the employees elsewhere, award a lucrative repair contract, and pursue litigation against the original contractor and architect. By June employees labored in safer quarters, and repairs commenced. Meanwhile, in September a grand jury concluded that "gross incompetence" on the part of numerous individuals and entities involved in courthouse planning had produced the mess but stopped short of handing down criminal indictments. For years only construction workers arrived each day at the building, until in December 1995 a rehabilitated courthouse reopened its doors. Eventually, the county recovered its money and gained a sense of what went wrong. "The courthouse was doomed to failure in its early stages of construction, which included mislaid brick work and improper insulation," one report detailed. "The result: Water seeped in, spurring the growth of mold and mildew," it added. "The spores traveled throughout the building via the air conditioning system. Walls, ceilings, wood and even paper files were contaminated."[33]

Just as the courthouse matter began to heat in 1991, another scandal that touched the county commission burst into view. In that instance, a joint state-federal law enforcement task force revealed a two-year investigation into a scheme by which businessman S. Norman Duncan several years earlier had solicited a $5,000 bribe on behalf of a county commissioner for a favorable rezoning vote. Convictions against Duncan eventually included perjury, attempted extortion, and conviction. Prosecutor Greg Kehoe later declared that "there's a serious problem in Polk County." The by-then former county commissioner named in the proceedings, Royce Ready, was not indicted and insisted adamantly that he never solicited any bribe while serving on the commission from 1980 to 1988. Kehoe acknowledged, however, that the federal grand jury had named Ready as an unindicted co-conspirator.[34]

Republican leaders watched with glee as Democrat officials writhed in political agony with these troubles. New GOP county chairman Jack Turner especially whetted his appetite for the upcoming contests of 1992, "preach[ing] his party's politics with an almost evangelical fervor." Turner, who in 1988 had founded the National Federation of Republican Men at Winter Haven, made no bones about his intention to "make

109. *Polk County commission members took a welcome break from government and politics in 1991 to lend their support to a lunch benefit for the Polk County Historical and Genealogical Library and Museum, located in the 1909 courthouse. Chairman Neil Combee is seated at center. Standing, from left to right, are Dan Costello, Marlene D. Young, County Administrator Ray Jackson, Bartow Chamber of Commerce Executive Director Mayme S. Burdin, Larry Libertore, and Robert Connors.* POLK COUNTY HISTORICAL QUARTERLY.

cratic crossovers. Instead, he bore down on what he described as the liberal leanings of local Democrat politicians. County commission chair Marlene Young offered his favorite target. "If Marlene Young walked in this door and said, 'Jack, I'm going to switch to the Republican Party and give it control of the county commission,'" he boasted, "I'd show her the other side of the door and say, 'We'll get it another way.'"[35]

Turner's optimistic outlook, as events proved, did not fail him or his party. In November 1992 voting, as one recapitulation suggested, "Republicans dominated local voting from the president to the school board." Party activist C. C. "Doc" Dockery summed the results up as "the best showing we ever had." All told, GOP candidates won eleven of seventeen races. Significantly, Republican Charles Canady, Jr., triumphed in a congressional election over Democrat Tom Mims, while Ken Richardson "stunned" incumbent Larry Libertore to become the first Republican ever elected to the county commission. Commissioner Neil Combee, a Democrat turned Republican, meanwhile scored a clear victory over opponent Dave Pretzsch. On the other hand, state representative Dean Saunders squeaked to a win over Republican Lynne Breidenbach by only a handful of votes. Accountant Joe G. Tedder offered the Democrats one of only a few bright spots during the polling when he captured the tax collector's job, especially since he defeated former GOP county chair Jean Burt to get it. Democrat Lori Edwards also narrowly retained her legislative seat, although some analysts claimed that the 3,000 votes afforded to "independent" John Paul Rogers "stole the election" from Republican Paul Senft. Edwards, realizing that Polk truly had become a two-party county, pointed a finger of blame at the Democratic Executive Committee. "There is need for improvement in organization," she in-

110. *Sheriff Lawrence Crow's status as a Republican officeholder served to provide a foundation for GOP advances during the 1990s. He is seen here with Republican party executive committee chair Jean Burt.* Jean Burt.

sisted." "There are problems there," Edwards added. "There is need for new energy in the DEC."[36]

The runup to the 1994 electoral season seemed eerily familiar. As the year commenced, scandal erupted when a county employee filed sexual harassment charges against the county administrator, leading to his departure under fire. Careful investigative work of the situation by Assistant County Attorney Karla Wright also had revealed "suspicious management decisions" by certain employees who had taken advantage of knowledge of the administrator's personal conduct. This led in August to dismissal of an official in the county building division and to further embarrassment for county government. Party switches grabbed headlines, as well, especially when Joe Viscusi chose to register Republican in order to oppose Representative Saunders. As these and other events transpired, many voters in the county, state, and nation felt resentments against Democratic rule rising with frustration. "People are letting this country go to hell because they're afraid," Bartow's Virginia Ford expressed for countless others. She added, "They don't care." A registered Democrat, she planned to mark her ballot for Republicans.[37]

When election day came around in November, Virginia Ford did not find herself alone. Polk claimed the state high for turnout with 73 percent, and, as votes still were being counted, the *Tampa Tribune* prepared to note the new state of affairs. "Polk is considered part of the conservative, Republican-rich Interstate 4 corridor," it declared. Even though county native Lawton Chiles moved toward re-election as governor, Republican Jeb Bush bested him in Polk 53 to 47 percent. Republican Congressman Charles Canady enjoyed an easy time of it over Democratic challenger Robert Connors. When Jerry L. Carter ousted incumbent Dan Costello, Republicans took control of the county commission with a three-to-two majority. They claimed the school board, as well, following newcomer Randy Wilkinson's defeat of longtime board member J. J. Corbett. Nancy Rouse Caldwell fared better than did fellow Democrat Costello and managed to edge past Mike Woodley for a county commission seat. Dean Saunders, Joe Tedder, and Lori Edwards also resisted the Republican tide to keep their offices. In Saunders's case, he did so only after Republicans protested the election results, demanded a hand recount, and unsuccessfully sued the county. Otherwise, the tide lifted only Republican boats.[38]

Few onlookers would have failed to credit conservative Christian groups and voters for their impact on these elections. Democratic operative Bob Grizzard put it into words after the 1992 results were in, expressing not a little political admiration—or envy—as he did so. "The so-called Christian coalition has worked its way into our politics," he argued. "It's an entire stealth organization." Anyone paying careful attention to local political controversies, though, would have known well the interest and effectiveness of the "religious right." At the school board, for instance, the question of a sex education curriculum produced sharply divided and voiced opinions with speakers such as Sue Russell of CARES (Concerned About Responsible Education on Sex) insisting on a strong message that abstinence was the only "safe sex." Over at the county commission and among other instances, the issue of public nudity in the form of "T-back" bathing suits worn by hotdog vendors and flower saleswomen as well as nude dancing provoked controversy, hard feelings, and political turmoil. When Commissioners Marlene Young and Robert Connors cast votes against the regulatory ordinance ultimately adopted, they risked alienation of support even as they backed individual rights against government intrusion.[39]

One final element of the political and electoral process as it existed in the early 1990s regarded the casting and counting of ballots. In 1992, officials required ten days to recount ballots in the Saunders-Breidenbach legislative contest, an excruciating wait for those concerned. In 1994, one of seven vote counting machines malfunctioned when something "went haywire" with the equipment. "We've had a disaster," Elections Supervisor Helen Gienau acknowledged. Faced again with a recount, Saunders sighed. "This is deja vu," he lamented. "I'm beginning to think I'm a jinx in the election process." The problem, though, underscored the concerns that opponent Joe Viscusi offered as justification for demanding another look at the results. "I want to know how many people voted, how many votes I got, and how many votes Dean Saunders got," he stated. "I don't think that's too much to ask." Viscusi added that his purpose was "to restore voters' faith in the process."[40]

Faith in the process doubtlessly offered a worthy goal, but, almost before the Republican grasp on county government could be formalized, faith in the party's integrity became a focal point for concern by some as a former state committeewoman found herself in legal trouble. In early January 1995, Alice Faye Redd found herself indicted on 295 felony counts of racketeering, fraud, grand theft, and securities violations for "accepting money under the guise of investments in her husband's medical practice, the prestigious Watson Clinic." Convicted of bilking 103 mostly elderly investors out of almost $3.6 million, Redd in March 1996 received a fifteen-year prison sentence. "She used the money she took from us to live high on the hog," victim Hazel Bullock argued. "I have no sympathy for her going to prison . . . because it's justice." Redd's daughter Rebecca Hagelin believed to the contrary that injustice had occurred. "I didn't expect a long history of misunderstanding of mental illness would change overnight in Polk County," she allowed. Whatever the truth of Hagelin's assertion, it appeared certain that Republican leaders found themselves on notice that Polk's long history of impropriety by political figures could reach out and touch them as well as Democrats.[41]

More Remembrances

The Gulf War of 1991 and Operation Desert Shield revived for county residents debates about the country's foreign policy and echoes of previous calls for service to the nation. Even opponents of the conflict such as the Polk County Citizens for Peace and Justice carefully articulated the nature of their criticisms. "An important message the group works to get across to the public," member Mercedes Fox observed, "is that it's possible to dislike violence and war and still support the military servicemen and women." Among the men and women serving in that military were members of Lakeland's Army Reserve Transportation Company and of the 325th Maintenance Company headquartered at Lake Wales. Additional residents belonged to Tampa's 810th Military Police Company and other units. Two members of the Tampa company, Sandy and Dennis Spicer were married. In civilian life Sandy served as a sergeant with the Haines City Police Department, while Dennis, a former Vietnam medic, had joined the company just to be with his wife.[42]

Individuals brought back with them to Polk tales of terrible conflict and also of heat, dust, thirst, and a yearning for home. Truck driver Dwight Staton of Winter Haven worried about his mother who "left the television on for days at a time waiting to hear what was going on." Lieutenant Colonel George Garner recalled "one day in the bleak desert" when he and his men assumed "the grim duty" of tending to enemy casualties. "I looked at wallets that had photographs of the Iraqi dead and their families," he related. "I realized right then and there that what happened to their families had happened to my grandmother [after the December 1941 attack on Pearl Harbor] and that somewhere in Iraq a family would wonder for years if their loved one would come back." Kathleen's Wanda Williams, just eighteen years of age, spoke for many others as to the lessons of her experience. "I think the most important thing I learned from being over there is my appreciation of my country," she recorded. "There are a lot of things we take for granted, and if you have never been outside the U.S. you don't realize how fortunate we are." Less sanguine were those who suffered wounds or, more commonly, health problems such as high blood pressure, sleep apnea, muscular disorders, headaches, and other afflictions common to the war's veterans. "It's just like Vietnam and Agent Orange," Auburndale's Bobby George charged. "What are they going to do—wait 30 years until we're dead to tell us what happened?"[43]

One Gulf War veteran came home to a very special welcome. Called to service in January 1991, Lake Gibson High School teacher Lonnie Smith served as an Air Force captain in the Persian Gulf monitoring Scud missile attacks. At home, his students and friends pressed his selection over ninety-seven other nominees as Polk County Teacher of the Year. "Thunderous cheers" greeted his return to the high school in April. "I don't deserve this," the teary veteran told well wishers following a parade, speeches, and a song. "Words cannot express all this love for just doing my job," he added. "I'm accepting this [honor] for the real heroes." Principal Richard Lewis had the final say. "Our family is back together," he shared. "Thank you, Lonnie Smith for coming home."[44]

Teachers in Polk, including Lonnie Smith, rarely received the honors or rewards that their labors merited, although the early 1990s saw a few other individuals and programs recognized for their worth. Among them, in 1991 The Florida Council of Teachers of English named Haines City High School's Barbara Clark as English Teacher of the Year. "Her students," one notice of the selection advised, "have won more state-level writing awards that those of any other English teacher in the state." The next year the National Council on Economic Education selected Lakeland High School's Wanda Joyce Calloway for a National Award for Teaching Economics. Five Polk teachers from three other schools earned honorable mention. Also in 1992, the "Polk is a Reading Zone" program, an initiative that had inspired students to devour two million books the previous year, received a national Gold Medallion Award from the National School Public Relations Association, with Alturas Elementary School and Lakeland Highlands Junior High School taking top honors in their divisions locally. Unfortunately, due to budget constraints, no school board officials could travel to Atlanta to accept the award, which subsequently arrived by mail.[45]

Women and African Americans continued to tally new marks of achievement in public affairs. When in 1991 Elizabeth Ann Toney accepted the position of city manager at Haines City, she took honors as the county's second woman to hold the position. Eagle Lake's Linda Weldon had pioneered the path earlier. Brenda Reddout pioneered her own path the following year, becoming the first female African American school board member. Ernest Tyler's acceptance of the Lake Wales city manager's job in 1992 also signaled a county first for African Americans. "I hope we continue to progress," NAACP leader Doris Moore-Bailey stated upon receiving news of the appointment. "I am pleased that Polk County, especially Lake Wales, is taking a leadership role and doing some positive things." Moore-Bailey added, "I hope that sets the tone and tempo for the rest of the county." Three years later Governor Lawton Chiles named Lakeland attorney and former prosecutor Timothy Coon as the first black man to serve as a judge in county history. "It feels good," Coon remarked. "I'm ready." Last but not least, in 1992 the African Methodist Episcopal Church honored Loughman-born Zedekiah L. Grady by electing him an AME bishop.[46]

Other milestones too numerous to list punctuated the era. Among them, Lakeland's Lee Janzen won the 1993 U.S. Open golf championship. In 1995, Lakeland inventor and businessman Allen K. Breed, founder of air bag manufacturer Breed Technologies, enjoyed recognition as National Entrepreneur of the Year. Also in 1993, the Cleveland Indians agreed to a ten-year contract for spring training at Winter Haven, replacing the departing Boston Red Sox. More good news came in early 1995 when the state Game and Fresh Water Fish Commission announced that "bald

eagles are making a remarkable comeback." Florida then contained more of the treasured birds than any other state except Alaska. The Kissimmee River basin in Polk and Osceola Counties, endangered species coordinator Don Wood explained, was "the best places to see bald eagles."[47]

111. *In 1995 Governor Lawton Chiles appointed former prosecutor Timothy Coon as Polk's first African American judge. Here, wife Marguerita and sons Joshua and Jasen enrobe Judge Coon.* LAKELAND LEDGER.

112. *Businessman, music lover, and Polk folklorist Carl Allen.* POLK COUNTY HISTORICAL
ASSOCIATION.

"the way people saw the world"

CHAPTER 13

At the Turn of a Century, 1995-2000

The saga of the final years of Polk's journey toward the twenty-first century mirrored in some respects its story at the twentieth century's beginning. During both times, a trail of economic devastation eventually led to an era of unrivaled prosperity as the county's natural resources lent themselves to reinvigorating a people and a place. Along the way, though, lawlessness, electoral scandals, questions about government's ability to resolve problems, and divides within the community had marked the calendar's turn. Reformist demands in each of the periods resulted in Polk offering leadership to the state and nation. At the century's beginning, that leadership derived from state senator—and later governor and United States senator—Park Trammell. At that century's end, it saw two individuals who proudly claimed intimate connection with Polk select the president of the United States.

Similarities with earlier times notwithstanding, the last half of the century's final decade repeatedly telegraphed to Polk's people that times were changing and that new generations and new ways of looking at things were taking precedence. The signals of the closing of an era echoed vividly, for example, in the period's human losses. In 1996 alone, the county witnessed the passing of Publix Markets founder George Jenkins, furniture magnate Wogan Badcock, and one-time Florida Senate president Curtis Peterson. Many of those departing carried hallowed names out of Polk's pioneer heritage. Thalia Johnson Gooch, gone in 1999, represented, as an obituary observed, "the last surviving child of the Lake Wales founding families." Daughter Lisa Koehler pointed out that "When [the family] came here, there were no schools, no churches, no hospital." Venetia Byrd Dees, whose death came the same year at age ninety-four, boasted roots than ran even deeper in the county's soil. Her Raulerson ancestors had pioneered settlement in the Green Swamp during the 1840s. "Strong-willed and determined, she lived alone until three years ago when she was injured in a fall," a reporter noted. He added, "The pioneer spirit ran in the blood of that family."[1]

Among the losses were individuals whose stories reached back more than 100 years, and whose lives had provided human ties with the nineteenth century as Polk looked ahead to the twenty-first. ReDora McGriff had seen 110 summers before she passed away in July 1996, one month shy of her birthday. She had lived in Lakeland for sixty-five years, where husband Arthur McGriff had predeceased her in 1978. Similarly, Lake Wales's Sam Jones had died in 1995, gone at 106 after marveling at the "improved relationships between whites and blacks." The county's oldest resident, 113-year-old Cindy Lincie Brooks, followed at Lake Wales in 1999. "I always honored my father and mother and loved them," she would tell friends, "and the Bible says if you honor your father and mother, your days will be lengthy." She had come to Lake Alfred from Alabama "in the early 1940s." "Although [mother] was raised before the birth of the automobile and never held a driver's license," son Ray Brooks recalled, "her favorite technological advance was the airplane." He continued, "At the age of 100, she made her first fight, from Tampa to Houston." Cindy Lincie Brooks summed up the experience for herself: "That's the best thing I've ever done."[2]

Carl Allen had wintered only seventy-eight years when he succumbed in March 1996, but residents would find their ties to Polk's bygone days ever more difficult to maintain in his absence. The "Original Florida Cracker," he embodied local heritage. "If a writer was in need of an expert in Polk County history, Cracker lore or a recipe for hush puppies," Mary Toothman insisted, "Allen was the man to call." Fortunately, Allen wrote well and often of the past, leaving a rich legacy. "One thing positive is that Allen didn't leave this Earth with much unsaid," Toothman explained. "While some of us lose relatives and say we really wish we had asked them to write their stories down, Allen's passing left us with many a tale about his childhood and Polk County's early days." One legacy, however, failed to survive him by long. Jewell Allen had stood with her husband for decades at Allen's Historical Café at Auburndale, with its "antique memorabilia, peculiar Florida menu, and bluegrass music." Her inspiration had led Carl to begin serving "real Cracker food," including "fried catfish, rabbit, armadillo,

112. *Businessman, music lover, and Polk folklorist Carl Allen.* POLK COUNTY HISTORICAL ASSOCIATION.

gator and rattlesnake, homemade grits, baked beans, 'sweet 'tater' patties, watermelon soup, and pickled peppers." By 1998, though, age and responsibilities compelled Jewell to close the place. "It represents the end of an era of old Cracker Florida," Lawton Chiles asserted. "The café had a quality of what old Florida is really about." Joe Spann, who played music as well as preserving the county's history, added his own thoughts. "No place will ever be exactly like Carl Allen's," he commented. "It's as unique as the person who created it."[3]

Sadly, Lawton Chiles outlived his friend Carl Allen only by a short time. On December 12, 1998, with less than one month remaining on his second gubernatorial term, the man who proudly called himself "the He-Coon" collapsed and died in Tallahassee at the governor's mansion. "Gov. Lawton Chiles' sudden death Saturday afternoon brought a cavalcade of emotion," the *St. Petersburg Times* reported, "enough to stop even the most serious business in Washington, D.C." Longtime associate Homer Hooks took the opportunity to recall the Chiles legacy. "His first concern was for that of Joe Lunch Bucket, and making sure those without real political power had their voices heard," Hooks expressed. "He was so devoted to children and their future. Every child that grows up healthy will have, in some respect, Lawton Chiles to thank for that." Friend Charles Canady, Sr., added: "He's the last of his breed, the last of the Cracker breed. I don't think we'll ever again see anyone like Lawton Chiles." Bob Graham, who had followed Chiles to the United States Senate, reflected, as well, on the meaning of the governor's death. "Lawton was part of a generation of Floridians who grew up when Florida was still a relatively small, relatively poor and still very remote state," he commented. "Lawton grew up with a lot of those values, including the way people saw the world and described it."[4]

The land and waters themselves almost seemed at times to be crying out as the county's past strove to be heard amidst the clang and clamor of development and the headlong rush toward a new century. From lakes ancient dugout canoes rose to remind residents of just how far back their heritage ran. One well-preserved example found in southeastern Polk measured nearly seventeen feet long and dated back more than a millennium to the Timucuan peoples or their ancestors. When crews dredged Lakeland's Lake Hollingsworth, portions of "about a dozen" canoes appeared. Discoveries of objects of all sorts became commonplace. "I get something out of the pump almost every day," dredge operator Ken Suttle acknowledged in 1999. By then most residents perceived even the World War Two era as ancient, giving a prominence to discoveries from that time not so long ago. To cite an example, two weeks prior to the twenty-first century's arrival A. R. Conner, while clearing land near the city's municipal airport, came across a rocket left from the Bartow Air Field days. The find literally came with a bang, as the rocket unexpectedly ignited and "took off straight into a chain-link fence." Conner fortunately avoided harm. "It sounded like dynamite," he declared with relief. "It exploded, hit the fence and dropped down and set the grass afire."[5]

Reminders of Polk's past such as that World War Two rocket loudly claimed attention, and, feeling with an increased sense of urgency the need to harken to the promptings, greater numbers of the county's people listened and responded. "Historic restoration" efforts emerged as the key to "revival" of downtown areas throughout the county. Bartow, Winter Haven, and Lakeland headed the vanguard. "Bartow's history is one of its biggest assets," Downtown Bartow's president Pat Crisman related, "and that's what we use to draw people to Bartow." Crisman added, "If we destroy history, we're going to destroy one of our biggest assets." A 1998 report from Lakeland confirmed the approach. "Renovation has long been the driving force downtown," the article described. "Long-neglected high-rises, such as the Lakeland Terrace Hotel and the Regency Towers, will soon see a sheen absent since the Great Depression."[6]

The county and some of those who were remaking its character tapped into the historical sensitivity. Polk undertook to market itself not so much for fancy attractions as for the wonders of nature, for "the

Great Outdoors." As one feature story observed, "Folks here think 'R & R' ought to be precisely that—Rest and Relaxation, nothing more." It continued: "Polk County's laid-back lifestyle beckons those who yen for adventure and those who simply seek reprieve from ringing telephones and airport delays. Real people live here, right in the heart of the Great Florida Birding Trail." The article concluded, "Fishermen, campers, and other nature enthusiasts marvel at Polk County's unspoiled open spaces." Perhaps the change in emphasis can help explain why in 1998 dwindling attendance forced the long-running Passion Play to close; yet, the Polk County Museum housed in the 1909 courthouse at Bartow could open to acclaim and Ray Albritton's delightful collection of essays *Recollections of Time Gone By* could enjoy such popularity. When backers announced plans for a massive retirement community to be located on 3,500 acres north of Bartow and adjacent to Lake Hancock, they understandably chose to market the development as Old Florida Plantation.[7]

Polk's African American communities too looked with greater intensity at the past to find steady foundations for the present and future. Excellent illustrations found their focus at Bartow. There, Clifton P. Lewis and wife Vendarae Lewis, who traced her ancestry to slaves brought to Polk during the Civil War, pondered rehabilitation of their Brittsville or West Bartow neighborhood, location of one of the county's earliest black settlements. They and friends subsequently organized the Neighborhood Improvement Corporation. Quickly, though, the Lewises perceived that the philosophy of "down with the old, up with the new" would not resolve the area's chronic blight. So, they took a different course. "We still intended to rebuild the neighborhood," Clifton Lewis explained, "but our revised strategy was to do so on a solid foundation of history." According to Lewis, Polk County Historical Association (PCHA) president Freddie Wright "put the whole organization behind us." Volunteers—many of whom such as Gloria McCoy, Charlie W. McNeill, Geraldine O. Watson, and Alvin B. Smith enjoyed longstanding ties to Bartow—joined in, as well, in projects ranging from cemetery cleanup to planning conversion of "shotgun houses" into senior citizen housing. The organization's scope expanded with successes to include all of Bartow and vicinity. One early triumph saw it save and restore, with widespread community support, the beautiful but derelict 1890s-era L. B. Brown house. The home and grounds now enjoy National Register of Historic Places endorsement.[8]

In several Polk communities history also became a tool for use in exploring, understanding, and improving race relations. Bartow again

114. *Local volunteers gathered in 1997 at Bartow's First Providence Missionary Baptist Church, one of the county's oldest, to begin the process of exploring community roots and revitalization through the recovery of history that many had thought lost. They are: (front row from left) Mable Leonard and Juanita Warner; (middle row), Clifton Lewis, Gwendolyn Strong, and Gloria McCoy; and (back row) Alvin Smith, Herman Burgess, and Pastor E. B. Williams.* LAKELAND LEDGER.

offered a good example. With assistance from the Florida Humanities Council, the PCHA, the City of Bartow, and other public and private bodies, the Neighborhood Improvement Corporation sponsored a series of public programs aimed at close and critical examination of Polk's race relations experience. The final program, held in May 2000, featured, among others, Florida A&M University historian Larry Eugene Rivers, one-time Florida NAACP field secretary Robert W. Saunders, Sr., former sheriff Monroe Brannen, local NAACP activist Doris Moore-Bailey, and Florida Southern College historian James M. Denham. In summarizing the program's impact in a front-page article, *Polk County Democrat* publisher S. L. Frisbie, IV, pulled from the discussion several quotations. "We don't do everything just like everybody else does" was one. Another read, "It is not a perfect place, but it is our place, and we love it." Doris Moore-Bailey added: "In each of our lives we experience personal gain when we establish relationships with people of different cultures. The mission is to work together for a common ground."[9]

At times people grew adamant about preserving the best of the past, sometimes nearly to the point of open conflict. This occurred, for instance, when church authorities suggested moving Fort Meade's lovely "Episcopal Gothic" Christ Church to Winter Haven or Lakeland. In the wink of an eye, passions flared. Pioneer descendant Etoile Altman, a Fort Meade Historical Society founder, voiced community reaction. "Over my dead body," she declared, "and I'm a Baptist." Something as simple as changing the telephone area code served to ignite controversy. When a switch from the 1950s vintage 813 prefix to 941 was announced in 1995, one writer indignantly argued that "the telephone company obviously has no respect for tradition." Four years later news came of another switch. Protests again erupted, but area code 863 soon debuted nonetheless. Even drive-in theaters gained from residents drawing lessons from the past. The county's only remaining drive-in, Lakeland's Silver Moon, celebrated its golden anniversary in 1999 by hosting the Drive-In Theatre Fan Club's national meeting. "What we're seeing is a lot of people coming to the drive-in these days because it's practical, not because of nostalgia," president Randy Loy commented. "They went to the drive-in as kids and now they're looking for ways to spend time together as a family." Loy added, "There's so many distractions these days, with other movies, the Internet and paid TV movies, but at a drive-in, families can stay together."[10]

Lest too much emphasis be placed on a growing sensitivity to history, let it be remembered that places filled with nostalgia fell by the wayside time and again as the march of progress made its way forward. Take the case of LaMond's Restaurant as an example. The Winter Haven landmark had stood "as one of the first culinary outposts on a once-lonely stretch of Cypress Gardens Boulevard" since 1953 when the widening of that avenue compelled LaMond's to shut it doors in 1999. Ceramic plates and old 45 rpm records that once adorned the walls vanished into storage, as the television celebrities who once delighted in the place during sojourns at Cypress Gardens went elsewhere. "I've been working in this building for 30 years, and I'm 36 years old," owner Robbie LaMond sighed. "To see it be demolished . . . is tantamount to going to your own funeral."[11]

Happy Times

The march of economic progress did traverse Polk's territory in the late 1990s, although the evolution involved overcoming roadblocks and continuing readjustments from past patterns. As late as spring 1997 one review of regional business conditions could assert that "Thriving central Florida has established itself as the region to watch" but add, "Polk County is a notable exception." Analyst Andre Henderson explained. "Its mainstay industries, citrus and phosphate, took hits in the last 12 months," he began. "Frigid weather in January incurred losses estimated at 3% to 4% of total juice yield (between $15 million and $20 million) and damaged a record citrus harvest in the making." Henderson continued: "Phosphate production had a strong year statewide, but Polk's reserves are depleting, sending industry titans into southern counties in search of greater lodes." Striking a more-positive note, he added: "Despite this, Polk is benefitting from its central location and an overflow of business from Tampa and Orlando. Unemployment stands at 7.0%, one of the lowest figures in the last two decades. Job growth is anticipated in food services, plastics, electronic components and distribution." The *Tampa Tribune* made the point even more bluntly. "The county is in transition from a citrus, phosphate and retirement economy," it declared. "This change is challenging, but there are new opportunities opening up as old ones close."[12]

It took a mere six to twelve months for those new opportunities to make their weight felt. By December 1997 Polk's unemployment rate had dropped to 5 percent, the lowest mark in seventeen years. Diversification, economists concluded, had worked the miracle. "The county's economy has branched out with many different businesses," Kevin Brickey advised, "with the fastest growth in retail sales, restaurants, trucking and warehousing, and local government." A business writer explored the matter further. "In addition to riding on the coattails of the soaring national economy, Polk is in the middle of the booming Interstate 4 belt," he observed. "Growth has continued between Tampa and Orlando, as evidenced by the increase in the number of trucking companies and warehouses." Eight "key" industries, a state report argued, would "continue to prosper significantly through 2005. They included local government, health services, agricultural services, grocery stores, restaurants, business services, social services, and trucking and warehouses. During 1998 matters improved to an even greater extent. "'98 Great For Polk's Economy" the *Lakeland Ledger* advised at year's end. Highlighting positive developments, the newspaper pointed to GEICO Corp. and State Farm Insurance Company, each of which had added "several hundred jobs to the Polk economy during the year."[13]

The long-awaited completion of the first section of the Polk Parkway, planned since the mid-1980s, added energy to the expansive atmosphere. Designed to carry east-west traffic south of Lakeland from points on Interstate 4, the limited access highway opened in August from South Florida Avenue to the Interstate just inside the Polk-Hillsborough County line. Construction proceeded eastward from South

Florida Avenue toward Auburndale, with the final link opening in December 1999. Riders only slowly gained familiarity with the new artery, but developers grasped its significance immediately. "The interest just continues to increase as we get closer and closer to the completion," real estate agent Gene Engle stated in late 1998. "It has just opened up a lot of land to development because the land now has good accessibility, and that's key to development, especially retail development." Before the final segment had received its first vehicle, two major projects already had been announced "that will transform the eastern leg over the next 20 years from a relatively rural area to a network of subdivisions, industrial parks, shopping centers, and offices." It was expected by 2000 that the completed parkway, soon to honor with its name World War Two medal of honor winner James Henry Mills, will forever change the face of Polk County."[14]

The century's last two or three years produced from a solid boom a truly remarkable one. Signs of growth in 1998 included, as one study detailed, "speculative distribution centers along Interstate 4, 13 hotels under construction or renovation, Tampa Electric Co. and Florida Power Corp. power plant expansions, and five new Wal-Mart 'supercenters' planned or under construction." Beyond that, automobile insurer Geico Direct announced that it would hire an additional 2,300 employees at its new Lakeland call center. East Polk Committee of 100 executive director Ron Morrow waxed positively enthusiastic. "This county cannot get out of the way of two great economic engines," he proclaimed. "One is called Tampa. The other is called Orlando." In 1998 the county began advertising itself, with some exaggeration, as "the center of the universe."[15]

Then things really started to heat up. As far as the *Lakeland Ledger* was concerned, "1999 Heralded a Boom in Construction, Employment and Consumer Spending." Its editors specified reasons for their conclusion. "This year was mainly the best of times for the Polk County economy with a little bit of the worst of times mixed in," the newspaper reported. "As the economy soared on the strength of a burgeoning stock market, fewer people were unemployed." It continued: "Consumers were spending money. Hotels were expanding. New jobs were created." Consumer spending offered the key to understanding the high times. "Total retail sales," the *Ledger* disclosed, "hit $4.1 billion for the first three quarters of 1999." It added, "Total retail sales were spurred by the addition of many new retail outlets in Polk." The downside mentioned by the journal concerned the bankruptcy of Breed Technologies following the death of its founder and the continuing travails of the phosphate industry. Yet another world drop in phosphate demand had produced a major restructuring of IMC-Agrico, layoffs, and job losses.[16]

Looking ahead at the century's turn, planning director Merle Bishop foresaw a county population by 2020 of 615,000. Given that "the baby boomers are starting to retire in the next couple of decades," he anticipated a continuation of aging trends to the point that, by 2010, Polk's elderly population (65 or over) would reach 22 percent. Developments such as Poinciana northeast of Haines City, Old Florida Plantation near Bartow, Ridgewood Lakes between Haines City and Interstate 4, and Oak Hill Estates between Davenport and Loughman aimed their marketing directly at such potential residents. Bishop estimated that, so great did growth in northwestern Polk appear, the area "near the Lake County line between U.S. 27 and County road 54, will be built out during the next decade with residents mixed between retirees and Disney World and tourist industry employees." Overall, he reinforced what others repeatedly expressed. "You will see continued growth pressure," he insisted, "from the Orlando and Tampa areas."[17]

Polk's towns and cities, following years of near-attrition earlier in the decade, now dealt with prosperity. This proved especially true at Lakeland. Summer 1998 reports detailed that "vacancy rates have dropped in the past three years, a startling turnaround for a downtown that was half-empty a decade ago." By New Year's 2000, phrases such as "the rebirth of downtown Lakeland" passed easily from person to person. Capping the excitement, the Lakeland Terrace Hotel reopened after extensive renovations and AmeriSuites finalized a 128-room hotel next to the Lakeland Center. Additionally, Lake Mirror Park achieved official rededication, and groundbreaking for the $1 million Hollis Gardens ensued thanks to a gift from former Publix Markets president Mark Hollis and his wife Lynn Hollis. During 2000, hopes ran so high that it seemed ice might no longer melt in the Florida sun or so the Lakeland Center's planners must have believed. When they called for yet another convention hall, they dreamed, as well, of Polk's first ice-skating rink.[18]

Winter Haven shared in the good times. "Downtown began experiencing a similar rebirth [to Lakeland's]," an observer recorded on January 1, 2000, "albeit on a small scale and later date." He continued, "The 1920s-vintage Ritz Theatre is being restored to its former glory, and should be open sometime this year as a community center and gallery [plus] the city got its first bus line this year, as the W.H.A.T. (Winter Haven Area Transit) busses were rolled out." Retail sales, though, lagged in the city. Lake Wales's newer Eagle Ridge Mall had snatched too much of

115. *Lakeland's new and beautiful Hollis Gardens.* POLK COUNTY HISTORICAL ASSOCIATION.

the Winter Haven Mall's business. As the onlooker noted, "The Winter Haven Mall finally succumbed to age and competition."[19]

The economic whirlwind touched down in parts of distressed south Polk as well as in the county's middle and northern sections. Bartow particularly appeared to benefit. "Bartow's Breakout: City in Line for Unprecedented Growth" one newspaper blared in September 1999. "Within 15 years, Bartow's population of 15,108 could more than double because of an influx of people attracted to new job opportunities," city officials estimated. Public Service Director Donnie True added, "We've had more interest in growth and development projects in the last year than we've had in the 10 years I've been here." Two potential developments headed local lists for future impact. Old Florida Plantation has been mentioned. In the second case, the Clear Springs Land Co. purchased 16,700 acres of mined phosphate land that surrounded the city from the south and to the east with the intention that it would be used "for industrial and residential development." City leaders embraced the idea of growth, but many desired to avoid the pitfalls of untrammeled development experienced elsewhere. "We have to keep some parts of Bartow unique," Mayor Leo Longworth asserted, "but we have to make sure to include all the neighborhood communities in the planning process." Commissioner Gail Schreiber agreed. "The possibilities," he pronounced, "are extremely great [but if] we don't do things about growth, other people will."[20]

Government and Politics

The decade's final half commenced, politically speaking, with a flurry of excitement and concluded with breathtaking electoral crisis. As mentioned in Chapter 12, early in 1995 Republican activist Alice Faye Redd had seen herself indicted for fraud and, ultimately, sentenced to prison. No sooner had the courts directed their attention to Redd than the scandal of "Eaglegate" burst upon unprepared residents. The always tumultuous community of Eagle Lake dealt with, according to an Associated Press recapitulation, "a break-in at City Hall, a wiretap and a scheme to blackmail the mayor using a prostitute." Grady Judd of the Polk County Sheriff's Department added detail. "They wanted to overthrow the current city government," he related. "The way they intended to do this wasn't through the democratic process. Instead, they planned to gather smut and dirt and extort the mayor." The coup failed when city commission candidate Walt Young approached a part-time police officer, then working undercover, for the city hall keys. Upon subsequently entering the building to tap City Manager Linda Weldon's telephone, he and campaign worker Earl Rice met unexpectedly with a warm reception

116. *Several of Polk's leading Republicans of the 1990s stand together in this photograph. From the left are party activist Jean Burt, state committeeman (and later state senator) John Laurent, state representative (and later Congressman) Charles Canady, attorney Parkill Mays, and future state committeeman and county commissioner Paul Senft.* JEAN BURT.

from the law. Although Young spent election day in jail, he nonetheless claimed one of every three votes cast in his race.[21]

The Eaglegate controversy and other incidents shone a spotlight on Polk in a manner that reflected a picture to the state and nation of a county marked by the bizarre when, during an earlier era, the exposure might have related to profound and sustained political power or else to the county's beauty or affluence. The popular comedian Leo Gallagher, on a visit home to Polk, once had vocalized what now seemed to capsulize its image. When asked if he derived his strange sense of humor from childhood experiences, he had responded: "Yeah, it's true. I got weird right here in Lakeland." By the mid-1990s and following Gallagher's lead, columnists and political analysts sometimes enjoyed a field day at Polk's expense. "Polk County has its quirks, its oddities and weirdness," one such pundit advised at mid-decade. "Sometimes the local flavor is endearing," she continued. "At times, though, it's weird living in a place where sinkholes have eaten homes and courthouses get deathly ill." Having addressed some more recent political goings-on, the columnist added, "You never know—cynical comics might start moving back home to roost."[22]

Had the United Nations flap occurred before the columnist wrote, likely she would have included it in her list of strange political happenings. The situation concerned special ceremonies scheduled in New York City during October 1995 to celebrate the fiftieth anniversary of the world organization. The United Nations had asked local governments to fly its flag on a particular day in honor of the occasion, in the process evidencing a temerity that enraged members of the resurgent and "arch-conservative" John Birch Society. Polk's board of commissioners initially agreed to the flag request, but Birch Society adherents thereafter threatened "controversy" and the bold panel reversed its position, earning thereby the glare of unwelcome attention. Commissioner Marlene Duffy Young refused to abide by the about-face and posted a United Nations flag on her office window. Beside it Young taped a sign. "We support world peace," it read, "even if it is controversial."[23]

With the Redd case, Eaglegate, and the flag flap setting the stage, the county launched itself into the 1996 electoral season. The year seemed guaranteed to produce fascinating politics since, beyond local concerns, Polk now found itself lumped with Pinellas, Hillsborough, Orange, Seminole, Osceola, and Volusia as the "Republican-rich Interstate 4 corridor." This meant that national politics would focus on the county's voters, particularly the campaign of Republican presidential contender

Bob Dole. "Polk County is very important in the state of Florida," local campaign chairwoman Cindy Ross explained. "We are number 14 in the number of registered voters in the state," she added. "We need to win in Polk County to take the state." Some experts such as University of South Florida political scientist Susan MacManus voiced a note of caution, however, for expectant Republicans. "The corridor is certainly the most competitive place in the state," she began. In words that most longtime Polk residents easily could comprehend, MacManus continued: "It's a far more independent group of people that can be swayed either way. They make their own decisions."[24]

To enliven the season further, several incidents punctuated the path to election day. First, Sheriff Lawrence Crow explained to reporters in April that for months his department had charged county jail inmates for toiletries, once again placing Polk in a less-than-appealing light. For the Republican sheriff, though, the policy merely reflected "life outside jail walls." As Crow noted, "If you want something, you have to pay for it." Then, County Administrator Richard Hedrick, who had taken office only in November 1994 after the last county administrator controversy, found himself acknowledging that he wanted to date Commissioner Nancy Rouse Caldwell once their respective divorces were final. This naturally resulted in demands for his resignation. He complied with the calls in May. "It's a sad day in the history of Polk County," Commissioner Jerry Carter observed. "It's another chapter we're going to have to live through." With questions about the judgment of local officials running high, residents then discovered that even a prominent minister might find himself in the same boat. Specifically, the pastor of one of the county's largest Baptist churches appeared to have "puffed" his resume with academic degrees that he did not possess. "It's been a smear campaign," the minister responded, but a church member felt differently. "You can feel it in the services," she declared. "I have looked around and there were people who were crying. It's so hard, because there are people you care about on both sides of the issue."[25]

The general election turned out to be as controversial as was the electoral season. In the presidential contest, Florida went Democratic for the first time since 1976, but Polk favored Republican Dole by a narrow plurality. Paula Dockery and Adam Putnam claimed legislative seats previously thought safe for Democrats, aiding a Republican tide that swept to control of the Florida house of representatives. This meant that, for the first time since Reconstruction, the Republicans controlled both houses of a southern state's legislature. School superintendent John

Stewart had opted not to seek re-election, and Republican Glenn Reyn-
olds, pledging "smaller administrative staff and stricter discipline," easily
bested Democrat Ken Addair. Meanwhile, Republican Jim Nelson defeated longtime incumbent Dan L. Moody in a school board contest.[26]

The controversy came on two levels. First, expectations of Republican consolidation of county government control proved ill-founded.
With Democrat Jim Miles very narrowly defeating Edith Yates and incumbent Democrat Brenda Reddout also narrowly retaking her seat,
the school board's three-two majority switched from Republican to
Democrat. Democrats E. D. "Bud" Dixon, Edwin H. Coleman, Helen
B. Gienau, and Joe G. Tedder retained the offices, respectively, of clerk
of courts, property appraiser, supervisor of elections, and tax collector
for their party. Janet L. Shearer also defeated Republican Lynne Breidenbach for a county commission seat.[27]

Shearer's win left control of the county commission hanging upon
whether Republican Bruce Parker, Jr., had ousted his party's favorite
nemesis Marlene Young from her seat, and therein lay the second level
of controversy. Initial returns placed Parker ahead by nineteen votes. A
series of recount demands convinced Young and others that tabulating
machines were providing erroneous totals. She demanded a full hand
recount. The canvassing board—made up of Republican Commissioner
Jerry Carter and Democrat Nancy Rouse Caldwell, plus County Judge
Michael Raiden—agreed, but Carter and Caldwell soon opted to ter-
minate the process and declare Parker the winner. As political turmoil
gripped the county, Young sued in circuit court. Judge Andy Owens ordered the recount to proceed and eventually declared Young the winner
by eighteen votes. A grand jury investigation took the canvassing board
to task but filed no criminal charges. A remarried Nancy Caldwell (now
Nancy Rouse Hedrick) meanwhile switched from Democrat to Republican, leaving the commission under narrow Republican control.[28]

The imbroglio carried some positive results. In September 1997 the
county commission created an elections study committee "to come up
with proposals to change state law." The panel placed particular emphasis on the grand jury's suggestion of a statutory change "so that improperly marked ballots don't have to be counted." Quillian Yancey chaired
the panel, which issued its recommendations early the next year. The
county commission quickly adopted the idea of nonpartisan contests
for the supervisor of elections. As *Tampa Tribune* reporter Bill Heery
detailed, several other recommendations were passed on to the legislative
delegation. They included "a mandatory hand count for any race where

less than two-tenths of 1 percent of total votes separate the candidates," placing appointment powers for county canvassing boards under "the chief judge of the judicial circuit"; and the curtailment, rather than expansion, of "the availability of absentee ballots."[29]

While the elections process received attention, so, too, did consideration of redesigning county government in light of changed times and conditions. Among others, Commissioner Marlene Young advocated adoption of a county charter or "mini constitution" as some called it. The commission agreed to appoint a fifteen-member charter board in October 1997. Headed by Chairperson Lisa Parks, the panel decided in good part to honor the status quo, specifically backing away from suggestions that the county commission appoint Polk's constitutional officers. The final draft nonetheless permitted recall of commissioners and constitutional officers, made the supervisor of elections a nonpartisan official, and authorized charter amendments and county ordinances to be proposed by voters through a petition process. The county, in turn, received all "municipal" powers, including the right to levy a utilities tax in unincorporated areas. "I just think this is a tremendous milestone for the development of Polk County and for Polk County government," Commissioner Young declared upon the charter's ratification by voters at the 1998 general election.[30]

All politically interested eyes, as these events were unfolding, looked eagerly toward the 1998 rematch between county Republicans and Democrats. An early taste of what the future promised came in February and March with primaries and special elections that became necessary when state senator Rick Dantzler resigned in order to run for the Democratic nomination for governor. Dantzler eventually would withdraw from the gubernatorial contest to join Buddy McKay's ticket as his running mate for lieutenant governor, but the resignation left his senate seat vacant. When state representative John Laurent announced to contest it, resignation opened his house seat as well. Laurent, a "moderate," grasped the GOP senate nomination despite a strong challenge from school board member Randy Wilkinson, the candidate of the Christian right. "They're kind of brutal," Laurent laughingly acknowledged on primary night. "I think I'm going to celebrate tonight by going to bed early." Democrat Tom Mims and Libertarian Carl Strang, a former Republican mayor of Winter Haven, challenged Laurent at the special election, with the Republican nominee capturing the seat with 57 percent despite attempts by some conservative Republican elements to undermine his campaign.[31]

Laurent's win suggested to more than a few Democrats that "the party's in even worse shape than it looks," but more bad news was to come. In the special house race, one-time citrus baron Ben Hill Griffin's grandson J. D. Alexander took the GOP nomination from Winter Haven lawyer Glenn Anderson. On the Democratic side, the voters selected another former Winter Haven mayor, Robert "Smitty" Smith, over physician Arturo Perez. Smith painted the race in class terms. "I think the difference between me and Alexander is I'm the middle class, common-man candidate," he insisted, "and he's going to be the Tallahassee lobbyist with the fat cat money." Given a relatively low turnout where Republican organizational skills proved themselves quite efficient, Alexander slid past Smith to win the house seat with 63 percent of the ballots.[32]

The spring races proved bellwethers of the November contests, the results of which once again illustrated the increasing strength of the religious right. Both county commission seats on the ballot went to Republicans who had ousted incumbents in the party primary. Bruce Parker retired Commissioner Jerry Carter before winning the seat over Winter Haven city commissioner Ann E. Darby. Similarly, Randy Wilkinson advanced over Commissioner Nancy Rouse Hedrick in the primary before beating Democrat Robert Connors. Margins of victory remained tight, though, with only 4 percent to 5 percent of votes separating winners and losers in the general election. In statewide contests, Polk backed the successful re-election bid of its one-time Democratic state senator Bob Crawford as agriculture commissioner and of Republican gubernatorial candidate Jeb Bush. A favorite daughter, Katherine Harris, also received the county's blessing in her successful run for secretary of state. Another

117. *Democrats such as Winter Haven's Robert "Smitty" Smith fought to keep their party's cause alive in Polk during the late 1990s. He appears here with campaigners including (left to right) granddaughter Lisa Woodard, wife Nancy Smith, and daughter Mary Kay Smith-Greene.* ROBERT *"SMITTY" SMITH.*

grandchild of Ben Hill Griffin, Jr., Harris had been raised in Polk but then served as a Sarasota County state senator.[33]

Unfortunately, the 1998 elections again produced frayed nerves and uneasy delays because of systemic problems. As previously, counting machines malfunctioned. "It was like pulling teeth to get results from the television," school board candidate Bob Macey lamented. "Finally, I hopped in my car and waited all night for the results." Elections official Barbara Osthoff explained that "improper coding on some absentee ballots" caused the malfunctions. This left workers "to hand inspect more than 11,000 absentee ballots until they found the faulty ones." Installed as a commissioner and soon the board's chairman, Bruce Parker made up his mind to do something to ensure the efficiency and integrity of Polk's voting processes. He pushed for the purchase of a new $1 million Accu Vote optical scanning system. When officials and voters tested it at primary elections in summer 2000, elections supervisor Helen Gienau pronounced the results. "We were very pleased," she expressed. "The voters liked the system, and the poll workers liked the system."[34]

118. *Agriculture Commissioner Bob Crawford and Secretary of State Katherine Harris, both individuals with roots running deep in Polk County soil, voted as members of the state's canvassing board to deliver Florida's electoral votes in 2000 to Republican George W. Bush over Democrat Al Gore, thereby affording Bush the presidency. They appear here in a 1999 portrait of the governor and cabinet. Present are (from the left) Comptroller Robert F. Milligan, Harris, Crawford, Attorney General Bob Butterworth, Governor Jeb Bush, Treasurer Bill Nelson, and Education Commissioner Tom Gallagher. FLORIDA STATE ARCHIVES.*

The county's new voting system stood ready just in time for one of the most controversial and hotly contested elections that the state or nation had seen, and it took place, insofar as Polk was concerned, in an atmosphere fraught with political bitterness. As the 1998 elections had shown, simple antagonism between Republicans and Democrats had evolved into a far-more-complicated situation where Republicans battled each other fiercely while Democrats continued to carry on their traditional intra-party bloodletting. The county commission especially had provided a forum for showcasing the mounting ill will. Commissioner Randy Wilkinson's attempts to redirect the commission agenda against Chairman Parker's resistance had sparked a feud between the two, with other commissioners finding themselves wading deeply into the fray. The situation had grown so bad—and public reaction to it so extreme—by summer 2000 that the board unanimously approved a resolution acknowledging that "the collective bad behavior of the commission has become a source of public embarrassment and ridicule." The panel added that it "condemns the behavior that has been exhibited in the past few weeks and pledges our renewed efforts to conduct ourselves in a professional and mature manner."[35]

Coming on the heels of scandals that had seen President Bill Clinton impeached but not removed from office, voters chose to hand the reins of power to Republicans who pledged to bring higher standards of behavior to government and lower taxes to the voters. "The Republican Party reigned in Polk County in 2000," one analysis of the results recounted, "taking complete control of the Polk County Commission and the local legislative delegation for the first time in modern times, if not in history." The dramatic turnaround from all-Democrat rule in 1940 and for most of the next half century stood out starkly. Auburndale mayor Jack Myers defeated Commissioner Marlene Young, while Lakeland city commissioner Don Gifford ousted Commissioner Janet Shearer. Incumbent commissioner Neil Combee achieved re-election. Marsha Faux stepped into the property appraiser's post, and Jim Thornhill took over as school superintendent. Democratic legislator Lori Edwards found herself barred by term limits from seeking re-election. Republican Marty Bowen captured the seat. Voters also approved two citizen-initiative charter amendments to express their disgust with the county commission. The first limited members to two consecutive four-year terms; the second slashed annual commissioner salaries from over $69,000 to $33,500.[36]

Whatever attention the Republican sweep received in Polk, for a short while most people looked elsewhere as Democratic candidate Al

Gore and Republican George W. Bush, brother of Florida governor Jeb Bush, battled over the state's electoral college votes and the presidency. Electoral mishaps—including votes tossed out, bad counts, "hanging chads" on punch-card ballots, improperly handled absentee ballots, and what have you—embarrassed the state and left an accurate count impossible to ascertain. Bush won Polk by more than 15,000 votes, and the county's new voting system appeared to have worked far better than those in some other counties. Still, as Judge Anne Kaylor expressed, "There aren't enough expletives to describe how this election has gone." Eventually, the United States Supreme Court overruled the Supreme Court of Florida and ordered recounting stopped. A five-to-four majority accepted the state canvassing board's certification that Bush had carried the state and the nation. That board's majority consisted of two individuals strongly identified with Polk. Arguably, Agriculture Commissioner Bob Crawford and Secretary of State Katherine Harris had elected the president of the United States.[37]

Standouts

Bob Crawford and Katherine Harris by no means represented the only Polk Countians who deserved to be remembered for their actions and accomplishments during the final years of the twentieth century. So large had the county become that no survey of those persons possibly could be properly inclusive. In the circumstances, a very few examples must suffice.

The field of education offers a starting point. The Polk school system—battered and beaten by major problems and challenges over the years—endured even more controversy in the decade's final half. Whether the issue involved charter schools, mandated uniforms for students, placement of Gideon Bibles in classrooms, or the proliferation of "portables," residents divided and argued their viewpoints. When chronic financial shortages complicated the mix, difficulties ensued for all concerned. In the circumstances, the achievement of high standards and quality work sometimes failed to obtain the recognition deserved. Certainly, Victoria Astley, a student in International Baccalaureate at Bartow High School, merited the spotlight. In 2000 she scored a perfect "36" on the American College Testing college entrance examination, the only student to do so in Florida that year and one of only twelve scholars to attain the level in the nation. Just as Victoria's efforts reflected the talents of many of her fellow students, so, too, did Odessa Johnson's mirror those of many other dedicated educators. A teacher of severely disabled children at Bartow, Johnson took strength from personal experience to touch meaningfully the lives of scores of pupils. In 1996, her contributions, despite the fact that her career was only beginning, brought recognition as Polk County Teacher of the Year. Then, in 1998, *Reader's Digest* proclaimed Odessa Johnson an "American Hero in Education."[38]

The schools and educators often from 1940 to 2000 had seen the difficulties of their work made ever more challenging by the county's struggles with relations between the races. Unquestionably, problems remained in 2000, but vast change had occurred as well. "We have been somewhere between the extremes," one-time Florida Board of Regents chairman D. Burke Kibler estimated as the twenty-first century opened. "There's still prejudice but not nearly as much." Former Lakeland mayor Carrie Oldham stressed the positive. "People now don't look at the color," she declared, "but at the quality of the individual." The progress, however far the distance that remained to be traveled, found recognition. On

118A. *On September 19, 1998, Polk Countians celebrated their rich heritage by dedicating the Polk County Historical Museum in the county's renovated former courthouse at Bartow. Seen here at the ribbon cutting are (from left) County Judge Anne Kaylor, Courts Clerk Richard Weiss, County Commissioner Nancy Hedrick, Polk County Historical Commission member William Ruster (behind Mrs. Hedrick), County Commission Chairman Jerry Carter, Congressman Charles Canady, State Representative Adam Putnam, Polk County Historical Association President Freddie Wright, County Commissioner Marlene Young, and Bartow's mayor Frank Smith (behind Mrs. Young). POLK COUNTY HISTORICAL ASSOCIATION.*

March 13, 2000, federal district judge Stephen Merryday dismissed the thirty-six year old racial desegregation suit of *Mills, et al.* v. *School Board of Polk County*. "Polk County schools," Merryday ruled, "have reached the point where they are not at this time identifiable by race on the basis of their overall student enrollments." An era truly had ended.[39]

A new era also had dawned between 1940 and 2000 when it came to women and the role of women in society and in government. Sheila Blount, as had others before, demonstrated abilities more than equal to that of men when in 1997 she became Bartow's first female mayor. The previous year Juanita Geathers had been selected as secretary of the Florida Democratic Party. At the century's turn, Sandra Graham Sheets of Haines City and a law partner at Holland & Knight in Lakeland presided over the League of Women Voters of Florida. Through the same years four female firefighters proved their willingness to risk their lives with the Polk County Fire Department, as did two women at Lakeland. Of Linda Walagorski, a firefighter at Bartow, colleague Jimmy Schaill observed, "I'd rather go into a fire with her than some of the guys." He added, "I have confidence in her ability." Governor Jeb Bush illustrated his confidence in attorney Karla Foreman Wright. During 2000, he appointed her as the county's first female African American judge. On a somewhat different note, one of the county's female leaders opted during the period to take a well-earned retirement or, perhaps better stated, partial retirement. Following fifteen years of service, Maryly VanLeer Peck resigned as president of Polk Community College in 1997 to become headmaster of Winter Haven's All Saints Academy. Trustees selected one-time Florida Southern College history professor and former Lakeland mayor Larry Durrence to succeed her.[40]

Also during the years from 1940 to 2000, crime—especially violent crime—increasingly had become a part of the fabric of life in Polk. The 1990s, although affording some relief in line with trends over the state and nation, nonetheless had provided more than enough loss, terror, and tragedy. Not all of the county's law enforcement personnel over time had managed to resist the temptation of impropriety or of unjustified violence, but many were the individuals who repeatedly risked their lives so that their fellow citizens could rest safely and more securely. Winter Haven police officer Johnnie N. Patterson, Jr.'s sacrifice on March 8, 1997, vividly proved the truth to that statement. After Walter Steven Norris fled an automobile that the officer had stopped, Patterson gave chase only to be shot in the face and killed.[41]

Others who routinely and quietly worked for the benefit of those less fortunate should be remembered, as well. Among the numerous charitable organizations and foundations that benefitted Polk, Help of Fort Meade served a community at times in the grip of economic calamity. The organization depended on volunteers to provide "basic needs and emergency services to people who have had temporary loss of income." Or, as director Beverly Ferris explained, it "fills the gap until unemployment checks or food stamps are issued." A thrift shop managed by Howard King permitted donations of clothing and other goods to be distributed equitably and efficiently, and the community responded accordingly. "We get plenty of donations," King assured. "It gets tough keeping up with it." In a similar vein, when Lakeland's Kimberly Laudon passed away from breast cancer in 1999, her husband Jim Laudon established the Kimberly Foundation "to bring hope and happiness to sick children by providing medical care and granting wishes." As foundation board member Kenneth Mundy commented, "Those of us who have been blessed need to reach out and help those who are having a hard time." Jim Laudon added of the kids helped by the Kimberly Foundation, "If I can brighten their lives right now, that's what matters to me."[42]

119. *As the twentieth century ended, history and heritage remained alive in Polk County, as these Oaks School students from Bartow discovered one beautiful day at Homeland Heritage Park.* POLK COUNTY HISTORICAL QUARTERLY.

Voices

Polk County's history does not end as does this volume at the year 2000, and the insights of historians of future days will be needed to aid those alive today and their successors to understand, beyond what this work has offered, the meanings and implications of the vast changes that have touched her and her people in the six decades that have preceded this point. It must be recorded, though, that generation upon generation of residents have considered "Imperial Polk," whatever its faults or mistakes, a very special place that offered a home of endearing value. When Beulah Pipkin passed away at age ninety-nine in 1995, an obituary touched on the experience as personalized by her journey through it. "She held many wonderful memories," it read simply, "but her life also was marked with hard times." As also was true with Miss Pipkin, however, Polk's experience ran deeper than that and with more profound significance.[43]

It may be that, until more time has passed and greater objectivity can be realized, the less said on the question the better; yet, one last moment spent reflecting on echoes of Polk's past might well be worth consideration and remembrance. The echoes derive from two Lakeland women who, in 1952, reflected upon their lives in the county and the changes that they had seen. Nell Swindell spoke specifically of home, but she did so in words that applied more broadly. "All my joys and all my sorrows have come to me right here in this house," she recorded. "The children would like me to give up the big old house and go into newer, smaller quarters," Swindell added, "but all my sentiments are tied up right here." Mrs. H. K. Hooks spoke with the same rhythm of thought and feeling. "Our family didn't have much money, and there was no chance to accumulate any," she began. "Many of our friends became wealthy and some of them left for more progressive communities," Mrs. Hooks continued, "but none ever had more contentment than we did, and none can have richer memories, now."[44]

Notes and Bibliography

Abbreviations

BPCD	*Bartow Polk County Democrat*
BPCR	*Bartow Polk County Record*
FML	*Fort Meade Leader*
FSA	Florida State Archives, Tallahassee
JFT-U	Jacksonville Florida Times-Union
LL	*Lakeland Ledger*
LWH	*Lake Wales Highlander*
MH	Miami Herald
MP	*Mulberry Press*
OS	*Orlando Sentinel*
PC	Polk County
PCHGL	Polk County Historical and Genealogical Library
RG	Record Group
SPT	*St. Petersburg Times*
TDD	*Tallahassee Daily Democrat*
TFS	*Tampa Florida Sentinel*
TT	*Tampa Tribune*
WHH	*Winter Haven Herald*
WHNC	*Winter Haven News Chief*

Notes

Introduction

1.. See Brown, *In the Midst of All That Makes Life Worth Living*.
2. *TT*, February 6, 1977; Brownlee, "Where De Water Drink Lake Cherry Wine," 2.
3. *LL*, March 27, 1965.
4. Ibid., July 10, 1952, March 27, 1965.
5. Brown, *In the Midst of All That Makes Life Worth Living*, xiii.
6. "Remembering Individuals Who Have Helped Polk County Historical Association," 4-5; *LL*, June 15, 1958.
7. Brown, *In the Midst of All That Makes Life Worth Living*, xiii-xiv.

Chapter 1

1. Brown, *In the Midst of All That Makes Life Worth Living*, 73; *SPT*, October 6, 1975; *County and City Data Book, 1994*, 88; *TT*, February 10, 1976.
· Except as otherwise noted, information contained in this chapter may be found in Brown, *In the Midst of All That Makes Life Worth Living*.
2. *TT*, February 10, 1976; *OS*, December 12, 1992.
3. Brown, *Florida's Peace River Frontier*, xvii-xviii.
4. See www.swfwmd.state.fl.us/green-swmp/greenswmp.html.
5. Miller, "Will Success Spoil the Central Ridge?" 54-55.
6. Brown, *Florida's Peace River Frontier*, 6, 23-23, 27, 35-36, 45, 6-70, 93, 131, 312-18, 427.
7. Mayo, *Seventh Census*, 11, 60.
8. Ibid., 61.
9. McNeely and McFadyen, *Century in the Sun*, 7-19; Mayo, *Seventh Census*, 83-89; "Native American and African-American Settlements," undated *Lakeland Ledger* clipping, African American file, PCHGL collection; Bur-

ton, "Teaspoon Hill"; idem, "Where is Moorehead?"
10. William Ellsworth, interviewed by James M. Denham, February 27, 2004, Center for Florida History collection, Florida Southern College, Lakeland; *FML*, March 1, 2002; Byrd, "Reflections," 9.
11. "Fighting from Within: Former Winter Haven Mayor Used the System to Fight Segregation and Racism," undated *Lakeland Ledger* clipping, c. 1997, African American file, PCHGL collection; *LL*, May 24, 1999.
12. "Fighting from Within"; *FML*, March 1, 2002.
13. *FML*, March 1, 2002; *JFT-U*, December 24, 1944; *Lakeland American-Press*, December 10, 1943; Hubener, *Lakeland Jubilee*, 318; Robinson, "Charlie Smith," 6-7; *BPCD*, August 26, 1938.
14. Brown, *In the Midst of All That Makes Life Worth Living*, 310, 320-22; *FML*, March 26, 2004.
15. Hubener, *Lakeland Jubilee*, 200, 231; Burton, "Dr. David J. Simpson"; idem, "Lakeland's Early Black Schools"; Brown, *In the Midst of All That Makes Life Worth Living*, 227-28; Frisbie, *Yesterday's Polk County*, 125.
16. McNeill, "Were They Pioneers Too?" 9-11; Lewis, "Bartow, West Bartow," 53-59; *BPCD*, January 27, 2000.
17. Burton, "Black Women."
18. Judith Breuggeman interview, November 11, 2001, notes in collection of the author.
19. Ibid.; Brown, *In the Midst of All That Makes Life Worth Living*, 264; Loquasto, *Celebrating*, 52-53; *BPCD*, March 4, 1999.
20. *LWH*, July 12, 1940; Brown, *Recollections*, 3, 81; Auburndale *Star*, January 21, 1954.
21. Brown, *In the Midst of All That Makes Life Worth Living*, 315; *Lakeland News*,

July 5, 1933; *TT*, October 2, 1938; Hubener, *Lakeland Jubilee*, 137.

22. *LL*, July 12, 1953; Lewis, "Bartow, West Bartow," 51-52; Brown, *In the Midst of All That Makes Life Worth Living*, 78; idem, *Fort Meade*, 38, 49, 60-61, 132; idem, *Florida's Peace River Frontier*, 334-35; Cushman, *Goodly Heritage*, 175-80.

23. Puckett, *History of First Baptist Church*, 17; Prine, *Kathleen*, 15.

24. Brown, *Florida's Peace River Frontier*, 334; McNally, *Catholic Parish Life*, 137-38; Holton, "If You Don't Start Your People," 6.

25. Cozens, *Florida Women*, 102.

26. Lauderback, *Consolidated*, 113; *LWH*, April 21, 1939; Brown, *In the Midst of All That Makes Life Worth Living*, 300-301, 306, 311, 323.

27. J. B. Berry to Fred P. Cone, March 2, 1939, Administrative Correspondence of Governor Fred P. Cone, RG 102, series 368, box 71, FSA; *LWH*, November 24, 1939, January 24, 1941.

28. Thrift, *Through the Decades*, 8-27; Hawes, "Charmer Promoted College."

29. *Lake Wales News*, September 3, 1981; *JFT-U*, December 27, 1941.

30. Bentley, *History*, 123-27.

31. Brown, *Florida's Black Public Officials*, 63-64; idem, *In the Midst of All That Makes Life Worth Living*, 178.

32. Brown, *In the Midst of All That Makes Life Worth Living*, 204-206, 229, 231, 244-45, 301-302.

33. Ibid., 204, 317.

34. Ibid., 301, 311.

35. E. E. Callaway to Fred P. Cone, November 12, 1937, box 71, Governor Fred P. Cone administrative correspondence; Bennett DeLoach interview, March 11, 2001; Burton, "Few Prominent Lakeland Blacks."

36. *Mulberry Press*, March 21, 1935; Stafford, "Sen. Spessard L. Holland," 16-18; "Special Report: Florida's Most Influential Men," 20; D. Burke Kibler

interview, February 12, 2004; *TT*, December 12, 1968.

37. Brown, *In the Midst of All That Makes Life Worth Living*, 314; *JFT-U*, August 17, 1939.

38. William Ellsworth interview; Caldwell, *Mountain Lake*, 103-105; Wright, "Polk County's First Poor Farm," 5.

39. "This Year's Pioneer Recollections," 7.

40. Hopkins, *Fifty Years of Citrus*, 172-76; *TT*, September 6, 1939; Brown, *In the Midst of All That Makes Life Worth Living*, 322, 324.

41. *TDD*, January 28, 1940; Hopkins, *Fifty Years of Citrus*, 176; Georg, "Notes on Florida Freezes," 3; "Ben Hill Griffin: Pioneer Citrus Baron," 55; William Ellsworth interview.

42. Brown, *In the Midst of All That Makes Life Worth Living*, 216, 275, 220, 282-85; *LWH*, February 5, 1929.

43. *OS*, May 3, 1986.

44. *TT*, January 1, 4, 1964; White, *History of Fort Meade*, 33-34.

45. William Ellsworth interview; *LL*, January 5, 1999.

46. *TT*, March 14, 1979.

47. *LL*, April 12, 17, 1950.

48. Pope, "Havenites Have Unique Program," 20-21; "Cypress Gardens," 4.

49. Brown, *In the Midst of All That Makes Life Worth Living*, 314-15; Burton, "Polk Players."

50. *OS*, April 8, 1990; Young, "Keeping Frostproof in the Dark," 9; Bowman, "Polk Theatre," 1-2; Craig, "Going There," 4; Hazel Bowman to the author, May 13, 2004, collection of the author.

51. Brown, *In the Midst of All That Makes Life Worth Living*, 212.

52. Ibid., 243; *LL*, June 11, 1961.

53. "Chalet Suzanne Day," 7; Ahl, *Lake Wales*, 117-18; Johnson, Chalet Suzanne," 4.

54. Watters, *Fifty Years*, 56-71; Burr, *History of Winter Haven*, 180.

Chapter 2

1. *LWH*, October 25, November 22, 1940.
2. Ibid., December 27, 1940; *JFT-U*, November 18, 1940; *TT*, December 12, 1968; Hubener, *Lakeland Jubilee*, 139, 160.
3. *TDD*, May 29, 1940, January 19, April 3, 1941; *JFT-U*, June 14, 1941; Burr, *History of Winter Haven*, 178; McKay, *Pioneer Florida*, II, 139, 1030, 1032. For a good look at Spessard Holland and his accomplishments as governor, see Stone, "Profile of Spessard Lindsey Holland."
4. Burr, *History of Winter Haven*, 178, 244, 346, 372; McKay, *Pioneer Florida*, II, 72, 718; *LL*, January 1, 1957; *LWH*, January 10, 1941; *BPCD*, December 3, 1964.
5. Reese, "World War II," 6.
6. *FML*, April 19, 2002.
7. *JFT-U*, December 14, 1941.
8. Kennedy, *Freedom From Fear*, 426-59; Tindall, *America*, II, 1174-75; *JFT-U*, June 11, 1941; Burr, *History of Winter Haven*, 180.
9. *LWH*, November 29, 1940; *JFT-U*, May 24, 1944; Hawk, *Florida's Army*, 276-81; "World War Two," 9.
10. Hubener, *Lakeland Jubilee*, 153, 157-58; Wright, "Civilian Defense," 1; Burr, *History of Winter Haven*, 180-81; *LWH*, April 25, May 2, 1941.
11. *LWH*, May 2, 1941; *TDD*, August 15, 1941; *JFT-U*, August 15, 1941.
12. *JFT-U*, May 27, 1941; Sage-Gagne, *Pilots in the Sun*, 2-30; Homan and Reilly, *Images*, 76-77.
13. *LWH*, June 6, 1941; Burton, "Polk County Blacks"; *"Pioneer Luncheon—2000," 4; JFT-U*, June 11, 1941, July 29, 1943.
14. Burton, "Polk County Blacks"; *OS*, April 8, 1990; "30th Annual PCHA Pioneer Luncheon," 7.
15. Reese, "World War II," 6.
16. *LL*, December 30, 1982.
17. *Tampa Daily Times*, December 12, 1941; *JFT-U*, December 27, 1941; Blankner, "World War II," 2-3; Burr, *History of Winter Haven*, 181.
18. *LL*, October 9, 1942.
19. Reilly and Homan, "Ruth Clifford," 65; Blankner, "World War II," 2; *MH*, January 3, 1993; *TDD*, February 6, 1942.
20. Reilly, "Florida's Fighting Minute Men," 417; Reilly and Homan, "Ruth Clifford," 64-66.
21. *LL*, April 21, 1963; *JFT-U*, October 27, November 2, 1945; *BPCR*, May 12, 1943.
22. *FML*, November 21, 2003.
23. *JFT-U*, April 25, 30, May 24, September 23, November 21, 1943, January 4, 15, February 26, May 7, March 7, June 26, 1944, April 2, June 8, 1945; *FML*, November 21, 2003.
24. *LWH*, September 4, 1942.
25. *OS*, July 16, 1997.
26. *TT*, January 30, 1944; Miller, "Reminiscences," 2-3; Burr, *History of Winter Haven*, 182; "Conscientious Objectors."
27. Billinger, *Hitler's Soldiers*, 19, 21, 25-26, 100, 203; Robert "Smitty" Smith interview, November 21, 2003; *OS*, August 14, 1994.
28. William Ellsworth, interviewed by James M. Denham, February 27, 2004, collection of the Center for Florida History, Florida Southern College, Lakeland.
29. Blankner, "Polk County's Participation," 4.
30. *FML*, December 3, 2002; Hazel Bowman to the author, May 13, 2004, collection of the author; Reese, "World War II," 7; Hubener, *Lakeland Jubilee*, 195, 197, 227.
31. *BPCD*, April 9, 1943; *LL*, September 19, 2001; Johnson, "Chalet Suzanne," 4-5; McKay, *Pioneer Florida*, III, 298; *MH*, April 13, 1986; Branch, "Florida With Flair," 8.
32. Howell, "WWII Experiences," 4-5.

33. *OS*, February 16, 1991; *LL*, August 17, 1966.
34. *TT*, September 2, 1945; Dewey, "Fickle Finger," 570; Carrie Oldham interview, February 13, 2004. On Brewster's black community, see Albritton, "Brewster Black Quarters" and "More About Brewster."
35. *JFT-U*, February 8, 1942, March 27, 1943, April 27, 29, June 23, October 12, 1945; *TT*, September 16, 1945, June 7, 2000.
36. *LL*, February 28, 1943; *OS*, October 7, 1951; McKay, *Pioneer Florida*, III, 348; Akerman, *American Brahman*, 325,
37. *BPCR*, January 15, 1943.
38. *LL*, January 4, 1959; "Polk Census Shows Gain of 28 Percent," unattributed and undated clipping, Polk County Clipping Scrapbook (1942-1944), PCHGL; *TT*, September 14, 1945.
39. Hubener, *Lakeland Jubilee*, 178; Holton, "Best Education," 33; *Lakeland American-Press*, August 13, 1943.
40. Holton, "Best Education," 33.
41. Report of Annual Branch Activities—1943, Lake Wales, Florida, Branch, Part 25: Branch Department Files, Series A: Regional Files: Special Projects 1941-1955, roll 15, National Association for the Advancement of Colored People Papers (available on microfilm at Coleman Library, Florida A&M University, Tallahassee); Holton, "Best Education," 34.
42. Burton, "Breakthrough Black Officers"; Hubener, *Lakeland Jubilee*, 190-91.
43. Green, *Before His Time*, 54; *TFS*, February 23, 1946.
44. McKay, *Pioneer Florida*, III, 152; Burr, *History of Winter Haven*, 265; *LL*, January 4, 1945; Hubener, *Lakeland Jubilee*, 189; *BPCD*, April 4, 2001. For an excellent memoir of one county resident's naval service, see Albritton, *Recollections of Time Gone By*, 173-224.

45. *TT*, August 28, 1999.
46. Misc. World War Two-era newspaper clippings, unattributed and undated, in "World War II Memorabilia Mulberry Area, Compiled by Mrs. Ralph Berry" scrapbook, PCHGL; Driver, *Bone Valley Comes to Life*, 244; *TDD*, January 6, 1943; Reilly and Homan, "Ruth Clifford," 67-71; "30th Annual PCHA Pioneer Luncheon," 7.
47. "Marshall G. Holloway," 5; Braim, *Will to Win*, 68-150; *SPT*, September 24, 1992; "Man of Three Careers," 2; Charles Elder Frederick biographical materials, Robert Hawk collection; Spann, "Humble Roots," 10-11; Norman, "Return to Iwo Jima," 5; *TT*, June 17, 1995.
48. *Auburndale Star*, January 21, 1954; *LWH*, August 10, 1945.
49. *LL*, August 20, 1944.
50. Misc. World War Two-era newspaper clippings, unattributed and undated, in "World War II Memorabilia Mulberry Area, Compiled by Mrs. Ralph Berry"; Reese, "World War II," 7.
51. Gannon, *New History of Florida*, 333; Reese, "World War II," 7.

Chapter 3

1. *JFT-U*, December 1, 1945, February 3, March 15, May 23, 1946.
2. Ibid., August 5, December 1, 1945; *TDD*, October 5, 1945.
3. *JFT-U*, October 27, November 2, 1945; *LL*, April 21, 1963; Hubener, *Lakeland Jubilee*, 226-27; *TT*, September 3, 10, 1945.
4. Kennedy, *Freedom From Fear*, 786-87.
5. *TT*, April 2, 2000; McKay, *Pioneer Florida*, III, 90, 186; Thrift, *Of Fact and Fancy*, 93.
6. *JFT-U*, October 7, 1945.
7. *FML*, September 12, 2003.
8. Joubert, "Florida," 185; *TT*, September 14, 1945; *Lakeland American-Press*, November 26, 1943; *JFT-U*, February 26, 1943; *LL*, December 31, 1996.

9. *TT*, August 14, September 14, 1945; "Introducing Florida Builder," 3; *LL*, January 2, 1949.

10. *LL*, January 3, 1947.

11. Hubener, *Lakeland Jubilee*, 227; "I. H. Green to Head Bartow Negro Chamber of Commerce," undated clipping from *Bartow Polk County Advertiser* in "1942-1944 Polk County Clippings" scrapbook, PCHGL.

12. *Lakeland American-Press*, October 15, 1943.

13. *JFT-U*, June 23, 1945, December 19, 1946, November 22, 1948, June 28, 1949, March 12, 1950; *LWH*, August 10, 1945; *LL*, January 3, 1950; Stavro, "Ben Hill Griffin," 55.

14. *TT*, September 2, 1945, August 6, 1958; *LL*, January 1, 1956, February 19, 1957; Dewey, "Fickle Finger," 571.

15. *TT*, September 16, 1945; *JFT-U*, February 9, 1946, October 26, 1948; Frisbie, *Peace River Pioneers*, 99; Dewey, "Fickle Finger," 574.

16. Mansfield, "Changing Tourist," 14; Cozens, *Florida Women*, 99; McKay, *Pioneer Florida*, III, 298; *JFT-U*, February 26, 1950; *TT*, October 22, 1946.

17. *LL*, January 5, 1947, January 2, December 25, 1949, January 4, 1959; *WHNC*, May 16, 1948.

18. *JFT-U*, March 15, 1946; McKay, *Pioneer Florida*, III, 238; *LWH*, July 18, 1947.

19. Scott Kelly, interviewed by James M. Denham, June 26, 2003, collection of the Center for Florida History, Florida Southern College, Lakeland.

20. *LL*, January 1, 1956; Sage-Gagne, *Pilots in the Sun*, 40; McKay, *Pioneer Florida*, III, 581; Burr, *History of Winter Haven*, 197.

21. Mayo, *Seventh Census*, 84; *Population of Florida*, 13.

22. McKay, *Pioneer Florida*, III, 598; *JFT-U*, March 21, 1961; Hall and Rise, *From Local Courts to National Tribunals*, 166; *LL*, April 25, 1996.

23. *Lakeland American-Press*, April 20, 27, 1945; Burr, *History of Winter Haven*, 203, 346.

24. Cotton, "Southeastern College."

25. *LWH*, April 4, 1947; Hubener, *Lakeland Jubilee*, 269, 292.

26. Hubener, *Lakeland Jubilee*, 265.

27. *JFT-U*, October 2, 1945; *LL*, January 5, 1947.

28. *JFT-U*, December 12, 1946, June 12, 1950.

29. Ibid., May 18, 19, 20, 22, July 29, 31, August 4, 5, 6, 8, 1948; *LL*, January 2, 1949; Burr, *History of Winter Haven*, 203.

30. *JFT-U*, March 4, 1951.

31. McKay, *Pioneer Florida*, III, 72, 572; *JFT-U*, January 15, 1950.

32. *LL*, December 20, 1949.

33. *JFT-U*, May 7, 1946; "Senator Holland's Fight to Ban Poll Tax," 10.

34. Saunders, *Bridging the Gap*, 20; Hubener, *Lakeland Jubilee*, 235, 242, 342.

35. Holton, "Best Education," 35; Holton, "Life Well Lived," 5; *JFT-U*, December 12, 1946; Hubener, *Lakeland Jubilee*, 264.

36. Hubener, *Lakeland Jubilee*, 318, 393; Egerton, *Speak Now Against the Day*, 415, 476-508.

37. Hubener, *Lakeland Jubilee*, 342; Newton, *Invisible Empire*, 121-22; *OS*, July 21, 1999.

38. *JFT-U*, December 12, 1946; *Lakeland American-Press*, September 21, 1945; Hubener, *Lakeland Jubilee*, 352.

39. Scott Kelly interview; Judith Brueggeman interview.

40. *OS*, April 8, 1990; *TT*, April 11, 1998.

Chapter 4

1. Tebeau, *History of Florida*, 431; *TT*, June 2, 1960; *JFT-U*, June 2, 1960; *Population of Florida*, 3, 13.

2. *JFT-U*, June 2, 1960.

3. Betty "Plum" Taylor interview, November 10, 2001.

4. Gannon, *New History of Florida*, 437; *LL*, January 1, 1965.

5. *FML*, September 26, 2003.

6. Betty "Plum" Taylor interview; Gannon, *New History of Florida*, 434-35; Derr, *Some Kind of Paradise*, 340-41; Burr, *History of Winter Haven*, 214.

7. Burr, *History of Winter Haven*, 215.

8. *TT*, December 1, 1964, May 6, 1965; Darragh, "Danger in Florida Land Developments," 12, 14, 16.

9. *LL*, December 31, 1954, January 2, 1955, January 4, 1959.

10. Ibid., January 4, 1959; *FML*, December 16, 2003, January 9, 2004.

11. *LL*, January 2, 1955; *JFT-U*, January 17, 1954.

12. *LL*, December 31, 1953, January 2, 1955; Robert Waters, interviewed by James M. Denham, January 19, 2004, Center for Florida History Collection, Florida Southern College, Lakeland.

13. "Interstate Highways in Florida," 9, 11; *JFT-U*, October 3, 1951; *LL*, January 1, 1956; Kendrick, *Florida Trails to Turnpikes*, 171.

14. "Have T-Square Will Travel," 18-19; "Inside Florida Companies," 61.

15. McKay, *Pioneer Florida*, III, 888; "Sikes Brothers at Lakeland Win Men-of-Year Honors," 67; "Businessmen in the News," 31.

16. *JFT-U*, January 18, 1950, March 21, August 19, 1952; February 4, 1954; *LL*, January 3, 1950; *WHH*, January 2, 1953; *MH*, June 23, 1950; *TT*, August 3, 1971.

17. "He Helped Automate Agriculture," 11-12.

18. *TD*, April 7, 2002; *JFT-U*, January 13, 1952, December 6, 1970; "Black Hills Passion Play," 6-7.

19. *TT*, August 8, 1981; "Sand Mountain," 2; White, *History of Fort Meade*," 43-44.

20. *LL*, March 20, 1953, January 1, May 6, 1956.

21. *JFT-U*, March 21, 1952, February 21, 1953, January 17, 1954; *FML*, January 23, 2004.

22. *JFT-U*, January 18, 1950, September 30, 1952; McKay, *Pioneer Florida*, III, 1030, 1032; Hall and Rise, *From Local Courts to National Tribunals*, 166; *SPT*, September 24, 1991; Burton, "Polk Players"; Frisbie, *Yesterday's Polk County*, 121.

23. *TT*, May 8, 1995; Orrick and Crumpacker, *Tampa Tribune*, 309.

24. *LL*, April 12, 1950, June 14, 1953; *TT*, May 7, 1950.

25. *TT*, August 6, 1958; "Conservation and the Fight Against Pollution," 20; Dewey, "Fickle Finger of Phosphate," 575.

26. *LL*, January 1, 1956.

27. Halberstam, *Fifties*, 78-86, 101-15.

28. Hawk, *Florida's Army*, 282; Burr, *History of Winter Haven*, 259.

29. *TT*, May 1, 1953.

30. Hubener, *Lakeland Jubilee*, 363.

31. *JFT-U*, July 3, 1951; Burr, *History of Winter Haven*, 259; *TT*, May 15, 1993.

32. *FML*, December 5, 2003, January 16, February 6, 2004.

33. McKay, *Pioneer Florida*, III, 262, 549; Homer E. Hooks, interviewed by James M. Denham, July 29, 2003, Center for Florida History collection, Florida Southern College.

34. *SPT*, September 24, 1992; *TT*, September 25, 1992; *OS*, February 1, 1954. On James A. Van Fleet's life generally, see Braim, *Will to Win*.

35. Barnes, *Florida's Hurricane History*, 182, 189, 192; *JFT-U*, June 18, 23, 1950, March 2, 4, October 6, 1951; *TD*, May 28, August 18, 24, 25, 1950, March 1, 1951.

36. White, *History of Fort Meade*, 43; *OS*, March 9, 1989; *JFT-U*, July 3, September 13, 1951, September 25, 1954; Frisbie, *Yesterday's Polk County*,

125; Johnson, *Famous Polk County Criminal Cases*, 85-115.

37. *JFT-U*, April 8, September 25, 1954.

38. Ibid., June 9, 10, 11, 13, 20, 23, December 18, 1954; *LL*, December 31, 1996.

39. Green, *Before His Time,* 5-11; *JFT-U*, December 14, 1950; Hubener, *Lakeland Jubilee*, 370; Newton, *Invisible Empire*, 129; *Miami Times*, December 14, 1952; Saunders, *Bridging the Gap*, 65-71.

40. Hubener, *Lakeland Jubilee*, 282-83; Burton, "Dr. David J. Simpson"; idem, "Breakthrough Black Officers"; Scott Kelly, interviewed by James M. Denham, June 26, 2003, Center for Florida History Collection, Florida Southern College; *LL*, January 2, 1955.

41. "A Civil Rights Pioneer: Oldest Lakeland NAACP Member Jesse Nesbitt Was One of Polk's First Black Deputies," *Lakeland Ledger* clipping, undated, Afro-American file, PCHGL; Burton, "Polk's First Black Deputies."

42. Robert W. Saunders, Sr., interview, August 5, 2002; Butler, "Black Man on the Thin Blue Line," 1; Burr, *History of Winter Haven*, 269.

43. Burton, "Polk's First Black Deputies"; idem, "A Few Prominent Lakeland Blacks."

44. *LL*, December 31, 1954, January 2, 1955; *WHH*, January 2, 1953.

45. *LL*, December 25, 1972; Hubener, *Lakeland Jubilee*, 391.

46. *LL*, February 23, 1997; *OS*, August 14, 1994.

47. *TFS*, December 5, 1953; Hubener, *Lakeland Jubilee*, 391, 414; Halberstam, *Fifties*, 422-23.

Chapter 5

1. See previous chapter.

2. Ibid.

3. Cozens, *Florida Women of Distinction*, 106; *Auburndale Star*, February 18, December 27, 1954; *LL*, January 2, 1955.

4. *LL*, May 30, 2004; *PCD*, May 31, 2004; Hazel Bowman to the author, June 6, 2004, collection of the author.

5. *TT*, July 18, 23, 1966; Burr, *History of Winter Haven*, 215.

6. *OS*, October 20, 1951.

7. "A Practitioner from the Past Returns to the Court," 6; D. Burke Kibler interview, February 12, 2004.

8. *JFT-U*, October 1, 1955; *LL*, January 1, 1956.

9. McKay, *Pioneer Florida*, III, 73-74.

10. *JFT-U*, March 21, 22, 23, 1956.

11. Scott Kelly, interviewed by James M. Denham, June 26, 2003, Center for Florida History Collection, Florida Southern College. Lakeland.

12. *JFT-U*, May 9, 17, 26, 1956; *BPCD*, December 31, 1959, June 6, 1962; *LL*, January 1, 1957, December 27, 1959, December 30, 1962, December 31, 1963.

13. Burton, "Key Whites."

14. Newton, *Invisible Empire*, 148, 150; *JFT-U*, July 21, 1956; *LL*, January 1, 1957.

15. *LL*, March 8, 1959; *WHH*, January 2, 1953; Klingman, *Neither Dies Nor Surrenders*, 157.

16. *JFT-U*, November 8, 1956; *LL*, January 1, 1957, March 8, 1959.

17. *LL*, January 1, 1957, May 6, 1964; Burr, *History of Winter Haven*, 219; McKay, *Pioneer Florida*, III, 78.

18. Burr, *History of Winter Haven*, 219; Scott Kelly interview.

19. *LL*, January 5, 1999; Frances Brown interview, February 14, 2004.

20. Thrift, *Of Fact and Fancy*, 111.

21. D. Burke Kibler, interviewed by James M. Denham, March 31, 2003, and Homer E. Hooks, interviewed by James M. Denham, July 29, 2003, Center for Florida History collection, Florida Southern College; Scott Kelly interview; Walter W. Manley II interview,

May 8, 2004; Orrick and Crumpacker, *Tampa Tribune*, 274-75.

22. Kibler interview, March 31, 2003; Hooks interview, July 29, 2003; *LL*, December 28, 1958, January 5, 1999; *MH*, December 8, 1987.

23. Tindall, *America*, II, 1331-32.

24. *FML*, January 9, 2004; Robinson, "Charlie Smith," 7; *LL*, October 8, 1997; Holton, "Best Education Provided," 41.

25. Holton, "Best Education Provided," 40, 95-96; *LL*, May 18, 19, 20, 1954; *JFT-U*, June 13, 1954.

26. Holton, "Best Education Provided," 96-97; *BPCD*, May 18, 1954; *FML*, April 23, 2004.

27. Pepper, *Pepper*, 229; *JFT-U*, November 17, 1954; Saunders, *Bridging the Gap*, 148.

28. *OS*, December 26, 1976; *LL*, February 23, 1997.

29. Holton, "Best Education Provided," 45.

30. *LL*, January 3, 1957, January 1, 1960; *JFT-U*, June 30, October 27, 1959; "A Civil Rights Pioneer: Oldest Lakeland NAACP Member Jesse Nesbitt Was One of Polk's First Black Deputies," *Lakeland Ledger* clipping, undated, Afro-Americans file, PCHGL; Burton, "Polk's First Black Deputies."

31. *LL*, January 2, July 2, December 22, 27, 1959; *TT*, January 4, 1959.

32. *TT*, January 4, 1959, July 8, 1998; "Wealth in Florida," 21; *LL*, January 1, 1957, January 1, 1960, December 28, 1982; *JFT-U*, February 14, 1958; McKay, *Pioneer Florida*, III, 299; *SPT*, February 3, June 28, 1998; *OS*, May 17, 1998.

33. *LL*, May 6, 1956, May 29, July 1, August 2, December 27, 1959; *BPCD*, February 27, 1958, June 29, 1959; Tindall, *America*, II, 1340.

34. Patterson, "Special Place," 19; "Florida Firms Enter Space Race," 7.

35. "How Far Behind?" 18-19; *LL*, January 2, 1960.

36. "Midwesterner Sparks Small Town Industry," 24-25.

37. Burr, *History of Winter Haven*, 216; Watters, *Fifty Years*, 120; *WHH*, March 8, 1957.

38. Watters, *Fifty Years*, 104; *WHH*, March 8, 1957.

39. *FML*, December 14, 2001; *LL*, February 14, 2004.

40. Brown, "Planes, Banks and Automobiles"; *JFT-U*, October 26, November 28, 1957; White, *History of Fort Meade*, 44.

41. *BPCD*, October 5, 1956; *LL*, October 7, 1956; *JFT-U*, January 31, 1957; Dewey, "Fickle Finger," 575-79.

42. *TT*, October 6, 1957, March 14, 1979; *LL*, January 21, 1959.

43. *LL*, December 28, 1958, December 27, 1959; *BPCD*, December 31, 1959.

44. *LL*, December 28, 1958; *BPCD*, February 9, 1959; *TT*, February 8, 1959.

45. *BPCD*, February 26, 1959.

46. *LL*, December 28, 1958, January 1, 1960; Burr, *History of Winter Haven*, 254, 360.

47. Collins, "Law and the Whole Man," 540; *Miami Times*, March 31, 1958.

Chapter 6

1. *TT*, June 2, 1960; *LL*, August 6, 1961, September 1, 1964.

2. *TT*, January 1, 1962.

3. *LL*, October 1, 1963.

4. Ibid., January 2, 1963, February 7, 1964, October 20, 1965; *TT*, December 28, 1963; *BPCD*, October 29, 1959.

5. "Inside the State," 10; *TT*, December 31, 1965.

6. *LL*, January 6, 1963.

7. Ibid., December 30, 1962, January 6, December 31, 1963.

8. Burr, *History of Winter Haven*, 232.

9. *LL*, May 16, 1966; Burr, *History of Winter Haven*, 233.

10. "Florida Turnpike Extension," 11; *LL*, December 30, 1962.

11. *LL*, January 2, 1949, December 31, 1961.

12. *FML*, February 6, 2004.

13. *TT*, March 14, 1979, August 8, 1981.

14. *TT*, January 1, 4, 1964.

15. Ibid., January 4, 1964; *JFT-U*, January 21, 1964.

16. *BPCD*, January 25, 1965; *TT*, April 16, 26, May 6, 1965; *LL*, August 26, 1965.

17. Wright, "Civilian Defense," 2-3.

18. *LL*, December 30, 1962.

19. *JFT-U*, June 16, 1963; *TT*, February 17, 1963.

20. *TT*, February 17, May 22, 24, 1963.

21. Ibid., May 22, 1963.

22. *LL*, September 7, 1966; *TT*, April 3, 1999.

23. *TT*, February 15, 1963.

24. Hetherington, *River of the Long Water*, 235; *TT*, December 27, 1963.

25. *Tampa Times*, March 11, 1974.

26. *LL*, December 31, 1961.

27. *Tampa Times*, March 11, 1974.

28. *TT*, December 4, 5, 1963.

29. Ibid., December 30, 1962, January 4, 1964, May 25, 1965, August 12, 1973.

30. *LL*, December 31, 1961.

31. Ibid., December 30, 1962, February 5, 1965.

32. *JFT-U*, February 23, 1963; *TT*, July 19, 1963.

33. *JFT-U*, December 20, 1963.

34. "Phosphate's Expansion Boom," 36; *TT*, December 30, 1964.

35. Hawes, "Town That Disappeared"; Albritton, *Recollections*, 33.

36. Gannon, *New History of Florida*, 363, 389; Franklin and Moss, *From Slavery to Freedom*, 495-501.

37. On Ossian Sweet, see Vine, *One Man's Castle*.

38. Vine, *One Man's Castle*, 264-66.

39. Burton, "Black Women Pushed Ahead."

40. Holton, "Best Education Provided," 38.

41. Ibid., 39; *JFT-U*, January 10, 11, February 26, 1962; *LL*, December 30, 1962; *TT*, December 30, 1965.

42. *TT*, January 26, 1961; "Fighting From Within: Former Winter Haven Mayor Used the System to Fight Segregation and Racism," *Lakeland Ledger* clipping, undated, Afro-Americans files, PCHGL; Burr, *History of Winter Haven*, 267.

43. *LL*, October 9, 1997.

44. Holton, "Best Education Provided," 29-65; *TT*, August 26, 1964; *LL*, August 21, 25, 1964; *BPCD*, August 27, 1964.

45. Holton, "Best Education Provided," 36; *LL*, December 30, 1962.

46. *LL*, January 1, 1961, October 24, 1963, January 19, 1964; *TT*, November 6, December 22, 27, 1963, January 4, 15, 1964, December 31, 1965; *BPCD*, January 16, 1964.

47. *TT*, August 4, 9, October 11, November 6, December 27, 31, 1963.

48. Scott Kelly, interviewed by James M. Denham, June 26, 2003, Center for Florida History Collection, Florida Southern College, Lakeland; Colburn, *Racial Change and Community Crisis*, 73; *TT*, May 6, 1964.

49. "Ben Hill Griffin, Jr., Legislator . . . Citrus and Cattle Tycoon," 21.

50. *TT*, June 12, July 16, 1964; *LL*, September 1, 1964.

51. *TT*, October 15, November 6, 7, December 31, 1963, January 1, 1964, January 4, 1965; *LL*, February 24, 1964.

52. *LL*, October 24, 1963; *TT*, October 29, 1963, July 24, November 3, December 31, 1965; *BPCD*, October 24, 1963.

Chapter 7

1. *TT*, November 3, December 31, 1965.
2. *MH*, November 7, 1965; Brown, "Florida Welcome to Reedy Creek," 36.
3. *TT*, November 3, 1965; Luhrs and Boyd, "Polk," 9.
4. Luhrs and Boyd, "Polk," 8-9.
5. Ibid., 9.
6. *LL*, January 6, December 30, 1970; Mayo, *Seventh Census*, 11.
7. *LL*, December 29, 30, 1970, January 1, 1971; *TT*, June 2, 1960; "Florida Adds Four New Metro Markets," 55.
8. Burr, *History of Winter Haven*, 230.
9. *LL*, March 26, 1966.
10. "Florida's Best Restaurants," 17, 19; *LL*, March 26, 1967; "Florida Trend's Third Annual Golden Spoon Awards," 37.
11. "Megalopolis," 16-19.
12. "Polk County: A Powerhouse of Potential and Progress," *SPT* article quoted in *LL*, September 7, 1966.
13. *OS*, January 1, 1967.
14. *TT*, May 23, November 22, 1967; *LL*, December 31, 1967; *OS*, January 2, 1968.
15. *LL*, December 26, 1969, December 23, 1970, December 27, 1998; *OS*, November 15, 1968; "Inside Florida Companies," 61.
16. *OS*, January 1, 1967; *LL*, January 4, 1970.
17. *LL*, January 4, 1970; Derr, *Some Kind of Paradise*, 342-43.
18. *LL*, January 4, 1970; Green, "East Polk," 9.
19. *TT*, February 11, 1966; *JFT-U*, January 6, 1966; Brokaw, *Greatest Generation*, 313; D. Burke Kibler interview, February 12, 2004; VanLandingham, *In Pursuit of Justice*, 87.

20. Colburn and Scher, *Florida's Gubernatorial Politics*, 178; *JFT-U*, March 21, 1961, May 26, 1971; Hall and Rise, *From Local Courts to National Tribunals*, 102, 165-66; T. Terrell Sessums, interviewed by James M. Denham, August 7, 2003, Center for Florida History Collection, Florida Southern College, Lakeland.
21. *SPT*, June 11, 2000; *LL*, January 5, 1999; Barnes, "Government in the Sunshine," 361.
22. D. Burke Kibler, interviewed by James M. Denham, April 7, 2003, Center for Florida History Collection, Florida Southern College; D. Burke Kibler interview, February 12, 2004.
23. Kibler interview, April 7, 2003; Kallina, *Claude Kirk*, 198.
24. *LL*, December 31, 1967; *TT*, January 1, 1968.
25. *LL*. December 31, 1967; *TT*, January 11, 1967.
26. *OS*, January 2, 1969; *LL*, January 2, 1969; Kallina, *Claude Kirk*, 93-102.
27. *LL*, January 2, 1969; *TT*, December 12, 1968.
28. *TT*, December 12, 1968; *LL*, December 27, 1970; *OS*, December 30, 1970.
29. *TT*, December 12, 17, 1968.
30. Ibid., December 31, 1965; Frasca, *Mulberry Tree*.
31. *OS*, March 15, 16, 17, 21, 23, April 15, May 13, August 24, 28, September 21, October 18, 1968, January 2, 18, March 14, 1969; *LL*, December 5, 2002; *FML*, December 6, 2002.
32. *LL*, January 1, 1965; *TT*, October 28, 1963.
33. *JFT-U*, June 9, 10, 1968; *OS*, January 4, 1970; *TT*, January 4, 1971.
34. *LL*, October 5, 1966, *JFT-U*, May 21, November 9, 1968, January 16, 1971; *TT*, January 1, 1968.
35. *JFT-U*, July 29, 30, 31, 1969; S. L. Frisbie interview, February 11, 2004; Walter L. Smith interview, February 13, 2004.

36. *TT*, December 31, 1963.

37. Polk County Vietnam casualties list, Robert W. Hawk collection; Burr, *History of Winter Haven*, 259-60; *LL*, December 26, 1970; *FML*, February 20, 2004.

38. Burr, *History of Winter Haven*, 259.

39. Ibid.; *FML*, February 27, April 9, 2004; *TT*, December 28, 1982.

40. *LL*, December 29, 1970, January 2, 1971.

41. Thrift, *Of Fact and Fancy*, 156.

42. James V. Holton to the author, June 19, 2004, collection of the author.

43. *LL*, January 3, 1971.

44. Ibid., December 23, 1970, January 6, 1971.

45. *TT*, May 21, 1965, February 9, December 29, 1969; *LL*, December 23, 24, 1970.

46. *TT*, December 31, 1965; *OS*, January 4, 1970; *LL*, December 31, 1967.

47. Holton, "Best Education Provided," 70-71, 166; Burton, "School Desegregation"; *FOMEHISO 1966*, unpaginated.

48. *FML*, October 3, 2003; *WHNC*, October 4, 2003; *LL*, October 2, 2003.

49. *TT*, November 27, December 4, 18, 1968, January 5, 1971; *JFT-U*, January 11, 1971; *LL*, January 5, 1971; Burr, *History of Winter Haven*, 257.

50. Holton, "Best Education Provided," 80-81; *LL*, December 31, 1970.

51. *LL*, December 31, 1970; Holton, "Best Education Provided," 98.

52. Walter L. Smith interviews, February 11, 13, 2004.

53. Holton, "Best Education Provided," 88-89; *TT*, January 1, 1994.

54. Holton, "Best Education Provided," 93.

55. *TT*, January 1, 1994.

56. *LL*, December 28, 1970.

Chapter 8

1. *OS*, October 2, 1971.

2. Ibid., December 31, 1989; Gannon, *New History of Florida*, 437; Morris, *Florida Handbook*, 571-72.

3. *LL*, January 1, 1972.

4. Green, "East Polk," 8.

5. Ibid.

6. *TT*, November 12, 1971; Green, "East Polk," 9; *OS*, January 6, 1974.

7. Green, "East Polk," 9; *TT*, February 13, 1973; *LL*, December 29, 1974.

8. *OS*, December 31, 1972; *LL*, December 29, 1972, December 30, 1973.

9. *LL*, December 28, 1970, January 1, 1972; *TT*, December 31, 1970.

10. *LL*, January 6, December 31, 1973.

11. *WHNC*, January 18, 1990; *LL*, February 13, 1997; *OS*, December 30, 1973, January 6, 1974; December 28, 1975.

12. *LL*, February 13, 1997.

13. *LL*, December 30, 1973, January 5, 1975, January 3, 1976; Miller, "Will Success Spoil the Central Ridge?" 56.

14. *LL*, January 3, December 27, 1974, January 2, 1976; *FML*, April 9, 2004; *OS*, January 6, 1974; *TT*, May 1, 1977.

15. "Will Success Spoil the Central Ridge?" 55; "Florida's Southwest," 80-81; *TT*, February 10, 1976; *LL*, January 1, 1976.

16. "Florida Leads Nation in Mobile Home Purchases," 54; *LL*, December 30, 1970, December 30, 1973; January 3, 1976.

17. *OS*, June 27, 1968, January 2, 1869.

18. Ibid., January 4, 1970.

19. *TT*, January 4, 1971; *LL*, January 1, 1971, December 31, 1982.

20. *OS*, December 31, 1972, December 30, 1973.

21. *TT*, June 13, 20, December 20, 1973; *OS*, January 6, 1974.

22. *OS*, December 29, 1974.

23. Ibid., January 7, December 30, 1973, January 6, December 29, 1974; *TT*, November 29, 1973.

24. *LL*, December 23, 1970; *TT*, November 23, 1973.

25. *LL*, January 1, 1972; *TT*, June 6, 1975, April 2, 1995; *SPT*, July 1, 1994; O. H. Wright to the author, June 1, 2004, collection of the author.

26. *OS*, December 31, 1972, January 1, 1982; *TT*, February 7, 1991; *LL*, January 1, 1974.

27. *TT*, December 28, 1979.

28. *SPT*, September 15, 1974, February 5, 1975.

29. *LL*, December 23, 28, 29, 30, 1970.

30. *TT*, May 23, 1971, July 2, 8, 1972.

31. Ibid., November 23, December 1, 1973; *OS*, January 6, 1974.

32. *LL*, January 3, 1974; *SPT*, September 1, 1991.

33. Tindall, *America*, II, 1407-10; Hawk, *Florida's Army*, 283.

34. *LL*, December 26, 1973, January 5, 1975.

35. Ibid., January 1, 1972.

36. Ibid., January 5, 1975, December 28, 1978, January 1, 1980; *OS*, March 9, 1989.

37. Spann, "Humble Roots," 11; *TT*, January 22, 1995.

38. *LL*, December 27, 1978.

39. *OS*, December 31, 1971; *LL*, December 31, 1971.

40. *OS*, December 31, 1972, January 6, 1974.

41. Loquasto, *Celebrating Florida's First 150 Women Lawyers*, 110; Johnson, "Black Lawyer's Mature Search," 24; *LL*, February 1, 2002.

42. Frisbie, *Yesterday's Polk County*, 125; *SPT*, August 7, 1998; Mary E. Jones biographical materials, Mary E. Jones collection; Hawkins, *African American Biographies*, 249; *OS*, December 29, 1974; *LL*, February 13, 2004.

43. *JFT-U*, January 7, 11, 1971; *TT*, January 5, 1971; *LL*, January 5, 1971, January 1, December 25, 1972.

44. *OS*, December 30, 1973, January 6, 1974, December 29, 1976.

45. *LL*, December 31, 1970; Holton, "Best Education Provided," 140; *OS*, January 7, 1973; Johnson, "Lakeland Is Going Somewhere," 33, 35.

46. Holton, "Best Education Provided," 181-99; *LL*, January 1, 1973; *OS*, December 28, 1975.

47. *LL*, December 27, 1974, February 16, 2002; *TT*, February 6, 1977; *OS*, December 29, 1973; Johnson, "Lakeland Is Going Somewhere," 41.

48. *LL*, January 1, 1972, January 6, 1973; *OS*, December 31, 1972; *TT*, July 20, 1996; Morris, *Florida Handbook*, 626; *People of Lawmaking in Florida*, 8.

49. *LL*, January 1, 1971; *People of Lawmaking in Florida*, 57.

50. *LL*, December 31, 1974; *OS*, March 2, 1990; *MH*, September 24, 1989, March 2, 1990.

51. *LL*, December 23, 27, 28, 1970, January 1, 1976.

52. *OS*, December 31, 1972, December 30, 1973, December 29, 1974.

53. *OS*, December 29, 1974, December 28, 1975; Susan Wadsworth Roberts interviewed by the author, March 1, 2004, notes in collection of the author; *LL*, January 1, 1976, January 1, 1977.

Chapter 9

1. *TT*, February 11, 1979, February 12, 1980.

2. Ibid., February 6, 1977.

3. Ibid.

4. Lawrence Sthreshley, interviewed by the author, February 14, 2003, notes in collection of the author. See also Burton, "Most Landmarks of Lakeland's Black Community are Gone."

5. *TT*, December 11, 1973.

6. Ibid., September 10, 1995.

7. *BPCD*, June 18, 1974; "Remembering Individuals Who Have Helped," 4-5; Hooker, "President's Message," 16; "PCHA Information," 6.

8. Hooker, "President's Message," 16; Frisbie, *Yesterday's Polk County*; Burr, *History of Winter Haven*; *LL*, January 1, 1977; *TT*, March 14, 1998.

9. *LL*, January 1, 2, 1977; *MH*, April 16, 1986.

10. *LL*, January 2, 1977, January 1, 1978.

11. Ibid., January 2, 1977, January 1, 1978, January 1, 1980; *TT*, August 3, 1980.

12. *LL*, January 1, 1976.

13. Ibid., January 1, 1976, December 26, 1976; *TT*, October 13, 26, 1976.

14. *SPT*, September 30, November 2, 1976; *TT*, August 26, 1976, October 13, 29, 1976; *LL*, December 28, 1978.

15. *LL*, January 2, 1977, January 1, December 12, 1978.

16. Ibid., January 1, 1978.

17. D. Burke Kibler, interviewed by the author, February 12, 2004, notes in collection of the author; *LL*, January 1, 1972; *SPT*, October 6, 1975; Selz, "Why the Phosphate Industry," 71.

18. *LL*, January 1, 1978.

19. *TT*, October 2, 1975; *SPT*, October 6, 1975, February 22, 1987.

20. *TT*, August 3, 1975; *LL*, January 2, 1977.

21. *LL*, December 27, 31, 1978.

22. Ibid., January 1, 1977, January 1, 1978, January 1, 1980.

23. *OS*, December 28, 1975; *LL*, January 2, 1977, January 1, 1978.

24. *LL*, January 1, 1977, January 1, 1978; Brown, *Recollections*, 81; Carrie Roberts Oldham, interviewed by the author, February 13, 2004, notes in collection of the author.

25. Holton, "Best Education Provided," 206; *LL*, January 1, December 25, 1978; "Fighting from Within: Former Winter Haven Mayor Used the System to Fight Segregation and Racism," undated *Lakeland Ledger* clipping, c. 1997, Afro-Americans file, PCH&GL; Carrie Roberts Oldham interview.

26. *LL*, January 2, 1977, January 1, 1978.

27. *TT*, July 14, 1977; *LL*, January 2, 1977.

28. *LL*, January 2, 1977, January 1, December 27, 1978; *TT*, November 9, 1984.

29. *LL*, January 1, 1978; Tucker, "Southwest Region," 134.

30. *TT*, April 2, 2000; *LL*, December 25, 1978, January 1, 1979.

31. Holton, "Best Education Provided," 206-224.

32. *TT*, November 9, 1984.

33. *LL*, December 25, 1978; *TT*, May 7, 1995, August 1, 1996.

34. Susan Wadsworth Roberts, interviewed by the author, March 1, 2004, notes in collection of the author.

35. *LL*, December 26, 1976.

36. Hall and Rise, *From Local Courts to National Tribunals*, 157; *LL*, January 1, 1978; *OS*, January 27, 1990.

37. *LL*, January 4, 1971; *OS*, December 30, 1973; *FML*, March 12, 2004.

38. Brokaw, *Greatest Generation*, 315-16; *LL*, December 29, 1973.

39. *LL*, December 26, 1976.

40. Ibid., January 1, 1979.

41. *OS*, December 28, 1975.

42. "'Doorman' Williams Plays Rare Instrument," undated *Winter Haven Herald* clipping collection of John R. Powell, Lake Wales.

43. *LL*, January 2, 1977, December 25, 1978, December 29, 1996; *TT*, October 30, 1994, March 31, 1996.

44. *OS*, December 31, 1971, December 31, 1972; *LL*, August 26, 1971, December 27, 1974, January 1, 1976, January 1, 2, 1977, January 1, 1979.

45. *LL*, December 23, 31, 1970; Stout, "Peace River Fun," 51, 62.

46. *LL*, January 4, 1971, December 26, 1973; *OS*, December 29, 1974.

47. *LL*, August 3, 26, 1971, January 1, 18, 1972, January 1, 1980; *TT*, December 29, 1979; Robinson, "Charlie Smith," 6-7.

48. Johnson, "Lakeland Is Going Some-where," 35; Carrie Oldham interview.

Chapter 10

1. *OS*, December 31, 1989.
2. *County and City Data Book: 2000*, 23; *TT*, January 26, 1991.
3. White, "Lakeland Looks," 58; *MH*, February 24, 1985.
4. *MH*, February 24, 1985; White, "Lakeland Looks," 58.
5. *TT*, February 12, 1980, February 9, 1981.
6. *LL*, December 30, 1981; *OS*, December 26, 1982.
7. Johnson, "Lakeland Is Going Some-where," 32.
8. *LL*, January 1, 1982, January 1, 1986; *TT*, April 28, October 28, 1982, February 8, October 2, 1983; *MH*, January 23, 1983; Selz, "Polk County," 89.
9. *TT*, February 9, 1981, October 2, 1983; *MH*, April 13, 1986.
10. White, "Lakeland Looks," 55; *LL*, January 1, 1986.
11. *LL*, January 1, 1986; *MH*, April 13, 1986.
12. Johnson, "Phosphate's Maverick," 57, 59; *TT*, February 11, 1979, February 8, 1983; Selz, "Why the Phosphate Industry," 70; *LL*, January 1, 1982.
13. *TT*, February 8, 1983; *MH*, May 27, 1983; *FML*, March 12, 2004; *Selz*, "Why the Phosphate Industry," 70; *OS*, August 25, 1985.
14. *LL*, January 1, 1982, June 18, 2001; *OS*, January 1, 1982, March 2, 1990.
15. *LL*, December 26, 1982; *MH*, July 2, 1984; White, "Lakeland Looks," 57.
16. *TT*, December 27, 31, 1983; Koenig, "Where Do Our Citrus Growers Go From Here?" 62.
17. *LL*, January 1, 1986; *MH*, March 23, 1985.
18. *LL*, December 30, 1984, January 1, 1986; *MH*, August 26, 1985.
19. *OS*, August 26, 1985.

20. Koenig, "Where Do Our Citrus Grow-ers Go From Here?" 60.
21. Pat Huff, interviewed by the author, February 11, 2004, notes in collection of the author; *MH*, January 13, 1986.
22. *SPT*, March 17, 1980; *TT*, February 9, 1982.
23. *LL*, January 1, 1981, December 29, 1983; Holton, "Best Education Provided," 233-34; *FML*, October 24, 2003.
24. *LL*, December 29, 1982; Stavro, "Buddy LeRoux," 58-59; *MH*, January 23, 1983.
25. *TT*, February 8, 1983.
26. White, "Lakeland Looks," 55-57.
27. *MH*, February 24, 1985; Selz, "Polk County," 90, 92.
28. *LL*, January 1, 1984; *OS*, October 13, November 8, 1987; Wilkening, "Not Just Fun and Games," 70.
29. *TT*, July 20, 1996; *SPT*, July 21, 1996.
30. *LL*, December 26, 1982; *TT*, December 26, 1983.
31. *LL*, December 30, 1984, April 18, May 3, 1985; *WHNC*, April 12, 1985; *TT*, July 26, 1985.
32. *PCD*, April 18, May 27, 1985; *LWH*, April 23, 1985; *TT*, May 24, 1985; *LL*, May 24, 1985.
33. *LL*, July 15, 1985.
34. Ibid., January 1, 1986; *OS*, November 2, 1985; Newton, *Invisible Empire*, 205.
35. *LL*, January 1, 1981.
36. Ibid., January 1, 1981, December 26, 1982.
37. *OS*, December 28, 1980; *LL*, January 1, 1981; *TT*, November 8, 1984.
38. *TT*, January 1, 1991; *TT*, November 8, 9, 1984.
39. *LL*, January 1, 1986; *OS*, January 1, 1982.
40. *LL*, January 1, December 26, 1982; *TT*, January 9, 1981, June 26, 1985; *BPCD*, June 27, 1985.
41. *TT*, December 26, 1983.

42. *MH*, February 10, 1985; *TT*, June 13, 1981.

43. *TT*, November 9, 1981; *OS*, November 30, 1985.

44. *OS*, December 28, 1980; *LL*, January 1, 1981.

45. *MH*, August 2, September 20, 1985; *LL*, December 29, 1983.

46. James M. Denham to the author, June 3, 2004, collection of the author.

47. *LL*, June 9, 15, 2004; Hazel Bowman to the author, July 14, 2004, collection of the author.

48. *LL*, January 1, 1982, December 30, 1984; *FML*, February 6, 2004.

49. *TT*, August 2, 2000; *LL*, December 28, 1997; Susan Wadsworth Roberts, interviewed by the author, March 1, 2004, notes in collection of the author.

50. *TT*, December 24, 1982.

51. *MH*, July 28, 1985.

52. *OS*, May 3, 1986.

Chapter 11

1. *SPT*, October 2, 1990; Aschoff, "Tough Times," 73-74.

2. Hagy, "Polk's Recovery," 75.

3. Willson, "Lakeland Makes the Most," 89-90; *SPT*, April 25, 1988.

4. *SPT*, April 25, 1988.

5. *OS*, December 31, 1989, May 24, 1991; *LL*, January 1, 1988, February 13, 1997.

6. *WHNC*, January 18, 1990; *OS*, December 31, 1989; *LL*, February 13, 1997.

7. Hagy, "Polk's Recovery," 76.

8. *TT*, October 20, 1993; Coletti, "Welcome, Florida," 40-41; *SPT*, April 25, 1988.

9. Willson, "Lakeland Makes the Most," 90; *LL*, January 1, 1987; *SPT*, March 2, 1987.

10. Hagy, "Polk's Recovery," 76; Blouin, "It Pays," 80; *SPT*, May 7, 1991; *TT*, November 9, 1988.

11. *MH*, September 13, 1986; Koenig, "Big Thaw," 58; Hagy, "Polk's Recovery," 75-76; Blouin, "It Pays," 80.

12. Longman, "Big Lie," 40-41; *SPT*, November 7, 1990.

13. *OS*, December 27, 1989; *SPT*, December 31, 1989; *MH*, April 22, 1990; *LL*, December 30, 1990; Aschoff, "Tough Times," 73.

14. Koenig, "Big Thaw," 60.

15. *SPT*, March 2, 1987.

16. Ashoff, "On a Mission," 52; *OS*, October 5, 1989, February 8, 1990, November 5, 1991; *SPT*, September 2, 1990.

17. *MH*, December 17, 1990.

18. Ibid., February 2, 1989.

19. *OS*, May 1, 1986; *LL*, January 1, 1987; *SPT*, February 12, 1987.

20. *SPT*, March 17, 27, 1988.

21. *OS*, December 31, 1989.

22. *LL*, January 1, 1986, January 1, 1987.

23. *OS*, December 30, 1990; *LL*, December 30, 1990.

24. *OS*, January 1, 31, February 6, 1988, April 29, 1989; *Tallahassee Democrat*, March 14, 2004.

25. *OS*, December 27, 1987.

26. *TT*, January 1, December 29, 1991.

27. *SPT*, May 9, 1990.

28. *LL*, January 1, 1987; *OS*, May 17, 1986, January 18, 1987.

29. *OS*, January 18, 21, 1987; *SPT*, January 21, 1987.

30. *OS*, January 21, 1987; *FML*, July 22, 25, 2003.

31. *SPT*, January 21, 1987; *OS*, January 21, 1987; *TT*, November 7, 10, 1988.

32. *SPT*, November 15, 1989.

33. *TT*, December 2, 1991; *MH*, February 19, 1987.

34. *LL*, January 1, 1987; *OS*, April 23, 29, June 11, 1986.

35. *OS*, June 11, 1986; *MH*, August 4, 1986; *LL*, January 1, 1987.

36. *TT*, November 5, 1986.

37. *TT*, November 9, 10, 1988.

38. Ibid., November 10, 1988.

39. *MH*, January 6, 1988; *WHNC*, June 15, 1989; *LL*, March 7, 1989.

40. Morris, *Florida Handbook*, 29-30, 609, 612; *OS*, November 7, 8, 1990; *TT*, November 7, 1990.

41. *TT*, November 7, 8, 1990; *OS*, November 7, 8, 1990.

42. *LL*, January 1, 1989, December 30, 1990; *TT*, November 7, 8, 1990.

43. *TT*, November 8, 1990, January 1, 1991.

44. Mary E. Jones biographical materials, Mary E. Jones collection; *LL*, December 31, 1999; *TT*, November 10, 1988, August 26, 1991.

45. *SPT*, November 7, 1997.

46. *SPT*, September 17, 1988; *OS*, September 20, 1988.

47. *BPCD*, November 14, 1985, June 26, 1986; Wright, "Homeland Heritage Park," 1-3; *TT*, November 9, 1988.

48. *LL*, January 1, 1989; *TT*, April 21, 1993.

Chapter 12

1. *County and City Data Book: 2000*, 23.

2. *TT*, June 29, 1992.

3. Ibid., August 23, 1991; *County and City Data Book: 1994*, 89; *City and County Data Book: 2000*, 71.

4. *County and City Data Book: 1994*, 88; *County and City Data Book: 2000*, 71.

5. *City and County Data Book: 1994*, 93; Aschoff, "Tough Times," 76; Miracle, "Beyond Theme Parks," 111; *Florida: 2000*, 224.

6. *TT*, January 26, 1991; *Florida: 2000*, 15.

7. *TT*, May 23, 1991.

8. Ibid., November 22, 1992.

9. *OS*, March 13, 1994.

10. *SPT*, September 1, 1991.

11. Ibid., April 3, 1990, April 28, 1991.

12. Ibid., January 7, April 28, 1991; *TT*, March 2, 1992.

13. *OS*, April 15, May 3, 1992.

14. Ibid., June 9, December 25, 1993; *MH*, August 12, 1993.

15. *OS*, January 28, March 1, May 19, 1994; *TT*, August 27, 1994.

16. *TT*, September 3, 1994.

17. *MH*, January 16, 1996.

18. Willson, "Anita Bryant," 29-30; *TT*, February 16, 1992; Miracle, "Long Climb," 72; *MH*, October 30, 1993, September 23, 1995.

19. Aschoff, "Tough Times," 74; *TT*, February 22, June 2, 1993, March 30, 1994, August 28, 1995; *SPT*, March 2, 1993, July 12, 1995..

20. *SPT*, June 9, 1995; *MH*, November 24, 1995.

21. *TT*, July 1, 1994; *SPT*, July 1, 1994.

22. *TT*, November 2, 1994, January 1, 1995.

23. Ibid., April 22, 1991.

24. *OS*, November 5, December 11, 1991; *MH*, November 1, 1991.

25. *OS*, June 15, 1992; *TT*, January 27, 1993.

26. *TT*, April 3, 1993, July 27, December 1, 1994.

27. *SPT*, September 29, October 2, 1990; *TT*, April 5, 1993.

28. *TT*, September 21, 1992.

29. Ibid., March 5, 1993.

30. *LL*, August 31, 1997; *TT*, May 27, August 21, 1992, September 18, December 19, 1995; *OS*, February 5, 1992; *SPT*, July 9, 1995.

31. *TT*, May 27, 1992, September 10, 1995.

32. Ibid., January 29, February 5, 12, 1992.

33. Ibid., February 26, April 7, 1992, December 25, 31, 1995, November 20, 1996.

34. Ibid., June 15, 1991, July 22, 2000.

35. Ibid., August 31, 1991.

36. *LL*, November 5, 6, December 31, 1992; *TT*, November 5, 1992.

37. *TT*, June 3, August 12, October 6, 1994, May 17, 1996.

38. *SPT*, November 10, 11, 1994; *TT*, November 10, 15, 22, 1994, January 1, 1995.

39. *OS*, October 1, 1992; *SPT*, October 1, 1992; *TT*, December 12, 1991, September 30, November 5, 1992.

40. *TT*, November 9, 15, 1994.

41. *OS*, January 6, 1995; *TT*, January 6, 9, 1995, March 12, 1996.

42. *TT*, January 8, 13, 14, March 1, 1991.

43. *LL*, January 17, 2001.

44. *TT*, March 3, April 3, 1991.

45. Ibid., November 3, 1991, June 29, September 27, 1992.

46. Holton, "Best Education Provided," 266; *TT*, September 21, 1991, January 30, 1992, October 18, 1995; *OS*, July 15, 1992.

47. *TT*, October 20, December 31, 1993; *LL*, February 2, 1995, December 31, 1999; *SPT*, February 13, 1995.

Chapter 13

1. *LL*, December 29, 1996, January 14, 1999; *TT*, April 25, July 20, 1996, December 24, 1999; *SPT*, July 21, 1996.

2. *LL*, August 1, 1996; *MH*, March 17, 1999.

3. *TT*, March 31, 1996; *SPT*, February 3, 1998; *OS*, May 17, 1998.

4. *LL*, January 5, 1999; *TT*, December 13, 1998; *SPT*, December 13, 1998; *MH*, December 12, 1999.

5. *TT*, July 16, 1998, December 14, 2000; *LL*, July 9, 1998, September 30, 1999.

6. *TT*, January 20, October 25, December 27, 1997, June 27, 1998.

7. "Polk County's Number #1 Attraction," 45; *TT*, September 5, 1998; *LL*, August 19, 2003; Albritton, *Recollections of Time Gone By*.

8. *TT*, March 28, 1999.; *LL*, September 1, 1997.

9. *BPCD*, June 1, 2000; *LL*, May 26, 2000; *TT*, May 21, 2000.

10. *TT*, May 8, 1995, March 14, 1998, January 28, May 22, 1999.

11. Ibid., April 3, 1999.

12. Henderson, "Ahead of the Game," 124; *TT*, November 15, 1996.

13. *TT*, February 21, 1998; *LL*, December 27, 1998.

14. *LL*, December 27, 1998, December 31, 1999; *TT*, December 10, 1999, January 1, 2000.

15. *TT*, January 4, 1999; *OS*, February 7, 1999.

16. *LL*, December 26, 1999.

17. *TT*, January 1, 2000.

18. Ibid., June 27, 1998, January 1, August 5, 2000.

19. Ibid., January 1, 2000.

20. *LL*, September 23, 1999.

21. Ibid., December 28, 1995; *MH*, October 23, 1995; *TT*, December 31, 1995, January 1, 1996, January 1, 2000.

22. *TT*, June 13, 1994.

23. Ibid., October 30, 1995, January 1, 1996.

24. *SPT*, October 28, 1996; *TT*, March 11, 1996.

25. *TT*, April 22, May 17, 21, June 7, 1996; *LL*, December 29, 1996.

26. *LL*, December 29, 1996; *TT*, November 5, 7, December 17, 1996.

27. *LL*, December 29, 1996; *TT*, November 7, 1996.

28. *LL*, December 29, 1996; *TT*, November 7, December 20, 1996, December 27, 1997; *SPT*, November 17, 2000.

29. *TT*, December 2, 1997, February 25, 1998.

30. *TT*, July 18, November 4, 1998.

31. *LL*, December 28, 1997; *OS*, March 15, July 1, 1998; *SPT*, February 11, 1998.

32. *SPT*, February 11, 25, March 11, 1998; *OS*, March 15, 1998.

33. *LL*, November 4, 5, 1998; *MH*, November 22, 2000.

Bibliography

MANUSCRIPTS

Bethune, Mary McLeod. Papers. Bethune-Cookman College, Daytona Beach.

Brown, John E. Historical notes and files. Fort Meade.

Florida Southern College Center for Florida History. Interviews collection. Lakeland.

Hawk, Robert. Historical notes and files. St. Petersburg.

Holland, Spessard. Papers. Polk County Historical and Genealogical Library, Bartow.

Jones, Mary E. Biographical and family materials. Fort Meade.

Lewis, Clifton. Historical notes and files. Bartow.

National Association for the Advancement of Colored People. Papers. Library of Congress, Washington, D.C.

Polk County Historical and Genealogical Library. Historical files. Bartow.

———. Polk County Clippings Scrapbooks. Bartow.

Powell, John R. Newspaper clipping collection. Lake Wales.

Saunders, Robert W., Sr. Papers. University of South Florida Library Special Collection, Tampa.

PUBLIC DOCUMENTS, PUBLIC RECORDS, AND MAPS

County and City Data Book, 1994. Washington, D.C.: Bureau of the Census, U.S. Department of Commerce, 1994.

County and City Data Book, 2000. Washington, D.C.: Bureau of the Census, U.S. Department of Commerce, 2001.

Florida. Governor, Office of the. Governors' Correspondence, 1929-1971. RG 102. FSA.

———. *Laws of Florida.*

Florida: 2000. Summary Social, Economic, and Housing Characteristics. Washington, D.C.: U.S. Department of Commerce, 2003.

Mayo, Nathan. *The Seventh Census of the State of Florida, 1945.* Tallahassee: Florida Department of Agriculture, 1945.

People of Lawmaking in Florida: 1822-1991. Tallahassee: Office of the Clerk, Florida House of Representatives, 1991.

Population of Florida. Tallahassee: Florida Development Commission, 1959.

U. S. Department of Commerce, Bureau of the Census. *Historical Statistics of the United States, 1789-1945: A Supplement to the Statistical Abstract of the United States.* Washington, D.C.: Government Printing Office, 1952.

NEWSPAPERS

Auburndale Star, 1953-*1954*
Bartow Polk County Democrat, 1938-2004
Bartow Polk County Record, 1943
Fort Meade Leader, 2001-2004
Jacksonville Florida Times-Union, 1939-1971
Lake Wales Highlander, 1929-1985
Lake Wales News, 1981
Lakeland American-Press, 1943-1945
Lakeland Ledger, 1942-2004
Lakeland News, 1933
Miami Herald, 1950-2000
Miami Times, 1952-1958
Mulberry Press, 1935
Orlando Sentinel, 1951-2000
St. Petersburg Times, 1970-2000
Tallahassee Daily Democrat, 1940-*1945*
Tallahassee Democrat, 2004
Tampa Florida Sentinel, 1946-1953
Tampa Times, 1941-1974
Tampa Tribune, 1938-2004
Winter Haven Herald, 1953-1957
Winter Haven *News Chief*, 1948-2003

SECONDARY SOURCES

Adams, William R. *Historic Lake Wales*. St. Augustine: Southern Heritage Press, 1992.

Addison, Morris S. "Lake Locke or Loughman: Things I Remember." *Polk County Historical Quarterly* 26 (December 1999): 1-3.

Ahl, Janyce Barnwell. *Lake Wales, Florida: The Golden Age*. Lake Wales: Lake Wales Library Association, 2000.

Akerman, Joe A. *American Brahman: A History of the American Brahman*. Houston: American Brahman Breeders Association, 1982.

——. *Florida Cowman: A History of Florida Cattle Raising*. Kissimmee: Florida Cattlemen's Association, 1976.

Albritton, Ray. "Brewster Black Quarters." *Polk County Historical Quarterly* 25 (June 1998): 2-3.

——. "Brewster Phosphates." *Polk County Historical Quarterly* 22 (March 1996): 7.

——. "More About Brewster Black Quarters." *Polk County Historical Quarterly* 25 (September 1998): 6-7.

——. *Recollections of Time Gone By.* Bartow: Polk County Historical Association, 1997.

Allen, Frederick Lewis. *The Big Change, 1900-1950.* New York: Harper & Row, 1952.

Aschoff, Susan. "On a Mission to Zap Your Chicken." *Florida Trend* 34 (March 1992): 52-56.

——. "Tough Times May Bring Rewards." *Florida Trend* 33 (April 1991): 73-76.

Barber, Bernice More. *From Beginnings to Boom.* Haines City: Cromer Printing, 1975.

Barnes, Jay. *Florida's Hurricane History.* Chapel Hill: University of North Carolina Press, 1998.

Barnes, Ruth Mayes. "Government in the Sunshine: Promise or Placebo." *University of Florida Law Review* 23 (winter 1971): 361-75.

Beeler, R. G. "A Brief Look at the Aviation History of Central Florida." *Polk County Historical Quarterly* 27 (March 2001): 1-3.

"Ben Hill Griffin, Jr.: Legislator . . . Citrus and Cattle Tycoon, His 'Progressive Conservatism' and Reputation for Sound Thinking Point Toward Governor's Office." *Florida Trend* 4 (July 1961): 21-22.

"Ben Hill Griffin: Pioneer Citrus Baron." *Florida Trend* 23 (June 81): 52-56.

Bentley, Altermese Smith. *History of the First South Florida Missionary Baptist Association (1888-1988).* Chuluota: Mickler House, 1988.

Billinger, Robert D., Jr. *Hitler's Soldiers in the Sunshine State: German POWs in Florida.* Gainesville: University Press of Florida, 2000.

"The Black Hills Passion Play." *Polk County Historical Quarterly* 3 (September 1976): 5-6.

Blakey, Arch Fredric. *The Florida Phosphate Industry: A History of the Development and Use of a Vital Mineral.* Cambridge, Mass.: Wertheim Committee, Harvard University, 1973.

Blankner, Leonard F. "Polk County's Participation in World War II Pilot Training." *Polk County Historical Quarterly* 12 (December 1985): 4.

——. "Remembering WWII Victory Gardens." *Polk County Historical Quarterly* 19 (December 1992): 6.

——. "World War II in Polk County." *Polk County Historical Quarterly* 12 (December 1985): 1-3, 6.

Blouin, Keith. "It Pays to Fight Back." *Florida Trend* 31 (1989 Yearbook): 79-80, 82-83.

Bowman, Hazel L. "'Imperial' in Polk Name Trace Back to 1914." *Polk County Historical Quarterly* 18 (March 1992): 1-3.

——. "Polk Theatre." *Polk County Historical Quarterly* 18 (March 1992): 1-3.

Braim, Paul F. *The Will to Win: The Life of General James A. Van Fleet.* Annapolis: Naval Institute Press, 2001.

Branch, Stephen. "Florida With Flair: Dick Pope and the Making of Cypress Gardens." *Polk County Historical Quarterly* 30 (September 2003): 1, 4-5, 8-9, 12.

Breuggeman, Judith. Interviewed by the author, Cortez, Florida, November 11, 2001. Notes in collection of the author.

Brokaw, Tom. *The Greatest Generation.* New York: Random House, 1998.

Brown, Arnetta. *A History of the League of Women Voters of Florida, 1939-1989.* St. Petersburg: League of Women Voters Education Fund, 1989.

Brown, Canter, Jr. "A Florida Welcome to Reedy Creek." In *Program of the Society of American Archivists 1998 Annual Meeting, Orlando, Florida.* Chicago: Society of American Archivists, 1998.

——. *Florida's Peace River Frontier.* Orlando: University of Central Florida Press, 1991.

——. *Fort Meade, 1849-1900.* Tuscaloosa: University of Alabama Press, 1995.

——. *In the Midst of All That Makes Life Worth Living: Polk County, Florida, to 1940.* Tallahassee: Sentry Press, 2001.

Brown, Frances. Interviewed by the author, February 14, 2004. Notes in collection of the author.

Brown, Jeffrey N. "Planes, Banks and Automobiles: The Great Bank Heist of 1957." *Fort Meade Leader,* June 17, 2003.

Brownlee, P. J. "Where De Water Drink Lak Cherry Wine: The Importance of Zora Neale Hurston's World in Polk County, Florida." *Polk County Historical Quarterly* 27 (June 2000): 1-3, 7.

Burr, Josephine G. *History of Winter Haven, Florida.* Winter Haven: Larry Burr Printing Co., 1974.

Burton, LaFrancine K. "Black Women Pushed Ahead in Lakeland." *Lakeland Ledger,* March 21, 2002.

——. "Breakthrough Black Officers Excelled in Lakeland Police Department." *Lakeland Ledger.* May 23, 2002.

——. "Dr. David J. Simpson: Lakeland Pioneer." *Lakeland Ledger,* April 17, 2002.

——. "A Few Prominent Lakeland Blacks Found Wealth on the Other Side of Law." *Lakeland Ledger,* May 3, 2003.

——. "Key Whites Stood Up for Polk Blacks." *Lakeland Ledger,* July 27, 2002.

———. "Lakeland's Early black Schools Started in Moorehead Community in 1880s." *Lakeland Ledger*, August 9, 2003.

———. "Most Landmarks of Lakeland's Black Communities Are Gone." *Lakeland Ledger*, September 21, 2002.

———. "Polk County Blacks Have Long History of Serving in Armed Forces." *Lakeland Ledger*, March 29, 2003.

———. "Polk Players Succeeded in Negro Leagues." *Lakeland Ledger*, November 30, 2002.

———. "Polk's First Black Deputies Chased Down Racketeers, Moonshiners." *Lakeland Ledger*, November 8, 2002.

———. "Teaspoon Hill Became Black Commerce Center As Lakeland Expanded." *Lakeland Ledger*, August 24, 2002.

———. "Where is Moorehead?" *Polk County Historical Quarterly* 27 (March 2001): 6-7.

"Businessmen in the News." *Florida Trend* 9 (July 1966): 67.

Butler, Macy V. "A Black Man on the Thin Blue Line: Lieutenant Frazier Neumon, Haines City's First Black Cop and a Polk County Law Enforcement Legacy." *Polk County Historical Quarterly* 29 (March 2003): 1, 6.

Byrd, Frank. "Reflections: Of A Time That Was." *Polk County Historical Quarterly* 26 (September 1999): 6-8.

Caldwell, John W. *Mountain Lake, A History*. Lake Wales: Mountain Lake Corporation, 1984.

Cauffiel, Lowell. "Bittersweet Victory: A Man, A House, a Murder–and a Trial That Rocked Detroit and the Nation." *Michigan: The Magazine of the Detroit News* (February 15, 1987): 8-13, 16, 22.

"Chalet Suzanne Daily to Benefit Polk County Historical Association." *Polk County Historical Quarterly* 23 (September 1996): 7.

"The Changing World of Citrus." *Florida Trend* 7 (October 1964): 26-33.

Colburn, David R. *Racial Change and Community Crisis: St. Augustine, Florida, 1877-1980*. Gainesville: University of Florida Press, 1991.

Colburn, David R., and Jane L. Landers. *The African American Heritage of Florida*. Gainesville: University Press of Florida, 1995.

Colburn, David R., and Richard K. Scher. *Florida's Gubernatorial Politics in the 20th Century*. Tallahassee: Florida State University Press, 1980.

Coletti, Richard J. "Welcome, Florida, to the 'Big Leagues.'" *Florida Trend* 36 (November 1993): 38-41.

Collins, LeRoy. "Law and the Whole Man." *Florida Bar Journal* 32 (November 1958): 539-41.

"Conscientious Objectors Still In Polk County Camp." *Polk County Historical Quarterly* 16 (September 1989): 3.

"Conservation and the Fight Against Pollution." *Florida Trend* 9 (January 1967): 17-23.

Cooper, Courtney Ryley. "Way Down West in Florida." *Saturday Evening Post* 212 (October 7, 1939): 14-15, 40, 42, 44, 46.

Cotton, Rickey. "Southeastern College: A Brief History." Typescript, 2004 (in collection of the author).

Cozens, Eloise N. *Florida Women of Distinction, Volume One.* New Smyrna Beach: College Publishing Company, 1956.

Cragg, Henry. "The Positive 'Triple-A' Program: Let's Eliminate the Negative and Accentuate the Positive." *Florida Trend* 10 (May 1967): 25-32.

Craig, Timothy E., "'Going There Was a Thrill . . .': Lakeland's Polk Theatre—A Movie Palace." *Polk County Historical Quarterly* 29 (March 2003): 4-5.

Cushman, Joseph D., Jr. *A Goodly Heritage: The Episcopal Church in Florida, 1821-1892.* Gainesville: University of Florida Press, 1965.

"Cypress Gardens: Swampland Turned Botanical Wonderland." *Polk County Historical Quarterly* 20 (June 1993): 4-5.

Darragh, Charles. "Danger in Florida Land Developments." *Florida Trend* 2 (September 1959): 12-16.

Davis, Edward D. *A Half Century of Struggle for Freedom in Florida.* Orlando: Drake's Publishing, 1981.

DeLoach, Bennett. Interviewed by the author, March 11, 2001. Notes in collection of the author.

Derr, Mark. *Some Kind of Paradise: A Chronicle of Man and the Land in Florida.* New York: William Morrow: 1989.

DeVane, Dwight. "Billy Bowlegs III." *Polk County Historical Quarterly* 14 (March 1988): 1-3.

Dewey, Scott H. "The Fickle Finger of Phosphate: Central Florida Air Pollution and the Failure of Environmental Policy, 1957-1970." *Journal of Southern History* 65 (August 1999): 565-603.

Donovan, C. H. "Florida." *Southern Economic Journal* 16 (July 1949): 115.

———. "Florida." *Southern Economic Journal* 16 (January 1950): 373.

———. "Florida." *Southern Economic Journal* 17 *(July 1950): 101-102.*

Driver, Raymond L. *Bone Valley Comes to Life.* Tampa: priv. pub., 1992.

———. "Reminiscing About Pierce, Florida 1906-1955." *Polk County Historical Quarterly* 23 (June 1996): 7.

Duncan, Mattie B. *There's Only One Frostproof, Including Frostproof Family Histories.* Frostproof: Frostproof Historical Committee, 1976.

Dunn, Hampton. *Yesterday's Lakeland.* Tampa: Bay Center Corporation, 1976.

Egerton, John. *Speak Now Against the Day: The Generation Before the Civil Rights Movement in the South.* New York: Alfred A. Knopf, 1994.

"Egg Producers Go Egg-Head: Modern Foods Inc. Installs Computer to Keep Watch on Daily Doings of One Million Hens." *Florida Trend* 9 (October 1966): 39-40.

Elkins, Ruth McKeown. "Cooperative Extension Home Economics in Polk County." *Polk County Historical Quarterly* 14 (September 1987): 1-3.

"Florida Adds Four New Metro Markets." *Florida Trend* 14 (February 1972): 55.

"Florida Leads Nation in Mobile Home Purchases." *Florida Trend* 6 (October 1967): 54.

"Florida Firms Enter Space Race." *Florida Trend* 5 (November 1962): 7.

"Florida Trend's Third Annual Golden Spoon Awards." *Florida Trend* 12 (August 1969): 37.

"Florida Turnpike Extension: Bond Refinancing Is Crucial Test in Bryant Administration." *Florida Trend* 4 (February 1962): 11.

"Florida's Best Restaurants." *Florida Trend* 10 (August 1967): 17-19.

"Florida's Building Boom Well Underway." *Florida Builder* 2 (February 1947): 5.

"Florida's Industrial Outlook: A Florida Trend Special Report." *Florida Trend* 9 (April 1967): 18-27.

"Florida's Industrial Parks: Their Status and Prospects." *Florida Trend* 7 (April 1965): 40-47.

"Florida's Railroad Revolution." *Florida Trend* 7 (September 1964): 25-31.

The FOMEHISO 1966. Fort Meade: Fort Meade High School, 1996.

Frasca, John. *The Mulberry Tree.* Englewood Cliffs, N.J.: Prentice-Hall, 1968.

Frisbie, Louise K. *Peace River Pioneers.* Miami: E. A. Seemann Publishing, 1974.

———. "Van Fleet: 'Greatest General We Ever Had'–Truman." *Polk County Historical Quarterly* 11 (June 1984): 6-7.

———. *Yesterday's Polk County.* Miami: E. A. Seemann, 1976.

Frisbie, S. L. Interviewed by the author, February 1, 2004. Notes in collection of the author.

Gannon, Michael F., ed. *The New History of Florida.* Gainesville: University Press of Florida, 1996.

Georg, James G. "Notes on Florida Freezes." *Polk County Historical Quarterly* 17 (December 1990): 1-4.

Green, Ben. *Before His Time: The Untold Story of Harry T. Moore, America's First Civil Rights Martyr.* New York: Free Press, 1999.

Green, Majorie. "East Polk: Where Disney World's Cup Runneth Over." *Florida Accent* (February 27, 1972): 8-11.

Haggard, Theodore M. *Florida Southern College: The First 100 Years.* Lakeland: Florida Southern College, 1985.

Halberstam, David. *The Fifties.* New York: Fawcett Columbine, 1993.

Hall, Kermit L., and Eric W. Rise. *From Local Courts to National Tribunals: The Federal District Courts of Florida, 1821-1990.* New York: Carlson Publishing, 1991.

"Have T-Square Will Travel: Central Florida Engineering Firm Spurs Hemispherical Growth." *Florida Trend* 3 (June 1960): 18-19.

Hawes, Leland. "Charmer Promoted College." *Tampa Tribune*, November 10, 1996.

———. "The Town That Disappeared." *Tampa Tribune*, May 17, 1992.

Hawk, Robert. *Florida's Army: Military/State Troops/National Guard 1565-1985.* Englewood: Pineapple Press, 1986.

Hawkins, Walter L. *African American Biographies: Profiles of 558 Current Men and Women.* Jefferson, N.C.: McFarland and Co., 1992.

"He Helped Automate Agriculture: Sam Killebrew Expands His Company Products to Meet Growing Demands of Agri-Industry." *Florida Trend* 9 (June 1966): 11-12.

Henderson, Andre. "Ahead of the Game." *Florida Trend* 39 (April 1997): 120-27.

Hetherington, Alma. *The River of the Long Water.* Chuluota: Mickler House, 1980.

Hetherington, M. F. *History of Polk County, Florida.* St. Augustine: Record Company, 1928. Reprint ed., Chuluota: Mickler House, 1971.

Holton, James V. "'The Best Education Provided': A Social History of School Integration in Polk County, Florida, 1963-1994." Ph.D. dissertation, George Washington University, 2002.

———. "'If You Don't Start Your People, Who Will?': The Wolfsons—Lakeland's Pioneer Jewish Family." *Polk County Historical Quarterly* 29 (September 2002): 1, 6-7.

———. "A Life Well Lived." *Polk County Historical Quarterly* 26 (March 2000): 4-6.

Homan, Lynn M., and Thomas Reilly. *Images of America: Lakeland.* Charleston, S.C.: Arcadia Publishing, 2001.

Hooker, Glenn. "The President's Message: Polk County's Bicentennial Present." *Polk County Historical Quarterly* 3 (June 1976): 16.

Hooks, Homer E. "Hungry World Needs Florida Phosphate." *Florida Trend* 10 (April 1968): 110.

Hopkins, James T. *Fifty Years of Citrus: The Florida Citrus Exchange,*

1909-1959. Gainesville: University of Florida Press, 1960.

"How Far Behind? Road Building." *Florida Trend* 3 (November 1960): 16-19.

Howell, Van D., Sr. "The WWII Experiences of Van D. Howell, Sr." *Polk County Historical Quarterly* 26 (December 1999): 4-5.

Hubener, Hal. "The Civilian-AAF Pilot Training Program and Central Florida." *Polk County Historical Quarterly* 1 (March 1990): 1-3.

———. *Lakeland Jubilee: The African American Experience, 1882-1954*. Lakeland: Lakeland Public Library, 1996.

———. "Siberian Saga: George and Tanya Grebenstchikoff." *Polk County Historical Quarterly* 21 (March 1995): 1-3, 7.

Hyman, Ann. "Polk County Ramble." *Florida Humanities Council Forum* 21 (spring 1998): 4-11.

"Inside Florida Companies." *Florida Trend* 9 (July 1966): 61.

"Inside the State." *Florida Trend* 8 (August 1965): 10-11.

"Interstate Highways in Florida." *Florida Builder* 2 (April 1947): 9-11, 39.

"Introducing Florida Builder." *Florida Builder* 1 (July 1946): 3.

"John V. Atanasoff, Ph.D.: Inventor of he Electronic Digital Computer." *Polk County Historical Quarterly* 13 (December 1986): 4.

Johnson, Jack O. *Famous Polk County Criminal Cases*. Bartow: priv. pub., 1987.

Johnson, Jan. "Chalet Suzanne--An Adventure in Good Eating." *Polk County Historical Quarterly* 29 (December 2002): 4-5.

Johnson, Robert. "A Black Lawyer's Mature Search for Power and Purpose." *Florida Trend* 22 (December 1979): 24-26.

———. "Lakeland Is Going Somewhere That's Good." *Florida Trend* 22 (November 1979): 31-45.

———. "Phosphate's Maverick." *Florida Trend* 23 (October 1980): 55, 57, 59, 61.

Joubert, William H. "Florida." *Southern Economic Journal* 12 (October 1945): 185-93.

Kallina, Edmund F., Jr. *Claude Kirk and the Politics of Confrontation*. Gainesville: University Press of Florida, 1993.

Kaucher, Dorothy. *They Built a City*. Orlando: Kirstein & son, 1970.

Kendrick, Baynard. *Florida Trails to Turnpikes, 1914-1964*. Gainesville: University of Florida Press, 1964.

Kennedy, David M. *Freedom From Fear: The American People in Depression and War, 1929-1945*. New York: Oxford University Press, 1999.

Kibler, D. Burke. Interviewed by the author, February 12, 2004. Notes in collection of the author.

Klingman, Peter D. *Neither Dies Nor Surrenders: A History of the Republican Party in Florida, 1867-1970.* Gainesville: University Press of Florida, 1984.

Koenig, John. "The Big Thaw in Citrus." *Florida Trend* 30 (March 1988): 58-62.

——. "Where Do Our Citrus Growers Go From Here?" *Florida Trend* 28 (June 1985): 60-64.

"Later Courthouses and County Governmental Buildings." *Polk County Historical Quarterly* 13 (December 1986): 3, 6.

Lauderback, Martha. *Consolidated, A Partial Story–Much Needs to be Edited and Added.* Jacksonville: Consolidated Naval Store Company, n.d.

Lavigne, Norbert F. "Our Citrus Industry: Present–Future." *Florida Trend* 1 (October 1958): 11-13, 29.

Lewis, Clifton P. "Bartow, West Bartow, and the Andy Moore Family: The Joy and Importance of Discovering African-American History." *Sunland Tribune* 24 (1998): 49-60.

Loadholtes, Joe. "Orange Belt League Semi-Pro Baseball in Polk County." *Polk County Historical Quarterly* 23 (September 1996): 3.

Longman, Phillip. "The Big Lie." *Florida Trend* 32 (July 1989): 40, 42-53.

Loquasto, Wendy S., comp. and ed. *Celebrating Florida's First 150 Women Lawyers.* Tallahassee: The Florida Bar and the Florida Association for Women Lawyers, 2000.

Lurhs, R. B., and M. L. Boyd. "Polk: A County in Jeopardy?" *Florida Accent* (October 1, 1967): 8-9.

"Man of Three Careers." *Polk County Historical Quarterly* 4 (June 1977): 2.

Manley, Walter W., II. Interviewed by the author, May 8, 2004. Notes in collection of the author.

Mansfield, Bill. "The Changing Tourist." *Florida Trend* 6 (October 1963): 14-20.

"Marshall G. Holloway, Ph.D.: Member of the Manhattan Team." *Polk County Historical Quarterly* 13 (December 1986): 5-6.

"Mary Frances Dewell." *Polk County Historical Quarterly* 24 (March 1998): 7.

McKay, Donald B. *Pioneer Florida.* 3 vols. Tampa: Southern Publishing Company, 1959.

McKennie, Bobbie M. "A Short Historical Sketch of Union Academy." *Polk County Historical Quarterly* 17 (September 1990): 6.

McNally, Michael J. *Catholic Parish Life on Florida's West Coast, 1860-1968.* Catholic Media Ministries, 1996.

McNeely, Ed, and Al R. McFadyen. *Century in the Sun: A History of Polk*

County. Bartow: Polk County Centennial Committee, 1961.

McNeill, Charlie. "Were They Pioneers Too?" *Polk County Historical Quarterly* 26 (September 1999): 10-11.

"Megalopolis: Florida Develops a Super City." *Florida Trend* 8 (February 1966): 16-19.

Meyer, Clarence C., and Phyllis A. McGill. *The Davenport Story.* Davenport: James L. Scanland, 1986.

"Midwesterner Sparks Small Town Industry: New Aggressive Spirit of Business Leaders Brings Manufacturing to Haines City." *Florida Trend* 3 (March 1961): 24-25.

Miller, Annetta. "Will Success Spoil the Ridge?" *Florida Trend* 23 (December 1980): 54-60.

Miller, J. Virgil. "Reminiscences of the CPS Camp at Mulberry, Florida." *Polk County Historical Quarterly* 22 (December 1995): 2-3, 7.

"Mining Is Mainstay." *Florida Trend* 10 (April 1968): 110-12.

Miracle, Barbara. "Beyond Theme Parks." *Florida Trend* 38 (April 1996): 104-111.

——. "A Long Climb to Catch the Rest of Florida." *Florida Trend* 36 (April 1994): 71-74.

Morris, Allen. *The Florida Handbook, 1991-1992.* Tallahassee: Peninsular Publishing Company, 1991.

——. "The '64 Governor's Race?" *Florida Trend* 5 (February 1962): 15-17.

"Most Likely to Succeed." *Florida Living* 10 (January 1968): 26-33.

Nerod, Felix. *An Historical Gazetteer of Imperial Polk County, Florida.* Lake Alfred: priv. pub., 1986.

"New Publisher Changes Lakeland Ledger Format." *Florida Trend* 7 (May 1964): 13.

Newton, Michael. *The Invisible Empire: The Ku Klux Klan in Florida.* Gainesville: University Press of Florida, 2001.

Nolan, David. *Fifty Feet in Paradise: The Booming of Florida.* San Diego: Harcourt Brace Jovanovich, 1984.

Norman, Dewey. "Return to Iwo Jima." *Polk County Historical Quarterly* 12 (December 1985): 5.

Oldham, Carrie. Interviewed by the author, February 13, 2004. Notes in collection of the author.

Olson, Gordon, and Frank Shubert. "You Never Forget It." *Polk County Historical Quarterly* 29 (June 2002): 1-3.

Orrick, Bentley, and Harry L. Crumpacker. *The Tampa Tribune, A Century of Florida Journalism.* Tampa: University of Tampa Press, 1998.

Patterson, Gordon. "A Special Place, Always: The Edge of the Continent Has Long Been on the Edge of History As Well." *Florida Humanities*

Council Forum 20 (winter 1997-1998): 19-21.

"PCHA Information." *Polk County Historical Quarterly* 1 (September 1974): 6.

Pepper, Claude. *Pepper: Eyewitness to a Century.* San Diego: Harcourt Brace Jovanovich, 1987.

"Phosphate's Expansion Boom." *Florida Trend* 7 (April 1965): 36-38.

"Pioneer Luncheon–2000." *Polk County Historical Quarterly* 27 (September 2000): 4-5.

"Pioneers Videotaped at the June Luncheon." *Polk County Historical Quarterly* 28 (September 2001): 4-5.

"Polk County's Buck Rogers Plant: Latest Automated Principles Are Built Into Bonnie Phosphoric Acid Plant." *Florida Trend* 6 (May 1963): 10.

"Polk County's Number #1 Attraction: 'The Great Outdoors.'" *Florida Living* 20 (November 2000): 44-47.

Pope, Richard D. "Havenites Have Unique Program for Enhancing City's Beauty." *Florida Municipal Record* 5 (January 1933): 20-21.

"A Practitioner from the Past Returns to the Court." *Florida Supreme Court Historical Society Review* 1 (spring 1985): 6-8, 15.

Prine, Harry Otis. *Kathleen and Nearby Residents, 1920-1940.* Kathleen: priv. pub., 1995.

Puckett, Paul. *A History of First Baptist Church, Bartow, Florida (1875-2000).* Bartow: Bartow Printing Co., 2000.

Reese, Iris Sullivan. "World War II and the Summerlin Class of 1945." *Polk County Historical Quarterly* 26 (March 2000): 6-7.

Reilly, Thomas. "Florida's Flying Minute Men: The Civil Air Patrol, 1941-1943." *Florida Historical Quarterly* 76 (spring 1998): 417-38.

Reilly, Thomas, and Lynn Homan. "Ruth Clifford and Dorothy Ebersbach: Florida Fliers During World War II." *Tampa Bay History* 20 (fall/winter 1998): 64-74.

"Remembering Individuals Who Have Helped Polk County Historical Association Reach Its Twenty-fifth Year," *Polk County Historical Quarterly* 26 (June 1999): 4-5.

Robinson, Odell. "Charlie Smith." *Polk County Historical Quarterly* 26 (June 1999): 6-7.

Rogers, William Warren, and James M. Denham. *Florida Sheriffs: A History 1821-1945.* Tallahassee: Sentry Press, 2001.

Sailer, Tom. "The Turpentine Industry in Polk County." *Polk County Historical Quarterly* 29 (June 2002): 4-5.

Sage-Gagne, Waneta. *Pilots in the Sun: Primary Pilot Training Schools in Lakeland and Avon Park, Florida, 1940-1945.* Lakeland: Friends of the Library, Lakeland, Florida, 1990.

"Sand Mountain." *Polk County Historical Quarterly* 8 (June 1981): 2.

Saunders, Robert W., Sr. *Bridging the Gap: Continuing the Florida NAACP Legacy of Harry T. Moore, 1952-1966.* Tampa: University of Tampa Press, 2000.

———. Interviewed by the author, August 5, 2002. Notes in collection of the author.

Selz, Michael. "Polk County Gets Serious About Economic Diversification." *Florida Trend* 28 (1985 Yearbook): 89-92.

———. "Why the Phosphate Industry May Soon Scrape Botton." *Florida Trend* 29 (September 1986): 68-74.

"Senator Holland's Fight to Ban Poll Tax." *Florida Trend* 6 (March 1964): 10.

"A Short History of Polk General Hospital." *Polk County Historical Quarterly* 15 (June 1988): 1-3.

Smith, Robert "Smitty." Interviewed by the author, November 21, 2003. Notes in collection of the author.

Smith, Walter L. Interviewed by the author, February 11, 2004. Notes in collection of the author.

———. Interviewed by the author, February 13, 2004. Notes in collection of the author.

Spann, Joe. "Humble Roots, Humble Hero." *Polk County Historical Quarterly* 30 (June 2003): 10-11.

"Special Report: Florida's Most Influential Men." *Florida Trend* 5 (December 1962): 14-25.

Stafford, Charles. "Sen. Spessard L. Holland: Statesman and Southerner." *Floridian: The St. Petersburg Times Magazine* (October 11, 1970): 14-20.

Stavro, Barry. "Ben Hill Griffin: Pioneer Citrus Baron." *Florida Trend* 24 (June 1981): 52-56.

———. "Buddy LeRoux: The Winter Haven Developer Keeps Batting 1,000." *Florida Trend* 25 (December 1982): 58-62.

Stone, Spessard. "Profile of Spessard Lindsey Holland." *Polk County Historical Quarterly* 29 (June 2002): 6-7.

Stout, Donna E. "Peace River Fun." *Florida Living* 7 (April 1987): 50-51, 62.

Sthreshley, Lawrence. Interviewed by the author, February 14, 2003. Notes in collection of the author.

Taylor, Betty "Plum." Interviewed by the author, November 10, 2001. Notes in collection of the author.

Tebeau, Charlton W. *A History of Florida.* Coral Gables: University of Miami Press, 1971.

"30th Annual PCHA Pioneer Luncheon." *Polk County Historical Quarterly* 39 (September 2003): 6-7.

"This Year's Pioneer Recollections." *Polk County Historical Quarterly* 30

(September 2003): 6-7.

Thrift, Charles T., Jr. *Of Fact and Fancy . . . at Florida Southern College.* Lakeland: Florida Southern College Press, 1979.

——. *Through Three Decades: At Florida Southern College in Lakeland.* Lakeland: Florida Southern College Press, 1955.

Tindall, George Brown. *America, Narrative History: Volume Two.* 2nd ed. New York: W. W. Norton, 1988.

Tucker, Jeffrey. "The Southwest Region Continues to Strengthen Its Economic Position." *Florida Trend* 21 (April 1979): 121, 124, 130, 134-35.

Turner, Gregg M. *Images of America: Railroads of Southwest Florida.* Charleston, S.C.: Arcadia Publishing, 1999.

Trinkner, Charles L., ed. *Florida Lives: The Sunshine State Who's Who.* Hopkinsville, Ky.: Historical Record Association, 1966.

VanLandingham, Kyle S. *In Pursuit of Justice: Law & Lawyers in Hillsborough County, 1846-1996.* Tampa: Hillsborough County Bar Association, 1996.

Vine, Phyllis. *One Man's Castle: Clarence Darrow in Defense of the American Dream.* New York: Amistad, 2004.

Watters, Pat. *Fifty Years of Pleasure: The Illustrated History of Publix Super Markets, Inc.* Lakeland: Publix Super Markets, 1980.

"Wealth in Florida: All That Glitters Is Not An Orange." *Florida Trend* 1 (September 1958): 20-22.

Weinkauf, Dayle Taylor. "It Was the Best of Times . . ." *Polk County Historical Quarterly* 20 (March 1994): 1.

White, Otis. "Lakeland Looks for a Silver Lining In Its Cloudy Economy." *Florida Trend* 27 (July 1984): 55-58.

White, Robert M. *History of Fort Meade, Florida.* Longwood: priv. pub., 1988.

Wilkening, David. "Not Just Fun and Games." *Florida Trend* 40 (April 1998): 68-72.

Willson, Elizabeth. "Anita Bryant, Where Are You Now?" *Florida Trend* 34 (June 1991): 29-32.

——. "Lakeland Makes the Most of Location." *Florida Trend* 29 (1987 Yearbook): 89-91.

"World War Two (1941-1945)." *Polk County Historical Quarterly* 30 (June 2003): 9.

Wright, Freddie. "Civilian Defense in Polk County." *Polk County Historical Quarterly* 24 (December 1997): 1-3.

——. "Homeland Heritage Park." *Polk County Historical Quarterly* 17 (March 1991): 1-3.

——. "The Living Was 'Great' in Phosphate Company Villages." *Polk County Historical Quarterly* 7 (March 1981): 5.

——. "Polk County's First Poor Farm." *Polk County Historical Quarterly* 8 (March 1982): 5.

Young, Lorraine, "Keeping Frostproof in the Dark: Life and Revival of the Ramon Theater." *Polk County Historical Quarterly* 30 (December 2003): 9-11.

Index

Index

Denham, James M., 228, 284
Denmark, James, 37, 90
Derr, Mark, 72
DeSoto County, 111, 173
Detroit Tigers, 21, 141
DeVane, Dwight, 172, 253
Dewell, Robert T., 8
Dewey, Scott H., 111
Dickson, John G., 57
Dieterman, Sonnie Dieham, 33
Diggs, Louise W., 43, 64
Diggs, Paul A., 43, 61, 64-65
Dimbath, Merle, 149-50, 161
Dingfelder, Jim, 226
Disney, Walt, 138-40
Disney World, 138, 140, 163-65, 171, 176, 196, 210, 288
Dixon, E. D. "Bud," 152, 190, 192-93, 253, 268-69, 293
Dockery, C. C. "Doc," 184, 252, 272
Dockery, Paula, 292
Doherty, John, 125
Doherty, William C., 121
Dole, Bob, 292
Domaingue, Ed, 145
Donnelly, Emmett, 86-87
Dorman, George, 132
Douglas, Rotha, 95
Dows, Harvey, 49
draft and draft law. *See* selective service
draglines, 55
Drane, Herbert J., 15
Drane Field, 34-35, 38, 50, 62. *See also* Lakeland Army Air Field
Draper, Lee, 249
drive-in theaters, 67, 285. *See also* names of individual theaters
drought. *See* water and water problems
drug abuse and drug-related crime, 156, 178-79, 192, 222, 226-27, 243
Duane, Jim, 168
DuCharme, Lucy, 251-52
Duffey, Motis, 241
The Dugout (Baseball City), 235
dugout canoes, 282
Dunbar, Elsie L., 43, 61, 64
Duncan, S. Norman, 271
Dundee, 6, 184-85, 197, 210, 258
Dunlap, "Pink," 21

Dunson, L. W. "Les," 134, 140, 149, 198
Dunway, Agnes, 92
Dupree, Jocky, 110
Durden, J. Willard, 86-87
Durrance, B. Lucian, 24
Durrence, Larry, 213, 233, 300
Dyckman, Martin, 147

E

The Eagle, 246
Eagle Lake (lake), 20, 27, 111, 120
Eagle Lake (town), 6, 51, 154, 168, 197, 210, 244, 258, 277, 290-91
Eagle Ridge Mall (Lake Wales), 288-89
Eaglegate controversy, 290-91
Eason, Sylvia, 185
East Bartow, 6
East Polk Committee of 100, 287
Ebeling, John, 229
economy and economic conditions: pre-1940, 3; in 1940, 17-20, 22, 25-26; upsurge of during World War Two, 41-42; during the post-World War Two boom, 52-58; in the 1950s, 106-110; in the 1960s, 116-17, 144-47; and the opening of Disney World, 164-71, 187-88; and the 1980s crash, 209, 211-16, 233-41, 257-58, 263-67; at the twentieth century's end, 283-89. *See also* employment and unemployment
Economic Development Council of Polk County, 220
economic diversification, 218-20, 234, 240, 286
Eden, Jane, 185
Edward J. DeBartolo Corp., 234
Edwards, John Sanford, Jr., 31
Edwards, Lori, 272-73, 297
Edwards, Thomas Clifford, 154
Eidson, Barbara, 197
810th Military Police Co., 275
Eisenhower, Dwight D., 99
elections: corrupt practices involving, 14-15; and white primary abolished, 43; postwar registration drives, 64; African American candidates in, 65, 87, 93; and county support for Republican candidates, 99, 148-51, 248-51, 290-98; irregularities concerning, 183-84, 274, 293-94, 296; and eighteen-year-old voting in, 206; adoption of optical scan voting system for, 296. *See also* Democratic party, Republican party, and politics and political affairs

368 ~ *None Can Have Richer Memories*

ᏨᎵ

About the Author

و~

Canter Brown, Jr., is one of Florida's most distinguished historians. He is the author of many works of state and local history, including prize-winning volumes such as *Florida's Peace River Frontier*; *Ossian Bingley Hart, Florida's Loyalist Reconstruction Governor*; and, with Larry Eugene Rivers, *Laborers in the Vineyard of the Lord: The Beginnings of the AME Church in Florida*. Three of his books are also published by the University of Tampa Press: *Tampa Before the Civil War; Tampa in Civil War and Reconstruction;* and *Family Records of the African American Pioneers of Tampa and Hillsborough County*, written with Barbara Gray Brown. In 2001, he wrote *In the Midst of All That Makes Life Worth Living: Polk County, Florida, to 1940*, the first of a two-volume county history commissioned by the Polk County Historical Association. Brown, who is professor of history at Florida Agricultural and Mechanical University, has received, among other recognitions, the Florida Historical Society's Rembert Patrick Book Award and the American Association for State and Local History's Certificate of Commendation. He is a native of Fort Meade, Polk County, Florida.